LIVING A SPIRIT

Seasonal Festivals in
Northern and Southern Hemispheres

An Esoteric Study

Revised edition 2016

Adrian Anderson

Threshold Publishing

Revised edition 2016
Threshold Publishing
www.rudolfsteinerstudies.com

Distributed by Dennis Jones P/L - Port Campbell Press
Bayswater VIC
Australia

ISBN 0-646-10285-0

Illustrations

Foreword to the second edition

Living a Spiritual Year, first published in 1992, was written in response to many requests from friends, who were seeking clarity about a new kind of festival, which Rudolf Steiner indicated was highly desirable. These festivals have as their focus the spiritual significance of the seasons, for people living in either hemisphere. Their aim is to help people become aligned to spiritual influences activated in each season, from the cosmos. As festivals are a social activity, in 1991 I submitted the manuscript to many groups and individuals, for their feed-back.

Now, in response to many requests, this book is being made available again. It was heartening for me to receive very positive responses from many of the readers of the first edition. However, it was not welcome by all groups. I am fully aware of the arguments against my book over two decades and have carefully assessed them, and included my response and conclusions in some foot-notes and in the text.

This process has further strengthened my confidence in the accuracy of the research presented here, and I am delighted now to offer my book in a new edition. I have added some additional material and graphics which further clarifies, from the work of Rudolf Steiner, the basis of the new festivals.

It is my hope that among my readers there will be some who will find this work of real value in creating new festivals, to help humanity to become once again attuned to the spiritual energies in the seasonal cycle of their hemisphere.

Adrian Anderson

2016

1

"Just consider, though, that when we here have St. John's festival in the summertime, that is, when it is the case that our souls can follow the Earth-soul which arises and unites itself with the stars; then the Antipodes, the Antipodeans, have their Christmas-Yuletide.

Whilst during summer in the north the Earth-soul goes forth, appearing to spiritual vision like a comet's tail which is drawing itself out toward heaven, on the other side the Earth-soul withdraws back into the earth and it is Christmas-Yuletide."

Rudolf Steiner, Oslo, May 21ˢᵗ 1923

CHAPTER ONE

LIVING EARTH, LIVING ATMOSPHERE

My subject in this book is the nature of a new festival cycle, arising from the spiritual-scientific research of Rudolf Steiner. This new cycle is the result of his research into the spiritual influences operative in the seasonal cycle of both hemispheres, together with the over-riding influence of the sun god, Christ. This concept in turn is derived from a core truth in Rudolf Steiner's anthroposophy, namely that this deity, 'the cosmic Christ', has become the in-dwelling, leading deity of our planet. A core aspect of these new festivals is that the great cosmic Christ being, with the help of four primary archangels, is monitoring the activity of multitudes of nature spirits and other beings whom together constitute the 'soul of the Earth'.

It is my hope that this book will assist in establishing a new cycle of festivals which are seasonal (that is to say hemispherical) and which also incorporates an esoteric view of Christianity. The basis for understanding the new festival cycle begins with the living Earth. We will consider the differences between the traditional Christian and nature festivals and then the relation between the individual festivals and the seasons.

But first we need to achieve an understanding of the life processes occurring in our planet, so we can picture more clearly the interaction between our planet and the cosmos during the cycle of the year. Then we can grasp the significance such processes have for humanity. The Earth is a living being. Like human beings, it has not only a physical body but as well those extra dimensions revealed by anthroposophy, namely an etheric body (a body of ethereal life-forces), and a soul (or 'astral body'). Hence the Earth has a soul; like us, the Earth is en-souled. Furthermore, since the resurrection of Christ, the great leader of the sun gods became incorporated in the Earth-soul; thus bestowing on the planet a spirit, or as Rudolf Steiner defines this, a (higher) ego or self.

The ether body, our concern in this first chapter, is a complex organism formed of subtle energies, life forces, concerned largely with nourishment, growth, and propagation. The ether forces of the world are of four distinct kinds, each manifesting in one of the four elemental states of being. Warmth, whether the heat of a flame or of a chilli pepper, derives from the warmth-ether. The light-ether produces visible light and physically manifests in gaseous substances. The chemical-ether produces the many different qualities or properties of chemical substances, whereby each is distinguishable from the other, and it manifests particularly in fluids, especially water. And it is through the fourth ether, the life-ether (called prana in the East), that the inner vitality of life processes on earth is maintained. The life-ether streams into us via the solar plexus.[1]

The human ether body consists of these four ethers, and so does the ether body of the planet. And just as our ether body extends a little way beyond our skin, so too does the ether body of the Earth extend up into the sky. The ethers arch overhead, 'behind' the physical atmosphere, sparkling and shimmering in the air. Rudolf Steiner taught that virtually all life on earth is dependent on the atmosphere – or more particularly, on the ether layers of the atmosphere. Indeed, according to Steiner, the Earth's interior was formed from the atmospheric ether layers.

A wonderful confirmation of Steiner's picturing of the outward extent of the earth's ether body came to light in 1957 when during the course of an American research project into the upper atmosphere a large specially constructed balloon with a one-man gondola attached was sent high up into the firmament, eventually reaching an altitude of over 18 miles (about 30 kilometres). There, suspended high above the Earth, the pilot witnessed a remarkable sight. The horizon was a brilliant iridescent blue, and above that the sky was a dark, velvety violet, several shades deeper than twilight,

> Then I saw something which at first I did not believe. Above the haze layer of the atmosphere, there were thin blue bands, sharply etched against the darker sky; they hovered over the earth like a succession of haloes. [2]

---

[1] In the Complete Works, vol. 93A, p. 18, lect. of 26th Sept 1905. (Note, the "Complete Works" will now be referred to as "GA".)
[2] *Life* Magazine, article, "*Man High*", 1957.

4

In earlier years, before the use of pressurized cabins in aircraft, pilots did at times have visions of such subtle, non-physical things, as if a slight 'etheric clairvoyance' develops in such situations. Now, through a careful study of recent scientific research into the structure and nature of the atmosphere, we can understand Rudolf Steiner's indications regarding the ether body of the Earth. Because of the difficulty of obtaining data from the upper reaches of the atmosphere, such scientific research has really only been possible since the 1960s.

It has become clear in recent decades that the continuation of life on this planet depends on the thin skin of the air layer (the troposphere) that encompasses the earth, a layer of life-giving gases only about 15 kilometres high. And since the middle of the century, it has been known that above this air layer are further atmospheric layers also vital for earthly life. In the stratosphere, for example, immediately above the troposphere, the gas ozone collects; industrial pollutants can seriously harm this layer. What other layers does our atmosphere consist of? What subtle, tenuous processes-not only physical but also ethereal-take place at higher levels?

The atmospheric ether layers
Rudolf Steiner describes the Earth's ether body as a remarkable layered structuring of the four ethers; he made a simple sketch of this, see diagram. He begins with layers of these energies inside the Earth, moving upwards or outwards from the innermost layer of warmth-ether, we would encounter layers of light-ether, then chemical-ether, then (at the Earth's surface) the very subtle life-ether. Then extending upward (outward) to the atmosphere, are five more layers, the Earth's ether aura.

As pictured in a 1920 Steiner sketch below, the ether aura begins after a 'fluidity zone' which means the oceans, and then an 'air zone' which is the atmosphere with its gases, that we breath. Then comes above the air layer, a warmth-ether layer, followed by a light-ether layer, then a chemical-ether layer (or tone-ether), then a life-ether layer, and finally a second warmth-ether layer, which he referred to as the "cosmic warmth layer".

My account through this chapter of the Earth's ether body builds on and in some important respects differs from the interpretations by a pioneering writer on this subject,

5

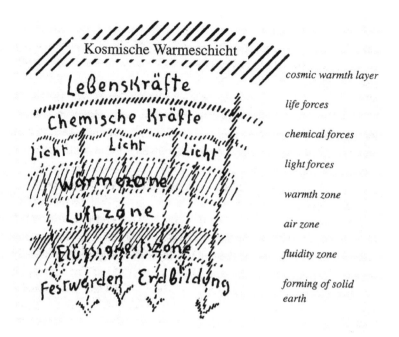

Kosmische Warmeschicht — cosmic warmth layer

Leßenskräfte — life forces

Chemische Kräfte — chemical forces

Licht   Licht   Licht — light forces

Wärmezone — warmth zone

Luftzone — air zone

Flüssigkeitzone — fluidity zone

Festwerden Erdbildung — forming of solid earth

Guenther Wachsmuth. Illustration 1 presents my view of the Earth's ether body; and is based on evidence from modern upper atmosphere research (Aeronomy) that is discussed in the following paragraphs.[3]

In the air layer, the troposphere, the higher one ascends the colder the temperature becomes, the gases sparser, more dilute. At the upper boundary of the air layer (at an altitude of 20 kilometres), the temperature falls to about -55°C. But above this altitude, the atmosphere is chemically different, simpler. Above the air layer an interesting phenomenon occurs: the temperature starts to rise and continues rising up to an altitude of 50 kilometres.

Warmth-ether layer

At the top of this band of warmth, the temperature reaches approximately 18°C in summer. Demarcated by its warmth, this is quite a separate layer from the air layer below; there is very little interaction between the two layers. This warmer band, extending from 15 to 50 kilometres above the ground,

---

[3] This illustration, from my Rudolf Steiner Handbook, replaces the earlier graphics used in the first edition.

6

corresponds to the warmth-ether layer. Above this band, the temperature once again falls. According to current scientific knowledge, the warmth of this band is due to the action of solar rays upon molecules of oxygen. The oxygen disintegrates to form ozone.

The ozone absorbs various other kinds of solar radiation and becomes warm. Then the ozone starts to disintegrate, releasing heat. But the question as to the nature and origin of ozone is still not fully answered; for recent aeronomical research has found ozone also formed above the band of warmth (the stratosphere), without any warmth being needed, or being generated.

In addition, as my **Rudolf Steiner Handbook** discusses, in this layer there occurs a mysterious phenomenon, called the mother-of-pearl clouds, or nacreous clouds. But they are not clouds at all, as we understand this word. Nacreous 'clouds' are formed from extremely tiny ice particles about 10 microns[4] across, forming between 15 and 30 kilometres up. Seen shortly after sunset or after sunrise, they are caused by water vapour in this layer being forced up from the troposphere, when winds encounter mountains.

But the warm, burnished colours are striking, and difficult to explain physically. Their iridescent colours are presumably due to the light being refracted through different sized particles, but why they have mainly warm orange-red colours is intriguing. They are also far more brilliant than true clouds, slowly curling and uncurling,

Light-ether layer
According to Rudolf Steiner's research, a layer of light-ether comes next above the warmth-ether. Light-ether produces our visible light, and it does so without producing any heat. Light, when created by this ether, in reaction to a solar ether force, is in effect cold light, and is not the by-product of a warmth process (such as a flame). And the process that generates this cold light also produces ozone, as a kind of by-product in the physical, chemical realm.

Hence phosphorus, which generates cold light and in so doing, chemically creates ozone too, is an earthly substance in which the light-ether is strongly present. Presumably, the mysterious 'ever-burning' (cold) lights described and even

---

[4] A micron is 0.001 millimetre in diameter, a human hair is about 75 microns thick.

found in tombs by the Greeks and Romans are evidence of the ether technology of ancient peoples. Reports of these lamps are not uncommon in earlier times. St. Augustine of Hippo mentions that in an Egyptian temple dedicated to Venus there was such a lamp which could not be extinguished by wind or rain. In about AD 1540, one of these lamps was found in a tomb on the Appian Way at Rome in the tomb of Cicero's daughter, Tulliola, who died in 44 BC. The lamp has been burning for some 1550 years. In Persia, another such lamp, enclosed in an air-tight vessel, was found by soldiers of king Chosroes, it was then 500 years, and still burning, or more accurately, shining.

The same light-ether force makes possible the phosphorescent (or cold) light emitted by fungi, glow-worms, and other plants and creatures. Do the atmospheric conditions above the band of warmth, above the altitude of 50 kilometres, indicate the presence of this band of light-ether? Before considering this question, we need to understand certain phenomena caused by the interaction of ether forces. Both sun and moon ray out ether forces into the Earth's atmosphere. The moon's rays consist of chemical- (or water-) ether rather than warmth, light, or life-ether; hence the moon's connection with terrestrial moisture processes. The sun emanates life-ether (prana) into the Earth's atmosphere.

As the lunar and solar ethers permeate the ether body of the Earth, layer by layer, each of the four ethers present in the Earth's atmosphere interacts with the incoming rays to create a particular, substance (in gaseous form) fundamental to life on earth. When the lunar chemical-ether permeates the Earth's light-ether layer, **hydrogen peroxide is created**. But when the same layer is permeated by the solar ether, ozone is formed. Similarly, as the lunar ether permeates the earth's chemical-ether, **water is formed**; but when the chemical-ether layer is permeated by the solar ether forces, **oxygen is generated,** as this diagram shows.

And at the upper boundary of the Earth's ether organism, hydrogen is formed from the action of the in-raying lunar chemical-ether and helium from that of the solar rays.[5] To return to the question of how the light-ether layer is indicated by the atmospheric conditions above the warmth layer-between the altitudes of 50 and 85 kilometres there is

---

[5] Reported by G. Wachsmuth, from a conversation with Rudolf Steiner.

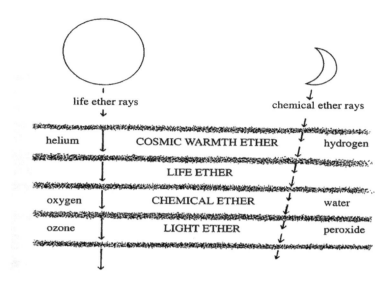

life ether rays

chemical ether rays

helium	COSMIC WARMTH ETHER	hydrogen
	LIFE ETHER	
oxygen	CHEMICAL ETHER	water
ozone	LIGHT ETHER	peroxide

another layer (the mesosphere) distinguished by several features, including temperature. It is cold. At the upper boundary of this layer, the temperature, which falls steadily the higher one rises, can be as low as -150°C.

Also, as that aeronomical research has indicated, ozone is formed in this layer. Regarding the connection between temperature and ozone formation, one experiment has discovered that when local temperature falls over several hours, the ozone level increases, sometimes as much as fourfold.[6] Because ozone is formed whenever the light-ether is active, we may regard this cold layer (between the altitudes of 50 and 85 kilometres) as representing the light-ether.

This correspondence is further confirmed by the strong presence here of hydrogen peroxide,[7] which is formed, as I have mentioned, when the lunar ether encounters light-ether forces. The presence of ozone below this cold band, that is, in the warmth-ether layer-we may regard as resulting from the complex chemical interaction between the ether layers. For example, the light-ether may ray down into the warmth-ether area.

---

[6] *Structure and Dynamics of the Upper Atmosphere*, proceedings of the Second Course of the International School of Physics, Erice, Italy, 23-27 June, 1971. p. 188.
[7] Encyclopaedia Britannica, 15th edition, 1983, vol. 2, p. 309.

150 kms	
105 kms	
85 kms	
50 kms	
20 kms	

Cosmic warmth layer

Life-ether layer (oxygen linked)

Oxygen & nitrogen ions

Thermosphere

Aurora

−150°C

Water-ether layer (water & magnetism linked)

Water vapour

Noctilucent wave clouds

Elf ring

Storm sprites

Shooting stars

Mesosphere

Light-ether layer (light & electricity linked)

Warmth-ether layer

Ozone

Nacreous clouds

+18°C

Stratosphere

AIR LAYER

Troposphere   −40°C

1 The four ether layers & the four bands in the atmosphere Warmth-ether layer: warm, with ozone; & nacreous clouds at times. Light-ether layer: shooting stars; sprites & elves can appear here. On the border: the shining, noctilucent 'clouds', with a velocity of 600 kms/hr. Water-ether layer: the watery aurora & also water vapour. Life-ether layer: a tenuous region, with ions of oxygen.

Also, as I wrote in the *Rudolf Steiner Handbook*, there are several strange and brilliantly radiant phenomena here, with qualities that indicate a potent etheric force. Firstly the so-called shooting stars occur here and only here. And these are extraordinary, for the shooting star's brilliant trail of light usually occurs between 70 and 100 kilometres above the ground, and will be seen by observers up to 500 kilometres apart, see Illustration One, for the over-all view.

This area corresponds to the light-ether layer and so one can ask, is the brilliant light we see due only to basic physical forces? For the material object that causes this visual phenomenon is about the size of the head of tiny pin ! And has a weight of about one hundredth of a gram or at the most, in some cases, just one gram.

Furthermore, mathematical calculations indicate that the density of this tiny particle is about that of water! The extraordinary radiance produced by such a tiny, semi-soft object is explained by science as the result of the speed with which it enters the atmosphere, about 45 kilometres per second, many times faster than a bullet. But the question arises whether the radiance of the shooting star might be enhanced by an ether force.

Meteors and shooting stars
This possibility gains credence when we consider that no solid rock has ever been produced by a shower of meteors. For these meteors are **not** solid objects, they never fall to the ground (it is the **meteorites** which do this, never a meteor). The meteor or shooting star is more energy (etheric energy) than matter. Is the light-ether here enhancing the radiance? Would you see a firecracker rocket even weighing five kilograms, from 500 kilometres away? Since light intensity fades with the {inverse square of the} distance from the light source, it is raises the question whether the brilliance of a tiny shooting star is enhanced by the etheric energies forming the matrix of this layer.

And also, in this band a very strange phenomenon was discovered. Whenever there is an electrical storm down here on the Earth's surface, then for a fraction of a second, far up in the light-ether layer, a huge and bright red shining tower of energy appears, called a 'storm sprite'. And even more amazing, above this tower of red energy, a bright circle of light appears too; this is actually called an 'elf-ring'. This link between these strange light-forms and the lightning produced in a storm is a mystery scientifically.

Noctilucent 'clouds'
But also in this layer, at the border of the next ether layer, there also occurs the fascinating and rare phenomenon of noctilucent clouds. These are brightly shining fields of tenuous energy (or 'clouds' for want of a better name) that are only rarely seen after dark in the summer, at an altitude of 80-85 kms.[8] At such a height and being so tenuous, in an area where very little material substances exist, they eluded scientific definition for many decades, and despite recent research projects, still remain unknown today. That their origin is in the activity of the band of light-ether in this layer seems likely.

A predominant theory is that tiny ice particles, perhaps with tiny dust particles from meteorites, enable a perceptible but very thin cloud-like structure to form. And then the sunlight reflects off them. In this theory, it is believed that ice particles are carried up there by strong, upward surges of the air in the lower atmosphere. However, alternatively, other academic experts have formulated the theory that tiny dust particles from meteorites (called meteor smoke) become these glowing 'clouds' by absorption of plasma material existing naturally up there.

Another fact very relevant here is that these clouds occur at the border of the light-ether layer and the water-ether layer. And in addition to this radiance, they also have a watery feature, namely the crests.

---

[8] The slight creeping up of 1% of these clouds to 88kms height, at the border between two regions is of no significance since these clouds straddle both layers; Megner, Khaplanov, etc. Annales Geophysicae 2009, *Large mesospheric ice particles at exceptionally high altitudes*; Megner, Khaplanov, etc.

For these are **wave-like crests,** and therefore both crests and dips exist in them, just like the ocean waves. In fact one of the earliest scientific articles about them invited readers to look at the photos supplied, turned upside down, because after 30 seconds one notices a distinct quality of three dimensional depth.

The chemical-ether or water-ether layer

Ascending still higher, above the altitude of 85 kilometres, we encounter yet another distinct layer of the atmosphere. This layer terminates at an altitude of approximately 105 kilometres, with an area of turbulence, above which again quite different conditions exist. According to the Steiner sketch, the chemical-ether layer comes above the light-ether. Steiner did not, however, give any indications as to the altitude of these layers.

What is then the nature of the atmosphere between the altitudes of 85 and 105 kilometres? One noticeable quality is the presence of an abundance of water vapour, relatively speaking. The atmosphere at this altitude is dilute; water, in the form of a fine vapour, predominates; gases are sparse. Above 105 kilometres, the water content abruptly ceases,[9] and below this layer there is very little water vapour, except of course in the air layer. Further, this layer above 85 kilometres contains more oxygen than any of the other layers except, once again, the air layer. Because the oxygen controls the chemistry and physics of this layer, scientific research has focused on the factors affecting oxygen content here.[10]

As I have mentioned, water and oxygen are formed through the reaction of the Earth's chemical-ether layer with lunar and solar ethers, respectively. We may therefore consider this stratum of the atmosphere between the altitudes of 85 and 105 kilometres the chemical-ether layer.

---

[9] *Intercomparison of Atmospheric/Mesopheric data,* COSPAR Interdisciplinary Scientific Proceedings, (Groz, Austria; Pergamin Press, 1985, p.75.

[10] *Dynamics of the Middle Atmosphere,* proceedings of a US-Japan seminar in Hawaii (Nov. 1982) (Dordrecht/Boston/Lancaster: D. Reidel Publishing Company, (1983) section on *Gravity Waves,* pp.140-45;see also Structure & Dynamics of the Upper Atmosphere...., chapter on *Global Structure,* sections 3-7.

Further evidence for this correspondence is the occurrence in this stratum of the aurora, the northern (or southern) lights. These startling light displays result from disturbances in the Earth's magnetic energies.[11] They occur in a broad band of the atmosphere, beginning at an altitude of 80 kilometres; the great majority, and the most intense, occur at approximately 100 kilometres.[12]

Rudolf Steiner's research established that as they become depleted through their activity, ether forces weaken and decay. The decay of chemical-ether induces magnetism.[13] The occurrence of the auroral lights, then, which is connected with magnetic energy, indicates the presence of decaying chemical-ether. As Rudolf Steiner discovered in his research,

> ...the electrical and magnetic energy streams which go around the earth.[14]

These streams indicate the existence of decaying ethers which form in the atmosphere, leading to these currents of magnetism and electricity. But furthermore, we noted that the water-forming ether is also called the tone-ether, as it produces and sustains physical sounds. And it is a fact that many people, but not all, who experience an aurora also hear strange sounds coming from it. It is also true that very sophisticated listening devices, especially deployed for this purpose in scientific research, have failed to detect any sounds at all from the aurora. The sounds heard will be in the ether, not in physical space.[15]

Ascending still further, beyond the turbulent upper boundary of the chemical-ether layer at 105 kilometres, we encounter yet another distinct area of the atmosphere. No more water molecules or hydrogen compounds; here we find primal simple gases, nitrogen and oxygen, diffused ever more sparsely in the atmosphere. Their molecules

---

[11] 'See H. Falck-Ytter, *Aurora*, for an excellent study of the aurora (Anthroposophic Press, 1985).

[12] The auroral lights do extend up beyond 105 kms, but only faintly, which I conclude is due to the persistence of the Earth's magnetic field (hence a kind of weak corona of the water-ether).

[13] GA 130, lect. 1st Oct. 1911.

[14] GA 98, lect. 7th Dec. 1907.

[15] In 2016, scientists made available sound recordings of electrical-magnetic waves from the aurora; but whether these are at all related to the etheric resonance is difficult to say.

continually fragmenting, disintegrating, recombining, the gases exist here in a less material state than in the lower atmospheric layers.

According to present scientific theory, gas molecules fragment when they interact with cosmic energies raying into the upper atmosphere. Whether the less material state of gaseous substance here is due to in-raying energies, or whether it is caused, at least partially, by the nature of the ether layer at this stratum, this is an interesting question.

The disintegrating of substances, called 'ionization', results in molecules and atoms becoming 'ions', that is, incomplete or less substantial atoms. The terms 'atom' and 'ion' (which I use to refer to fragmented energy points) are taken from conventional science. I am aware that the idea of the atom is constantly being reviewed scientifically and is viewed in various ways by Rudolf Steiner. But my intention in this chapter is simply to give a sketch of the scientific view of the atmosphere that is sufficient to allow the emergence of an anthroposophical view. For this purpose, ionization could be considered as the beginning of a dematerializing or etherealizing (ether-generating) process. Thus the oxygen and nitrogen present in this atmospheric layer are increasingly less material with altitude.

At this atmospheric stratum, between the altitudes of 105 and about 150 kilometres, we reach the last of the four ether layers, the life-ether. Beyond this layer, we encounter the outermost sheath of the Earth's ether aura, which is more a cosmic than a telluric layer; this is the cosmic warmth-ether layer. To define the life-ether band further, it is helpful to consider first this outermost sheath, which does not seem to begin at a clearly defined altitude, but gradually emerges then predominates in the upper region of the life-ether layer. Scientists are still researching this outermost sheath, the gases of which are in an even less material state than are those in the life-ether area.

Indeed this outer area is regarded by science as consisting of energy rather than matter; it is defined as consisting of plasma, that is, an energy state, like that in a flame, rather than tangible material substances. We may describe the gaseous substances in the outer sheath as ions; they are in an unstable, energized state. They are more points of energy emission than they are substance. The energy we may describe as warmth energy.

The atmosphere is described as becoming very hot at altitudes above the life-ether layer. For example, at an altitude of about 200 kilometres, the temperature is said to be approximately 700°C, and at the outer boundary of this energy sheath, at an altitude of about 3,000 kilometres, the temperature is said to reach 1700°C ! But at such altitudes we would encounter only rarefied energy points of gases, not a tangible gaseous atmosphere. And because there is no air to conduct the 'warmth', the human warm sense would not detect any heat. Temperature readings are taken at these altitudes by complex rocket devices, which register the energy state of the semi-material ions as temperature.

The energy state manifests as warmth within the tiny semi-ethereal speck of gaseous substance, but, again, human skin would not sense any warmth. So we picture an area with intense inherent warmth-an ethereal warmth mantle around the ether layers of the earth. This cosmic warmth-ether layer consists, chemically, at first of incomplete or semi-ethereal (monatomic or ionic) oxygen, then at higher altitudes (above about 500 kilometres) of helium, and finally of hydrogen in ionic state.

Helium is formed when the sun's in-raying life-ether permeates the warmth-ether; and hydrogen is formed when the warmth-ether is permeated by the moon's chemical-ether. Thus hydrogen and helium should be present also in the lower, first warmth-ether layer.

We do find hydrogen present there, in various forms, but not helium. Perhaps this lack is connected to the operation in the lower warmth layer of powerful chemical processes involving ozone. Thus we may regard this outermost area of the atmosphere as a cosmic warmth-ether area, confirming Rudolf Steiner's research of 1923. He stated that,

> ....the warmth-ether {band} consists of two parts, two layers, the one being the layer of earthly warmth, the other that of cosmic warmth, and these two continually play into each other.[16]

We can now complete our brief consideration of the life-ether layer. So far, we have noted only one quality of this layer, that its gases are beginning to ionize. Thus if one were to descend through the atmosphere, one would encounter

---

[16] GA 230, lect. 3 (*Man as Symphony of the Creative Word*).

16

first the virtually nonmaterial cosmic warmth-ether layer, then an area where a tangible gaseous atmosphere develops. One would in this area encounter the material earth for the first time, even though the substances are gases in a fluctuating volatile state. This is the life-ether layer. There is no specific chemical evidence for its presence. But it is the life-ether that condenses solid matter, (called the 'earth element', in alchemical terms), out of the ether realm.[17]

Thus it was through this ether that in Lemurian times the material globe was formed, condensed out of an ethereal state. Matter in this sense means any tangible substance, including gases, anything that is no longer ethereal, not only a rock or soil. On the Earth's surface, this condensing ether produces the more earthy, more angular, leaf forms, the needles of the pine tree, for example. The life-ether layer, then, begins at an altitude of about 105 kilometres and extends upwards for perhaps 50 kilometres before gradually merging into the cosmic warmth-ether layer. Precise measurements here are difficult.

Finally, we can note here that a small amount of electricity is present in plants also, where the ether energies are so strong and alive. Electricity is created as light-ether decays. When one views electricity and magnetism from this perspective made possible by Rudolf Steiner's research, one comprehends the harmful nature of modern technology, based as it is on electromagnetic energy. For example, the use of solar cells to generate electricity from sunlight depends upon the direct destruction of light-ether.

Note: an update of the description given here is available in my *Rudolf Steiner Handbook,* together with a number of coloured images from NASA of mysterious upper atmosphere phenomena which is very supportive of my conclusions given here.

The seasons and the breathing of the hemispheres

The complex, many-layered ether atmosphere is a vital part of the living Earth. And the various changes that occur in the ether layers during the cycle of the year demonstrate, substantially, that the seasons are hemispherical phenomena. In the wintertime of either hemisphere, we experience a variation in the colder temperatures; the days can be at times mild, at times very cold. But up above in the

---

[17] GA 123, lect. 12th Sept. 1910, (*Gospel of St. Matthew*).

atmosphere, throughout the warmth-ether layer, the temperature falls and stays low until the spring. Thus, at an altitude of 15 kilometres, where it is -55°C in summer, it will fall to -80°C in winter.

And at an altitude of 50 kilometres where the temperature is +18°C in summer and then it falls to -20°C in winter. Higher up at 65kms, the temperature in summer is around -40°C, it falls to -80°C in winter. These temperatures are averaged out, as the temperatures in the layers above the polar regions are different to those above the equator. But the temperatures given here are representative of the differences in the summer and winter hemispheres.

But it is fascinating to know that these very different winter-summer temperatures also occur simultaneously; one set for the hemisphere having its summer time, the other set of temperatures for the hemisphere having its wintertime !

And as Illustration 2 shows, there are also these 'mirror-opposites' occurring in the air-pressure readings, wind currents and other factors operative in the atmosphere ! (Higher up, beyond the light-ether layer a temperature variation does occur which is beyond the scope of this book.)

Then as the equinox condition approaches, bringing spring on one side of the Earth and autumn on the other, a remarkable uniformity or equilibrium of temperatures develops over the entire globe. The atmospheric warming over one hemisphere is accompanied by a simultaneous cooling over the other hemisphere; a rhythmical global contrast that astonished the scientists who discovered it.[18]

Scientists discovered yet another indication of the marked inner difference between summer and winter hemispheres when they directed radar signals into the upper atmosphere at different times during the year. In summer, the signals were echoed back strongly, from an altitude of about 80 kilometres, which is near the top of the light-ether layer. In the winter, there was only a weak echoing back of the radar from what we can define as the whole range of the light-ether layer.[19]

---

[18] "Structure & Dynamics..." chapter on *Global Stratospheric Temperature fields*, Lindzen, pps. 172-3; and *Introduction to 3D climate modelling*, Chapt.2, (W. Washington, C. Parkinson, 2005). The global contrast in temperatures was discovered through a 10-year research project involving 200 probes of atmospheric conditions.
[19] *Dynamics of the Middle Atmosphere*, p. 77ff.

Discoveries such as these demonstrate what scientists call the mirror image situation in the contrasting seasonal dynamics of the two hemispheres. Seasonally, opposite meteorological situations-including direction and strength of wind currents, air pressure, temperature, and chemical interactions between gaseous substances-prevail on either side of the globe.

It becomes clear that the seasonal cycle of the year is a powerful hemispheric reality, that the alternating atmospheric phenomena are indications of processes in the ether layers above the hemispheres. The seasons are a major rhythm in the life of the Earth, and the cycle of the year is a reality for the entire ether body of the globe, not only amongst the flora and fauna on the ground.

Two processes are at work causing the seasonal cycle, one discovered by science and the other through the spiritual science inaugurated by Rudolf Steiner. The scientific explanation is based on the well-known astronomical relationship of the Earth to the sun. Because our planet is tilted a little on its axis, one hemisphere is more exposed to the rays of the sun than the other hemisphere at certain times during the Earth's orbit. Thus in December, the northern half of the globe is pointing away from the sun, while at the same time the southern half is pointing toward the sun and is therefore having its summertime.

The reverse is the case in June. In the summertime position, the hemisphere receives the sun's rays more directly, more intensely. The sun will also rise higher in the sky than at any other season, so the more direct rays are also permeating the atmosphere for a longer time in each 24 hours, see Illustration 3. The factors are of course all reversed in the winter. According to Rudolf Steiner, the seasonal cycle is caused by the breathing of the Earth; a process in the ether aura similar to our inhaling and exhaling.

This breathing process affects the earth's soul: as new growth develops in spring, the ethereal and soul forces-in the springtime hemisphere-begin to ascend out of the Earth. They are exuded or exhaled into the atmosphere.[20] This exhaling of subtle energies continues into the summer; then

---

[20] GA 223, lect. 31st Mar. 1923 (*Cycle of the Year as Breathing process of the Earth*).

2 June - December atmospheric mirroring

The polarity of winter & summer is reflected in the middle atmospheric layers, as in a mirror-image.

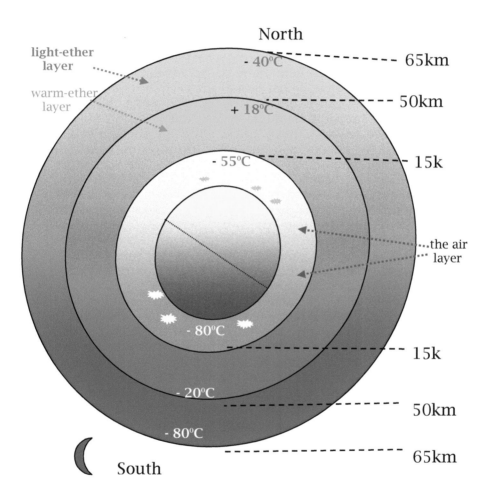

North

light-ether layer

warm-ether layer

- 40°C — — — — — — — 65km

+ 18°C — — — — — — 50km

- 55°C — — — — — — — 15k

...the air layer

- 80°C

- 20°C

- 80°C

15k

50km

65km

South

The strong temperature differences (averaged) between the two hemispheres near to the solstice. But this opposite mirror-imaging also occurs in the air-pressure, wind currents, and other factors. The opposite nature of the seasons in the two hemispheres extends high up into the atmosphere's structure, on many levels.

in autumn the hemisphere begins to inhale its forces, and by the winter these forces are again drawn down into the physical body of the Earth.

In summer the life processes occur mainly toward the top or periphery of the bushes and trees. From there scents and colours ray out into the sky, where the busy winged insects work ceaselessly. The air seems somehow 'full' not clear, as in winter, and not only because of the waves of heat oscillating through it, but also because of some subtle presence. The air and all the layers of the ether aura are permeated with the fully out-breathed forces and elemental powers of the hemisphere.

But all this is drawn down into the ground by winter. How subtly empty the winter sky seems, how little activity is occurring in the plants above the ground ! Yet beneath our feet, in the body of the earth, an intense activity is developing, which will enable the new life of the spring to unfold. In this book we will consider the breathing process of the Earth in detail. It is important to note that this exhaling and inhaling process has a definite rhythm; which is harmonized with the astronomical motions causing the seasons, **it is this which enables a particular relationship to develop between the sun and the Earth.**

As the hemisphere becomes increasingly pointed toward the sun, elemental forces are at the same time exhaled, and the interaction between earth and sun is thereby intensified with the involvement of ethereal and soul elements.

Likewise, as the hemisphere is turned away from the sun as the planet moves through its orbit, the hemisphere's elemental forces are drawn down into the interior of the Earth, which is impermeable to the sun. Is there any evidence of this exhaling and inhaling of the telluric ether forces? Yes, in that atmospheric phenomena are, as we have seen, connected to activity in the ether body of the Earth. Careful study of meteorological and aeronomical data can reveal to some extent the occurrence of a rhythmical pulsing or breathing in the Earth, dynamically similar to the ethereal hemispheric breathing process.

The pulse beat of the living Earth
Meteorological research undertaken over the last two

3 The two causes of the seasons

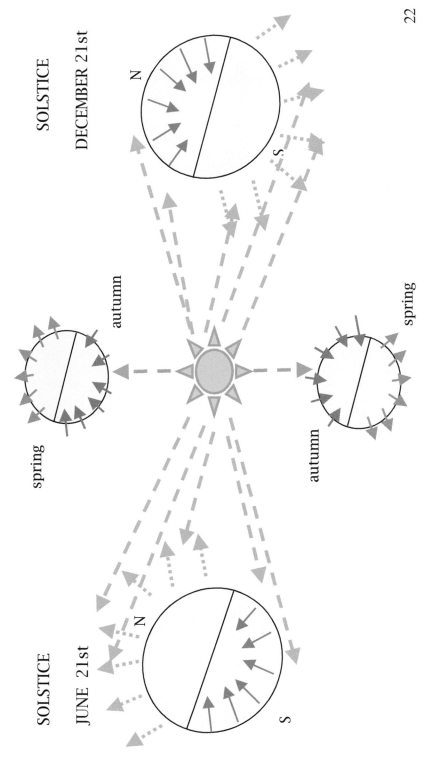

SOLSTICE
DECEMBER 21st

N

S

autumn

spring

spring

autumn

SOLSTICE
JUNE 21st

N

S

centuries has discovered many aspects of the interaction between the Earth's atmosphere and the cosmos, especially the sun. For example, there is, as one would expect, during the day a response to the sun's energies, in the course of which the air heats up and a wave of high pressure moves through the atmosphere. However, the daily timing for this response is irregular, as is its intensity.

And our perception of this response is obscured by other atmospheric processes occurring in the air layer closer to ground level. But here on the surface of the Earth, we cannot experience this once-a-day surge of high pressure.[21] In addition to this daily response of the atmosphere to the sun, there occurs another more mysterious atmospheric phenomenon that has puzzled scientists for about two hundred years.

Some activity, some surge of energy, causes a maximum of air pressure, a wave of high pressure, twice daily, always at the same times – between 9 and 10 am, and between 9 and 10 pm. This remarkable rhythm would appear to derive from some force not connected with that once-a-day heating up of the air by the midday sun. This semi-diurnal pressure wave was studied by such great pioneers of modern science as Laplace, Lord Kelvin, Goethe, and Humboldt, who remarked that this development of high pressure each morning and evening was so regular that his barometer could serve as a clock!

Until a few decades ago, this phenomenon was regarded by scientists (including Guenther Wachsmuth) as a tropospheric process; that is, as a process occurring only in the air layer. But since the 1960s it has been discovered that this process, involving twice-daily (or 'diurnal') pressure waves and the winds which they generate, takes place in the atmosphere: and this is from ground level, right up to an altitude of approximately 120 kilometres ![22] That is, this regular energy pulse oscillates through a major part of the atmosphere, affecting all four layers of the Earth's ether body (remember that the fourth layer, the life-ether layer begins at an altitude of approximately 105 kilometres).

---

[21] Chapmand and Lindzen, *Atmospheric Tides*, (Dordrecht, Holland D. Reidel Publishing Co. 1970, p. 17ff).
[22] Dynamics of the Middle Atmosphere, section on *Tides & Oscillations;* linearized calculations of semi-diurnal Tides.

What actually happens each day? What is the significance of this process? At midmorning, a surge of energy manifests in the atmosphere of the eastern side of the Earth, the side facing the sun. This wave of energy arises at this time in both northern and southern hemispheres (although each is in a different season), causing, physically, higher air pressure and consequent wind currents and other effects throughout the ether layers. Then again in the mid-to-late evening, with clocklike regularity, the same energy surges in the western side of the Earth or evening sky of both hemispheres.

Because the sun's influence is minimal at midmorning and late evening, researchers over the last two centuries have naturally considered that this semi-diurnal energy wave cannot be due to the daily heating of the atmosphere by the sun. What then is causing it? The answer was intuitively grasped long ago by that outstanding scientist, Johann Wolfgang von Goethe, who thought that it derived from an activity occurring within the Earth, a living planet. The Earth is breathing in and out at these times, he wrote.[23] Through his spiritual research, Rudolf Steiner confirmed Goethe's conclusion.

The anthroposophist Guenther Wachsmuth conversed with Rudolf Steiner on this subject and proceeded to research the available scientific data for confirmation of this viewpoint. He was not fully aware of the structure of the Earth's ether body, and there was no scientific knowledge of the upper atmosphere at that time, the early 1920s. Still his careful study of the changes in the troposphere each morning and evening revealed that some of the subterranean chemical-ether layer is exhaled and later inhaled at these times. The four ethers, it should be remembered, also exist under the ground, inside the Earth.

The chemical-ether has an affinity with moisture. This daily rhythm, the breathing in and out of the Earth's chemical-ether, causes (as Wachsmuth pointed out) a remarkable rhythm in the generation of atmospheric water vapour, which forms most strongly, becomes maximal, twice each day, a few hours after sunrise and then again a few hours after sunset. This rhythm follows closely the 9 am and

---

[23] In Naturwissenschaftliche Schriften, *Versuch einer Witterungslehre* 1825, Hamburger Ausgabe, 1955, edit. Trunze, C. Wegner Vlg, Hamburg vol. 13, p.308.

9 pm rhythm of the global energy pulsations. Hence it is not surprising that even today science cannot find the explanation for this rhythmical moisture formation.

Having discovered the cause for the rhythmical generation of atmospheric water vapour, Wachsmuth wanted to understand the twice-daily pressure wave (or energy pulsing) as also caused by the ascent and descent of the Earth's chemical-ether. This conclusion was in error, for as I have explained, the pressure wave oscillates throughout the entire ether aura, it is not restricted to the air layer. But Wachsmuth's deduction is understandable in view of the lack of scientific data in the 1920s.

Just as the pulsing in our wrists does not cause the circulation of the blood through the body, so too the morning and evening humidity maxima do not cause the powerful energy surges through the Earth's ether body. The subterranean chemical-ether forces do not ascend higher than the air layer-the moisture-forming process occurs only in the air layer.

The twice-daily pressure wave that arises throughout the ether layers of the earth is a powerful rhythmical dynamic; it is a pulsing activity which develops ethereally, and then physically, within the 24-hour rhythm of day and night. It is the pulse beat of the living earth. The accompanying chemical-ether ascent and descent can serve to portray the larger scale seasonal in- and out-breathing of ether and soul forces. The daily process is one aspect of the telluric in- and out-breathing dynamic, a 'pulsation' (as Steiner called it), "a manifestation of an inner life, an inner power of the earth".[24]

Some scientists have theorized that, the twice-daily pressure wave-between 9 and 10 am and between 9 and 10 pm-is part of the complex response of the ozone layer to the midday build up of heat in the atmosphere. However, it is acknowledged that the mathematical calculations upon which this explanation is based cannot account for important aspects of the pulsing; for example, its seasonal variations, which researchers describe as remarkable. The pressure wave is stronger; its amplitude twice as large, its phase tending to lag; in the hemisphere experiencing winter than in the one experiencing summer.

---

[24] GA 163, lect. 4th Sept. 1915 and GA 58, 21st Nov. 1914 and GA 174, 28th Jan. 1915.

This is an interesting discovery when one reflects that in winter the hemisphere's ether and soul forces are within its physical body, that the Earth-soul is awake or intensely active then (see Chapter Two for further discussion of this theme), whereas in summer, the hemisphere is 'out of itself' or half asleep. Our pulse, too, is stronger, quicker when we are active and alert.

ADDENDUM

Guenther Wachsmuth's view of the Earth's ether layers

Wachsmuth's understanding of the ether layers, from the 1960's, is quite different from that presented in this volume. He does agree that there are four ether-layers inside the Earth, but he understands the Earth's ether aura as consisting of only three layers. But the number and order of the layers above the earth's surface needs to be clarified. Apparently Wachsmuth never saw Steiner's sketch of the structure of the ether aura, but instead had to interpret the somewhat ambiguous description Steiner gave of this sketch in a 1923 lecture:

> We have the light-ether and the warmth-ether, which consists of two parts, two layers, one being the layer of earthly warmth, the other that of cosmic warmth, and these continually play one into the other...Then bordering on the warmth-ether is the air {layer}. Below this would come water and earth, and above {*above what?*} would come chemical-ether and light-ether.[25]

Wachsmuth decided that the chemical and light-ether layers come immediately above the air. The air to him did not mean the air layer, which Steiner knew about, which modern science knows about. In the 1920s the layered structure of the atmosphere had not yet been recognized, the troposphere and adjoining stratosphere had not yet been identified. Hence Wachsmuth defined 'air' as a band of the troposphere immediately above the ground, a few kilometres perhaps in height. For Wachsmuth, the chemical and light-ether layers come between this lower part of the troposphere (above it, that is) and the warmth-ether layer. And this warmth layer itself was unclear to him; that is, its beginning point and its extent. His diagram of these layers has no altitude indication.

But Rudolf Steiner was saying that the chemical and light-ether layers come above the warmth-ether layer, not the bottom section of the air layer. Wachsmuth was misled by another factor, namely that in the air layer the light-ether is

---

[25] GA 230, lect. 27th Oct. 1923 (*Man as Symphony of the creative Word*).

active (or 'reflected'), and that in the moisture of the air and of the oceans the chemical-ether (from high above) is reflected. Further, Wachsmuth's diagrams show that he was unaware that there is a layer of life-ether up above the Earth, arching overhead like the other ether layers. In addition to evidence I have already presented to establish the presence of this layer, let me recall Rudolf Steiner's direct comment about "the life-ether that weaves around the Earth".[26]

---

[26] GA 145, lect. 23rd Mar. 1915.

CHAPTER TWO

NATURE SPIRITS

So far, we have considered only the more external aspects of the seasonal processes of nature. The full significance of the seasonal out- and in-breathing of the hemispheres becomes clear when we realize that the tangible, sense-perceptible processes of nature are brought about by living beings – the so-called nature spirits, not distinguishable by our physical vision. For when the aura of the earth is breathed out, certain kinds of nature sprites ascend with it up into the atmosphere, arising ever higher on into the summer; then they begin to descend back down to the soil during the autumn, as the currents in the ether body of the Earth, reverse. During this ascending and descending, the altering of the consciousness and functions of these sprites contributes considerably to the changing inner moods of the seasons, to the seasonal influences upon us.

Prior to our modern human consciousness, it was the common traditional experience of humankind that these living or en-souled beings are active in the various seasonal processes of nature. These beings, now called 'fairies' or 'nature spirits' (though these terms are used rather loosely), exist as ethereal entities and or soul entities, and are hence invisible until perception of the ether forces has developed. Perception of such beings was universal in earlier times, when humankind possessed a natural psychic faculty. Thus a worldwide fairy lore does exist, remarkably consistent in its major details. We need to understand the nature of these beings in order to develop an understanding of the significance for us of the cycle of the year.

We have seen that the four elemental states of being; earth (solid), water (fluid), air (gas), and fire (warmth), are each the expression of one of the four ethers. That is, the life-ether, chemical-ether, light-ether, and warmth-ether. Each of the four ethers is brought into activity by one of the four kinds of nature spirits: in earth, called **gnomes**; in water, called **undines**; in air, called **sylphs**; and in fire, there are the **pyrausta** or fire spirits. These are soul beings; they are minor entities in relation to the hierarchies of creative beings (or gods, as they were called in earlier times), for unlike the divine hierarchical beings, they have no spirit in the higher divine sense.

There are many different kinds of such soul beings in nature, for example, those active within musical tones, or in electro-magnetism (sinister beings), or in the regulation of the moon's phases. The four kinds of spirits I have just named are more accurately called 'elementals' or 'nature elementals', as they are each active around plant life (and elsewhere) via one of the four elements.

Though the term 'elements' today calls to mind the four states of matter we have mentioned, it really refers to the four ethereal forces that produce these states, and to the corresponding soul world dynamics (or more technically, the astral forces) that create the four ethers. Thus the gnomes, undines, sylphs, and pyrausta inhabit the ether and soul realms, and working with the elements or ether soul forces, maintain the external, physical-material world.

This special connection makes the term 'elemental being' preferable to 'fairy' or 'nature spirit'. From Rudolf Steiner we have the deepest and clearest information about these beings. From his teachings, we can see that, in a precise usage of words, the term 'spirit' is inappropriate for these beings. This is because he has pointed out that they do not have a spiritual kernel. This is not to say, however, that other, higher, greater beings who direct these lesser sprites do not have a spirit.

As we will see, Rudolf Steiner regarded the lack of living knowledge of these beings as a serious defect in modern Christianity, and in its festivals. Apart from the gnomes, undines, sylphs, and pyrausta, there are many other nature beings, some little sprites, some powerful beings; overseeing particular processes in the kingdoms of nature. These beings, unlike the four elemental nature beings, are not focused in special ethers, but have tasks within the general ether aura of the Earth. The modern term 'fairy' appears to refer to nature sprites other than the elemental beings.

The subtlety of the substance of which the bodies of these beings are composed – they can have virtually any form or colour they please – intensifies our confusion. Only to the trained vision of an initiated seer is their real form perceptible. A vision of a fairy by an untrained person need not be a reliable description of the actual being involved. For example, experienced clairvoyants have pointed out that a 'winged' figure is not a being with fine gossamer wings;

rather, surging around behind the figure, is a stream of forces that can appear as a wing. In one case, a girl who would see fairies from time to time commented in great delight upon the graceful, beautiful appearance of several aerial sprites. On one such occasion these sprites suddenly became intensely ugly and hostile then disappeared.[27]

Here we will consider the nature of the four types of elemental beings, with the help of a pastel drawing by Steiner, entitled "Elemental Beings", see Illustration 4. Then we can return briefly to the enigma of elves and fairies. The perspectives I present here concerning elemental beings are based on Steiner's spiritual research.[28]

Gnomes

The gnomes are active in the solid material, the solidifying processes, of nature. They work with the life-ether in mineral-chemical processes, especially in the soil and in the root systems of plants. They also work to maintain the structure of the mineral kingdom, of the rocks, crystals, and metals. The word gnome, derived by Paracelsus from a Greek word for 'knowing', is appropriate, for these beings gain an immediate insight into whatever aspect of the physical body of the Earth they are working with.

They do not have to deduce facts through logical processes of thinking as we do. This difference probably is a major reason for their tendency, well known in earlier times, to derive pleasure from mocking human beings and even playing tricks on them – tricks that indicate their power to intervene in the physical-material world. Rudolf Steiner confirms their mischievous nature, so widely reported in the fairy lore.

But the gnomes are also ready to be helpful; especially to those people who have a positive attitude toward the realm of faery, or "the middle kingdom" (as the Celts called the world of nature beings between humans and the gods); that is, toward the living beings behind nature. Traditionally they were helpers of miners, guiding them, for example, in the search for veins of valuable metals. The farmer also needs

---

[27] From A. Doyle, *The Coming of the Faeries*, (N.Y. Samuel Weiser, 1972, p.120).
[28] In particular, GA 230, (*Man as Symphony...*) and GA 98.

4 **"Elemental Beings"** by Rudolf Steiner. Pastel, Nov.1923, original size 64x 71.5 cm. Reproduced in original size by Rudolf Steiner Verlag, Dornach.

The view is of a river bed, hovering in the water (itself not visible), are three undines; emerging from the soil, near a shrub, are several gnomes. Above them are several sylphs, near two birds; above these are two 'pyraustas' in the vicinity of what are presumably several butterflies. On the left an ahrimanic human face; on the right a Luciferic face.

the goodwill of these beings, whose activity in the roots and germinating seeds of plants plays a significant role in the success of a crop. The term 'Kobolds', 'rock (or mountain) elves', 'dwarves', or 'leprechauns'- usually refer to the gnomes. The gnomes are especially active in winter, and we will refer to them again when considering the winter festival. They can be seen in Steiner's pastel drawing as little mannikin figures, bluish in colour and moving up out of the ground, which to them is no barrier at all, into a bush.

Undines

The term for the water sprites, undines, was also coined by Paracelsus, from unda, Latin for 'waves'. Undines manifest in watery, moist environs, such as lakes, rivers, mists, waterfalls, and rain. In the plant realm these beings, working with the chemical-ether (also called 'tone ether'), direct the flow of moisture in plants, helping the formation of leaves and buds. They appear as delicate, beautiful beings; similar to young women who are just taking on a form, for their appearance is always changing, unless expressly held in the nymph form.

These beings are the famous nymphs or nixen of fairy lore, perception of which was regarded as dangerous (for the male viewer !) in olden times, their beauty being so entrancing. The undines are especially active in nature during springtime. Rudolf Steiner's drawing depicts them as young feminine forms (possibly with one masculine undine) in green and yellow shades. If one considers the left side of the picture, where the soil slopes away, to be a riverbed, then the undines are within the water of the river (the water being omitted from the picture).

Sylphs

The air elementals were called sylphs by Paracelsus. It appears that he combined the word nymph with the word sylvestris ('of the woods'). In any event, the inner mood or gesture of this word, its vowels and consonants, is appropriate for air elementals. They are manifest in the physical world in the air, in the wind. When they are moving in the sky they move like little meteors, lightning swift, according to Rudolf Steiner. They have significant tasks in connection with the bird life, usually journeying with the birds in the sky if possible. In the plant life, they have the important task of directing the light-ether into the growing plant, working together with the undines, to weave the archetypal form of the plant into its physical substance.

The appearance of the sylphs is even less fixed, less definable, than that of the undines, although they can have winged fairy form, according to some psychics. So in the Steiner drawing, one sylph has a rather tangible winged form, whereas the other two sylphs (in blue, amidst the blue sky) are almost spherical (two brown birds are flying near them).

The sylphs are especially active in the autumn, when the plants begin to lose their form, wither, and decay. For then their task is to transfer the idea, the archetype, of the plant's form down into the realm of the gnomes. There under the Earth it is the task of the gnomes to perceive this 'form-archetype' and to preserve awareness of it within themselves. Thus the gnomes can prepare during the winter for the form's re-emergence in material substance, as the seeds (or dormant buds) of the plant once again begin the growth process in the new year.

Pyraustas
The elemental beings who active in fire, that is, in warmth processes, use the warmth-ether to bring about fruiting and seed formation in plants. The fire elementals were called 'pyrausta' by the Greeks. They are mentioned by Pliny, a first century Roman, as nature sprites that 'live in fire'. In another context, writing about a salamander-lizard common in Europe and Asia Minor, Pliny records the superstitious 'fact' that the creature is so cold it can walk through fire, unharmed. Gradually, the name of this 'fire-proof' lizard was given to the pyrausta; Paracelsus, for one, used the term 'salamanders' to refer to the fire elementals.

Rudolf Steiner at first used this term also. But presumably he came to feel that this term is not so fitting, for in later lectures he ceased to use it. He did use the term 'fire spirits', however, because the pyrausta, being the most evolved of the elemental beings, may be regarded as having a spiritual (or 'devachanic') essence. (The term in anthroposophical literature for 'spirit' is 'devachanic'; it refers to Devachan, the actual spiritual realm beyond the astral realm.) And also the word 'spirit' is culturally used for any non-material entity.

Like the sylphs, undines, and gnomes, the pyrausta influence the tone of human consciousness. Especially active

34

in the summer, the fire elementals gather up the warmth, present through the warmth-ether, and bear it into the blossom of the plant. Hence seeds-and within seeds, oil-can develop; plant oils, with their rich golden colour, are the result of the pyrausta's alchemical transforming of the warmth-ether.

In Illustration 4 the pyrausta are drawn, in a relatively defined form, as golden-yellow winged beings, high up in the atmosphere; but as with the sylphs, two of them are depicted in a more or less formless state, in a bright red colour. Perhaps these formless pyrausta, like the formless sylphs, are in rapid motion. (The two humanlike countenances, to the left and right in the drawing, will be considered in Chapter Four.)

Fairies and Elves

What is the relationship of the four elemental nature beings to the classical fairy or flower sprite of the eighteenth and nineteenth centuries? The term 'fairy' or faery, is a generalized, vague expression today; it derives from the Latin word for one of the three 'fates', entities involved in guiding human destiny. This term, fatum, was used in the Middle Ages to form the term fatare, "to enchant". And this word, as a past participle, fae in French, meaning 'enchanted', gradually became the noun 'fee' or fairy, designating any nature being in the enchanted realm of the middle kingdom.

There are many different kinds of beings in the alluring, colourful realm of ethereal and astral (soul) forces which sustain nature and humankind. There are nature beings who oversee the development of trees and shrubs, and there are the flower elves or flower fairies who nurture the blossoms of plants. The sylphs and undines may be regarded as flower elves to some extent; that is, when they are in a more formed state and are active around a plant.

But normally the flower fairy is a different kind of nature being, having less power than the sylphs, undines, and other elementals, and not so intimately connected to our normal ego consciousness. (Also, as we have noted, the gnomes, undines, sylphs, and pyrausta work each with one specific ether or elemental force, whereas the flower fairies and the many other nature sprites are active in a more general way in the subtle life forces of the Earth.) The flower fairy, in fact, is usually directed in its activity, only carried out during the night, by a particular sylph.[29]

The sylphs revel in the light of the sun, working with the light-ether to produce visible light. But old traditions tell of the flower elves, and others of the non-elemental nature beings, that they may not be exposed to the sunlight, which has a benumbing effect on them. So these beings manifest in the physical world as evening begins – they work from their ether-astral realm into nature during the night, ceasing this activity as dawn approaches, the coming sun resounding for them in majestic cosmic tones through the ethers. The visions (or sightings) of nature beings can occur at night, and a special instance is the dance of the flower fairies under the moonlight, in a quiet clearing.

The flower elves are referred to in Shakespeare's *A Midsummer Night's Dream* (Act 3, scene 2), when Puck reminds his master Oberon that morning is approaching. If the initiate inspiring this the playwright had not formed it with a major emphasis on the nature spirits, then the English-speaking world would have had almost no literature of renown which preserved awareness of the world of faery.

Sightings of nature sprites do occur in midsummer, we shall consider this again when exploring the St. John's festival. Goethe's Faust, directly refers to the flower elves and their need to avoid the daylight. Ariel, the ruler of the nature sprites, utters these words as the dawn approaches,

> Hearken ! Hark – the day hours careering !
> Sounding loud to spirit hearing,
> Now is the newborn day appearing !
> Rocky portals grating rattle
> Phoebus' wheels rolling, clatter!
> In pandemonium the light draws near !
> Drumbeats roll and trumpets blaze!
> Eye is blinking, ear amazed:
> The Unheard may no one hear!
> Slip within each blossom bell,
> Deeper, deeper, quiet to dwell,
> In the rocks, beneath the leaf,
> If it strikes you, you are deaf !   (Part 2, act 1, scene 1)

(*Translated by Bayard Taylor, revised by the author*)

---

[29] GA 224, lect. 23rd May 1915, and GA 172, lect. 22nd May 1915.

Demonic elementals

There are also elemental beings that are demonic, born from the disharmonious thoughts and feelings of humanity, and enlisted into the kingdom of evil through the activity of fallen spirits. The old traditions of nature catastrophes being the manifestation of evil elemental beings are quite accurate. In the succeeding chapters we will consider such beings as the storm giants and trolls.

The intimate interweaving between humanity and the elemental beings during the seasons is clear when we learn that the sum of the ether substance of the elemental beings constitutes the ether body of the Earth.[30] And the human ether body is connected to the entire sphere of the nature beings around us; it is through the activity of these beings that our ether body is created, during the incarnation process.[31] The yearly breathing of the hemispheres includes as a major aspect, the rhythmical dynamic affecting the existence of elemental beings, as the hemisphere undergoes its in-breathing and out-breathing process. One can see from this, how the breathing process of the hemispheres is directly sustained in the Earth's etheric body.

Our connection to the elemental beings is deeper than we may think. Our feelings are connected to the element of air; our breathing can have an immediate impact on a strong emotional state. Our ether body has a connection to the element of water, as have all life (ether) processes in the plant world. Our physical body is of course formed from the earth element. And our higher faculties of will and inspirational thinking are related to the element of fire. The elemental beings are not just 'out there' in nature.

We feel that our faculties, feeling, thinking, and willing, are inherently connected to higher, divine beings. We can think of the message in St. John's Gospel, that the human spirit has its origin in the Logos. We can resolve this paradox, that the innermost being of our soul is influenced and moulded by forces from the 'middle kingdom', when we consider that our higher (spiritual) faculties of thinking, willing, feeling, manifest in us through our personality, the veil of our soul. Our personality, in turn, manifests through our ether and physical bodies. The elemental beings exert their influence in the astral (or soul) world, and in the ether

[30] GA 136, lect. 4th April 1912.
[31] GA 158, lect. 22nd Nov. 1923.

realm and the physical plane. And, again, it is the elemental beings who, under the guidance of higher beings, form our new bodies as we incarnate. The kind of interaction we have with the elemental beings during our life affects our consciousness. Our attitudes, feelings, and thoughts influence the elemental beings, and they in turn affect our soul life.

Our thinking life is only possible through the activity of the gnomes and pyrausta. The gnomes' activity, in the life-ether, enables the brain to bring our thoughts to consciousness, and the pyrausta – like messengers of the gods – bring spiritual (inspired) thoughts into the sphere of the human being.[32] How deeply our life is affected by the experiencing or non-experiencing of a certain thought ! What a different dynamic arises for our future, for spiritual development, if we are able to experience spiritual thoughts ! Intuitive thoughts, flashing into our consciousness, are mediated for us by the pyrausta. The activity undertaken by the gnomes and pyrausta is not constant but varies during the year. The outer darkness of the winter brings the danger of a corresponding inner darkness to the gnomes.

Rudolf Steiner described the elemental beings as the 'servants', 'messengers', or 'artisans' of the divine hierarchical gods. The position of the elemental beings as intermediary between humankind and the hierarchies, is expressed in a wonderfully deep way in Nordic-Germanic mythology. In the so-called younger Edda, in skalda 35, we learn of the wondrous boat Skidbladnir which the dwarfs (gnomes) fashioned for the god Freyr. This vessel can journey out into the universe, having always a fair wind, no matter in what direction one is sailing; yet upon returning, this vessel can fold up into a small box.

Rudolf Steiner has explained that this vessel represents the faculty of the human soul allowing it to expand into the cosmos at night then return into the skull and realign itself with the brain in the morning. The relationship of our soul to the brain, which depends upon the way in which the elemental forces build up in our body, makes possible our link with the spiritual world each night.[33]

My purpose in this chapter has been to provide an overview of the nature and the roles of the elemental beings, so that

---

[32] GA 230, lect. 4th Nov. 1923.
[33] GA 121, lect. 17th Jun. 1910.

both those interested in the ecclesiastical or Christian festivals and those wishing to renew the old pagan festivals of the yearly cycle may share a common understanding of the middle kingdom. My design is also to provide guidelines for the study of Rudolf Steiner's many lectures on the subject of the elemental beings; I have based this chapter on those lectures, without itemizing each reference.[34]

The following story, a poignant fairy tale from the Harz Mountains of Germany,[35] which I have revised slightly, reminds us of the interdependence between humanity and the ethereal inhabitants of the elemental kingdoms.

The Three Tree Fairies
The great plain north of the Harz Mountains was not always the smiling fruitful tract of land the eye now beholds. Long ago, a large lake covered much of it, and the land around this lake was swampy and unfruitful. Dense forests of noble oaks and beech trees covered the higher land and the mountains. But in the deep green foliage of these woodlands where the foot of man seldom wandered, this sacred stillness of deep shadows, this lush undergrowth, these flowering bushes, undisturbed by the bustle and noise of human kind, were nevertheless inhabited. Beings of delicate form and rare beauty, not so material as man, not so tenuous as air, wafted lightly through the woods, as if borne by gentle breezes. Flower fairies lived in the forests, their existence intimately interwoven with that of the trees they inhabited, growing with the trees, drooping and dying with them.

When the moon rose high into the blue throne of the night, and cast her pure silvery glance over the silent noble forests, it was as if the trees lightly quivered, and then appeared the delicate maiden forms of the tree fairies. In the pale moonlight they moved amongst the majestic trees on the mountainside or descended to the lake and the river Bode, where they could meet their kindred, the water sprites. As happy and innocent as themselves, the water sprites

---

[34] In particular, Rudolf Steiner, *Man as Symphony of the Creative Word* and GA no. 98, *Natur und Geistwesen; ihr Wirken in unserer sichtbaren Welt.*
[35] T. Lauder, *Legends & Tales of the Harz Mountains*, (London, Hodder & Stoughton, 1881).

played and danced above the gentle waves, beneath the smile of Queen Luna.

But as the years passed by, these joyous dances were interrupted by the human race, which penetrated the forests, mercilessly cut down everything that stood in the way of its progress, and made these peaceful regions the stage of its ambitions and aims, never dreaming that with every tree that was hewn down a life, pure and beautiful, was destroyed. Soon the joy of these fairy rites was changed to sorrow, and when the moonlight called the fairy forms of wood nymphs and water sprites into life, they wept together over their vanished sisters and friends, and not one was sure that the following day the same fate would not be hers.

Now a powerful Kaiser had come into the district with a vast retinue and an army, built himself a burg on the banks of the Bode, and bestowed the land on his followers, who were to cut down trees, drain swamps, and transform the wilderness into a fruitful plain. Soon, the forest gave place to bare fields, and the groves of maiden trees grew ever smaller. On the mountain west of Thale, where the bones of huge ancient beasts had been found, an old soldier received permission from the Kaiser to clear the land. He toiled unweariedly, dug the soil, felled the trees one after another, until of the sacred grove only three trees were left standing.

"Now, only these three trees left", thought he to himself, stretching wearily in the grass to rest a minute and strengthen himself for the last stroke. But fatigue overcame him, so that he sank into a deep sleep, not waking until the moon and stars shone in the heavens.

Then half awake, half asleep, he beheld the forms of the three tree fairies, silent and mournful. Their eyes were moist as if dewdrops hung in their drooping eyelashes, and they uttered plaintive tones like the rustling of the night wind in the leaves.

"Let us say farewell to each other", lisped softly the voice of one. "Our time has come. When the rosy dawn awakens he will come who cut down our sisters, and as they are fallen so must we. Desolate will be the spot that saw us so oft united in joy, lonely the moonlight that shone on our dance. The nymphs of the lake and the river will look out for us, longing for our coming, and ask, "Where are our friends of the mountains? Why do they not descend when the Queen of the Night illumines our watery palace?" Happy sisters, ye are as yet safe from our mournful fate for ye are secure, in your deep waters, from the destructive deeds of humankind".

"Weep not, sister", said another of the tree maidens, lightly moaning, "weep not over our fate. 'Tis not that we must die that grieves me, but that with us the last of our fairy race will be gone; this it is that fills my heart with woe. That our race might continue I would live on, and if I could appear to him who will come in the morning with his axe, I would entreat him to give us the blessing of life, and surely he would not refuse my plea ! But only night gives us a form comprehensible to man. The day confines us, stiff and formless, in our narrow house".

"Ah, if only we could appear to him !" added the third. If we could only appear to him and beg him for life, we would not plea in vain. I have been sad, mourning the fate of the beautiful forest. And what benefit would it be to him to destroy us also? What benefit has it been to him that our sisters are destroyed? Will the products of such soil as this repay the labour of tillage? Ah, we would gladly, though invisible, help him to cultivate the fertile land of the plain, during the hours when we may have a form, if he would only take pity and spare the last of our ancient race !"

The old soldier who had listened, amazed, to this sad plea could contain himself no longer. "By the sword of my Kaiser", he cried, springing to his feet, "cursed be the hand that would do you an injury, ye innocent beings. Destroy you I will not, no, but protect you and defend you with my goods, my blood, and my life !"

"But who are ye? Was it then a dream that had charmed my senses?" For astonished, the fairy maidens had vanished at his first words. Then as a gentle glow developed in the eastern sky, their voices resounded from the trees once more: "No dream has deceived you. You have seen the last of the wood nymphs that adorn this mountain. If you will protect them, then spare the trees that still remain, and we will thank you". Dawn broke over the mountain, and the voices became silent; they sighed in the morning breeze, but the old soldier could not understand the tones.

At first he was inclined to hold all for a dream, but what he had heard stood so clearly in his mind he finally doubted no longer, and zealously defended the three trees. On his dying bed, he bade his sons to care for the trees and never to sell the land. Long did the fields near the trees thrive above all others, and at night the three maiden forms could be seen, hovering above the furrows that had been ploughed that day.

But alas, years later, the trees and land came into the hands of an owner who held the story of the three tree fairies for a fable, and he cut the trees down. Since then the fields have been barren, unfruitful, and the three sisters have not been seen above the furrows.

CHAPTER THREE

CHRISTIAN FESTIVALS, NATURE FESTIVALS, NEW FESTIVALS

We have glimpsed the inner reality of nature by considering the beings that exist behind the sense world, knowledge of whom derives primarily from Rudolf Steiner's spiritual research. The subtle effect of each season is different, for the nature sprites, responding to changes in the cosmic forces operative in each season, influence the hemisphere and humanity in different ways, throughout the year. In order to define the themes of a renewed cycle of festivals, we need a deeper understanding of these influences. But in this chapter we must address a question that has been waiting for us: What is the relevance of such matters to Christianity – not only to theological Christianity, but also to esoteric Christianity?[36]

The seasonal festivals that Rudolf Steiner was indicating need to be created from the anthroposophical perspective – how is it that they would be spiritually nourishing? One wants the festivals to have a connection to the cosmic reality of Christ, a deep connection; not simply a Christian gloss applied externally. To people with a deep past connection to ecclesiastical Christianity, as it was developed in the Middle Ages, the very concept of a seasonal festival, such as could be envisaged from the brief outline of 'the middle kingdom' I have so far presented, may appear of little value.

The interest of these people is in maintaining and deepening their relationship to the events described in the Gospels. In this regard, we can recognize the enormous value of the traditional Christian festivals, in that they are meditations, so to speak, on the deeds of Christ. But other people feel more of a connection to the old nature festivals of Europe, especially those of Celtic Europe, and sense that the cycle of the year has a deep significance for our soul.

Now that anthroposophy offers a deeper perspective on both Christianity and the seasons, we may reconcile these

---

[36] To learn more about esoteric Christianity, see Steiner's *Christianity as Mystical Fact*, and my *Rudolf Steiner Handbook* and *The Hellenistic Mysteries & Christianity*.

two contrasting attitudes. The term Christianity has an extended meaning in anthroposophy. The term Christ does not refer to the god-man of normal theology, but rather to a divine being, a god. Steiner's spiritual scientific research revealed that the baptism in the Jordan of Jesus of Nazareth by John the Baptist is the event through which this god, this cosmic being whom we call Christ, descended to the Earth.

The Christ is then the sublime god known to the ancient Greek initiates as the firstborn son of God, the divine consciousness permeating the cosmos. The Christ is a being immensely evolved, that is, having an infinite capacity for love; love in this context meaning selflessness in the will, not only sympathy and a warm compassion. The Christ is a being dedicated to bringing into expression the intentions of the Father-god whose very being, according to Steiner, is selfless will or love. But Rudolf Steiner's esoteric Christology is not the subject of this book.

However, for an understanding of the esoteric Christian perspective underlying the book, we do need to differentiate between the Logos, which is part of the primal Trinity, and the sun spirit, the foremost of 'the Powers', an order of the celestial hierarchy. When I speak of "the cosmic Christ" here I am usually referring to the Sun-spirit; the Logos is present in this being.[37] Rudolf Steiner taught that the Christ is a solar deity, that is, a sun god. (That the evangelists themselves, also understood this to be the truth, is presented in my book *The Hellenistic Mysteries and Christianity*.)

Even for those of us who are more inclined to seasonal festivals, discovery of the esoteric Christian reality can mean that the traditional, ecclesiastical festivals will provide us with profound spiritual nourishment, deepening our connection with the immensely significant events that occurred in old Palestine about two thousand years ago, and in turn strengthening our devotion and commitment to the Christ being today. The festivals commemorate events in the life of Christ, events that occurred on the physical plane but which were in essence an expression of a spiritual intention of the cosmic Christ.

But for those already more inclined toward Christian festivals, the situation is quite different. They find in the

---

[37] Rudolf Steiner has given invaluable understanding of the Hierarchies in his many books; my *Rudolf Steiner Handbook* helps the reader to understand his challenging, esoteric ideas.

cycle of the year simply qualities that stimulate our interest in knowledge; that is, of the ways of nature, and our feeling for beauty, our artistic sense. To be of value, seasonal festivals must somehow bring the participants into a closer connection with the Christ being. But how becoming attuned to the seasonal dynamics in the Earth-soul could be 'Christian' remains a riddle, for the traditional Christian sees the actual spiritual essence of a festival as developing in the human soul as it immerses itself in contemplation of the deeds of Christ-in the crucifixion, the death, and the resurrection of Christ on Golgotha Hill (called by Steiner the Mystery of Golgotha).

Should there be a nature process which appropriately symbolizes the theme of a Christian festival, such as the springtime reappearance of plants, which traditional Christianity sees as symbolizing the resurrection, which is held to be a theme of the Easter festival, then that aspect of nature is incorporated into the Christian festival symbolism.

And it is true that we form a connection in our minds between the season of the year and the Christian festival that shall at that time be celebrated. But apart from these considerations, the Christian festivals are not connected with nature. And so it is that in the southern hemisphere, Christmas is regarded as occurring on the 25th of December, even though it is then summertime.

It is a different thing, of course, to acknowledge that the traditional Christian cultures have tolerated nature festivals, when they were too popular with newly converted peoples to be banned, or when their content was perceived as being indifferent, thus not a threat to, Christian values.

The Christian festivals
Let's see a list of the festivals that constitute the traditional Christian cycle.

Christmas: The birth of Jesus, on December 25.

Epiphany: The three Magi visit Jesus, on January 6.

The Transfiguration of Jesus Christ: On August 6, the perception by the three disciples of an aspect of the cosmic Christ within Jesus.

Easter. The crucifixion and resurrection of Christ. At this time, according to Steiner, "when the blood flowed from the wounds of the Redeemer, on Golgotha, the entire the ether aura of the Earth took on another form, another colour".[38] According to Steiner's research, Easter marks the descent and sacrifice of the cosmic Christ, renewing the connection between humanity and the logos, between April 3 and April 5, A.D. 33.

The Ascension of Christ. Processes inaugurated at the resurrection are completed.

Pentecost. Because of the nearness of the Christ to earthly humanity, the descent of the Holy Spirit can now occur. This being, assisting those in the quest for spirituality, came first to the disciples.

Of the other, minor festivals in the ecclesiastical cycle, one which has as its focus the great initiate who worked as a woman; namely Mary, the mother of Jesus (of St. Luke's Gospel), would be important. For reasons that will become clear, I have not listed either St. John's Tide or Michaelmas among the ecclesiastical festivals.

The seasonal festivals
A festival cycle that seeks to assist humanity to perception of and spiritual nurture from the spiritual forces within each season is, of course, of an entirely different kind. In earlier times, such festivals were celebrated at the spring equinox, at midsummer, at the autumn equinox, and at midwinter. Through such festivals, initiates, who because of their greater wisdom were acknowledged as cultural leaders, strove to assist the spiritual development of the community. Experiencing the rhythmical interweaving of cosmic and telluric (earthly) forces during the year, the trained seership of the priests sought to help the members of the community draw near to beneficial influences and to distance themselves from pernicious influences.

The high priests of old Egypt, of Greece, of Persia, and of the Celtic lands of Europe would have felt a deep disquiet at the prospect of a culture devoid of such seasonal festivals.

---

[38] Rudolf Steiner described this on a number of occasions, e.g., lect. 21st June 1908 (*Apocalypse of St. John*).

Such ancient cultures were of course not Christian; the Christian civilizations have always avoided such activity. Today, however, there is a resurgence of interest amongst those born into the Christian world, and seasonal festivals are emerging; but separate, of course, from the ecclesiastical cycle. Large crowds gather before dawn on midsummer's day at Stonehenge or in midwinter at the Externsteine in north Germany. The longing for a renewal of the capacity to commune with the Earth-soul during the cycle of the year is growing stronger.

However, even if it were possible to exactly recreate the old pagan festivals, doing so would be pointless. For human consciousness has changed greatly over the centuries. Humanity used to experience livingly the inhabitants of 'the middle kingdom' and whatever spiritual influences were active in the Earth-soul. But the clairvoyance which was once humankind's birthright, has faded away.

New seasonal festivals could be formed, but they would only have a real meaning if we were to strive toward a new spiritual sensitivity (that is, clairvoyance). And not only has human consciousness changed; the Earth-soul has also undergone an immense change. At the resurrection of Christ, this sublime god became the indwelling planetary ego, the highest aspect of the planet's spiritual nature.

Still, to draw the conclusion that since the advent of Christianity, the Christian festivals have removed the need for seasonal festivals would be incorrect. For while the Christian cycle has as its purpose the strengthening of our awareness of the significance of the life of Christ, we are given the opportunity to call to mind the events of that life. But such a cycle does not include an important aspect of life, namely our latent capacity to experience the connection to the spiritual and elemental processes of the living Earth.

Such a seasonal festival cycle would assist the development of a new spiritual sensitivity by stimulating an active interest in the cycle of the year, an interest in the dynamic prevailing seasonally, and hemispherically, in the aura of the Earth. Such a seasonal festival cycle would promote the development of a new clairvoyance, and the cycle would also need human beings to start to develop new faculties of perception.[39]

---

[39] My book, *The Way to the Sacred* provides a substantial guide to the process of spiritual development, as taught by Rudolf Steiner.

The new festivals

Rudolf Steiner sounded the keynote for any endeavour to develop new festivals. The yearly cycle, he taught,

> becomes the archetype of the human being's own soul processes..... By finding the right {seasonal} festival mood, we will once again link human existence to divine existence.[40]

Clearly, Rudolf Steiner regarded the striving to consciously participate in the cycle of the year as a sacred task, and his words indicate the power of the new seasonal festivals to attune the community in general to the spiritual processes underlying the seasonal changes. Becoming attuned should lead gradually to the development of a conscious relationship between the individual and the Earth-soul.

Still that question remains, though. What would be the relevance of Christianity, to a new seasonal cycle of festivals? The answer is that, based in the initiation wisdom offered by anthroposophy, such festivals would be profoundly Christian, although not in a way that Christian churches can recognize; and this religious aspect would be actually a spiritual-esoteric aspect. Thus participants could develop a relationship to the Christ reality in a way that transcends religious boundaries. Not only would the spiritual essence of the festivals still develop in the human soul; it would expand to involve the Earth-soul too.

The goal I set for myself here is, again, to indicate how such esoterically 'Christian' seasonal festivals could be a reality. To achieve the insight necessary for these new festivals, we start from the same fundamental truth that forms the basis of the traditional festivals. Namely, that through the Easter event, that sublime being who is the very origin of the human spirit became the guiding being or ego of the planet. But now a new question arises: What is the influence, the activity, in modern times, of the indwelling Christ, that is, as regards the life processes of the Earth?

Rudolf Steiner's research emphasized the awesome meaning of the words of Christ, at the Last Supper, when he offered pieces of bread to the disciples: "Take, eat; this is my body". Since the planet is now imbued with the Christ being,

---

[40] GA 243, lect. 23rd May, 1923.

the life-processes in its ether and astral aura, which manifest for example as the seasonal cycle, will be nurtured by him.

This is not a nominal activity, like that of modern monarchs ! For neither this Earth nor humanity has simply evolved and developed, just through the passage of time. The gradual development of the human into an ego-endowed, independent being, living in an appropriate environment, is the result of intensive, creative activity by many spiritual beings of the hierarchies, who bring to expression the intentions of a primal Trinity. The great sun god (the Christ-being) was foremost in this task of ensuring that human evolution proceed correctly. And he was worshipped under various names prior to his descent to Earth, when he was still in the remote sphere of the sun gods.

It is important to strive to become aware of the inner reality of the seasons, in words of Rudolf Steiner,

> for thereby forces intermingle with our thoughts that enable humankind to once again 'hold a dialogue' with the divine beings in the cosmos,

and then,

> every little firefly will be for the person a mysterious revelation of the cosmos; every breeze in the air in midsummer will proclaim the cosmic element within the telluric.[41]

Is such teaching not in harmony with Christian mystical ideals? There is a reason for the absence of a seasonal aspect in Christian festivals: they came into being at a time when the old inherited clairvoyance was fading. By about the fourth century it had lost its power; and precisely then the church fathers were busy giving to the festivals a form and content that would be acceptable to the developing orthodox theology. From the fourth century onward, humanity entered an increasingly materialistic phase of evolution. As the old psychic tendencies faded, so too did our rapport with the living milieu of the elemental kingdoms.

In this isolation, humankind could develop the individual ego sense. The feeling of being an individual could arise,

---

[41] Lect. 1st Oct. 1923.

now that people were no longer feeling themselves to be part of a vast living reality. As perception of the 'middle kingdom' faded, our consciousness became focused on the material world. Thus our connection, through time, to the spiritual worlds faded; the pre-birth descent to Earth and the post-death ascent back to the spirit were no longer felt. And our connection through space was lost as we came to perceive the sparkling shimmering ether layers overhead as only a mixture of gases.

This materialistic phase was needed, for it has enabled the ego to develop powerfully, so that it may now re-establish its awareness of the spiritual reality through its own inner strength. This phase of evolution, this age of inner darkness, ended in 1899. Called Kali Yuga in Sanskrit, this 'Age of Darkness', or of iron, rather than gold, began about 5,000 years ago. It was not a zodiac age. Now humanity can, and must, redevelop the communion with the spiritual reality behind material nature processes.

> We must develop the perception that, just as there is a soul in our bodies, so too in everything that occurs outside us – the rising and setting of the stars, the bright sunlight, the twilight – there dwells something spiritual. And just as we are inserted into the air through our lungs, so are we inserted into the spiritual reality of the cosmos through our souls.[42]

Steiner spoke further of the spiritual importance of nature experiences:

> When we achieve our awareness of nature through spiritual science, we realize it is a great privilege to be in the spiritual reality of nature. And that is a privilege...especially when we recall just how many people today because of their environs cannot be near the creations of the nature beings. And when we contemplate nature with a gaze clarified through spiritual science, then we know how intimately that which we call the spiritual life, the highest moral aspirations, are connected to that which we sense in nature. It is paradoxical, yet true, that the city dwellers who must lose knowledge of what oats, rye,

---

[42] From lect. 13th Mar. 1917 (*Cosmic & Human Metamorphoses*).

or barley grains look like, will also unfortunately become separated, in their hearts, from the deepest moral source of our existence.[43]

How different is this perspective from the attitude, found amongst some students of anthroposophy, that we modern human beings no longer have any significant connection to nature ! Steiner is not referring to pleasurable indulgences obtained through nature, but rather to experiences that arise through the soul being open to the inner quality of what we see and hear. It is precisely one of the results of the path to spiritual development as given in anthroposophy that awareness of the elemental world re-awakens. This awareness is not simply a matter of experiencing "something out there". For our connection to these forces is quite intimate:

> Only the coarseness of our perceptions prevents humanity from sensing what, in themselves, is dependent upon this external cycle {of the elemental beings ascending and descending} in the out/in breathing process of the Earth.[44]

Indeed, the modern seeker of the spirit can bring this awareness so far as to feel spoken to by the seasons cycle, "as if a friend's soul is communicating" in different moods.[45] It is the spiritual seeker, who is engaged in the process of esoteric development, who will be the pioneer of this renewal of the clairvoyant nature consciousness.[46]

What connection do such new possibilities have with the Christ reality? Let me restate part of a Steiner passage I have already quoted from,

> "We must develop the perception that just as there is a soul in our bodies, so too in everything that occurs outside us.....and we will find that the cycle of the year, with its secrets, belongs to the Christ being, that being that underwent the deed on Golgotha Hill".

---

[43] GA 130, lect. 19th Sept. 1911.
[44] GA 223, lecture of 1st Oct, 1923.
[45] ibid.
[46] ibid.

The profound connection of the Christ reality to nature is also strongly expressed in these words from another Steiner lecture:

> We must again learn to understand the language of nature, in its entirety....our Christianity must be widened through being permeated by a healthy paganism.[47]

In speaking of the relationship of the Christmas festival to the winter season, Steiner makes a very central point, which indicates the essence of the new festival cycle,

> One will indeed have to soar up to {achieve} a correlation of that which occurred historically on earth in the events of Golgotha with the great secrets of the world {that is, the seasons}....Thereby one livingly experiences parallel to the cycle of the year the image of the mystery of Golgotha.[48]

But what is this connection; what real connection can there be between the seasons and the Christ-being? At this point, we may recall that the traditional Christian festivals were formed at a time when there was no longer a real connection to nature. The festivals were then further developed, into their present form, during the Middle Ages. By then, the Europeans involved in consolidating Christian beliefs were insensitive to the elemental forces. Furthermore, they were unaware of the southern hemisphere. They lived on what they understood to be a flat Earth.

So when European colonists settled in the southern hemisphere, they simply kept celebrating their festivals on the dates established for the northern hemisphere. The cycle of the year was quite irrelevant. Insofar as these festivals have no conscious relevance to the seasons, that was logical.

But in that there is a connection between the indwelling Earth-spirit and the life processes of mother Earth, the custom of the colonizing Europeans of following the dates of the northern hemisphere has had remarkable results ! It has caused, now that the feeling for nature is re-awakening, an intense questioning in the southern hemisphere. From this questioning, the new festival cycle can arise, uniting –

---

[47] GA 190, lect. 29th Mar. 1919.
[48] Lecture, 13th Mar. 1917.

52

conceptually at first, then experientially – the Christ reality to the life of the Earth-mother, for people in both hemispheres. The uncertainty for people in the south is simply a conscious manifestation of the non-understanding which prevails globally – that is, also in the north.

The new festivals will be Christian in a special sense; they will enable us to relate to the cosmic sun god Christ as he is today. In this sense, the new festivals will contribute toward the reappearance of Christ. When Steiner declared that 'there is a need to soar high enough to correlate what occurred historically on earth with the cycle of the year', he also commented that this "will be demanded of us in this time, in which the reappearance of Christ will occur". This significant statement is strengthened by his words to a Scandinavian audience:

> Prior to the mystery of Golgotha, humanity had beheld nature, en-souled, permeated with spiritual reality. After the mystery of Golgotha, humanity must strive to make this {experience of} an en-souled, spiritualized nature constitute the following of Christ {that is, the leading of an actively Christian life}. So that all the nature beings are perceived through this following of Christ; for without him, they cannot be seen.[49]

We shall explore further crucial teachings given in the lecture from which this quote comes, (Oslo, of 21st May, 1923) in detail, later in the book. Here we can start to explore what this extraordinary revelation means. Namely that the seasonal dynamics, manifested by the elemental beings, are maintained and vivified by the Christ being – for both hemispheres. Again, Steiner on this theme:

> The astral body of our Earth undergoes transformations throughout the year. The changes are **the opposite in each hemisphere**....The astral body of our Earth {hemisphere} is involved with the natural world during the time of new plant growth. It takes care of things when plants grow...and in autumn, when a kind of sleep condition comes over

---

[49] GA 226, lect. 21st May, 1923.

the earth, the astral body of the earth {hemisphere} passes to its spiritual creativity.[50]

Note: Rudolf Steiner seldom used the word 'hemisphere', even when referring to the seasonal dynamics; there are some times when he did use this word, but often he simply said 'earth'. So in quotes from Rudolf Steiner, if he uses the word 'earth', obviously referring not to the entire planet, but the local environs, I have put in brackets the term 'hemisphere', to make it clear that he means one hemisphere; and usually he means the local area of that hemisphere, where people are living. Thus in the above quote, "*The earth {hemisphere} has given its soul to the cosmos the soul of the earth strives toward the stars...*" adding the word 'hemisphere' in brackets it makes very clear that he is referring to a seasonal condition, which is a hemispherical reality. And it is important that this is made clear, otherwise scores of his references to a hemispherical seasonal process, could be missed.

All of the plant life is governed by the elementals, as we have seen; these in turn are governed by various high spiritual beings. These elementals, and the many faeries or etheric-astral nature spirits, such as those that look after a specific plant, or tend to its blossoming have an etheric body, and often an astral aura, too.

The difficulty in understanding this living etheric-astral breathing process, leads to confusion about, or opposition to, the new festival concept. We can see this clearly in the erroneous nature of the description given of the seasonal cycle and the two hemispheres by a Christian Community clergyman, F. Benesch; whose writings, despite his many errors, were recently recommended as a guide to this topic.[51] As I wrote in the **Rudolf Steiner Handbook**,

> Benesch's primary lecture on this subject is, "Does one celebrate Christmas in summer?" (*Weihnachten*

---

[50] GA 136, lect. 4th April, 1912 (*Spiritual Beings in the Heavenly Bodies*).

[51] M. Samson, p. 69. Benesch, who joined the church in 1947 and rose to become its most powerful figure over decades. But the competence of Benesch to represent anthroposophical ideas was rejected by many people after 2004, when Holocaust historians in Rumania and Leipzig University reported that he was a fanatical Nazi, participating with Himmler's SS troops who carried out the extermination of Jews and others. See the author's e-booklet *Opponents and Critics of Steiner*.

im Sommer feiern?), this was later expanded to a full-size book. Early in his lecture Benesch declares that,

> "...this yearly breathing-in and out, which actually produces the seasonal cycle, is therefore in the soul (astral) realm {of the Earth}, **it is not at all in the etheric realm**.."[52]

This is one of many statements in his lecture which are obviously contrary to Steiner's teachings. For Steiner describes how the nature spirits who, as we saw earlier, carry out the seasonal processes of the in-breathing and out-breathing, **actually compose the Earth's etheric body**.[53]

But Rudolf Steiner also described how the nature spirits and their plants exist within the astral aura of the hemisphere. So the nature spirits are within both the etheric energies of the planet and within its astral aura. As he once told an audience, "The plant's astral nature is part of the astral aura of the Earth".[54]

We can note here too, that Benesch also gives his opinion,

> "....with regard to the unitary nature of the Earth given again and again in decisive indications from Rudolf Steiner that, the Earth **really does not consist of two hemispheres**. This is a pure abstraction, rather it comprises in its bodily shape, four 'mental' (i.e., devachanic) archetypes".
>
> (emphasis mine A.A.)

Benesch then proceeds to refer to the irrelevant argument that the Earth is a tetrahedral object, owing to the shape of its tectonic plates, and the crystalline minerals found in these.[55]

Continuing with our exploration of the theme of the living Earth, wit its two, very real hemispheres, and the great numbers of spiritual beings that sustain the seasonal processes, we find in Rudolf Steiner's teachings that

---

[52] The German text of this cleric, Friedrich Benesch,"Dieser Jahresatemzug, der eigentlich das Jahreslaufgeschen bewirkt, ist also das Seelische, es ist gar nicht das Ätherische..."
[53] GA 136, pages 39, 46.
[54] GA 98, p. 143, & GA 60, p.172.
[55] F. Benesch, "*Weihnachten im Sommer feiern?* p.20, Vlg. Urachhaus, 1998.

included amongst these beings are high deities, such as the Archangels and the Powers and the even beyond these ranks. But these beings are in turn directed by the Earth-spirit, who through these many lesser beings oversees the life processes of the planet.

This being, the Earth-spirit is, as Steiner taught, the Christ-being, who therefore made profound statements about his mission at the Last Supper. At that time, Christ speaks of his body and blood as being shed for humanity, but connects these to bread and wine; both products of the living Earth (see John 6:56, Matt 26; 26-28 and Mark 14: 21-22). But the deepest revelation of this core cosmic Christology in anthroposophy, is pointed to by these comments of Rudolf Steiner,

> Who is the 'spirit of the Earth' ? This 'spirit of the Earth' designated himself as the Earth-Spirit then when He said, "Whoever eats my bread treads me underfoot".

These comments are referring to a sentence in the gospel of St. John, 13:18. It reads as follows in the New International Version, (the NIV) as follows,

> "I am not referring to all of you; I know those I have chosen. But this is to fulfill the scripture: 'He who shares my bread has lifted up his heel against me.'

To say, "lifted up his heel against me" means in ancient Hebrew to become a dangerous enemy. But Rudolf Steiner gives the above version of this, "Whoever eats my bread treads me underfoot". In doing exactly this, he is in effect, dismantling the Biblical idiom so it becomes thereby a harmless statement. And a statement which implies being walked upon.

This situation has presented a considerable difficulty for those representing his viewpoint, since people were unable to reconcile Steiner's use of the sentence with the obvious meaning. An official of the Christian Community has written that Steiner's understanding of the Gospel text was in error here.[56] However, from a close analysis of the sentence from

---

[56] Friedrich Schmidt-Hieber in, Das Goetheanum Wochenschrift, 2008, N.24/08. My *The Hellenistic Mysteries and Christianity* includes an unveiling of the initiatory meaning in this sentence in St. John's Gospel.

its Hebrew origins, through the version in the Septuagint and then in the New Testament Greek of St. John, I have been able to demonstrate how this sentence does indeed state, on its veiled initiatory level, that the Earth has become the body of the cosmic sun god, (referring to its etheric, astral and spiritual levels).

We cannot go into the details of this theme here, but my book, *The Hellenistic Mysteries and Christianity* presents the full analysis of the ancient Greek and Hebrew basis of the gospel sentence and the cultural context behind the gospel. Here we can note that a sacred, initiatory layer of meaning is hidden in the sentence, which allows us to translate it as this,

> **"The one who is consuming living plant foods ....**
> **is eating that which belongs to me;**
> **and those same persons are walking across me."**

> *(across the surface of the Earth, which shall soon become my body.)*

The implication of this hidden gospel teaching and Rudolf Steiner's words, is that the cosmic Christ is active in the elemental processes taking place behind the seasonal cycle of each hemisphere. Awareness of the inner reality behind the seasons will arise from a meditative participation in the yearly cycle; and formation of the new festivals will greatly aid humanity on the path to experiencing the contemporary presence of the cosmic Christ in the life of our planet. In so doing, these festivals will also assist us in the development of a new clairvoyance.

When we are exploring the new spring festival concept, we shall also consider a question as to what Steiner presented about this new festival cycle. This question is focussed on the perspective that Steiner often mentions, namely how modern humanity is not connected inwardly to the nature cycle of the year anymore.

It is interesting to note that awareness of this concept of humanity being able to become attuned to the spiritual in the natural cycle of the year was present in Emil Bock, an early leader of the Christian Community church; a church which today is opposed to this concept. Many conversations occurred between Rudolf Steiner and the people who were the pioneering of this church. One question put to Rudolf

Steiner came from the very respected Rev. Friedrich Rittelmeyer, "What can one do in order to prepare oneself in advance for an experience of Christ, similar to that which St. Paul had, on the road to Damascus?" This is referring to experiencing Jesus Christ (briefly), in the ethers, through what requires, in effect, a moment of etheric clairvoyance.

In the first edition of my book, I referred to this, quoting from Emil Bock. Steiner's answer was, as Bock gave it: "*Through the meditative experience of the cycle of the year. The mysteries of the seasons are the gifts of nature for the meditating person, who seeks the realm of the Christ.*" A few years after my book was published, a correspondent informed me that the report was not correct in its details, because Bock's words about this had been published in a defective way, obscuring who actually said what.

The first sentence are the actual words of Rudolf Steiner, "*Through the meditative experience of the cycle of the year.*"[57] But the next sentence was actually a commentary from Bock himself, explaining and commenting on these words, as given during a lecture some years later. But this situation was impossible to discern, because of the incorrect layout of the published book. Thus anyone reading this would have been misled on this point.

So in fact the next sentence, "*The mysteries of the year are the gifts of nature for the meditating person, who seeks the realm of the Christ,*" is **not** from Rudolf Steiner. But when Rudolf Steiner replied "*Through the meditative experience of the cycle of the year*", he used an ambiguous German expression (*Jahreslauf*); it could mean either the liturgical festival cycle of a church, or the seasonal cycle of Nature. One would normally assume, since he is talking to the leader of the church, that Steiner meant the liturgical festival cycle.

Since Emil Bock was a leading member of the church, one would also assume that his commentary would refer to the church festivals, such as Easter, Ascension and so on. But Bock doesn't; he says, in effect: *the gifts of nature, that is, the mysteries of the seasons are the way to find the realm of the Christ for the meditating person.* Whether Bock misunderstood the words of Steiner, or was exactly correct,

---

[57] Memoir manuscript of the founding priests of the Christian Community: *Erinnerungen an die Begründungsereignisse der Christengemeinschaft*, Stuttgart 1984, p. 318.

is today unknowable; but his interpretation is in accord with our views here.

In an Easter lecture, Steiner approached this theme from the perspective of the old European myth of Baldur. Baldur was a beautiful and radiant god, beloved of all, whose celestial dwelling was called Breidablick, ('radiant expanse'). Baldur made possible the old clairvoyance and became its symbol. The following extract from Steiner's lecture describes the intimate connection of Christ with a renewal of perception of the 'middle kingdom', the world of faery:

> When people in earlier times beheld the meadows, the elemental beings appeared to them there at certain times. That was no mere seeing, that was not a passive reception of something seen, rather it was united with a living feeling, with a living perception. People went through the forests, they gazed at these sprites, at the elemental beings, but they did not merely see them. I could say, they absorbed the essence of these sprites into their souls; that is, they felt their 'breath' like a draught of refreshment for soul and spirit. The people said: "Baldur is there".[58]

The time came when this sensitivity faded, the enchanted world of the elementals disappeared. Baldur was killed, and a tragic mood spread amongst the north Europeans; the "twilight of the gods" had come. The lecture continues:

> Today as you look at nature, you see the green of the plants, the blue-green of the forests, the blue of the heaven, the many-coloured brightness of the flowers. Imagine that a revolution were to come, so instead of seeing colours, the whole of nature would appear as only grey on grey, grey meadows, shades of black and grey for the flowers, then you would have a comparison for what in fact happened when the possibility of beholding all the manifold elemental beings of nature disappeared. The priests proclaimed, Vanished is Baldur's kingdom of the sun". Then came the news of Christ. "He calls Baldur to life. Christ has brought to life again that which was once yours through Baldur's power", proclaimed

---

[58] Lect. 2nd April, 1915.

the priests. "The Christ impulse of Golgotha will call Baldur to life. Wait, wait, till he rises again, the re-awakener of Baldur".

The renewal of interest in, and the perception of, the denizens of the middle kingdom – the elemental beings, the flower elves, and the others – arises in human beings through the effect of the Christ impulse. Before we consider, in Chapter Four, the springtime as an expression of the contemporary reality of the Christ impulse, I should again stress that the new festivals will be hemispheric; so there will be a six-month gap between for example, the springtime festivals of the two hemispheres, north and south. The timing requirement of the traditional festivals is very different ! They are global, based on the calendar, not the seasons.

By commemorating the events at a time agreed upon, globally, the traditional cycle strives to bring humanity into a deeper awareness of the significance of the events that two thousand years ago became imprinted into the flow of earthly time. With an agreed date, all Christians can be engaged in the same contemplative reverence at the same time, no matter where they are living on the Earth.

Centuries of negotiations and discussion have resulted in the present universal dates for the Christian festivals. Because we know that on a certain day a sacred event is to be contemplated, we can inwardly anticipate the event, and the festival thus becomes a powerful reality in our soul. Hence from the viewpoint of the traditional festivals, wherein the seasons are not consciously involved, Christmas day, which in this traditional context means the festival of the birth of Jesus, is to be celebrated on December 25th, whether one lives in Australia or Iceland.

Indeed, when in the future, some people are living for some months on the moon and on Mars, and when it is December 25th in earthly time, it will be the time for those astronauts or technicians, if they are Christian, to remember the wondrous birth stories of Luke and Matthew. A globally harmonized, that is, simultaneous timing process would be senseless for these new Christian seasonal festivals. Rudolf Steiner was asked by an anthroposophist from the southern hemisphere, Lute Drummond, a woman living in Australia, for indications about the festivals in the southern hemisphere.

60

Steiner's answer: "You are the preparers of the preparers of those who will renew the festivals". That is, he foresaw that three generations would be needed, the three generations that have brought us to the present day. The time is at hand. May these new festivals, with all their social healing qualities, arise through the work now being done on this question, especially in the southern hemisphere.

A valuable study of the over-all theme of these new festivals, and the errors that arise by approaching this theme from the viewpoint of the traditional church festivals, has been carried out by an Australian author, D. Skewes, in his book, "*Towards a Cosmic Cultus*".

An excellent, but unfinished, smaller book on this subject is available in manuscript form, by Geert Suwelack, *The New Dialogue with the Spirit of the Earth.*

CHAPTER FOUR

THE SPRING FESTIVAL

As winter gradually gives way to spring, nature's powers of growth and fertility intensify; the hemisphere teems with sprouting life. The abundance of produce that ripened during the preceding summer and autumn were the culmination of the previous spring. Now that winter has gone, and the sun draws nearer, as it were, the life forces of the earth will be renewed. The yearly cycle begins again.

It is not only the increasing exposure of the hemisphere externally to the light and warmth of the sun that makes possible the spring. The ether rays of the sun can now permeate the hemisphere's own ether body, replenishing its forces. For as the hemisphere becomes more exposed to the sun, the Earth-soul in that half of the globe begins to exhale its forces; currents of ether and astral forces begin to ascend upward, from that half of the globe, ever higher above the ground. With this process of out-breathing the penetration of the Earth's aura by solar forces and (indeed) beings becomes ever more intense.

So from the interplay of sun beings and the Earth-soul arise the major dynamics of the springtime – the fertility of nature and the yearly renewal of life for each hemisphere. Without the penetration of solar ether forces into the Earth's ether body, there could be no true spring; and the penetration by solar forces can only occur, to such an extent, when the hemisphere exhales its forces. Were the earth to bring forth plants without any solar or cosmic forces present, then all the flora would become like mushrooms, which are unwholesome earth fungi. In such fungi, which grow at night, the esotericist may see an image of the malignant lunar and earth forces prevailing inside the Earth.

After the spring equinox, the solar ether forces are not only a stronger influence than the lunar ethers in a general sense; they also become predominant within the moonlight, within the moon's rays themselves. Moonlight consists of lunar ethers and some solar ethers, as well as physical sunlight. According to Rudolf Steiner,

What is mirrored to the Earth as sunlight, via the moon, is after March 21st {thus September 23rd in the south} entirely different from that {light} which is reflected before then.[59]

This phenomenon may be one reason for the movable dating formula for the Easter festival. In any event, most earlier cultures regarded the spring equinox as the start of the new near, and this was the case in Europe too, until the sixteenth century. In earlier times people were aware that with the exhaling of the Earth's auric forces the multitudes of elemental beings, that during winter were relatively inactive under the ground, experience a renewal of their powers and gradually ascend further into the heights as summer approaches.

The undines or water sprites are especially active in spring, working with the moisture-forming chemical-ether. They busily whir around the developing plants, working in the process of leaf formation and general growth. Old legends tell of how the undines or 'nixen' love the moonlight and of how they may be seen revelling in the play of moonlight on the waters of a lake or in the misty veils around a waterfall.

A common theme in ancient spring festivals was the 'marriage of the sun to the Earth'. Understanding how the solar rays penetrate the ascending elemental forces in spring, we can appreciate the deep truth of this expression. We might look upon all the new life and growth of spring as an expression of the creative powers of the sun beings, who are the regents of the solar system. Through these great beings, the foremost of the sun beings manifests its creative powers. Steiner refers to this being as the World-spirit (or Cosmos-spirit). Such truths were known in earlier times, and people naturally felt a reverence for life and nature, which every spring undergo such a rejuvenation.

Something of this mood can be re-attained, along with an understanding of so-called sun worship, through the following meditative words:

Where do we see the world spirit {in summer}? We behold this being, when we are able to recognize where it is that he beholds himself ! Verily does this

---

[59] GA 167, lect. 18th April, 1916.

being create during summer those organs through which he may behold himself. He creates external sense organs ! Let us learn to understand what it is that from springtime onward decks the earth {hemisphere} with its carpet of verdant plants, bestowing on the earth {hemisphere} a renewed countenance. What is it? It is a mirror for the solar Cosmos-spirit...all plant life; bud, blossom and leaf, are but images which portray the pure Cosmos-spirit, who sees himself reflected in his work, which he has conjured forth out of the earth.[60]

But it is not only the world's flora that owes its existence to the sun's forces. Specific aspects of the human organism are closely connected to the sun. Our eyes, for example, are solar organs; ancient wisdom's association of the eyes with the sun is profoundly accurate. Our eyes have been empowered by the sun's forces; and we gaze at a world rendered visible by the sunlight. A proof of this empowering connection may be seen in the case of animals that migrate into large caves, spending entire lives there. Over several generations, these animals lose their eyesight.

Before humanity and the Earth entered into the material phase of evolution; that is, when the planet was still a delicate ethereal organism, physical vision was not yet developed. As the environment became more dense, the sunlight gradually developed the physical eyes in human beings. Hence the day came when the first sunrise was experienced, so to speak. Instead of being aware, clairvoyantly, at sunrise of the inner reality of the sun growing stronger, the human being now perceived the outer radiance of the sun's physical body.

This truth was alive for the people in earlier cultures who celebrated the renewal of the sun's regency over the Earth in springtime. An echo of this initiation knowledge is found in an apocryphal text, *The Books of Adam and Eve*,

> On the first day {after the fall} Adam turned his face toward the east, and saw the sun rise, in flowing rays, and felt the heat thereof on his body. And he was afraid of it, and thought in his heart that this flame came forth to plague him....in as much as

---

[60] Lecture, 21st Dec. 1909.

64

while he had been in the garden {of Eden – that is, in the ethereal condition}, he had heard the voice of God...he never had seen the brilliant light of the sun, neither did the flaming heat thereof touch his body.[61]

The following meditative verse from Steiner's Calendar of the Soul also speaks of our close springtime connection with the sun's forces.

Into our inner being
Is poured the senses' rich abundance.
The spirit of the world thus finds itself
In mirror image of the human eye
Which from this spirit
Must form its strength anew.[62]

The spring festival activities of earlier times had various leitmotifs, some of which are especially puzzling to modern non-clairvoyant humanity. For example, the rite of the "boat cart". This remarkable vessel, a kind of boat that could also travel on land, because it had wheels, would be paraded through the villages in central Europe in springtime. During the days that this procession was passing through the region, no fighting was allowed; it was a time for rejoicing. This was a sacred occasion, for the priests taught that they undertook this activity when the great mother goddess Nerthus, descended to the earth. (According to Steiner, the god Nerthus was originally masculine and feminine, that is, androgynous.)

It appears that a similar rite was undertaken in Egypt, in honour of Isis. Behind this ritual was an understanding; and indeed, earlier on, even a direct perception of the processes through which the human soul, descending to birth, became en-clothed in a material body. Hence the vehicle of the god could traverse the sea of the soul world, and yet it was also able to function on the Earth too. The process of incarnating was thus the focus of this festival. Such boat wagons were constructed as late as the twelfth century, but by then the procession had become decadent; erotic fertility dances were performed. In the course of time, such rites gave rise to the

---

[61] *The Books of Adam & Eve*, chapter 15, in Lost Books of the Bible.
[62] The translations are my own, made in the 1970's and revised recently.

carnival festivities. We will meet a similar theme when we explore the new spring festival.

Another remnant of earlier spring festivities is the Valentine's Day custom, which derives from the ancient Roman spring festival of fertility, the Lupercalia. One rite of this festival involved the creating of temporary lovers. The names of young women were placed in a box, from which the young men made random selections. The church weakened this custom by placing the commemoration of a saint, Valentine, on that day.

The suppression by the church of the religious or festive traditions of cultures being converted to Christianity did often result in the irretrievable destruction of valuable information and artwork. But even noble rites degenerate, and the spring fertility customs were especially susceptible to a malignant decay process. Take the Walpurgis Night scene in Goethe's Faust. This evening, on April 30, is referred to as Walpurgis night, because May 1st is, in the church calendar, the day of St. Walpurga, the abbess of Heidenheim, who died in about the year A.D. 778. This scene, in its sinister eroticism, portrays the striving of evil beings to create a malignant version of the sacred fertility rituals of the Nerthus priesthood.[63]

Additional springtime customs, arising from the natural, spontaneous response to spring and its beauty, are Maypole dancing and flower arranging. These customs are usually enacted on May 1st in Europe, through a natural merging with the old Celtic Beltain festival, which was held on that date to celebrate the beginning of summer.

A significant aspect of the earlier spring festivals concerned the opposition from spiritual powers seeking to influence humankind. In some cultures, the festival preparations began with the performance of strictly observed cleansing rites and also with actual physical bathing. Old utensils and clothes were burnt. This spring cleaning activity was not just a pragmatic matter of hygiene; it was designed to ward off unwanted influences. The concern with opposing powers was also expressed in both Europe and North America in a remarkable custom, the rite of' 'the snatchers'. As a part of this rite, people equipped with long, extendable shears would snatch at the headdresses of unwary passers-by during processions. The

---

[63] Lecture 21st Dec. 1916.

esoteric significance of these various customs will be considered later in this chapter.

An additional theme of the spring festivals concerns the attitude toward nutrition. In Judaism and in Christianity, one aspect of the springtime festival is fasting, or the renouncing of pleasurable foods. This custom introduces a remarkably stern or ascetic quality, which contrasts markedly with the external mood of nature. Still another theme of early spring festivals was "the first fruits". Throughout the world, it was an earnest duty of the priesthood to offer an unblemished sample of the first of the crops to the god or gods. The fruits of the Earth could not be consumed until this offering was made; the produce from nature, arising in spring through the activity of ether forces, was not to be eaten until the people were reminded of the divine beings from whom the Earth's creative powers derive.

The rituals conveying this perspective on the spiritual reality of life were powerful and solemn. Severe penalties were imposed on anyone who broke the taboo on the new spring produce. Such customs, which may at first puzzle us, become comprehensible when we have researched the nature of the various middle kingdom forces involved in plant growth processes.

The tradition of the Easter bunny that brings eggs is one non-Christian spring festival custom still practiced, un-metamorphosed, within the general context of the Easter festival. Originally, the custom involved a hare, not a rabbit, for the hare's fertility is an expression of the life-renewal processes of spring, and it is in February and March, in the northern hemisphere, that the hare begins to breed. Furthermore, the hare expresses in its nature something of the selfless giving needed for the bestowing and renewing of life. The outpouring of life forces from the sun is, spiritually considered, a ceaseless act of sacrifice. A hare will place itself at risk as a decoy when another hare is on the point of being caught by its pursuers; and the hare is herbivorous, it does not take the life of any animal.

The linking of eggs with the hare seems unnatural, but in the context of the renewal of life on Earth it is profoundly valid. For the egg is not only a symbol but as well a physical expression of the world. The egg shape can represent the form of both the Earth and the solar system. Radio-astronomical research has revealed the presence of various enveloping energy fields around the earth, which appear to be oval in shape. The five ether layers would also form an oval or roughly egg-shaped 'shell' around the earth.

Radio-astronomy has discovered such enveloping integuments around other planets too. Although it is not yet possible to detect this kind of subtle energy shell around the solar system, it is known now that other suns are surrounded by oval-shaped corona, which scientists take to be the beginnings of planetary systems, prior to the formation of separate planets. Further, entire galaxies reveal a similar oval integument, when they are viewed not in visible light but on the level of the energy body, so to speak – that is, when their x-rays, radio waves, infrared radiation are mapped. Thus, as the ancients knew, in their initiation wisdom, the cosmos is egg shaped. And hence the egg-bringing Easter hare portrays the fructification of the Earth sphere in spring.

The upsurge of life forces in the springtime hemisphere brings much activity to the middle kingdom. The elemental beings and nature sprites are involved in manifesting the new growth within all the kingdoms of nature. But this upsurge of ether forces gives increased powers to the fallen; that is, demonic-elemental beings, too. It is for this reason that the springtime festivals of earlier cultures had a certain solemnity, emphasizing the need for purification and cleansing.

Lucifer & Ahriman

The pastel drawing by Rudolf Steiner, 'Elemental Beings', shown in Chapter Two, includes two humanlike countenances, as we have noted. On the left, nearer to the ground, is one that has a heavier, older quality. On the right, up in the air, amidst the sylphs and pyrausta, the other countenance is younger and has a naive quality. These two images, with their distinctive characteristics, picture the influences, respectively, of Ahriman and Lucifer in the middle kingdom and thus on humankind.

Humanity is placed in the midst of three dynamics. On the one side, is an alluring, selfish light (referred to as 'luciferic') as Rudolf Steiner calls the leader of this first group of beings, Lucifer. On the other side There is darkness (referred to as 'ahrimanic'), as Rudolf Steiner calls the leader of this group, Ahriman. This influence causes human beings to be subject to the 'darkness', of hate, violence, etc. 'Ahriman' is in fact a name for a primary evil being in the Persian texts of the old Zoroastrian religion. Zoroastrianism permeated the Hebrew culture, and its ideas and terms became widely known to Jewish people, in the time of the Babylonian Captivity. The term Ahriman was probably seen by the Hebrews as an equivalent to the Hebrew Satan.

But, between these two factors, there exists a true light, in other words a truly ethical way of being; this is Christ reality. In the luciferic state, souls can be carried away with a potent desire to have some experience which is personally irresistible. This is a highly attractive and egocentric, but not directly evil, form of inner 'light'; leading to goals which are driven by self-indulgent selfish desires. But both of these influences are sources of misconduct that lead to social disharmony.

However through Lucifer, humanity developed the capacity to experience its own self, its own ego-ic reality. Consequently, we developed the capacity for both good and evil. Rudolf Steiner teaches that the intention of these beings was not to create evil as such, but it was to stimulate the ego-sense of the human being, in a way which would take humanity into ways of being that were no longer an automatic reflection of the divine. But naturally if its influence is too potent, this could, and often does, lead to specifically evil results. (See the *Rudolf Steiner Handbook*, for more about these beings, and their effect on humanity.)

These two fallen gods have the power to convert inhabitants of the faery world into demonic elemental beings. Folklore describes many of these demonic entities, for example, the trolls and pookas.

In springtime, as the out-breathing process develops, elemental beings rise ever higher into the air. High up in the ether layers of the atmosphere, in the radiant warm sheath, exist the fallen luciferic spirits. These beings have ensnared elemental beings that also exist above the ground, in the atmosphere; especially sylphs and pyrausta, which presumably congregate in the (first) warmth-ether layer and the light-ether layer. As the normal elemental beings ascend, they undergo a dulling of consciousness, coalescing into clouds of shimmering sleeping beings, and "thus the possibility is created that the luciferic spirits take control of the elemental beings". In the realm of the elemental beings this dynamic of the luciferic powers is real and strong.

Thus in springtime the disharmonious self-centred emotions and desires, which are part of our nature, the so-called lower self, can become stronger. This dynamic was inaugurate by the 'Fall of humanity', when luciferic beings were cast to the Earth sphere-. Indeed, Rudolf Steiner observed that in springtime "the human countenance wrestles away from the luciferic principle".[64]

The force of ahrimanic elemental beings also increases in springtime. For the foremost phenomenon in spring, in the physical world, is the creation of matter; that is, the condensing, from light and air together with solid substances from the soil, of new material organisms. The growth of plant bodies and the development of new embryos in the animal world is in effect the creation of further solid matter. Millions of tons of substances come into being each springtime. This is an activity that involves the undines and gnomes, because within material substances, ether forces are active.

But this activity also involves the ahrimanic powers, through which matter as such comes into being. The enabling of life and growth necessarily involves the creating and moulding of matter, as we are part of the material world. The fact that the ahrimanic powers have a role in the condensing or materializing of matter means that these beings, when they are kept in check, serve the spiritual purpose of the Earth's existence. The physical world, with its three-dimensional spatial quality, was created by the gods, but Ahriman is necessary for the condensing of solid matter into the ideal forms of this physical plane. Ahriman, however, strives to harden such matter so as to make it unfit to be an instrument of the spirit.

The ahrimanic powers have many elemental beings serving them; the gnomes in particular, can become ensnared by these powers which are connected to the interior of the Earth. There is no more dense material place, no area less permeated by sunlight and the spiritual reality behind the sun, than the subterranean depths of the Earth. Hence the gnomes are working in a realm subject to sinister influences.

In a lecture titled 'The Easter Imagination', in core *Four Seasons and the Archangels* lecture cycle, Steiner detailed the nature of the ahrimanic and luciferic activity of the

---

[64] In Supplement no. 19 to the GA, p.4.

spring. And in his notebooks, Steiner recorded that in spring these beings strive to bind the higher functions of the human being to the earthly reality. Ahriman strives via the dark malicious gnomes to cause a materialistic quality in our thinking, and Lucifer, with ensnared sylphs and pyrausta, to engender self-centred disharmony.

In early spring both Ahriman and Lucifer have enhanced powers, their activity is stronger. This is one reason for earlier humanity looking forward to the spring equinox; in early spring, up to the time of the equinox, the growth processes – that is, the ether forces active in them – are especially accessible to ahrimanic and luciferic elementals. After the equinox the solar forces again come to predominate.

As the out-breath begins, some weeks before the equinox, with growth and fertility processes already underway, the demonic beings become active. In early springtime the moon still has a strong influence in the ether processes involved in growth, in the plant, animal, and human realms, through the activity of elemental beings in the Earth-soul. This influence is carried over from the winter, when the sun's ether rays are at their yearly low. The fact that the winter hemisphere is somewhat isolated from the solar rays has considerable significance for humanity, because in the Earth's ether body, below ground level, malignant ether forces are present, especially lunar ethers of an evil kind.

These remained when the moon was incompletely cast out of the Earth.[65] The moon has benign forces, which govern life (growth) processes, and also malignant forces, which were previously in the Earth, prior to the extrusion of the moon. During winter and on into early spring the malignant lunar forces reinforce the influence of the malignant subterranean ethers. These ethers, having become activated at this time, are used by the ahrimanic gnomes.

But after the spring equinox, when the sun's path rises higher in the sky than that of the moon, and the hemisphere is in the out-breath process, the solar ethers can gain predominance over other ether forces active in the planet. Behind this seemingly automatic process an intense drama occurs.

---

[65] Rudolf Steiner taught that the moon was cast out, in the mid-Lemurian Age, some 18 million years ago.

For it is the intention of the ahrimanic powers to use the materialistic attitudes, the thoughts that arise in the soul, to eventually remould the human body in such a way as to prevent the incarnate person from awakening to his or her spiritual potential. This remoulding means nothing less than the forming of a semi-human batlike body, the bat being derived from an intensely 'ahrimanized' animal group-soul. The horrid intentions of the ahrimanic powers, revealed to us by Rudolf Steiner, may perhaps never be realized, but their materialistic influence is real.

Again, the activity of the two fallen powers, Lucifer and Ahriman, has been moderated every springtime by the solar ether forces. From the spring equinox onward, the sun's influence predominates; after the equinox the sun's path reaches higher into the sky than the moon's. This outer physical fact expresses the predominance in the elemental world of solar forces over the lunar and earthly forces. In spring, "the sun takes over the nurturing of life on earth",[66] and even the sunlight reflected to Earth by the moon has a different quality.[67] The moon itself then becomes a channel for the sunlight which is now inherently more potent for the earth.

The relative outer, astronomical positions of the Earth, moon, and sun create corresponding dynamics in the elemental world. Such truths serve as a bridge between the external illusion of nature and the inner ethical reality of our soul. The cycle of the year has a direct influence on our spirit, our consciousness. Steiner elaborated in an April 1923 lecture:

> When the spring comes {that is, in March for the northern hemisphere and in September for the southern hemisphere} there ascends from the depths of the earth with the growing plant world, permeating this sprouting plant life and also humankind all that is brought about by these ahrimanic spirits. In past ages humankind...{had}... a divine heritage {of spiritual consciousness}, which enabled it to withstand the impact of these ahrimanic powers... In springtime, with the growing and sprouting, a kind of intoxication will befall

---

[66] Ibid.
[67] GA 167, lect. 18th April, 1916.

72

humankind {that is, from the fifteenth century onward} with regard to the spiritual reality of life and take from humanity the awareness that a spiritual world at all exists.[68]

The two human countenances in Steiner's pastel drawing, (Illustration 4) express the springtime reality as reflected in humanity. We see the one figure, the heavier, older one, struggling with the materializing influence of Ahriman; we see the other figure, the young and naive one, threatened by the self-centred dreaminess that Lucifer promotes. It was the purpose of the ancient spring festivals to protect the community from the influences of the fallen elemental beings. Considering the intentions of the ahrimanic and luciferic powers, we can understand why the initiates in ancient times gave the meditation "know thyself" to their pupils, as a guiding thought for the season of spring.[69]

In such meditative activity, we encounter another aspect of the old seasonal festivals, an aspect still valid today: the opposing of the consciousness that arises in us through the forces of nature with a spiritually conscious attitude toward the season, with the conviction that going beyond 'maya' (the word for illusion, in Oriental terms), with some effort, we can become attuned to the higher influences of the season.

How can we attune ourselves to the higher influences of springtime? Is there some specific spiritual influence we can contemplate, so as to tread the middle path between the forces of Ahriman and Lucifer at this time? To a certain extent we have already answered this question, for it is to the in-raying solar ethers and, even more, to the Earth's indwelling Christ-being that we may look for support of the spiritually conscious attitude. To elaborate this answer, to develop the foundation for the new spring festival, we must consider more deeply the relationship of the indwelling Christ to the springtime, the seasonal basis for Easter and earlier springtime religious festivals.

In Christian lands of the northern hemisphere, the exact date of the Easter festival is movable, tied to the springtime processes in nature. But it is considered a historical festival, as it commemorates the event of the death and resurrection

---

[68] GA 223, Lect. 1 (*The cycle of the year as breathing-process...*).
[69] Ibid. lect. 5.

of Christ. This is an extraordinary paradox: the dating of this historical festival has not been connected with historical day in question ! The actual date of the historical Easter event has not been established by the church; in a sense, the event, as history, has been ignored.

The death days of many saints are commemorated after being established by the church on the basis of less historical data than is available regarding the Golgotha event. But no definite date has ever been decided upon for Easter. Instead, a remarkable movable dating formula has been followed, so that Easter is celebrated sometime after the 21st of March each year. The nature and purpose of this formula has not been questioned; in the absence of a conscious understanding of the formula, we have attributed to it a cosmic nature.

Passover: a seasonal and prophetic festival
Passover, the springtime festival of the Jewish religion, of all the ancient spring festivals, is closest to Easter. The Jewish people were preparing for the Messiah, for the Christian reality. In March and April in Palestine, as the springtime brings the barley crops to ripeness, the shepherds take their flocks out of the shelters into the fields, for the nights are not so cold. The spring rains come, the snow melts from the mountains, and the Jordan begins to swell. In the fields the wheat is ripening, carob trees are bearing their pods. In fertility the land responds to the powers of spring.

In Old Testament times, when the time of the spring festival approached, the roads and bridges were repaired, to facilitate the travel of people to the temple with their lambs, which were to be sacrificed then. Purification, both ceremonial and pragmatic, was carried out; sepulchres were whitened, to make them easily identifiable, so people could avoid them and thus remain free of a subtle uncleanness.

Then, at the time of the first full moon after the spring equinox, the people set out for the temple, where after a threefold trumpet blast, the lambs were killed. Certain rituals were performed at the temple to commemorate the Passover, then the people returned home and ate the Passover meal, the roasted lamb and bitter herbs. Why this rite? It had a historical basis. It reminded the people of the miracle long ago in Egypt, when Jehovah had sent "the destroying angel" to smite the Egyptians in their houses with disease.

Each house where the Jewish people lived had been smeared, above the doorway, with the blood of a lamb; the inhabitants had thus been protected from evil forces, which 'passed over' their houses. The festival of Passover, was understood as a festival to honour Jehovah, who ensured that the Destroying Angel passed over the sons of Israel at the plague of Egypt.

Such was the message of the priesthood. Thus the yearly leitmotif, the picture manifested through the Passover festival: Through the sacrifice, the outpouring, of an innocent life (a lamb), humanity, insofar as the forces of the lamb are present on the 'house', is protected from pernicious influences.

In old Israel, after the one-day Passover, there came a week-long festival of unfermented bread. Only insipid, unleavened bread was permitted during the week, so that people would remember that they were once in bondage to dark powers (the Egyptian Pharaoh), and that only through the intervention of Jehovah had they escaped the times of affliction. At the end of the week, the first fruits of the harvest (wheat, for example) were dedicated to God, and only then were people permitted to eat of the new crops. In connection with this festival, great numbers of animals were sacrificed as an offering to Jehovah.

Both of these festivals, Passover and the Festival of Unfermented Bread, had a historical basis; they both looked back in time to historical events. But the festival rites I have described also had a deep seasonal relevance, which we may begin to appreciate by considering the role of food, that is, nutrition, in the festivals. Take the reverential gratitude invoked by the first fruits ritual, for example. As we have noted, this spring ritual is still practiced in tribal communities today. This ritual has a metamorphosed existence in the custom of saying grace at the table. The grace, like the mood in which one prepares a meal, encourages the subtle power of our food to influence our mental attitude.

The dietary requirement, that is, the consumption of only bitter and insipid foods, also affects the physical body and hence our consciousness. This spring ritual appears in Christianity as the pre-Easter fast, Lent. We begin to see a purpose behind these spring festival activities; their focus is on a particular part of our being, namely the physical body. Rudolf Steiner revealed the correspondence of the four seasons to the four aspects of our human organism: In summer, it is the ego that is highlighted, as it were, by the seasonal processes; the ego in its manifestation via our deep volitional drives, our will impulses.

In autumn, the astral body (soul) is primarily affected by the elemental dynamics. And in winter, the ether body. In spring, processes focus on the physical body and its influence on our mental attitudes.[70] It was Steiner's perspective that from season to season each of these aspects of our organism, in their relationship with the indwelling Christ-being, would in turn become the focus of a new festival.

In springtime, then, our physical-material body, like the other physical-material aspects of creation, is subject to a powerful interplay of forces. The body is exposed to the rejuvenating life forces activated in spring, permeating the springtime hemisphere. All four groups of elemental beings, together with the other nature sprites, draw upon the ether energies that arch overhead in layers to bring about the growth and new life of spring. And because spring is the time when the earth-soul breathes out its elemental forces, the sun's ether energies are strongly attracted or drawn into the hemisphere's ether layers.

The solar life force can thus permeate our physical body, vivifying it. But the other dynamic is possible, that the physical body becomes subtly harder, coarser, denser, through the activity of ahrimanized elemental beings attempting to imbue plant life with their ether forces in order to induce in us this intoxication, which blinds us to the reality of the spiritual aspect of life.

The solar ether, which in springtime must permeate our physical body, is the life-ether, "the finest ether energy of all"; it streams out from the sublime ether organism of the sun beings, "the divine life-ether, pulsing through the world".[71] This life-ether rays out from the sun, together with the chemical (tone) ether; they are interwoven with each other, and bear within a reflection of the music of the spheres, the planetary forces governing life on Earth.[72] The life-ether (prana) is the inner force of life, the mysterious subtle principle that bestows life on Earth's creatures.

---

[70] In Supplement no. 19 to the GA, p.2.
[71] GA 123, lect. 3rd Sept. 1910, (Gospel St. Matthew).
[72] Ibid.

When the life-ether withdraws from the plant realm, and when decaying light-ether accumulates, then the mineral realm arises.[73] If our ether body and thus our physical body were deficient in life-ether, a subtle coarsening would result. It is essential that each springtime we assimilate the fine solar ether energy. For the residual lunar ether forces in the Earth are used by ahrimanic gnomes and hence are not receptive to the solar life-ether.

Indeed, if the elemental substances which later condensed into the solid moon had not been cast out of the Earth, then the Earth's ether body would have become impervious to the life-ether rays of the sun, and consequently the physical-material planet, and hence humanity's physical body, would have become hardened, coarse, increasingly non-human.[74]

It is necessary that material substance be available for the creation of our physical body, but this process must be governed by spiritual forces working in the life-ether. The finest of the ethers must govern the forming of matter, for the spiritual influences that create the music of the spheres can ensure that the process does not become excessively earthbound. Thus we find ourselves, in the spring, physically, between the solar life-ether used by the (benign) gnomes and the old ahrimanic lunar ether activated by 'dark gnomes'. The dietary requirements of the unfermented bread festival and of the Lenten season derive from these secrets of the springtime.

Hebraic initiation wisdom

I have noted that in spring, the earlier initiates experienced a marriage between sun and Earth; "the sun beings draw down to the earth" as Rudolf Steiner noted.[75] It is surely the perception of this process which underlies a springtime tradition in New Guinea, in the southern hemisphere. The indigenous peoples there construct in springtime a ladder with seven steps and carved birds symbolizing the dawn, to facilitate the union of the sun (beings) with the Earth.

To become attuned to the new solar life forces as opposed to the earthbound ethers from the subterranean dark elves: this was the striving of the acolytes of earlier times. The Hebrew initiates encouraged this striving by referring to the

---

[73] Archive lecture: Aug. 1905.
[74] GA 123 (*Gospel of St. Matthew*).
[75] In Supplement no. 19 to the GA, p.5.

miracle that occurred during the exodus from Egypt; that is, when manna descended from heaven to nourish the people. Leaving aside the many aspects of this miracle, we have the motif of celestial nourishment for the body, which was linked to the new life forces of spring.

The rabbis in esoteric Judaism, taught that in announcing to Moses that manna would be given, God said, "until now you have eaten of 'the bread of poverty', but from now on your bread shall emanate from another, distant realm; I will rain down bread from heaven for you". The rabbis taught that this phrase "from heaven" means "from the very centre of grace, and not, as previously, from the blemished moon".[76]

The people received a form of high spiritual nourishment, not the normal life forces, rayed down by the moon. The rabbis taught that every springtime, at Passover, this spiritual nourishment is available. It comes, they said, from heaven. Rudolf Steiner referred to this same process in the *Soul Calendar*, in a verse for the period around the spring equinox. The *Soul Calendar* consists of 52 verses (one for each week of the year) which indicate the inner spiritual processes that occur during the year, in the hemisphere. Verse 52, for the week between the spring equinox and Easter, reads:

> When from the depths of the soul
> The spirit turns toward the world
> And beauty wells forth from space around,
> Then drawing out of distant heavens
> The force of life streams into human bodies,
> Uniting through its power
> The spirit's nature with the being of the human.

The force of life rays into us in the springtime, after March 21 in the north, and after September 23 in the southern hemisphere. The esoteric commentary of the old mystery wisdom of Judaism said of the dating formula of the Passover festival, which is the forerunner, in a sense, of the Easter festival: "At this night, as the moon receives the full light of the sun, the 'holy wedlock' occurs, which gives

---

[76] These two quotes are from The Zohar, Mantua version, English translation in the Soncino Press edition, vols. 3 and 5.

78

protection for all from the Destroying Angel".[77] In other words, the solar life-ether becomes predominant after the spring equinox (even in the lunar energies, as we have noted) and bestows on humankind the healthy renewal of the physical body.

To sense livingly this springtime dynamic is a profound experience. This meditative verse, believed to be written by Thomas Aquinas, who had a high clairvoyance, indicates something of this dynamic,

> O bread to pilgrims given, O food that angels eat, O manna sent from heaven, For heaven-born natures meet; Give us, for Thee long-pining, To eat till richly filled, 'Till, earthly pleasures resigning, Our earthly wishes all are stilled.[78]

The secret of transforming and spiritualizing, the material-physical body (of achieving that spiritually conscious attitude), so that the primal divine will forces of the human spirit may manifest unimpeded through it, is contained in this verse. Through striving to experience with gratitude and reverence the inner nourishment that our food contains, and thereby overcoming sensuality in regard to eating, we may gradually spiritualize the human body.

Again, the renewal of the Earth's ether forces by solar life-ether every spring is not an 'automatic' process. As the Judaic temple ritual indicates, a sacrifice by (or of) a young lamb is needed. Thus, the Passover festival centred on a protection from malignant influences, through absorption of the immensely alive solar life-ether. Further, the festival sought to stimulate awareness that this absorption of solar life-ether was only possible through a deed of sacrifice, through connection with "the blood of a lamb". This drama unfolds each springtime, to ensure a wholesome renewal of life. It takes some effort for us modern human beings – who may not directly perceive the intense living reality behind the processes of the Earth – to realize that the cycle of the year is not an automatic thing !

The pre-Christian Passover, again, was celebrated on the first full moon after the spring equinox; the 14th or 15th of

---

[77] Ibid.
[78] Translation by R. Palmer ca. 1850, it appeared in a hymn book in 1858, and has a close affinity to Aquinas' Summa Theologica, Q.75.

the month of Nisan, which occurs in March/April by our calendar and started with the new moon (by fourteen days the moon is full). Easter is celebrated on the first Sunday after the first full moon after the spring equinox. The dating formulae for the two festivals are, then, nearly identical; indeed in the East they were identical for a long time, the Eastern churches did not delay Easter until the first Sunday.

The Easter dating mystery

If the Old Testament Hebraic culture had occurred in the southern hemisphere, then the Passover festival would have been observed in late September, or early October. But what of the Christian dating formula, different only by the requirement that one must wait for the Sunday? It is generally agreed amongst students of anthroposophy that this Easter dating formula is connected with the cosmic forces that are involved in the Easter festival. But what does the term "cosmic" mean here? This word can be thought of in an abstract way.

Rudolf Steiner stressed the importance of the movable, cosmic nature of the dating formula, but only rarely did he reveal the basis of this formula. In one lecture he stated that,

> The Easter festival is joined to the relationship of sun and moon"; [79] in another lecture he taught that "the Easter festival was determined by certain cosmic requirements, that is, the reciprocal relationship of sun to moon". [80]

These, like many similar statements, refrain from indicating just what kind of cosmic conditions are the basis of this festival. To reveal that the dating formula for this festival, used for so long unconsciously, was actually seasonally based, and hence applied to each hemisphere separately, is initiation wisdom that is only assimilable to those who are inwardly free of their cultural traditions.

Contemplating this puzzle, as to why the original, historical Easter event is commemorated according to 'cosmic' time, we usually come to the conclusion that on

[79] GA 169, Lecture, June 6th 1916.
[80] GA 167, 18th April, 1916.

that cosmic day some kind of life force becomes animated on the Earth, and that this annual renewal of the Earth is the right time to remember the original deeds on Golgotha hill. We conclude that the rejuvenating force of that one 'cosmic' Easter day applies to the whole Earth, apparently without regard for the seasonal differences between the hemispheres. But is this assumption, which was not taught by Rudolf Steiner when he spoke of his research into Easter, true?

Regarding the esoteric basis for the Easter dating formula, Rudolf Steiner taught that,

> The sun is the outer expression of the spirit of our world, the resurrecting spirit of our world. Such things as this must become living {in our souls}: the inner unity between the reflection of the world spirit in the moon and that which is the world spirit itself, in the sun. There must once again become living, how the Easter festival is determined {that is, dated} through the relationship of the sun and the moon in spring.[81]

In a different lecture, Steiner commented that,

> ...in the Easter festival, the spiritual significance of the world saviour was brought into connection with the physical sun and the awakening, re-arising life in springtime.[82]

And of course, spring is a season, and thus a hemispherical phenomenon. In a private conversation, when questioned about the late or early appearance of the new spring growth, he told his student:

> The later or earlier onset of plant growth in spring is connected to that grouping of forces through which also the Easter festival is dated.[83]

A Steiner notebook entry for the lecture regarding the Easter Imagination reads,

[81] GA 203, lect. 27th Mar. 1921.
[82] GA 96, lect. 12th Oct. 1907.
[83] Speaking with W.J.Stein in his book, *The Ninth Century*.

The sun beings draw down to earth; the Christ lives thusly with them; the luciferic and ahrimanic {elements} become strong; the human being inwardly inclines to these.[84]

As we have seen, all that is described as an Easter activity in the earth's soul refers to the season of spring. This discovery, central to the understanding of the new seasonal festivals, is confirmed by another Steiner reference to Easter,

When the Earth-spirit departs up into the heights, which is indicated by the Easter festival, then one related this going away from the earth {hemisphere}, this passing into the astral element, to the relationship of sun to moon.[85]

The new Christian spring festival
We have considered how behind the delightful colours and refreshing days of spring, an inner drama takes place. The sinister fallen elemental beings wish to influence our consciousness, but throughout the ages, the powerful solar life-ether rays have always brought a wholesome quality to the teeming, sprouting springtime world. This solar life force is an aspect of the great sun gods through whom the Earth came into being, and has ever since been nurtured in its separate evolution.

Foremost amongst these great hierarchical sun gods is "the lofty sun spirit, Christ", as Rudolf Steiner described him. This being is the highest of 'the Powers' or Spirits of Form as Rudolf Steiner calls this rank of being. This great being incarnated into the Earth sphere in order to prevent the increasingly powerful influences of Lucifer and Ahriman from undermining the connection between our normal ego-hood and our spiritual potential or higher ego.

According to Steiner's research, it was the inspiration of Christ, working unconsciously in the souls of the church fathers, at the Council of Nicea in A.D. 325, that brought about the instituting of the dating formula and the springtime placement for the Easter festival. A study of Steiner's lectures can help clarify the reason for this placement.

---

[84] In Supplement no. 19 to the GA, p. 5.
[85] GA 143, lect. 16th May, 1912.

Considered as connected to the seasonal cycle of the year, Easter is then a springtime festival, and as such **it is a hemispherical phenomenon**. Just as spring occurs twice each year, once in each hemisphere, so too should this esoterically defined 'Easter' occur twice each year. Once we know why that festival which commemorates the events of Golgotha was placed in the springtime (but varying each year, depending on the moon's cycle), it will be possible to create the new spring festival for each hemisphere as a esoteric 'Christian' festival. Of course, the new anthroposophical festivals will not be in conflict with the traditional ecclesiastical festivals. They are of interest to those who wish to participate in the activity of the Christ-being in the evolution of the Earth-soul.

The Easter festival, ecclesiastically, has two great themes: the incarnation, the sacrifice of entering into matter, which is the realm of death, and the resurrection or triumph over the influence of matter, over the influence of Lucifer and Ahriman. If we seek to understand the actual living connection of the Christ-being to the cycle of the year, then we discover that the focus of each Christian festival, its main theme, has a relevance to a particular season.

For example, the birth of Jesus (as described in St. Luke) and also the birth into the world of the cosmic Christ via the baptism in the Jordan have as a leitmotif or theme a relationship to the wintertime – not a poetic, symbolic relationship, but a very real organic connection. Now that we are in the twenty-first century, these truths of Christian initiation wisdom are seeking expression through the forming of the new seasonal Christian festivals.

Let us consider two extracts from a lecture by Rudolf Steiner, from the lecture cycle entitled *The Cycle of the Year as Breathing Process of the Earth*, wherein the contemporary activity of the cosmic Christ in the season of spring is revealed. Steiner's words in the second extract refer to the northern hemisphere, but just prior to this passage, in the first extract I will quote, he points out that what he has to say **refers to the seasonal breathing process, which is a hemispherical phenomenon**. It is precisely these words, and many other similar ones, that are not grasped, if one does not perceive the new festival concept. The first extract reads:

> We can, of course, always only consider one part {hemisphere} of the Earth in connection with this

breathing {process}. We consider that part of the Earth which we ourselves inhabit. On the other side of the Earth {hemisphere} exactly the opposite conditions apply.

The seasonal conditions and their attached festival

The words, "the other side of the Earth" means the other hemisphere; and confirms that Rudolf Steiner is talking about a seasonal process occurring in either of the two hemispheres. There are many such times when Steiner spoke of the opposite season occurring in the two hemispheres.[86] The German word, for 'opposite' (*entgegengesetzt*) means exactly that; just as the two poles are on opposite points of the globe, (contrary to M. Samson's interpretation). Steiner once spoke of seeing the astral aura of the Earth being on the one hemisphere, withdrawn in winter, whilst on the other hemisphere, it was extended out into space. And the word 'conditions' means of course the differing physical, etheric, astral and spiritual dynamics; **it is these which provide the basis for the new festivals**.

The primary point about the new festivals is that the seasonal cycle of in-breathing and out-breathing creates these different conditions in the hemisphere; **and that it is the spiritual dynamics inside these conditions which are the basis of the new festivals**. The 'conditions' and the 'festival' **are thus almost the same thing**, for the festival is, for human beings, a social activity which presents the seasonal conditions, in a meditative, artistic way.

But this concept would not be acceptable to any person to whom a festival is what the church has established. In this way of thinking, under no circumstances could the seasonal conditions be the basis of a religious festival; the two are seen as entirely separate things. (This does not prevent poetic considerations of nature, or Creation, being linked to a church festival).

But the traditional church festival view is, in essence, that the actual spiritual reality of a festival develops **within the remembering human soul** as it immerses itself in

---

[86] As post-graduate scholars of German (incl. medieval and Gothic) & accredited translators of German, such as myself, are aware '*entgegen*' when combined with the verb '*setzen*' can **never** mean 'leaning towards' or 'inclined towards', etc.). It loses that nuance, which it has with other verbs.

contemplation of the deeds long ago, of Christ in the Crucifixion, and the Resurrection on Golgotha hill.

Whereas in the new spiritual-esoteric festivals, inspired by high initiation knowledge, the actual spiritual essence of a festival **exists in the effort of spiritually striving people to sense the nature spirits and cosmic forces, guided by the cosmic sun god, that are active in the conditions of each hemisphere's seasons**, and how these affect the human soul.

It also needs to be mentioned here that this book is placed into a cultural context, in terms of anthroposophical groups. Rudolf Steiner had taught that the two organisations, the Anthroposophical Society and the Christian Community church have different missions in the world, and so must be kept apart. It is then, inappropriate for the Christian Community church to try to exert any influence in the debate about this theme, as Rudolf Steiner taught that the church's role is connected to church matters, and to church festivals, but not to what esoteric initiation wisdom has to offer to the world, whether in regard to festivals or any other subject.

But this requirement from Rudolf Steiner has been ignored in recent decades, and the two organisations are now even closer, with the creation in 2015 of a new Section of the Anthroposophical Society; one for religious renewal. This is in addition to the already existing sections for mathematics-astronomy, literature, medicine, education, agriculture, etc.

The confusion caused by an ecclesiastical view being imposed on the spiritual research of Rudolf Steiner, is demonstrated by another error of Benesch, "The Easter event is something that is valid in a unified way for the entire Earth; it is completely irrelevant whether it is summer or winter, spring or autumn."[87] The very important point here is that since this clergyman is unaware of the new festival concepts, his remarks are harmful to the intentions of Rudolf Steiner in regard to this theme, but, if he were here to restrict his comments to the church's memorial festivals, then he would be quite accurate.

Now returning to the second extract from the lecture about the activity in the seasonal cycle, where earlier Steiner had emphasized that he would be speaking about one

---

[87] F. Benesch, "Weihnachten im Sommer..." p. 24.

hemisphere; and therefore he was indicating that the same spiritual conditions would apply six months apart to the other hemisphere. He tells people about the interweaving of the cosmic Christ in these hemispherical processes;

> Whereas since December {*or June in the south*} the Christ-impulse has been intimately bound to the earth, to the soul forces of the Earth, we now {that is, in the spring} find that this Christ-impulse with the out-streaming soul forces {of the hemisphere in its springtime} begins to irradiate the earth {hemisphere} with light. That which as Christ-permeated astrality streams forth into cosmic heights, must now encounter the power of sunlight itself.
>
> And so, this picture arises in the mind: the Christ who has since December astrally withdrawn into the earth {hemisphere}, so as to be isolated from cosmic influences, now begins to let his forces breathe out, with the out-breathing of the earth {hemisphere} itself. He lets his force extend out to receive the solar force which rays toward him...
>
> The Christ begins to work in conjunction with the solar force at Easter time. Easter therefore occurs in the time of the out-breathing of the earth {hemisphere}... And the human being, feeling this, should say regarding Easter: If I have united myself with the power of Christ, then my soul flows out, too, into cosmic expanses {above the hemisphere} with the out-breathing force of the Earth-soul, and receives the sunlight which the Christ brings to human souls-from the earth sphere; just as he, prior to the mystery of Golgotha, had directed it to these human souls, from the cosmos. (March 31st, 1923)

Rudolf Steiner refers here not to the outer physical sunlight, but to the inner light, the pure transcendental ether radiance from the spiritual world, which maintains our life on Earth. The annual receiving of this inner light is now made possible through the cosmic Christ. Rudolf Steiner, as the great Christian initiate, experienced clairvoyantly the interweaving of forces between the elemental powers in the aura of the hemisphere and the guiding Earth-spirit (that is, the Christ being) in springtime. He reports how the need for the

Christ's presence is very real in each hemisphere's spring. It is as if the incarnation into the material world, the sacrifice on Golgotha hill, re-occurs:

> The mystery of Golgotha…had indeed to enter into the history of the earth as a unique event; but this event is renewed each year in a certain way, for humanity…the being of Christ…he appears every year in spring… in his resurrection form, between Lucifer and Ahriman, as…the Easter phenomenon… the Christ who works in human evolution so that we may be wrested from the luciferic and ahrimanic powers at the very time when we could most readily fall prey to them, that is, in the Easter; in the springtime.[88]

As prophetically proclaimed in the powerful images of the Old Testament Passover festival, the "lamb of God" each springtime sacrifices his forces, keeping at bay the harmful influences that are strongly activated then. Indeed, learned Jewish commentary refers to the lamb as "his body", as the body of a divine being.[89] A further Steiner notebook entry expresses this 'Easter dynamic' in springtime terms. The entry reads, "The word: fructification of the terrestrial lunar forces through the sun".[90] That is, through the sacrifice of the cosmic Christ or Logos force, both the lunar and earthly life forces are renewed by having access to the solar life-ether.

Changing Steiner's words

The extracts I have just quoted from Steiner's *Cycle of the Year* lecture include the expression "irradiate the hemisphere in light". The term 'earth' here means 'hemisphere', as we have so often noted. This conclusion is shown decisively by the drawing Rudolf Steiner made on the blackboard when giving the lecture; see below. Sadly, in the published English translation, this phrase is translated to read, "encircles the Earth". This translation is incorrect to

---

[88] Lect. 7th Oct. 1923 (*Four seasons & the Archangels*).
[89] The Mishnah, pesh, 10:3, quoted by Edersheim in The Temple and its Services, (London, 1874, Religious Tract Soc.).
[90] The German here: „Das Wort: Befruchtung der Erden-Mondekräfte durch die Sonne".

the German, and it reveals the difficulty that the student of anthroposophy has in thinking in a real way about these dynamics.

For the 'Easter' reality as we have seen, when using the term in the esoteric way that Rudolf Steiner does, concerns one hemisphere at a time only. The German verb used here is, *umstrahlen*, which means "to irradiate" (or bathe in light). But in German, the word 'encircle' would be "*einkreisen*" or "*umfassen*" or "*umgeben*".

The phrase in question is therefore saying that a radiance develops in the ether-astral atmosphere of the springtime **hemisphere** from the out-breathed soul forces and the Christ light; as shown in the blackboard drawing. It is **not** saying that the Christ-being encircles (or journeys around) the entire globe, thereby magically invoking an abstract, global Easter. The illustration made by Rudolf Steiner during this lecture confirms my interpretation. The Christ forces do not encircle the Earth, they do not curve around the globe; they ray out above one hemisphere at a time.

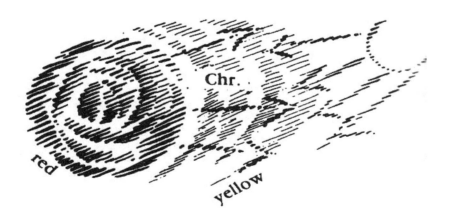

Through the sacrifice made each springtime, by the indwelling Christ being, the life-ether from the sun is received into the Earth's ether aura and into our ether bodies, pushing back the influence of the fallen gnomes. This process is in turn affected by our attitudes to the world; a striving away from the emotional and intellectual illusions about life that so strongly but subtly arise in spring, has a direct effect, of a beneficial nature, on the elemental beings. When we consider the activity of the guiding archangel of springtime, Raphael, in Chapter Nine, we will have more to say about the significance that these processes have for healing and health.

Resolving the enigma: the festival of incarnating

As we have already noted, the ecclesiastical Easter festival has two leitmotifs, the incarnation and the resurrection. The incarnation theme is present in the sense that the events of the last week of the Christ's life on earth – Passion Week – together with the actual Crucifixion, portray an increasingly intense immersion into the world of matter. That is, a kind of incarnation into the material world, albeit not by birth. Both of the themes, incarnation and resurrection (the latter in metamorphosed form) can lead us to the right theme for a Christian seasonal springtime festival.

The conscious motivation I have just mentioned, which looked to the springtime for support of the resurrection theme, is contrary to the perspective given by Rudolf Steiner. Indeed such a viewpoint is really materialistic and simplistic, for such a spiritual process as the resurrection of Christ, or the spiritual rebirth of a person through initiation, is not truly symbolized by material growth processes, as Rudolf Steiner pointed out.[91] Instead, the resurrection motif should be celebrated in autumn, and was so celebrated for centuries by pre-Christian religions.

At such festivals, a statue of a God was placed in a kind of grave for three days and then 'resurrected' out of it. In autumn, in contrast to the material resurrection of springtime, there is a subtle force, an elemental power enhancing our inner strength, bringing a greater capacity for spiritual activity through the strengthening of our will forces (see Chapter Six).

But by the fourth century AD, as humankind had lost its previous instinctive perception of the inner, elemental dynamics within the seasons, the autumnal resurrection and renewal rites were transferred incorrectly to the springtime ! If the autumn festival were to be renewed, we would

---

[91] GA 233a, lect. 21st April, 1924.

incorporate as an initial theme the historical resurrection of Christ, insofar as all contemporary spiritual renewal processes may be considered as connected to the triumph over sinister influences which seek to undermine humanity, by the cosmic Christ in the resurrection. This metamorphosing of the ecclesiastical Easter festival, that is, its resurrection aspect only, making contemporary our relationship to the triumph of the Christ being over Ahriman, is the connection of Easter to autumn.

Such an autumn festival we would call a Michael festival, referring to the great archangel Michael, who as a vessel of the Christ light, is active in the autumn. In this sense, defining it as a festival of resurrection, Rudolf Steiner did occasionally refer to Easter as an autumn festival, naming the same themes as for the autumn Michael festival.

Of course, the *ecclesiastical* Easter festival can still speak of spiritual renewal or triumph. But this theme should then be seen as connected not with the springtime nature renewal but rather with processes occurring in the vast time scale of human evolution; for example, the union of the great sun god, the cosmic Christ, to the Earth, which assured the triumph of the spirit over matter. In essence, our present ecclesiastical Easter festival will lead to the development of a new spring festival, which will centre on the theme of incarnation, descent into the material world. The other theme of the ecclesiastical Easter festival, that is, resurrection, will merge with an inner understanding of the dynamics of autumn, creating a festival of spiritual triumph, centred in the processes occurring in autumn.

The motif of incarnation is, as we have noted, the theme of the new spring festival. Why this motif? What is the connection of the present Easter festival to such a theme? What process made the historical Easter possible? Incarnation ! When at the baptism in the Jordan, the Christ descended to 'overshadow' Jesus, this was the beginning of an increasingly deep penetration into the physical-material world, until the cosmic Christ had united his consciousness to that of earthly humanity.

Then, in the crucifixion, in the death process, this incarnating reached its deepest point, wherein transcendental cosmic consciousness became narrowed into the travail of death. Only thereby could the needed spiritual light permeate the earth reality. The ongoing, upward leading development of humanity begins with the

90

incarnation. Thus can a conscious contemplation of the esoteric reality of the incarnation provide a contrast, a powerful counterbalance, to the messengers of 'maya', of subtle materialism, who approach us in spring.

Considered esoterically, the material plane is 'hell'; so for a sublime hierarchical god, the narrowing and drying up of consciousness that is necessary for functioning in the world of matter would be a 'hell-ish' state. With this point in mind we can comprehend the definition Rudolf Steiner gave of this first aspect of the Christian spring festival:

> The Easter concept...the descent into 'Hell' and, through this descent, the conquering of the {path to} the heavens for humanity. In this sense, 'He was laid in the grave, He is arisen'.[92]

That is, the cosmic Christ incarnated into matter, and overcame it, and thus humanity in its ongoing development in the material world will eventually achieve the goal of evolution. The theme of resurrection is present in this Easter-spring thought, but it is muted; it is taken up more strongly in the autumn festival, the theme of which Steiner states this way:

> The human being has arisen {through the fact of the resurrection} and therefore can confidently be laid in the grave {because he will be able to arise out of death}.[93]

The process of restoring a balanced spiritual attitude to spring through contemplation of the historical incarnation is the first phase of the new festival. Then we can develop a further significant aspect of the festival, and of our own relationship to the Christ being, when we contemplate the contemporary springtime reality of the Christ. The relationship of the Christ-being to the inner drama of springtime, both before and after the events of Golgotha, was sensed by St. Paul. In the spring of AD 33, the disciples gathered together with Christ on the occasion of the Jewish Passover festival.

But their Passover meal was different from that of their fellow Jews; Christ, who was about to be arrested and

---

[92] Lect. 1, in *The Cycle of the Year as breathing process...*
[93] Ibid.

crucified, spoke to them at this Last Supper, indicating that he would sacrifice his being to become the inner life of this planet. Thus would humankind be able to assimilate his light during earthly life; "this bread is my body". Some years later, in a spiritual experience given him by the risen Christ, in contemplating the Last Supper, St. Paul uttered the immortal words, "for indeed, Christ, our Passover {lamb} has been sacrificed for us" (Cor. 5:7).

The first phase of the new springtime festival involves then bringing spiritual (holistic) thoughts to consciousness of such a nature as to counterbalance certain attitudinal tendencies of the season. The second aspect of the festival involves experiencing the connection of the Christ to the seasonal processes as real, contemporary, and existential. As we have seen in this chapter, the activity of the Christ in spring may be considered an incarnation process.

That is, when in springtime in each hemisphere the Christ-being encounters the upsurge of life forces in that hemisphere (including that within fallen ahrimanic elemental beings) and pours out his forces to ensure that the pure solar forces predominate in the spring, it is a kind of incarnating or entering into the very essence of material existence of that hemisphere.

Describing this dynamic brings us close to another aspect of the guiding, nurturing influence of the indwelling sun spirit of the Earth. Scientific research and anthroposophy agree that the sun will gradually lose its powers, that it will weaken and fade. In anthroposophical knowledge, this deterioration process will not take such a long period of time as science today says. One factor hastening this weakening of the sun's forces is the active absorption by the Earth of these solar energies (presumably this is especially so when each hemisphere has its springtime). But,

> through the presence, since the events of Golgotha, of the sun spirit in the Earth, it will always be possible for the reducing solar forces to be supplemented.[94]

We can grasp the full significance of these words when we have clarified the relationship of the Christ being to the midwinter processes. Additional aspects of the theme of

---

[94] GA 150, lect. 23rd Mar. 1913.

92

incarnation are important as themes of the new spring festival – in particular, the pre-birth mysteries, the processes whereby the human being descends back to incarnation. The descending journey through the cosmic spheres of the returning soul was contemplated in the ancient mystery centres in springtime, and this timing is still valid, although it needs to be considered in the light of the esoteric Christianity given to us by Rudolf Steiner.

Considered in this way, this theme would include esoteric embryology – the cosmic processes in embryonic development – and the relationship of the incarnating child to its developing body. Steiner expressed this aspect of the incarnation theme:

> There where nature is in a growing phase, there the human being should commemorate his {or her} descent into physical reality. There, where nature is in decline, there the human being should commemorate his ascent, his resurrection in the spirit.[95]

In such words, we can conclude that the Nerthus mysteries of old Europe are finding a new Christian expression. Springtime thoughts and elemental beings.

Springtime thoughts and elemental beings
But spring is a time for rejoicing, too ! Not only the beauty of the flowers delights us, but a sense of well-being glows in us also. Rudolf Steiner describes the happiness that arises from sensing the powerful creative forces our planet is blessed with:

> As springtime begins, as the sun moves into such a relationship to the earth {hemisphere}, that through its forces the plant seeds can germinate and arise out of the womb of the Earth-mother, then the human soul begins, inwardly, to jubilate, as if in the radiance of heaven. Because it knows that forces are moving through the cosmos, which with each new year, in cyclical succession conjure forth, from the womb of the earth, that which is necessary for external life and also for the life of the soul. So that the human

---

[95] GA 233, lect. 19th April, 1924 (*Easter Festival in relation to the Mysteries*).

being during Earth evolution may be able to go his way, from the beginning of this Earth evolutionary period until its end.[96]

To grasp such spiritual perspectives with our thinking is of great significance ! Our thoughts about nature are important, for ourselves and for nature, for the elemental beings. We have seen that experiencing the theme of incarnation in the new 'Christed' spring festival helps to push away the ahrimanic influences in the thinking life, influences which seek to develop in us an attitude of materialism. This sinister springtime dynamic has its purpose, even if that purpose is not fully comprehended by the ahrimanic gnomes who carry it out.

They are relatively minor members of the shadow side of the middle kingdom. We can gaze at the teeming, sprouting beauty of springtime, asking what kind of ether force is active, asking which planetary or zodiac forces are especially involved with the plants, and because 'thoughts are things', when our gaze falls upon a plant, for example, the nature sprite or elemental being involved with that plant will be protected from 'the dragon'; that is the demonic beings in the elemental realms.[97]

In a future time cycle the Earth will etherealize, we will live in an ethereal body, no longer needing the life lessons of a material (flesh) body. Those nature beings, which through humanity are ensnared by Ahriman, are unable to work toward this goal;[98] whereas those that are protected by humanity are thereby free to become especially active in the elemental substance of the Earth, wherein this new planet of light will develop.[99]

We begin to see how significant our attitude to nature is, and how intimately we are connected to the elemental kingdom ! If we view the plants, especially in the springtime, with the kind of thoughts Rudolf Steiner suggests, we are working with another aspect of the incarnation theme ! For then the underlying concept is that plant and animal growth is only possible because an intention to incarnate arises in

---

[96] Rudolf Steiner in GA 150, lecture of March 23, 1913.
[97] GA 223, lect. 28th Sept. 1923 (*The Cycle of the Year as Breathing process...*).
[98] Ibid.
[99] Ibid., see also the cycle *The Spiritual Hierarchies and their reflection in the physical world.*

the group soul or guiding intelligence of the animal or plant species. That is, from the spiritual realm, the group soul of, for example, the animal species carries out the impulse to incarnate on the Earth, raying its forces down into the earth sphere from the cosmos.

Themes of the new 'Christian' spring festival

We remember: the incarnation of Christ, his descent into matter; the outpouring of his life has countered Lucifer and Ahriman, that is, their influence through past ages.

We contemplate: the season of spring, the hemisphere out-breathes its forces; life-ether forces from the sun stream in, rejuvenating the physical body; fallen elemental beings become powerful; again, through a sacrifice of Christ, the springtime influence of Lucifer and Ahriman is held in check. The incarnation echoes on, through the Earth's own life rhythm, the cycle of the year.

We realize, we observe: the descent into matter; when a human being is born, when animals have their young, when young plants arise-then from higher worlds, a descent occurs. Thus this new festival, which we could name the Christian spring festival, occurs on the first Sunday after the first full moon after the 21st of March in the northern hemisphere and after the 23rd of September in the southern hemisphere. The structure of the festival calendar will become clear, with regard to both hemispheres, when we have completed our study of the new festivals.

Apart from the two festival cycles mentioned so far, there is also the purely historical "name/date calendar", which lists key historical events and the birth and or death dates of outstanding people. In this calendar the actual date of the events on Golgotha, the 3rd to the 5th of April in A.D. 33, according to the research of Rudolf Steiner, can be entered.

We should note that the new festivals are different in their inner dynamics from the traditional commemorative festivals. In the ecclesiastical (commemorative) festivals and sacraments, the priest(ess) through carrying out the rituals invokes spiritual powers down into the earthly sphere. The dynamic that creates the new festival is the reverse of this. In the new festival the theme is presented in an artistic performance, in meditation, and esoteric commentary.

Then the people present strive to grasp and then contemplate the spiritual truths (thoughts) within these presentations. This intuitive thinking, intensely focused on such esoteric realities, lifts the consciousness of the participants up to a spiritual sphere. Steiner termed this kind of activity "the reversed cultic act", that is a reversal of the liturgical rituals of the church.[100]

Review of the dating formula

That the festival is to occur for each hemisphere on the first Sunday after the first full moon after the spring equinox is very important ! The moon is significant for our life, especially for all the processes carried out by the ether body; this includes growth, healing, and bringing thoughts to consciousness. Its motions around the Earth govern the way in which life processes manifest on our planet. Yet the ether forces that we use derive primarily from the sun. From late autumn until the spring equinox, the moon has the predominating influence over the hemisphere's ether processes. During the same period, the solar ethers have much less influence, for until the springtime out-breathing the hemisphere is not so receptive to them.

But by the time of the spring equinox the sun has become the predominating influence because of the out-breathing process. And it also predominates over the moon through the astronomical process, the path of the sun across the sky, of that hemisphere, reaches higher than that of the moon, from the equinox day onward. This fact, as we noted, has its corresponding elemental reality, the solar ethers will have a greater influence than the lunar ethers.

Further, the moonlight, and each full moon which occurs after the vernal equinox, will become ever more a vessel for the strengthening solar energies, rather than exerting its own influences. The first full moon after the equinox begins this process; its light, even in its own night sky en-clothes the rays of the sun. Steiner expressed this fact in connection with Easter,

> Those whose souls are open to the impressions of the spiritual world know that our earth does not become different just because the vegetation buds

---

[100] *In Awakening to Community*, GA 257, lectures 6 & 9.

forth in spring and in autumn is harvested; rather that part of the earth which is illumined by the moon is different from that {part of the} Earth which is not illumined by moonlight. We must picture to ourselves that it is not the case that above in the firmament there moves the silver globe or the silver sickle, rather that there is a 'web of light' around us, of a spiritual nature, in which we are living and swimming and 'weaving', with our soul, just as we swim in water with our body. And that which lives and weaves in the earth, changes continually, according to the relationship of the moon to the sun.

The sun is in an entirely different relationship to the Earth after the 21st of March than before the 21st of March {the 23rd of September in the southern hemisphere}. And that which is reflected, as sunlight, to the Earth, by the moon is entirely different from that which is reflected before then. The first full moon after the spring equinox, which gives back to us the initial power of the sun which is now once again resurrected, is quite different from all other full moons.[101]

But what then is the significance of waiting for the Sunday? Then we are relating this yearly renewal of life, especially the activity of the indwelling sun spirit in reaction with the sun's ether rays, as they stream into the material world, to the flow of time. Without the element of Sunday, the festival would arise simply from a spatial consideration, regarding the positions of the sun, moon, and earth in space. Through the waiting until Sunday, the cosmic dynamic between these three living organisms is related to the experience of time, the flow of time.

Time is another aspect of our relationship to the cosmos; while we orient ourselves in space, we have a feeling for the flow of time, hence for rhythms. The flow of time is, like the spatial relationships of the planets, an expression of the spiritual reality behind the world. The spatial relationships of the planets, whether they are in opposition or conjunction, and their distance from each other, and from the sun-brings to expression a spiritual reality.

---

[101] Rudolf Steiner lecture April; 18th 1916, GA 167.

So too in the rhythmical flow of time does a spiritual force come to expression. The seven-day week, a small time cycle in itself, is an image of the spiritual significance of the seven classical planets in the flow of time experienced on Earth. This correspondence of the seven days to the seven planets has no spatial basis; it exists simply in the flow of time.

Thus the rationale for the Easter formula, wherein we wait until Sunday: A process develops that is connected to the sun, the realm of the sun spirits, and we contemplate it at that moment of time when the sun is present, projecting into our time flow. This is another way we attempt to attain a perception of the process as spiritual, transcendental. For where does the dynamic occur if not beyond our world, beyond the spatial, three-dimensional world. Spiritual processes exist in a realm where space, as we know it, ceases to exist, but where time, in a different manner, does exist, as eternity; past, present, and future existing simultaneously. So we gain a closer relationship to the spiritual process by connecting it to its own rhythmical time functions.

Is humanity still spiritually linked to the natural year?
People at times object that there are statements from Rudolf Steiner to the effect that we are not connected to the seasons inwardly any more, and that we therefore cannot obtain any spiritual nurture from the seasonal cycle. We shall refer to this topic in various chapters of this book. But here we want to note that the reference to humanity not having any real inner connection with Nature, in a certain sense, was made in a lecture given on 31st Dec. 1922, in the lecture cycle, *Man and the World of Stars.*

There Rudolf Steiner taught that in the way our soul moves out of its body at sleep, and then back into it in the morning, as we awaken, causes both winter and summer dynamics to occur in us at the same time. That is, when our soul is drawn down into our body, and awakens, there occurs a similar dynamic as in a hemisphere at wintertime, in that the earth-soul is then drawn down into the soil.

The soul and ego however, are at this time, (i.e., when we are awake in the body) consciously open to whatever stream into them as perceptions of the external world. But this latter dynamic is just like the summertime condition of the hemisphere, for it is then that it opens up to receiving impressions from the cosmos. Now one can see from this viewpoint that both winter and summer dynamics occur inside us simultaneously.

What is difficult for those who are not clear about the new festival concept, is that the entire theme in this lecture does not refer to the spiritual beings and forces of a season, it refers only to the dynamics involved in an out-and in-breathing process.

For, here Rudolf Steiner is **not** teaching that we humans have the **spiritual reality** of the summer hemisphere (the nature spirits and divine beings) all occurring inside us, while at the same time we also have all the winter **spiritual reality** with its varied beings, going on inside us too. The theme of this lecture has nothing to with these wonderful spiritual processes, it is simply pointing out an analogous condition, a parallelism in the dynamics, between humanity's sleeping/waking processes and the seasons.

So the 'inner freedom' of humanity from the specific rhythms of Nature, does not prevent us from being influenced by the seasons in our astral and spiritual being-ness.

Nor does this suggest that we should be separate from Nature; on the contrary, it emphasizes that we need **all the more** to be gaining access to the higher spiritual influences in the seasons, and that we may do so with inner freedom. To conclude that such beings and realities do not affect our soul-life, just because our physical-etheric nature has this subtle 'intermingling' process is entirely incorrect. Such a conclusion would have as a consequence that, simply because of this intermingling of in-breath and out-breath dynamics all the cosmic and elemental beings of summer and winter ray out their forces into the our aura simultaneously, at any time of the year; and furthermore, it's all irrelevant.

These conclusions have no validity, because two entirely different matters are under consideration. One is the potent and intimate interweaving in our subtle 'bodies' of seasonal spiritual realities; the other is simply that our conscious mind does not automatically mirror the dynamics which underpin the natural processes. Whether a person is interested in becoming conscious of these processes and working with them is the point, our freedom comes into relevance at this point.

Spiritually striving people find it possible to sense something of the inner realities of a season, and then seek to be receptive to that aspect of the divine world which is manifest then. People who are not ready for such experiences will seek to remain distant from such an interface with these higher realities. He many times pointed out that we human beings can and should become re-attuned to the divine influences operative in our hemisphere's seasonal cycle. For example, after an entire lecture on this topic he stated,

> And really, just as we human beings participate through the tenor of our inner life, in what occurs in our blood circulation, so do we actually participate in the entirety of our human nature, in the cycle of the year....People must again have an inner understanding of what this connection to the natural yearly cycle can mean for humanity.[102]

We can now explore the fascinating spiritual forces which become in the summer time.

---

[102] GA 223, lect. 1st Oct. 1923.

CHAPTER FIVE

THE SUMMER FESTIVAL

In springtime, the solar forces begin to interact with the ever more active life processes of the hemisphere. The hemisphere's own forces, from which the new growth of spring develops, begin more actively to interweave with the sun's forces. This regenerative interplay of solar and terrestrial activity is the fundamental dynamic of springtime. The basic dynamic of winter, on the other hand, involved the divine beings who constitute the Earth-soul and the Earth-spirit working together with the inner, spiritual life forces of the sun.

Now as summer approaches, we experience the gradual predominance of warmth and light, because of the increasing power of the solar ethers. We have seen that in the summertime the hemisphere is most exposed to the solar influences because it is then most exposed to the sun (because of the tilt of the Earth's axis) and also because at this time the hemisphere is completing its out-breath. All the growth and fruiting processes, produced by the springtime through the interplay of sun and earth, can now culminate under the sun's influence.

The hemisphere now appears drowsy, as the increasing solar forces, manifesting as warmth and light, enable fruits and grains to mature and ripen, ready for the harvest. The impression we take in summer of a sleepiness in nature might seem illusory, for there is obviously an activity associated with the ripening and maturing of the "fruits of the earth". Nevertheless, the impression that nature is also somehow asleep, is correct.

The out-breathing process has carried the numberless multitude of spiritual beings, from elementals to great hierarchical gods, up into the heights of the atmosphere, and thus the earth; the physical body of the planet, that is, has been to a great extent vacated. In summer the hemisphere is in a situation similar to the sleeping human being, for at night we vacate the body, leaving it empty. This image of summer as the sleep time of the hemisphere is a deeply valid image for the spiritual changes that are also occurring, for the consciousness processes involved. For when we are awake, when we are in our body, we have maximum consciousness, but our growth and healing processes are minimal. In the winter hemisphere, likewise, there is an intense wakefulness in the middle kingdom, but minimal reproduction and fruiting in the plant kingdom.

In summer, the situation prevailing in the hemisphere is opposite to the experience of an awake human being. For in summer, consciousness becomes muted while ether processes connected with growth intensify. Just as the fruition processes are maximal in nature during summer, they become maximal in us during sleep, when we are also out of the body. Then vegetative life processes predominate; the rebuilding of cells and general healing can occur while we sleep.

There is an additional parallel between sleep and the summer out-breath of the Earth, namely that when we leave the body in sleep, ether forces from the sun stream into our ether body, to enable the rejuvenation process to occur.[103] This activity, wherein the life-ether permeates our sleeping physical ether organism, is directed by spiritual beings of the sun sphere.[104] Meanwhile our soul rises into the spiritual worlds; cosmically considered, our nightly journey takes us through the planetary spheres and into the sun sphere and the starry heavens.

The spiritual reality behind the sun, which has created the entire solar system, and nurtures all beings on its planets, is immensely great. The spiritual reality of the sun is much deeper than that of the planets, as indicated by the greater physical-ethereal presence of the sun. The sun's immense life-evoking, life-sustaining powers encompass the entire solar system. There is a deep truth to the ancient saying that human beings are sons and daughters of the sun.

In summer, the Earth-soul in that hemisphere undergoes its sleep phase, the multitude of elemental beings and gods depart from their 'body', and the vegetative processes are maximal. The seeds and flowers formed in spring can now culminate in mature crops ready for harvesting. As the summer out-breath proceeds, the hemisphere's ether layers are flooded with in-streaming solar forces, making possible this culmination of the growth capacity of the hemisphere's

---

[103] See Rudolf Steiner GA 112, *The Gospel of St. John in relation to other Gospels*, lect. 26th June 1909.
[104] Ibid., Lecture 27th June.

ether body. The consciousness of the Earth-soul changes in summer. Elemental beings undergo a dimming of consciousness, as they ascend into the sky.

By the summer solstice, they have entered a dreamy sleep state and have coalesced to form clouds of de-individualized sleeping elementals, high up in the ether aura above the hemisphere.[105] Some of these sprites then traverse the globe and descend over the other hemisphere; see Chapter Ten for further consideration of the interweaving of these beings between the two hemispheres revealed by Rudolf Steiner.

The sleep state of the summertime has still a further correspondence to our human sleep state. Just as we reunite with the high spiritual realities of the sun sphere during sleep, albeit without our normal ego consciousness, so too does the Earth-soul of that hemisphere in summer encounter and reunite with the beings and forces from the sun, although in a dream state, as it were. As Steiner describes,

> ...in summer, the process of out-breathing is at its height. The earth {hemisphere} has given its soul to the cosmos...the soul of the earth {hemisphere} strives toward the stars, it wants to know about the life of the stars {and planets}. And, in its own way, it is most united with the movements of the stars, through the light of the summer sun, at St. John's time.[106]

In springtime, as we have noted, the elemental beings of the middle kingdom are intensely active, working at the new growth processes, bringing to expression the zodiac and planetary influences behind the plant and animal species. These influences could be regarded as thought forms or picture thoughts deriving from higher beings in the cosmos. The summer out-breathing process carries all these living thoughts and feelings, which appear as images in the astral body of the earth, up into the heights.

Up there, these are perceived by the sun beings, as the summer is a time when they can 'read' the will-forces manifested in that hemisphere, as it were. And since much of what has developed during the spring and summer

---

[105] Rudolf Steiner GA 223, *The Cycle of the Year as breathing-process of the Earth,* lect, April 2nd 1923.
[106] GA 226, lect. May 21st 1923.

derives from the springtime permeation of the hemisphere by solar forces, the sun gods are thus able to contemplate the outcome of their guiding, nurturing influence. Steiner again:

> The earth devotes its forces to all that which streams down from the sun, and forms this under the influence of the solar forces. In summer the earth {hemisphere}, together with all its forces, enters into the sphere of influence of the sun. The spiritual researcher sees in that which occurs between the earth and the sun, through the help of the plant {elementals}, the wonderful interweaving of a cosmic thinking, feeling, and sensing realm.[107]

This interweaving activity in the Earth-soul, now high above the summer hemisphere, is a cosmic process, for the sun beings are now present in the Earth's aura, permeating it with their soul forces, with their thoughts and feelings. As Rudolf Steiner taught,

> In ancient times, people knew that the 'summer sleep' was of such a nature that they could say: 'during the summer the earth is enveloped by thought pictures'. And they expressed this by saying: 'the upper gods come down {to the earth} during summer and hover around the earth {hemisphere}; whereas during winter the lower gods ascend out of the earth and hover around it'.[108]

Understanding the subtle processes occurring in summer will greatly assist us in discovering the themes of a new Christian festival for the season. Walking through nature on a summer's day can be a fascinating, rewarding experience. The air seems so full of a subtle presence, and everywhere flying insects are whirring on their busy way. Apart from those that plague human beings in their search for food, such as mosquitoes and flies, most insects avoid or ignore us.

The dragonfly is a notable exception. Unless we walk right into it, the dragonfly, so named for its voracious appetite for small insects, will calmly continue its activity. To a sensitive

---

[107] GA 60, lect. 8th Dec. 1910.
[108] GA 219, lect. Dec 1st 1922 (*Man and the world of stars*).

observer, it is evident that the human being is a welcome presence for the dragon fly. Why is this?

In summer, the increased solar forces that now have access to the hemisphere's atmosphere, energize the ether layers overhead. In particular, the warmth-ether layer and the light-ether layer appear to be vivified by the forces of the summer sun. In Illustration 1, we saw a depiction of the interaction between the layers of ether forces in the atmosphere, and the surface of the Earth. The chemical-ether layer reflects, as it were, into the oceans and moisture processes here on the ground. The light-ether layer works into the troposphere; the band of air, of breathable gases, that sustains us, that forms the world's weather. It is the task of the light-ether to create visible light from the in-streaming solar ethers; science calls this 'cold light', that is, light formed without any of the invisible radiations such as infrared light, which happen to be warmth generating.

The warmth-ether layer envelops the Earth like a protective mantle; from it all the warmth processes in nature derive their heat. The pyrausta (fire spirits) are especially active in summer, for it is their task to ensure the continuation of life on earth; they enable the reproduction process in all the realms of nature to achieve its goal. Warmth is a vital part of reproduction; in the plant kingdom, the seeds are formed through the presence of the warmth-ether, hence the oils too are a result of the summer.

As Rudolf Steiner taught,

> "...the fire spirits {pyraustas} whir around the plant, concentrating the cosmic warmth into the tiny seed points."[109]

We need this warmth-ether too, for we must be able to draw upon an inner warmth for life and consciousness processes; although we can create this through our nutrition, the warmth-ether forces in our own ether body need to be maintained. As we noted in Chapter One, the entire warmth-ether layer above the summer hemisphere becomes warmer, while above the winter hemisphere it cools; this warmth streams down onto the earth during the summer.

Now, with the help of Steiner's research, we may understand the role of the dragonfly. This insect transmits

---

[109] GA 230, lect. 2nd Nov. 1923 (*Man as symphony of the Creative Word*).

the warmth, the warmth-ether, into the earth, into the ethereal aura of the earth, into our human ether body. A Steiner verse describes this wonderful summer mystery.

Summer
In radiant heights,
Where, glistening in the sun,
The friendly dragon flies are
Flitting out rays of warmth
Which blend into the space around,
There, tarry thou, my soul;
For, thinking of me, they weave
From sadness, strength.
Already I can feel
How they are sensing me;
How warmth streams from them,
Permeating me.
The Spirit dissolves
In cosmic interweaving,
The earthly heaviness
Into light of the future.

The warmth-ether forces, growing stronger in summer, not only bring higher temperatures but also have an effect on a substance that contains warmth-ether forces, namely, sulphur. Rudolf Steiner's research found that sulphur exists in fine vaporous clouds, so to speak, homoeopathically dilute, in the atmosphere. In confirmation of Steiner's research, recent sophisticated scientific research has discovered the presence of clouds of a sulphur compound, dimethylsulfide, in the air. This substance is added to the atmosphere as the sun's rays evaporate sea water; it is produced by plankton, which is sea algae, that exist in vast quantities in the world's oceans. In summer, with the evaporation of more water, there is more of this sulphur in the air.

The enhanced state of the warmth-ether forces during the summer cause the sulphurous presence in the atmosphere, which is now maximal, to become more sulphurous, or inwardly intensified. The ether-astral forces within the sulphur begin to glow, creating an ethereal radiance in the aura of the summer hemisphere. For a being on another planet with etheric clairvoyance, a remarkable radiance would be seen to develop in and above the summer side of the Earth; the hemisphere has the appearance of a comet, for as the planet moves through the cosmos, a radiance trails behind the summer hemisphere.[110]

In particular the people living in the summer hemisphere appear radiant, for their inner being starts to shine, through the presence of the enhanced sulphur forces.[111] There are many substances, trace elements, present in the air in dilute, semi-ethereal form. But iron and sulphur appear to be especially present, for both these substances manifest in condensed, tangible form in the air. Iron appears in the form of the meteorites and shooting stars that vaporize in the air; and we have just considered the material presence of sulphur in the atmosphere.

Modern science has recently begun to discover this atmospheric sulphur, after a century of ignored meteorological reports indicating its presence in the atmosphere. Dozens of reports have testified that sulphurous rain can occur. And vicious storms can also carry so much sulphur that they cast a disagreeable odour along their path.[112] We also hear of pieces of ice found which smell of sulphur. There have been occasions, too, when clumps of sulphurous matter have been seen to fall to the ground out of a clear sky, in situations where the possibility of pollution from a nearby industrial source must be discounted.

It is reported that this happened, for example, at Pultusk in Poland, in 1868 a mass of burning sulphur, the size of a human fist, falling onto a road, where it was stamped out by a crowd of villagers.[113] Now, it is known that raindrops form with the help of the tiny particles of sulphur vapour; as the chemical-ether condenses into water, it utilizes the sulphur particles to form raindrops.[114] The condensing of sulphur into a material state from a fine ethereal state is no doubt the cause of such phenomena; a similar process occurs with regard to iron, creating meteorites.

---

[110] lect. 5th May 1923 (*Man's being, his destiny and World Evolution*).
[111] GA 229, lect.5th Oct 1923 (*Four seasons and the Archangels*).
[112] Some instances of this have been published in *The Complete Books of Charles Fort*, pp. 68, 236, 301, Dover Books 1974.
[113] ibid.
[114] See, *Phylogenetische und Ökologische Untersuchungenan Bakterien desOxidation und Reduktiven Marinen Schwelfelkreislaufs...* A, Teske, Max-Planck-Institut für Marine Mikrobiologie, Bremen, 1996.

Meteorites are formed in various ways. Modern science has not yet discovered all their secrets. We will consider further the significance of sulphur and iron when we explore the autumn festival. Sulphur is the biblical 'brimstone', and earlier initiation wisdom associated sulphur with demonic elemental forces. I refer to sulphur here as an example of the intensified power of the warmth and light-ether layers in summer. Sulphur also contains light-ether forces and thus is able to generate light under certain conditions.

A further sign of the summer effect on these layers, especially the light-ether, is the fascinating phenomenon of fireflies (more correctly: glow beetles). A number of insects and marine creatures have, all year round, this eerie capacity of glowing brightly, but coldly, as no heat is generated. The glowing, flying beetles exist especially in the tropics, where the solar ethers are at a maximum (this also prevents the appearance of the aurora there); in temperate zones, such insects are especially active in the summertime.

Glow beetles appear, with their cold flashing lights, on midsummer nights, increasing the magic mood of those evenings. They are a familiar sight in Europe, China, and North America. In Germany, such beetles have received the very appropriate name of Johanniswärmchen, "St. John's Tide glow worms". In India, it was the custom for travellers who had to journey at night to fix a number of these glow beetles to their hands and feet, thus providing much needed illumination for walking in the dark landscape.

The increased existence of such cold light-processes is an indication of the animated state, in summer, of the light-ether forces. The complex chemical substances that enable the beetles to glow contain phosphorus compounds (such as adenosine triphosphate) and sulphur compounds (such as luciferin) that combine to manifest cold light. Wachsmuth identified phosphorus as a substance in which the light-ether is present; it generates a cold light, and when chemically active can form ozone.[115]

There is another unearthly radiance that attracts our attention in summer (and also at other seasons); the rapid streak of light caused by a shooting star. Many superstitions have become attached to the phenomenon of the shooting stars; their significance for humanity is considerable, and we

---

[115] G. Wachsmuth, *Etheric Formative Forces in Cosmos, Earth and Man*, 1926, Dornach.

will study them in detail in Chapter 6 when treating the autumn festival.

The out-breathing process that culminates in summer also causes a remarkable mirror situation. The beings and forces that constitute the Earth-soul absorb and interweave with the beings and forces from the sun high above the planet's surface, and act like a mirror to the in-streaming solar and cosmic forces. This interaction between the hemisphere and the cosmos, occurring up in the firmament of the summertime hemisphere, tends to block the influences of the sun beings from reaching down to the surface of the earth.

This mirror effect causes the astral aura of the hemisphere, at ground level and somewhat above, behind the mirror as it were, to become insulated from the astral forces that stream down from the sun, and from the Christ being, who has risen into the heights as well. The solar ether rays do exert a strong influence during summer on the processes occurring on the surface of the earth, but the higher sun influences, that is, the sun's astral and spiritual forces, have little influence there. Another Steiner verse expresses the result of this summertime mirror effect.

> Asleep is the soul of the earth
> In summer's heat;
> Then, the mirror of the sun
> Brightly shines
> In external space.
>
> Awake is the soul of the earth
> In winter's cold;
> Then, the sun's true being
> Is spiritually glowing
> In the earth's inner being.

This summer situation, wherein the divine beings of the Earth-soul are absent, leads to an increased presence of the ahrimanic powers in the vicinity of the ground. There is a shadow side to the middle kingdom; many elemental beings are of an ahrimanic nature. In winter, these "sprites of egotism" manifest in the vicious, destructive storms. Yet they also have their place in the economy of nature, for they are involved in growth processes, and will continue to be involved, until the material earth transforms into an ethereal organism. They assist the condensing of matter out of the ether world, and are active in spring and summer.

They do not enter the sleep state, for in summer they are required to participate actively in the summer growth, in the maturing of the fruits of the earth. Although the power of these beings is fundamentally held in check, they experience a sense of freedom in summer, through the absence of the higher beings of the Earth-soul, an absence due to the out-breathing process and to the insulating mirror effect. Hence they,

> revel in a kind of ecstasy in the unfolding of their strongest forces... during the summer, around midsummer, these lowly elemental beings revel in an ecstasy, like a paroxysm.[116]

In Chapter Six, in connection with the Michael festival, we will discuss further the significance of these ahrimanic influences that develop in summer. An additional quality of the summertime is the magical mood of the summer nights. Shakespeare wrote his famous play, *A Midsummer Night's Dream*, on the basis of the inner, elemental reality that creates this mood. In Chapter Two, we reviewed the many kinds of elemental beings and nature sprites that exist in the astral and ether body of the earth, in the middle kingdom: blossom fairies, and tree and bush sprites, and the beings that each work in one of the four elements, that is, the gnomes, undines, sylphs, and pyrausta. In the middle kingdom we also find the spirits of the elements, beings higher than the gnomes and the other elemental beings.

A Spirit of the Elements is a kind of group-soul or guiding being for the elemental beings.[117] Through the activity of such higher, guiding beings in the middle kingdom, who serve the intentions of the hierarchies, including the sun gods who dwell in the sun sphere, a counterbalance to the ahrimanic elementals is created.

In the summertime, the activity of beings such as the spirits of the elements, working through nature sprites that remain around the earth's surface, brings higher spiritual forces indirectly on to the earth, but only during the day hours. During the summer nights, such nature spirits find

---

[116] lect. 7th May 1923.
[117], lect. 24th August 1909, (*The East in the light of the West*).

that the forces which were working through them in the daytime, from higher realms, withdraw.

As a result, they are free to follow their own inclinations, to express their own being.[118] So these beings from the world of faeries are especially active, busy with mysterious rites and dances, thereby giving an extraordinary, magical quality to midsummer nights: a dreamy, bewitching quality quite different from that evoked during the Holy Nights of winter.

In earlier times, these processes and their effect on the middle kingdom and hence on mankind were contemplated in the midsummer festival,

> ...at the peak of summer one felt most clearly of all, how one is dependent on one's ether body, and how oneself, together with the earth {hemisphere} goes through an extraordinary life process.[119]

This brief statement was elaborated in later years,

> One was hungry in midsummer, when it was St. John's Time at high summer, to experience those days, at least in such festivals which released humanity from its earthly restraints, {and which} gave to human beings the consciousness that they were not banished to the earth; rather that they could 'arise' and gaze out into untrammelled realms of the world, into the ether.[120]

One aspect of the St. John's Festival is to help people to develop an awareness and understanding of what is happening in the ether and astral aura of the hemisphere then,

> The spirits of the earth {hemisphere} withdraw in spring, in order to ascend into cosmic heights. In autumn, these beings descend again; one saw this, in olden times. In those days it was natural to indicate this, namely that a situation exists which is like the absence of the earth's own spiritual reality. Instead, there takes place a 'leaping up' of nature elementals,

---

[118] lect 8th April 1923 (*The Cycle of the Year*).
[119] 23rd March 1913 (*The Effects of Spiritual Development*).

[120] GA 143, lect. 24th June 1923.

as if in a paroxysm...one could not portray this better than by placing St. John's festival precisely in this time, in order to indicate that, just now, the leaping nature sprites are active, whilst the actual spirits of the earth {hemisphere}, that is, the ego and the astral body of the earth {hemisphere}, have departed.[121]

These words make it clear that the major processes occurring in the elemental forces of the earth will be themes of the new midsummer festival, which Steiner defined as the St. John's festival. This festival, which is also called St. John's Tide ('tide' is the old English word for 'time') is no longer part of our cultural life. It is no longer understood, except as a historical, commemorative festival in the church calendar.

The name 'St. John' refers to John the Baptist, and shortly after midsummer's day (June 24th in the northern hemisphere) the church festival assists people in Christendom to remember the birth and life of this remarkable prophet. On this day the Christian churches in both hemispheres recall the life of the Baptist. Since the ecclesiastical festival cycle is not connected to the seasonal reality, the observation of St. John's day in the southern hemisphere on the same day as in the north, although it is then winter there, is quite consistent.

But the question arises for us, what connection is there between St. John the Baptist and midsummer's day? Further, what can we do today to create a contemporary, meaningful midsummer festival? And how can such a festival be brought into a relationship with the indwelling cosmic sun god (Christ)?

Understanding the esoteric significance of St. John can lead us to answers for these questions. But it is first necessary to consider other aspects of the summertime. So far, we have characterized the midsummer festival as involving the ether forces and elemental powers and the dynamic arising in the soul because of the summer out-breath. There is, of course, more to the festival, but already it is obvious that focusing on these themes will assist us to achieve an important feature of the new festivals, namely, an

---

[121] GA 143, lect. 16th May 1912.

alert, spiritual perspective in opposition to the simplistic nature consciousness.

In the summer, when a dreamy sleepy tendency dulls our consciousness, it is important to maintain an inner alertness, to remain aware of the dynamics in nature and the effects in our soul, the subtle changes in our feelings. Otherwise, we pass through the summer in a state of soul lethargy: "We need to use all of our soul forces, so that we do not lapse into the sleep of the earth {hemisphere}".[122]

This soul lethargy arises for two reasons: the predominance of vegetative ether processes, carried by the intensified warmth-ether forces, causes difficulties for our thinking, which is the focus of our consciousness; and additionally, the ascending forces breathed out by the earth, tend to draw along our auric forces, thus lifting us 'out of ourselves'. Rudolf Steiner describes this process in verse 7 of the *Soul Calendar*:

> My self, it's threatening to flee,
> Attracted powerfully by cosmic light:
> Now enter, my divining,
> With strength into your rightful realm;
> Replace for me my thinking's power
> Which in the senses' bright illusion
> Wants to lose itself.

As the summer out-breath draws us out as well, it becomes increasingly difficult to think clearly, but the faculty of divining or intuition can function well. It is through this faculty that we experience flashes of intuitive thoughts; such insights are mediated to us by the pyrausta, which are especially active in summer. To perceive, to experience, the inner reality of the summertime, through intuitive insights, we need to develop a certain sensitivity to the spiritual forces of the planet.

This is a challenge similar to that of being aware of what dreams we have had during the night and what their symbolism is communicating. We need an artistic sensitivity, in order to assist an interaction between our soul and the 'dreaming' Earth-soul. Verse 8 of the *Soul Calendar* expresses this situation:

---

[122] GA 162, lect. 23rd May, 1923.

The power of the sense grows
in union with the Gods' creating,
It presses thinking's clarity down
to dreaming's dimness.
If the Divine would unite to my soul,
human thinking must tacitly yield itself
to dream existence.

The dynamic which we enter in summer has a similarity to that of dreams in our sleeping state, which could be called 'the summer mood of the soul'. To strive toward a greater sensitivity to the significance of our dream life is a process similar to remaining alert in the time when the Earth-soul is sleeping. This is a wonderful, renewing process:

> People who do not intermingle at least something of the 'summer mood of the soul' in their awake, day consciousness so easily become 'dry'. A dry academic... is that kind of person who does not like to absorb that which is not fully conscious; who does not like to assimilate something from the summer mood of the soul.[123]

On the basis of the processes we have discussed so far, it would still not be possible to develop a new esoteric Christian festival. We can find the way to this new festival by recalling the correspondences between the seasons and the aspects of the human organism that I listed in Chapter Four. The seasonal festival should have as its central theme that aspect of the organism that the natural processes are bringing into focus. In *autumn*, the focus of the festival should be on the astral body (the soul), on its resurrection as supported by the elemental dynamics.

In *winter*, the focus of the festival should be on the development of the Life-spirit through the union of the inner sun forces to the Life-spirit of Christ.

In *spring*, as we have discovered, it is a question of the renewal of the physical body, amidst the regeneration of matter, through access to solar life-ether due to the deeds of the Christ being.

In *summer*, finally, it is important to cultivate an awareness of the elemental powers active during the out-breath and of

---

[123] GA 150, lect.14th March 1923.

the effect of the summer on the warmth and light-ethers. But further, we must address the ego, the significance of summer for our ego, its relationship to the sun and St. John.

A pastel drawing made by Rudolf Steiner in the summer of 1923 depicts the inner reality of the summertime. This drawing, showing what the clairvoyant consciousness of an initiate beholds in the Earth's aura at midsummer, contains images depicting the underlying spiritual dynamic of summer. The drawing is entitled "St. John's Tide Imagination". The word 'imagination' means here an astral clairvoyant image, or imagery which a healthy, trained clairvoyance forms, not a fantasy picture.

Over the years, some parts of the drawing have faded. Against a background of warm red and orange, the sun looms large and strong above the brown soil, in which large bluish-white crystals are placed. Yellow and white radiance streams forth from the sun, and cascades down through the atmosphere.

In addition, swirls of yellow form a bright band in the middle-right of the picture; this is possibly a row of three trees, or just clouds of ethereal sulphur. At the bottom left, three 'ahrimanized' elemental beings are bounding across the ground in a rapid leaping motion. Above them, in a warm orange-red, a lion can be seen; the symbol of the ether body and of the solar ethers. Immediately next to the lion is a stag, although this figure has faded so much as to be virtually indiscernible.

The association of the lion with the sun, and hence the zodiac sign Leo, is well known; through anthroposophy it is possible to comprehend the reality behind this association. For example, when our ether forces ray out beyond the skin, the tendency to hair formation arises; the quite strong outpouring of ether energy from our head results in the predominance of hair there. The lion's ether body has an exceptionally strong outpouring of ether force around the head; hence its mane. Since the sun is constantly renewing the ether forces of the Earth, the lion is quite naturally a symbol of the sun.

The stag or deer is also a deeply significant representation of the sun forces. It is a symbol of the sun in many ancient religions. The antlers reveal to a sensitive observer the presence of a remarkable solar influence in the deer. Unlike the horns of cattle and sheep, deer antlers are deciduous; they are shed and regrown each year. They are not a static bone structure with a layer of horn substance.

Antlers derive from dense knobs having a vascular structure; fluids nourish cell growth and flow throughout these knobs, causing them to grow. During the growth process, more and more calcium is deposited until the antlers become solid, and their skin dies away. Each year growth processes reoccur inside the antlers, near the skull, and thus they regrow.

This life process, connected to the animal's blood stream, occurs in, and triumphs over, a dense, hardened area of the body; and this triumph of the life forces occurs above the head, where the least alive part of the organism has its domain ! As Rudolf Steiner pointed out, the rhythmical system in the body trunk and the limbs, has far more movement, and life force, than that of the less vital head area, where the brain is developed, where most damaged cells cannot be repaired.

The stag is thus the symbol of the life-bestowing role of the sun; a deer, whether a hind or a stag, has often been regarded as a sacred being, an embodiment of the sun forces, an emissary of the sun gods on Earth. From their awareness of these facts, the priesthoods of earlier cultures created such beautiful expressions as "the hind of the morning" to describe the dawn. The rays of light which stream out above the eastern horizon before dawn were likened to the out-raying antlers of the deer. This term is used in Psalm 22, as the title of its melody. Such truths are known in the esoteric Christian traditions. There are churches in which carvings of a stag represent Christ.

The legend of St. Hubert embodies this motif. Hubert, who is hunting animals on Easter Friday, is confronted by a stag with a crucifix between its antlers. The stag speaks to him, admonishing him to become a Christian. Several passages in the Old Testament are also based on the esoteric significance of the deer: "The Lord is my strength, who makes my feet as nimble as a hind's and sets me to range the heights."[124]

So far, the themes in the pastel drawing do not provide any assistance in developing a midsummer festival in which

---

[124] *The Book of Habbukuk* 3:19, 18:33.

5 The "St. John's Tide Imagination" by Rudolf Steiner. Pastel, July 1923, original size 55 x 72 cm. Reproduced in original size by the Rudolf Steiner Verlag, Dornach.

The various etheric and astral summer phenomena: John the Baptist (pointing to the sun), the 5 'descending' zodiac forces. In the foreground, three ahrimanized elementals bound along, behind them a lion and behind it (not longer visible) a stag. Above these two are the 3 Cabiri entities; 2 faintly in yellow, 1 bolder, in blue; below this is a human face. (Some now-faded facial details have been slightly enhanced, for clarity.)

the significance of our ego, and its relationship to the Christ reality, would be expressed. Indeed, the features of the drawing, so far considered, refer to processes in the ethereal or astral aura of the earth. They are helpful contemplations of that aspect of the new summer festival concerned with the ether body of the earth and humanity. This elemental aspect of summer is certainly a theme for the new festival.

The other, higher theme of the midsummer festival is depicted in the middle and upper part of the drawing, in an interaction between humanity and the sun forces. Before considering that part of the drawing, we must reflect on the midsummer festivals created by the initiate priesthoods of earlier cultures. Rudolf Steiner's research again makes it possible to discover what took place in Europe (and probably elsewhere) some millennia ago, at midsummer.

> In the earliest midsummer festivals, that is in the celebrations at the time of the summer solstice, which later became our St. John's festival, the participants were guided so as to develop a musical-poetical activity, consisting of many highly rhythmical round dances, accompanied by song. Certain kinds of performance and portrayals occurred, which were full of special musical recitatives accompanied by primitive musical instruments. Such a festival was steeped in music and poetry. What human beings had in their dream consciousness was poured out, as it were, into the cosmos in song, music and dance.[125]

The term 'dream consciousness' refers to the fact that we human beings, in remote ages, did not possess the individualistic ego-hood of today's humanity. We felt ourselves, in earlier times, to be part of the family group, or small nation. In that sense, we were in a dream state; we had only a semiconscious awareness of our own ego. Rudolf Steiner's sociological discovery is of great value to us in understanding history; it explains why there is so little emphasis, amongst earlier civilizations, on having a truly individual personal name. Often a person's name indicated his or her place in the sequence of offspring, or the age of

---

[125] Rudolf Steiner, *The Cycle of the Year*, lecture 4.

118

the extended family's oldest member at the time of the child's birth.

Or it was a term of power designed to ward off evil influences, or enhance the family's wealth. Hence, for earlier humanity, the ego was 'outside' or remote, existing in the spiritual world; it was only a potential reality, compared with the ego state of modern humanity. The earlier humans could not have formulated such definitions about their ego situation, any more than a young child, who has not yet awoken to its own self, and hence cannot use the word "I," could analyse its state of consciousness. It was precisely the purpose of the old midsummer festival to assist humanity to develop an awareness of the ego.

The sacred dances and chanted poetry, which were in some ways a primeval predecessor of today's eurythmy performances, formed the first part of the festival. When this was over, the participants had to become inwardly quiet and still, and strive to listen to, or 'divine', what was occurring on a spiritual level in the heights above them.

In the first phase of the festival, people 'let arise' into the heights, into which the Earth-soul had arisen and the sun beings were active, their very being, the quintessence of their soul. Through the sacred dances and other activities people brought to expression deep questions of life; they inaugurated a dialogue with the divine, hierarchical beings from the sun sphere. Then, in active, sensitive inner listening they waited for the response from the heights. What was created in the first half of the festival,

> streamed up, as it were, into the cosmos, just as water on the earth streams upward {as vapour}, then forms clouds in the sky, and descends as rain. Likewise the effects of the festival activity streamed upward and came back, as something which manifested the power of the ego to the people... At midsummer then, at the festival of {what we now call} St. John's Tide, through the celebrations arranged for a section of humanity who were willing to take part in them, the ego consciousness flashed up. When the midsummer celebrations were over, and July and August came again, people had the feeling: We have an ego, but this ego remains in Heaven; it is up above; it 'speaks' to us only at

midsummer... when heaven opens 'the great window of heaven' at midsummer.[126]

So this spiritual process through which the spark of divinity, that is, the potential ego, drew nearer to the human soul, was only possible at midsummer, when the out-breathing process and the greater exposure of the hemisphere to the sun coincided, to create what is poetically referred to as "the great window of heaven". In summer, the great beings behind the sun's visible light and ether forces, its inner reality, draw near to the planet. Our higher ego is intimately connected to the sun, to the inner or spiritual sun. We need to understand this concept in order to create the new Christian summer festival.

An ancient legend from Ireland reporting a conversation between a druid high priest and a Christian priest is of help in this matter. At one point the Druid gestures toward the sun and says, "It is your god and mine." To which the Christian priest replies: "That fiery ball there is simply the lamp of the world, and woe to that man, who can not distinguish the torch from the torchbearer."[127] The sun worship of earlier cultures, which is so misunderstood today, was a natural result of the awareness that existed in previous ages, concerning the inner nature of the sun.

Through Rudolf Steiner's research it is possible to gain a deep understanding of the link between humanity and the sun. He describes in his great work, *An Outline of Esoteric Science*, how the creation of man can be viewed as that event in which the divine aspect of the ego (or higher ego/higher self) emerged from the lap of the deity and descended toward the Earth in Lemurian times.[128] The developing bodily and soul organism of humanity was by then made capable of achieving a connection with the true higher ego; although this higher self remains as a potential, which has to be merged with the earthly ego-sense.

Although it is our understanding that the ego came from God (or the Trinity), it is also true to say that it came from the sun. For God, or the Trinity, manifests in the physical world through the sun's immense powers of life and light.

---

[126] ibid.
[127] A legend quoted by F. MacLeod, referred to in C. Los, in *Die Altirische Kirche*, Stuttgart, Verlag Urachhaus.
[128] This process occurs over some millions of years, commencing some 18 million years ago (see my *The Rudolf Steiner Handbook* for more about this.

Further, the creative deeds and intentions of the Trinity come to expression in the physical world via the divine hierarchies. It was through the great beings called by St. Paul, the Powers (in Latin, Potentates; in Greek, Exusiai) that the human ego emerged into independent being, and began to enter earthly existence.

These beings, the Powers, are known in Hebrew as the Elohim; it is these beings to which Genesis is referring when the creation of man by the deity is described. And medieval Christian wisdom identifies the Powers as the regents of the sun sphere, whereas the Angels, for example, are the regents of the moon sphere.

The summertime union, then, between sun and earth is actually a reunion between creator and created; the divine gods of the spiritual sun and their offspring, humankind, are drawn near to each other. We need to contemplate this dynamic and bring it to life in the soul as the summer draws near. Doing so is not so difficult when one recalls the fact that the entire Earth is itself an offspring of the sun. Modern science is aware that the physical Earth, in a tenuous semi-ethereal state, was cast out of the sun. Through a study of anthroposophical cosmology, it becomes clear that the elemental and spiritual (devachanic) substance of the planet also came from the sun.

That is, when the Earth was cast out the sun, its spiritual essence was included as well. So the summertime brings us nearer to the origin or source of our own ego. Although we are unaware of them, those spiritual forces from which our ego derives are nearer to us in summer. This situation is expressed in verse 9 of the *Soul Calendar* (for early June in the north, for early December in the south):

> Forgetting my own will,
> The cosmic warmth, in heralding the summer,
> Fills all my soul and spirit:
> To "lose myself in light"
> Commands my spirit's inner vision,
> And strongly now intuitive-sensing proclaims to me;
> O lose yourself, to find yourself.

This verse expresses the contemporary reality of the summertime, which is entirely different from that of several millennia ago. For early humanity, the task was to try to awaken to an individual ego-hood, in which something of the true, higher ego is reflected. In today's world, this ego-hood is strongly felt, and the challenge is different. The summer dynamic is again expressed in a few meditative words by Rudolf Steiner in a notebook:

> "High summer: the impetus to the spirit, the ego, resting in the lap of divinity, receives this {from} the second hierarchy".[129]

In the summer, it is as if our ego is at rest in the matrix of its own being; that is, with the Powers, part of the second grouping of hierarchical beings. (The second hierarchy includes the Powers, the Virtues, and the Dominions.) For ancient humankind, of course, it was not the case that in summer their normal ego seemed to be once again drawn near to the spiritual matrix of its being.

Rather, since the ego was still within the lap of the gods, it was as if, because the gods drew closer, the people could at least glimpse their (future) ego, and receive an impetus toward the spirit, their own ego. But for those who were striving for spiritual development in ancient times, the mystery centres gave a meditation for the summer: "Receive the light".

Such people had already developed ego-hood, to some extent; they understood that they should strive to become aware of the real spiritual reality of the ego. Such a person might have thought, "During the peak of summer, I stand before (I feel the potential for) enlightenment".

Enlightenment is an especially appropriate term for that process in the journey to initiation which brings awareness of the true, higher ego. An aspect of this ego is the Spirit-self, the wisdom of which fills the soul with a supernal radiance. In summer this radiance, an objective reality on the spiritual level, permeates the hemisphere's out-breathed aura, for the great hierarchical beings from the sun sphere possess such wisdom, it emanates from their being.

Rudolf Steiner describes the radiance that the ego is permeated by in the summer as deriving from "cosmic intelligence". This unusual expression means in effect, the spiritual wisdom of the gods, as he once explained,

---

[129] A more literal translation is "High summer: the moral impulses". In German: Hoch Sommer: die moralischen Impulse – die im Schosse des Göttlichen rühende Ich empfängt sie–2.Hierarchie" from Supplementary vol. 19 of the Complete Works.

In times when people were more accurate with nomenclature than the present day, people called the subjectively active wisdom in humanity 'intelligence', distinguishing it from the objective cosmic wisdom.[130]

For these initiates and for modern seekers of the spirit, verse 9 of the *Soul Calendar* (which I have quoted) is relevant, if the true ego-hood is to be found; then the normal earthly ego-sense will have to be transcended. The bright outer sunlight is a symbol of, an outer vestment of, the inner, spiritual light of the sun gods, from which our ego in a sense derives. '

This challenge of the midsummer is described further in verse 11 of the Soul Calendar. To translate this verse requires a great deal of skill, for several reasons. Firstly, as we are discovering here, the spiritual dynamics of summer and the link between these and our human nature are the most difficult of the four seasons to understand.

Verse 11

But also I have found, in the years since this book was first published (1992), that my translation needs to be revised to reflect new insights that arose after I discovered that there is a printer's error here. This is found by comparing the hand-written manuscript of this book, with the original German edition. Also, verse 11 was uniquely given a late revision by Rudolf Steiner, in pencil, just before it was sent to the printers; resulting in two versions, as it were.

The deep message of this verse becomes clearer when both versions are considered and the printer's error is corrected. The earlier version reads like this,

It is incumbent on you in this solar hour
– whilst surrendered to the beauty of the world –
to feelingly live-through, within you
these words of wisdom:
"The human ego can lose itself
And find itself within the cosmic ego".

---

[130] The Gospel of St. John cycle, lect. 20th May 1908.

Here we are clearly being urged to let the less intellectual, more 'feeling-sensing' faculties prevail, and to *live into* the effect on us of the sulphurous warmth, the nearness of the solar beings, and the out-breathed hemisphere in general. The soul should in these conditions contemplate its immersion in the solar reality, a herald of the cosmic ego. Then in the final draft it reads,

> It is incumbent on you to recognize in this solar hour the words of wisdom,
> {whilst} surrendered to the beauty of the world, {and} within you, feelingly living-through your self:
> "The human ego; it can lose itself
> And find itself within the cosmic ego".

The words in brackets are added by me, to clarify the meaning. Here the message is certainly similar to the earlier version, but with the added nuance that the spiritual seeker should seek *to recognize* the significance of the 'words of wisdom', in regard to the inner dynamics of the summer time. It is a more difficult version, that is why I have added two words, in brackets. So my new translation varies from others for several reasons. One is that, in the hand-written manuscript of Rudolf Steiner, there is no colon placed after the verb 'to recognize'. [131] This was presumably added in error, by the printer.

Most translations will also refer to '*experience* the self within you', but the verb here is very unusual and actually means 'to live-through' rather than 'experience', as such.[132] The "cosmic ego"; this expression refers to that aspect of the Christ being which manifests through the sun sphere and thus the sun gods, as they guide the evolution of the Earth and of the solar system in general.

Another process occurring in summer is the perception of the Earth's inner being by the sun beings. The 'window' that opens in summer also enables the beings above to gaze downward, to become more aware of the hemisphere then.

---

[131] Also the additional word, 'self' is possibly not actually there; only a few faint letters in pencil are visible; they might possibly be the word 'thyself', it is uncertain.

[132] In my planned book, *The Soul Calendar of Rudolf Steiner - a new translation with commentary,* this will be discussed in more detail.

Verse 10 of the Soul Calendar speaks to this 'sensing' of us by the higher beings:

> Into summer heights
> Rises the sun's radiant being,
> It takes my human feeling
> Into its wide expanse of space.
> Intuiting, an inner sensing stirs
> Which faintly unto me proclaims;
> One day you will become aware:
> A god has sensed you now.

In summer, a sublime being from the sun-sphere perceives our inner being. How, then, will the new midsummer festival offer the possibility to gain insight into the deeper aspects of our ego? And what connection will the festival have to the perceiving of our inner being by higher beings? The creation of this new festival is a challenging task, for its focus is on a part of our being, the ego, not so easily perceived or taken in hand; not just normal self-awareness but the deeper levels of the ego, in effect, the true or higher ego.

It is the higher, real ego which rays into us from beyond the threshold of normal consciousness. It is the higher ego which guides our footsteps through life, bringing us into encounters with those people whom we need to meet, in accordance with our destiny, our karma. The guiding motifs of our life, which come to expression through our motivations or will forces, are a manifestation of the deeper aspects of our ego. Because the higher ego is active in these deep-seated will forces, we can begin to approach the ego by contemplating our will. How do we respond in a particular situation? What leads us to significant decisions in life?

Midsummer: an interplay of will forces

In our quest to form the new summer festival of the ego, we receive little help from the remnants of earlier midsummer festivals, which basically involve looking at and dancing around bonfires. But the festival of a community in Tunisia, North Africa, had a significant feature. There the menfolk would leap over a fire, which had been lit in three places by young women. As they went over the fire, they called out, "We shake onto you, lady Ashur, fleas and lice and the illnesses of the heart, and also those of the bones. We shall pass through you again next year, and in the following years, with safety and health."[133]

A similar custom existed in Greece; there the women would call out, while jumping over a fire, "I'll leave my sins behind me".[134] In Schwabia it was the custom for the people, when departing from the bonfire, to throw a weed into the fire, saying, "It is going away, and with this, all my misfortune will be burnt up".[135] The significance of these old customs becomes clear when we understand the most important process that occurs in the summer, a process, connected to our will forces, that Steiner described in detail in his October 1923 lecture cycle, *The Four Seasons and the Archangels.*

He told how the gaze of the initiate in summer is drawn down into the subterranean rocks and minerals beneath the soil. The dense crust of the earth is not a barrier to spiritual vision; it appears translucent, glowing with a deep blue colour. This blue background is everywhere suffused with crystalline forms; lines, planes, and angles permeate the amorphous blue of the earth's interior. But these lines and planes, which gleam with a silvery radiance, are crystal-like outlines or forms of objects, not complete objects. They are the archetypal forms of the rocks and minerals of the earth's physical body.

These archetypal forms are created in Devachan, and then are brought into the elemental (astral and ether) forces of the Earth. From there they guide the forming of the mineral kingdom. As Steiner indicated in his book *Theosophy*, these silvery lines are the product of what is called the "first elemental realm". It is likely that these energies are closely linked to that underlying subtle physical energy-template of the body called 'the Phantom' by Rudolf Steiner. In any event, the same process is involved in the forming of our skeleton, which is the most dense or mineral part of our being. These silvery-glowing form-giving forces are especially strong and visible in the summer, they are somehow inwardly vivified when summer comes.

Today we realize that our thoughts and feelings have a significance, an impact on the world. What comes to

---

[133] Sir James Frazer, *The Golden Bough*, 13 vols. London Macmillan, 1978.
[134] ibid.
[135] Grimm's *Deutsche Mythologie*, Vol.1, p. 515, Ullstein Materialen, Frankfurt 1981.

expression as an elemental force in us, in our aura, rays out into the environment. Most people feel the after-effect of a repeated or intensely expressed feeling in a room. For example, the mood in an old church is easily perceived. Our will forces also ray out from us.

When we make a decision and carry out a deed, our will forces become active in us, and through our limbs, we do something in the world. But this process also has an objective consequence on a spiritual level, for an act of will engenders a subtle force that rays out from us. Steiner described this process in a midsummer lecture: "The earth continually sends out rays of will force, the will {forces} from all the people who live on the earth".[136]

The subtle forces which ray out from our aura, released by our will impulses, also stream downward, into the earth. There, in the earth, the auric emanations have an effect on the elemental substance of the planet's physical-mineral body, on the elemental forces maintaining the form and the nature of the physical Earth. That is, they affect those silvery-coloured sparkling lines and waves that weave their patterns into the substratum of the Earth's own being, and which become stronger in the summer. Why do the subtle energies invoked by our will forces affect the very foundation of the earth's being, the elemental forces that form its physical body?

Those elemental forces that bring the physical, mineral body of the planet into being are the instrument of the will of the hierarchies, and therefore, ultimately, of God. It is through the will of the hierarchies that the Earth exists. When a living being incarnates into the physical-material plane of existence, this is through a deed of will. It results from that being's intention to exist, to be. Hence our physical body, especially the skeleton, is an expression of our will, our will forces. But these will forces, like those of the Earth itself, are in essence, on their deepest level, divine (that is, Devachanic). The will forces that brought our body into being are in effect part of our higher ego, our true self. Much of what we will derives from our normal earthly ego, but our decisions can be the expression of our higher ego, of the divine will potential in us.

---

[136] GA 213, lect. 25th June 1922.

Hence Steiner's description of the human being feeling a connection to the spiritual forces behind the rocks and minerals of the earth:

> One feels that as a human form, one had grown out of the blue depths of the earth's crust, and one feels inwardly permeated with strength {in summer} by the silver-gleaming lines of force. And if one asks oneself: How is it that these silvery lines of forces are working within myself? What is it that lives and is active there, silver-gleaming in the blue of the earth? Then one knows: That is cosmic will. And one has the feeling of standing upon cosmic will.[137]

A profound experience, through which the seeker of the spirit can begin to approach the mystery of God, that being through whom the substratum, the foundation of the world derives. In summer, when so much of the earth's soul force is drawn up into the heights, this subterranean force, the silvery radiance through which cosmic will forces manifest, also ascends into the heights.

We have seen how, late in the springtime, the elemental beings are drawn ever higher into the heights, coalescing into 'clouds'; they bear with them this gleaming, silvery will force, and a radiant silver sheen envelops them as they ascend. This radiant will-force, arising into the upper layers of the hemisphere's aura, carries along the forces released into the earth by the finest, most selfless deeds or will impulses of humanity.

This substance of human spirituality is interwoven with the cosmic will-substance of the earth, which rises up to where the sun forces are streaming through the atmosphere. There, it is united to the spiritual essence behind the sunlight raying into the atmosphere in summer. Thus, in summer, elemental forces from the hemisphere's crust, which nurture its mineral-physical existence, are permeated by cosmic forces from the sun sphere.

But this process is not a natural result of the summer out-breath; the silvery will forces from the hemisphere are actively drawn upward. When the seer gazes into the bright, warm summer sky to discover what it is that draws these forces upward, he beholds a radiant being, a great archangel

---

[137]GA 229, lect. 12th Oct.1923 (*Four seasons and the Archangels*).

in whom the radiant spiritual forces of the sun gods are especially present. This archangel has been known to initiates for millennia as Uriel, a Hebrew name referring to the radiance and fire of God.

It is through the activity of this great being that the will forces from the earth and humankind arise at summertime, to be permeated by the golden inner sunlight, or one could also say, by the wisdom of the sun gods. Wisdom is an alternative term for the divine spirituality or Spirit-self, it is a radiant tangible reality in the spiritual world. To the gaze of the initiate, this union of spiritual sunlight with the hemisphere's aura in summer is directly perceptible; a golden-coloured radiance permeates the upper reaches of the sky and streams into the atmosphere, casting a golden glow over the clouds of drifting elementals.

We see in this process a nurturing and strengthening of the Earth's inner being. That an archangel is the guiding being of this process is not a situation unique to the summer; the central process of each season is guided and nurtured by an archangel. In springtime, the archangel Raphael manifests over the hemisphere, bringing healing forces to humankind. In winter, it is the task of the archangel Gabriel, who appears over the hemisphere then, to mediate between our ether body and the Life-spirit forces of winter.

The archangel of autumn is the great Michael (who still has this function even though he is now gradually rising to the rank of principality); his activity will be considered in Chapter Six. In Chapter Nine, we will explore the particular seasonal significance of each archangel as well as the interweaving of the archangels with each other.

The summer interaction between forces of sun and earth is of considerable significance, because what the hemisphere thereby receives is drawn down by the autumn in-breath into the earth, where it affects the life forces that are so active in winter. Through this process, the future, transformed, non-material body of the Earth will develop. (We will also consider the development of the new Earth or New Jerusalem in connection with the Holy Nights festival.) Each winter the Earth's ether aura is vivified inwardly, so that the new Earth globe can develop. In this process then, the archangel Gabriel is active. However, for the future spiritualized Earth to arise, the summertime vivifying of its physical body, that is, of the will forces behind it, is also necessary.

These truths are indicated in those fragments of previous initiation wisdom that have survived for posterity in the neglected apocryphal texts. In one such text, which discusses the end of the world and the ascending of good souls to a new world, it is said that,

> ...then Gabriel and Uriel form a column of light, and go before them {the elect} into the sacred realm, and bid them to eat of the Tree of Life and to put on white raiment.[138]

The working together of both archangels is necessary for the development of the new condition of the Earth, that is, what they are able to accomplish during the summer (Uriel) and during winter (Gabriel). We will discuss the activity of archangel Gabriel further in the later chapters.

Archangel Uriel serves the aims of the great hierarchical beings from the sun sphere; he brings about the permeation of the Earth's aura with forces from the spiritual sun. Through this process, which is also connected to the will impulses of humanity, the cosmic Christ, who is now the indwelling spirit of the Earth, works to bring the Earth and humanity into the New Jerusalem, the future age called by anthroposophy, the Jupiter aeon.

That the summer process is also, like the other seasons, guided and maintained by the indwelling Christ being, is also indicated by Steiner:

> And that which heaven could give to the Earth, in order that the Earth may spiritually receive what it does receive anew every summer, through the strengthened power of the sun, this the Earth has received from the Christ.[139]

The purpose of the mystery of Golgotha we could describe as being to ensure that the summer interaction of earth {the hemisphere} and the sun occurs. Only through the presence of the cosmic Christ in the Earth-soul can the hemisphere receive, during the summer out-breath, spiritual (or devachanic) substance from the sun, that spiritual substance

---

[138] From *The Apocalypse of Elias*, in Buttenweiser, Die Elias-Apokalypse.
[139] GA 150, lect. 21st Dec. 1913.

from which are created the elemental forces that underlie the Earth's physical-mineral existence. This process is only possible through the activity of the archangel Uriel, who draws up from the otherwise inaccessible realm these silvery elemental will forces. This is quite different from the spring process, wherein life-ether rays are directed into the Earth's ether body.

As we will see, the activity undertaken by the Christ being during the winter depends on this summertime process, during which the solar life-ether forces unite with the aura of the Earth. In the lecture cycle from which I quoted in Chapter Four, *The Cycle of the Year as Breathing Process of the Earth*, Steiner gave the following description of this process,

> Continuing our study of the yearly breathing cycle of the earth, we find that the earth {hemisphere} has completely out-breathed. All its soul forces have been poured forth into cosmic expanses, and are permeated with the forces of the sun, with the forces of the stars. The Christ, who is united with these soul forces of the earth {hemisphere}, now unites his power also with the solar and star forces, which are flowing into the hemisphere's soul, that has given itself up to the cosmos. (lect. 31st March 1923)

How very different is the spiritual reality of the summer from that of the wintertime ! A midsummer festival, celebrating these summer processes that have their most significant expression in the striving of the archangel Uriel, would be a Uriel festival. Such a festival can only be celebrated, according to Rudolf Steiner, in the summer. Just prior to speaking the words I have just quoted from the *Cycle of the Year* lecture, Steiner indicated, yet again, that he was referring to the particular process as a hemispherical phenomenon:

> Then we find, how in June the earth {hemisphere} passes into a third state {that is, after winter and spring}. The earth has, on that part which we are now considering, completely 'out-breathed'. It is {now} St. John's Tide.

Of course, in this lecture, Steiner was considering the northern hemisphere. The archangel Uriel may be regarded as an emissary of the sun sphere; hence he is involved with warmth and light processes, not just on the level of the ethers, but also on the level of their devachanic or spiritual essence. Uriel is connected with the sun sphere rather than a planetary sphere, according to rabbinical teachings, wherein he is regarded as a sun being, like the archangel Michael, and his day is Sunday.[140] That Uriel is connected to the sun sphere is also indicated in an initiatory text from the Hebraic mystery schools:

> And also Uriel showed me twelve doors, which are open, in the circumference of the sun's chariot; through these the rays of the sun break forth, and from them warmth is diffused over the earth, when they are opened at their appointed season. [141]

The expression, "The sun's chariot" appears to refer to the geocentric journey of the sun around the Earth during one year. It follows quite organically, then, that the outer reaches of the Earth's aura would be the area where Uriel's activity occurs, as Rudolf Steiner describes it.

This understanding is also taught in the esoteric Hebraic teachings. In the course of a commentary on the Creation account in Genesis (1:20) with regard to the words "God said: 'Let the birds fly above the earth, across the expanse of the sky' {or, in old English: the firmament of heaven}," Uriel is mentioned. The commentary says that the 'face' of the sky's expanse (or the 'face' of the firmament), refers to Uriel.[142] The question has arisen as to whether Uriel is from the Saturn sphere; this is not the case, but there is a connection to this planet (see addendum 2 at the end of this chapter).

Now we can approach the question of developing a contemporary summer festival. It is only necessary to proceed one step further in order to understand a major theme of the new summer festival and, likewise, the remarkable old customs connected with jumping over the summer bonfire. Let us return to Rudolf Steiner's

---

[140] M.Schwab, *Vocabulaire de L'Angeologie* (Paris: Acadmie des Inscriptions et Belles-Lettres, 1897.
[141] Book of Enoch, (1st century BC) 75:4-5.
[142] The Zohar, Mantua version, (New York) Soncino Press 1970, vol.1, n.46.

description of the presence of Uriel in midsummer. One beholds up above, this great archangel, and the interweaving of the golden-coloured spiritual forces of the sun sphere with the ascending will forces, sparkling and silvery.

Then one perceives that the ascending 'Earth-will' forces are transmuted into the same golden radiance as that which the sun rays out. The hemisphere's forces are metamorphosed into a spiritual substance such as exists normally in the higher levels of the sun; and it is with this increased presence of inner sunlight that the earth's soul forces return during the autumn, to reach the centre of the earth by midwinter.

But while beholding this wondrous cosmic alchemy, Rudolf Steiner describes in the *Four seasons and the Archangels* lectures, that one becomes aware how Uriel is gazing down toward the Earth (that is, the hemisphere in its summertime) in a particularly earnest manner. Feeling a deep yearning to understand why this earnest gaze is directed downward, one turns one's gaze also down into the earth. There, amidst the silver lines of force, one sees various shapes; strangely irregular forms that have a disturbing effect on the viewer, "shapes which are in a certain sense disturbing, they continually gather and dissolve, gather and again dissolve away."

Then one understands what these forms are, namely the errors of humanity, the effect of ethical imperfections in the elemental substance of the earth, working against the geometrical harmony that underlies the physical existence of mother-earth. It is to this that Uriel's attention is directed, to the disharmony in the will forces of humanity. When the will is subject to the dictates of the lower self, it releases forces in the middle kingdom that oppose the activity of the divine powers sustaining the physical existence of the earth. Such opposition to this physical activity of the divine powers will in turn hinder the spiritualization of the Earth; indeed, negative will forces could create an opposing tendency inside the planet.

Uriel has an additional significant task, one concerning the deeper layers of the Earth, below the area where the silver lines of force occur (see addendum 1 to this chapter). Rudolf Steiner indicates that the conscience has been strengthened through the subconscious perception by humanity of the "earnest, admonishing" quality of Uriel. This strengthening of the conscience in turn has given rise

133

to the old customs described earlier, wherein people exclaimed that "all my misfortune will be burnt up", or that "I'll leave my sins behind me". A particularly important theme of the new midsummer festival is therefore a striving toward an enhanced awareness of our will forces; an effort to become more aware of our potential for disharmonious as well as selfless, humanitarian acts; an effort to enable the higher ego to come to expression ever more fully in our innermost being, in what we will.

In midsummer it is thus especially appropriate that we take the time to review our year, with a view toward discovering what kind of social or anti-social tendencies emerged during the events of the previous twelve months. with a view toward bringing the higher self ever more into the mysterious recesses of our personal leitmotifs and life priorities. This resolve is surely what lived in those people of olden times, who placed their yearning for freedom from the disharmony of the lower will before a bonfire, the symbol of the spiritual light which has brought forth and which nurtures the world.

In addition, the contemplation of the nature of our will forces becomes a meditation on the divine beings from whom our higher ego derives; this is, ultimately, God. The first section of Steiner's Foundation Stone meditation is especially relevant to experiencing the midsummer on a spiritual level: "For the Father-spirit of the heights holds sway, in the depths of the world, begetting being".

Such meditative activity is appropriate to the midsummer, when deep in mother-earth, and in us, the primal forces that sustain existence in the physical world are especially active. One notes here that in anthroposophy the term 'God' has a deeper and more comprehensive meaning than in the normal cultural life today. A glimpse into this deeper concept of God is given in a verse which was found inscribed in a rock cave used by Cathars: "What is God? We who came here are tranquilly silent. His name we do not utter. Quiet we stay; quiet we pray; whoever would say who he is must be who he is."[143]

The dynamics of the summertime, around which the new St. John's festival will be formed, are more difficult. Rudolf Steiner has given the following meditation to assist us in

---

[143] Quoted by Rudolf Steiner; the last line could also be "must be like unto him".

grasping these deep mysteries. I provide here an expanded translation of the meditation, adding explanatory words {in brackets} to the extremely condensed, brief original.

{*in the heights*}

Behold our weaving,
the radiant arousing,
the warming life.

{*in the depths*}

Let live in you the
sustaining force of the earth,
and that which has,
in breathing, developed form
as the essential prevailing element.

{*in the midst: the inner
being of the human*}

Feel thy human bones
with divine radiance shining in the
prevailing union of worlds.

We can now try to gasp something of what is being indicated in these enigmatic words. That which is proclaimed as the summer dynamic in "the heights", that is, above in the sphere of Uriel, should be readily understood in the light of our considerations in this chapter. What is said of the dynamics in "the depths" is more difficult to grasp. It is a plea that the divine forces that sustain earthly being, the physical existence (or body) of the Earth and of humanity, be the predominating force.

The divine forces should be the real or actual prevailing force, the 'essence' of the force that prevails over the physical existence of the earth and our physical body. Thus the term "essential" means 'of the essence', of the true, fundamental element. These divine will forces in the depths should not be weakened by the negative will forces from the lower self, for then the body will become subtly coarser, harder.

Further, part of the "prevailing element" is in us, that which has developed our body's form through the breathing process. This is a deeply esoteric matter, which it is not necessary to examine in great detail here. This theme is connected to the Philosopher's Stone, the esoteric preparation that would assist one to overcome the denser substance in the physical body. If one considers that the breathing process has played an important role in the development of the physical body, in that it conveys subtle ether forces into the body's growth processes, through uniting with the blood, then one can begin to contemplate the meaning of the verse.

The breathing process has been involved in the development of the present-day dense physical body, and it will be involved in the reversal of this process. Spiritual development processes assist us to quicken the pace of spiritualizing the body so that the earthbound will loses its hold on us and the higher ego can manifest in the normal ego.

The same processes also contribute toward the forming of the future physical body, which will be a radiant, ethereal organism. Hence, in the third section of the meditation provided by Rudolf Steiner, the call is made to feel these profound realities of the summertime, to feel the skeleton glowing with this unearthly radiance. This result is only possible through the increased strength in summertime of elemental forces deep in Mother-earth's inner being. These elemental forces are the bearers of divine will forces from the Father-god, from those hierarchical beings through whom the 'first cause' or God brings his will to manifestation.

The transcendental Father-god and the Earth-mother, the two realms of being that they represent, are united now. From this union of worlds, the indwelling Christ being, through Uriel, works toward the future spiritualization of the earth. The process taking place, then, at midsummer involves the inter-working of these three great cosmic beings or principles. The archangel Uriel is, in effect, a vessel for the Christ being. It is significant that a day for the Trinity, Trinity Sunday, was placed in the church calendar in the summer.

The meditative verse we have been considering finishes with three brief summarizing thoughts: "Substances are condensed, Errors are judged and rectified, Hearts are sifted". These three phrases are to be imagined as resounding in the cosmos, "as though with organ and trumpet tones". They bring us back to the activity of Uriel, above the sulphurous, shimmering summer sky.

The midsummer festival and John the Baptist

If in the summer one practices "spirit remembering", which is contemplating the past year with the aim of attaining deeper insight into one's will forces, for the good of the Earth, one is striving to 'change one's mind for the better', to 'amend one's way of being'. Such an activity has always been part of the spiritual path, and these definitions are translations of a Greek term for this inner exercise, namely metanoia. Metanoia can be expressed in one English word: 'repentance'. This is the original meaning of the word repentance, which is well known because of its biblical usage. Perhaps the best known and most striking occurrence of the term repentance is its usage by John the Baptist.

The Baptist urged people to undertake this inner activity in order that they be able to participate in the new world reality that the coming of the Christ would bring about. We see, then, that there was a poetic validity in the Christian churches' decision to connect the midsummer festival day of the non-Christian cultures they were converting with John the Baptist.

Rudolf Steiner confirms the view that the ecclesiastical St. John's Tide is a pagan midsummer festival that has been taken over by the church. He also refers to the midsummer festival as the "St. John's Tide festival", as the various quotations from his lectures show. Is there more than just a poetic relationship of John the Baptist to a midsummer festival, in which the role of the sun is predominant?

The history of this festival is obscure. It was, however, already in existence in the time of St. Augustine, who denounced the mixing of old pre-Christian traditions for the 24th of June (bonfires, and so forth) with the commemoration of the birth of the Baptist. The church had a difficult struggle with this problem in southern Europe and Asia Minor, and in the land of the Celts and Germans it was just as difficult. For the 24th of June was especially important in the calendar of these peoples. As the sun went down, from every hilltop huge columns of flame rose into the air, illuminating the villages and towns. In A.D. 841 at the battle of Fontenay, both armies resolved to have a truce on June 24, so that the sacred rites of this day – partly Christian and partly pagan – could be observed.

In addition to the old traditions for this day, which have been described earlier, there were also customs in Christian lands that linked this day, and the inner spiritual processes guided by Uriel, to the Baptist. In Italy, for example, as the boys jump over the fire they call out: "St. John, preserve my thighs and legs !" In such a custom, which we could consider as merely a reflection of a muddled mixture of Christian elements and pagan traditions, it is also possible to see an unconscious linking of the Baptist to the summertime call for metanoia, for an increased awareness of the significance of our will forces. But as we have seen, our will is in essence a spiritual reality, part of our true, higher ego, which originates from the sun, from the sun spirits (the Elohim).

What is the connection between the Baptist and the deeper, hidden aspect of our will? Does the Baptist have a connection to the inner reality of the sun? Because such a possibility seems to require that the Baptist be more than merely human, we may be inclined to dismiss this line of thought. However, a study of the theme of St. John the Baptist and the sun, as presented in the Gospel of St. John, indicates that there is indeed a connection between the sun and the Baptist.

First, there is the description of the Baptist by Christ: "He was a burning and a shining light; and you were willing, for a time, to rejoice in his light" (John 5:35). The solar nuance is unmistakable ! These words conjure forth an image of the sun, especially the summer sun.

There is also the remarkable statement of the Baptist himself, concerning his connection to Christ: "He must increase, but I must decrease" (John 3:30). These words can be interpreted in a straightforward historical way; that is, to mean that the Baptist's task is coming to an end while that of Christ is on the increase. However, scholars have noticed that these words can be regarded as describing the dynamic between the outer sun, which reaches its peak of activity at midsummer, and the inner sun, which was revered in pagan winter festivals.

This winter sun begins to increase, as it were, after the summer solstice, when the summer sun begins to wane. This seasonal interpretation has support in the fact of the six-month difference between the birth dates of Jesus and the Baptist, the Baptist having been born around the 24th of June.

But this is an abstract, theoretical idea, unless one has a living spiritual feel for such expressions as "the inner sun". The study of esoteric Christianity makes it clear that the inner sun forces – which, as we will see, are present in wintertime – are connected with the cosmic Christ. But no such cosmic connection can be discovered between the outer sun and the man who was born as John the Baptist. However, already the prophecy of Malachi (3:1), "Behold, I will send my messenger {angel, that is} and he shall prepare the way for me", is an indication that an angelic being was overshadowing the Baptist. Steiner confirmed this reading, showing that it was the task of that angel to help humankind toward true, individual ego-hood, which would become possible once the Christ being united to the earth.[144]

However, there was also present in the Baptist a higher spiritual force, a hierarchical being, the spirit of ego at that time in human evolution when the ego was shared by entire groups of people.[145] This was a being connected to God from whom we come, to the Elohim or Powers, those hierarchical beings who are the sun spirits and from whom the spiritual substance of our ego derives.

For long ages, humankind's ego was, as we have mentioned earlier, up above in the spiritual world. It hovered over the incarnate person. It was a potential capacity of the individual, and people gained a stronger awareness of it at midsummer, when the sun forces draw near to the earth. In the Baptist there was present a being connected with the sun gods who are the origin of our "ego substance". This spiritual matrix of our ego became at first the basis of the group egos of the various "nations" of early humanity. Over the ages, the group egos gradually individualized into the separate human beings, though they did not really become aware of this process, and of the full potential of the ego.

So John the Baptist was a vessel for an exceptional angel, whose task was to inspire John in his work of preparing people for the descent to the Earth of the cosmic Christ, the highest of the sun gods. And also 'in' the Baptist was the high spiritual being who is connected to the sun sphere, from whence the ego had its origin at first as a group ego. These two beings witnessed and prepared the descent to the Earth of the highest of the sun gods or Powers, the Christ being, in whom the innermost essence of our ego exists. With the descent of the foremost of the sun spirits, the Christ, humanity began the process of developing a

---

[144] GA 127, lect. 25th Feb.1911, and lect, 17th Sept. 1912 in the cycle, *the Gospel of St. Mark* (GA 139).
[145] Lect. 17th Nov. 1912, in GA 130.

conscious ego-hood. And it is the presence of the Christ being in the Earth-sphere that shall make possible the spiritualizing of the ego. The more humanity develops a conscious relationship to the true, higher ego, the sooner the inspiring spirit of John the Baptist will cease to have a task with humanity; for then humanity will have assimilated the spiritual force constituting the ego. Then, under the guidance of the Christ being, we will become conscious of this force as a spiritual reality and undertake to bring it into full manifestation as the spirit self.

Thus the more external summer sun is a symbol, and the physical manifestation, of the group ego of mankind, of the ego that is not awakened, and hence of the not-yet-conscious ego-hood. The Baptist is, therefore, a representative of the summer sun; and "he must decrease", that the inner sun may increase. The spiritual reality behind the Baptist is "a burning and a shining light", and we were willing, for a time, to rejoice in his light !

If we look once again at the "St. John's Tide Imagination" by Rudolf Steiner, the large translucent silvery-blue crystals speak to us of the enhanced will force moving through the earth's crust, strengthening our body. But these crystals are also an image of the future, transformed physical body of humanity, which shall arise as the life-ether or prana force becomes, via the breathing process, a stronger factor in our existence. And up above in the drawing, near to the sun, is the head and arm of a man, pointing toward the sun. The pointing gesture of the figure is similar in quality to that of the Baptist.

Is this figure who is pointing, not to the Christ or an inner sun but rather to the outer sun, a representation of the 'inspiring spirit' that was present in John, from the ego-bestowing sun sphere? Is it perhaps saying to us now, "behold the origin of your being as it draws near each summer, to imbue the Earth's inner being with further strengthening forces, from its radiant inner light. What has been the effect of your own ego's actions for Mother-earth during the year? Are your deeds a true reflection of the will that, sun-born, now has become yours, in that it seeks to manifest in your earthly ego?"

Above this figure in the drawing, there are to be seen, although not clearly, five echoes of this being, or five human countenances. It appears to me that the depiction of these five, semi-formed countenances confirms that a major

140

leitmotif of the new St. John's festival is indeed the connection of our ego to the sun beings. For these five countenances indicate that humanity has not yet assimilated, from the forces of the powers, the entire substance of the higher ego. We may understand the significance of the five human images, which are incompletely formed, and which incline toward the sun, when we study the connection of the ego to the zodiac.

The division of the zodiac into five and seven signs is a highly significant matter. The following seven signs: Aries, Taurus, Gemini, Leo, Cancer, Virgo, and Libra, are known, esoterically, as the 'day' or 'ascending' signs, whereas Scorpio, Sagittarius, Capricorn, Aquarius, and Pisces are known as the 'night' or 'descending' signs. If we consider a diagram of the human body with all twelve signs placed in an order corresponding to the influence of each on a part of the body, then we see that the five night signs start at the region of the reproductive organs and continue down the legs to the feet. This lower part, which has been called the less noble part, of the body, is that section of the body in which the less conscious, more instinctive impulses come to expression.

We can gain the feeling that in the upper part of the body, from the hips (Libra) up to the crown of the head (Aries), impulses come to expression that represent a truer, clearer image of our soul. The seven 'day' signs, as reflected in the body, indicate that the soul has received and integrated the spiritual potential in these seven zodiac forces into its own being. This state of affairs comes to expression during the time that the embryo is being formed, in a process occurring in response to the forces in the soul body of the person who is preparing for birth.

In this situation, the seven signs have called forth an echo from humanity, their forces are no longer just descending into the Earth sphere; there is now a response. They are now 'ascending back' into the cosmos, from the viewpoint of the sun gods who direct these forces onto the Earth. In this context, that is, the term 'ascending' has no connection with the seasonal cycle of the year; the use of 'ascending' here does not derive from the time during the year that the sun is in these signs. The term refers to processes occurring in the human soul, regardless of the hemisphere where one is living and its seasons.

The situation is reversed for the five 'night' signs; their influence is still descending, there is no echo yet from humanity. Our consciousness has yet to assimilate these five influences, we have yet to form a conscious connection to them; so we regard them as night forces. And we note that so much of our subconscious will, our instinctive behaviour, comes to expression through that part of the body formed by these five zodiac forces.

This cosmic perspective arises when we take a longer-term view of the zodiac and humanity. We are not referring to the normal astrological qualities of the zodiac; there is in this sense no inequality between people of the two groups of five and seven signs.

It is also possible to see the 'night' and 'day' quality of these two groups from a study of the twelve senses of humanity. The five senses deriving from the five night signs are less conscious than the others. Although we normally consider that there are only five or six senses, there are in the anthroposophical view, twelve senses in all, these twelve senses derive from the zodiac forces. The senses of ego-hood, concept, speech, and sound are, for example, quite conscious, but the senses of our own movement, of balance, and odour are much less conscious. These latter senses derive from the influence of the night signs, while the former derive from that of the day signs.

The five semi-formed countenances near the sun in the Steiner drawing very likely represent the ego forces from the night signs of the zodiac, forces that are not yet integrated into our being, for zodiac influences are mediated to us by the sun. The St. John's Tide festival is, then, concerned with the further development of humanity, particularly with respect to the increasing mystery of our will forces. It is concerned with the development of a conscious awareness of the higher ego.

This conclusion is further supported by the inclusion in the drawing of the three Cabiri deities, grouped near a human countenance. These are to be seen in the middle of the drawing; the human face having faded here, I have made it a little darker so that it may be seen. Above this face is the strongest and broadest of the three Cabiri; there are two more below and to the left of the human countenance.

These deities, whose cult was especially prominent on the island of Samothrace, was part of the Mysteries integrated into the Greek culture. Rudolf Steiner reports that they

142

represent the forces of Mars, Mercury, and the Sun in the elemental substance of the Earth and thus also in humanity. Illustration Six shows three carvings of these entities, made by Rudolf Steiner, who also taught that there were three such forms in the shape of jugs; from which smoke from incense could arise, and this was a help to the priests in contemplating these entities. The development of the human being, from the primal beginnings of the first human through the ages up to present humanity, and beyond, was the central concern of the Cabiren mysteries.

A Cabiren vase from the fourth century BC depicts amongst other figures, an ugly dwarf-like being whose name, Pratolaos, appears to mean "the earliest generation of the human". In Rudolf Steiner's words,

> The Cabiri were worshipped in remote antiquity as the guardians of those forces which are connected with the genesis of the human, and with the ongoing development of the human.[146]

Hence they are connected to the Mysteries of the Earth-mother too; archaeological excavation on Samothrace has revealed evidence of the worship of the Cybele, an ancient form of the Earth-mother.[147] So the inclusion in the drawing of images of the three Cabiri is a further indication of the relevance of the midsummer festival to the great drama of the spiritual evolution of humanity.

It is also significant in this connection that the cult of the Cabiri, about which little is known, as it was a truly esoteric cult, included the rite of "confession"; the laity were to confess their imperfect deeds.[148] This rite is not to be confused with the later Christian (Catholic) rite! But it is perhaps an indication of the earnestness with which the Cabiren mysteries strove to assist people to work with the spiritualization of the will forces. In any event, the recognition by the Greek people of the profound ethical renewal attained by the participants in the Cabiren mysteries was unequivocal, according to Diodorus Siculus, a Sicilian writer from the first century BC,

---

[146] Lect. 17th Jan 1919, (in GA 273).
[147] This is reported in e.g., the Encyclopaedia Brittanica, vol. 19. p. 983.
[148] Plutarch, in "Apoptheg. Lacon." quoted in Hastings Encyclopaedia of Religion and Ethics, vol. 7, p. 631, Edinburgh, T & T Clark, 1908.

It is especially attested of the Samothracian mysteries, and of these alone, that 'those who had partaken in these mysteries became more pious and more just, and in every respect better than their past selves'.[149]

In the Cabiren mysteries it was the task of the participants to contemplate the interweaving of the planetary influences with the elemental forces in humanity and the Earth, and to assist the underlying spiritual intentions behind this process. Verse 13 of the *Soul Calendar* (for the first week of July in the north and the first week of January in the south) expresses many aspects of the midsummer mystery, the St. John's festival:

> And when I am in the senses' heights,
> then there flames forth in my soul's depths
> from the fire-realms of the Spirit,
> The Gods' Word of truth:
> In spirit depths seek intuitively
> to find yourself as spirit-kindred.

Now let me summarize the various themes of the new St. John's festival. This festival, of course, must be celebrated in the summer. On this point Rudolf Steiner remarked that "the Christmas festival belongs in the winter, just as the St. John's festival belongs in the summer".[150] And in another lecture Steiner told an audience, "Whoever knows how to live with the spirits of the earth, that person celebrates, for example, the festival of St. John in summer."[151]

Themes of St. John's Tide
We *remember:* the mission of John the Baptist, which was to assist the union of the high sun spirit, Christ, with the Earth and humanity via the proclamation of Christ and the baptism of Jesus. In the Baptist, witnessing the descent of Christ, was a divine hierarchical spirit from the sun sphere, from whence our higher ego derives.

---

[149] Diodorus Siculus in his *Bibliotheca Historica.*
[150] GA 143, lect. 7th May 1912.
[151] GA 158, 7th Jan. 1913.

6 **The Cabiri** as modelled by Rudolf Steiner for use in a production of Goethe's Faust.

These three images depict what Rudolf Steiner described as the entities which the initiates at Samothrace perceived in their rituals, in plumes of smoke. They represent the forces of Mars, Mercury and the sun.

We *realize*: at first the ego was 'above' human beings, who felt therefore themselves to be part of a group. As humanity assimilates the spiritual substance of the ego from the sun sphere, then those beings, for example, the "inspiring spirit of the Baptist", will no longer need to provide the matrix of our ego.

We *contemplate*: the summertime, its dynamics. The sun's influence is maximal; the out-breath is complete; the Earth-soul, in that hemisphere, its great beings, and the Christ have ascended to the heights. There amidst the sun forces, elemental beings drift in 'sleep', and the hemisphere's aura mirrors back into the cosmos the astral radiance it receives. On the ground, lowly elementals revel and leap; warmth and light-ethers intensify, enhancing sulphurous and phosphorescent activity.

And archangel Uriel draws upward, from the depths of the earth's being, elemental forces derived from will forces of the creator; amongst these are also interwoven forces arising from the noblest deeds of humanity. In the heights these forces are permeated by the in-raying light of the sun beings and transformed, becoming like the spiritual radiance 'behind' the sunlight.

We *seek to experience*: the ego development of humankind. Uriel gazes into the earth, while guiding the union of the sun's inner radiance with that of the earth, knowing that the union of creator and created is affected by the disharmony inside the earth, resulting from imperfect deeds of humanity. Like a call from the conscience, the need arises to let the light of the higher ego shine into our being. By reviewing our deeds of the past year, while the 'eye of heaven' gazes down upon us, we seek to know the will forces that through our deeds became part of the earth's being. We respond to the summertime call for a yearly metanoia.

It should now be clear that each hemisphere has its own breathing process. St. John's Tide festival occurs in December in the southern hemisphere. When Rudolf Steiner spoke about the seasonal festivals, he used the term "the earth" to mean any one hemisphere. The following quotation emphasizes this; and confirms the basic concept which I have seen in Rudolf Steiner's works, and which is being presented in this book,

146

> We now want to consider the participatory experience of mankind with the Earth {during the yearly cycle}; in fact only one hemisphere comes into consideration there....Actually the spirit of the Earth is never really in sleep {that is, in the summer}. Rather, when it lets its waking activity pass over into sleep for one hemisphere, it then transfers its waking activity to the other hemisphere.[152]

One can only consider one hemisphere, one season, at a time; thus Rudolf Steiner dealt with the seasonal process of just one hemisphere, not with two opposite seasons, in any one lecture. We experience our own hemisphere's season, not the season of the other hemisphere, even though the Earth-spirit experiences both seasons simultaneously.

There are specific indications for the celebration of St. John's festival. In particular, eurythmy and music are important mediums for its themes. And the dynamic between a trinity of powers active in summer, the Christ being, the Earth mother, and the profound will forces from the Father-god (that is, the creator), could be brought to expression dramatically with the help of clouds of smoke, artistically utilized.

---

[152] Lect. 23rd Mar. 1913 in *The Effects of Spiritual Development.*

ADDENDUM ONE

Uriel and the interior of the Earth

The spiritualizing, or inner 'coarsening', of the Earth is the result of the kind of subtle forces generated on Earth, especially by humanity. When the future age of the ethereal, non-material human body is reached, then the Earth too will be etherealized to the fullest extent possible. A significant contemplation of this theme occurs in an ancient initiatory text, called the Sibylline Oracles, where the end of this world order and the arising of the new Earth is prophesied. The resurrection of the physical body of human beings is proclaimed (although in a material sense, which is incorrect), and then Uriel's role is described:

> And then shall Uriel break in twain the colossal bars of hard, very dense stone, at the massive gates of Hell, and cast them down forthwith; and then He shall bring forth to judgment all the afflicted entities there; above all, firstly, the old Titan figures.[153]

Although in some translations the word 'diamond' occurs instead of 'hard stone,' that is a scribal error. The original Greek text refers to adamantine, which is not a specific mineral, but a term for the very hardest of stones. These oracular words are in reference to the further aspects of spiritualizing the Earth; namely the need to overcome the most 'hardened' or ahrimanic forces in the world. We need not elucidate the deeper esoteric aspect of this matter here, where our task is to present the nature of the new festivals.

ADDENDUM TWO

Uriel and Saturn

To resolve the connection of Uriel to the sun and to Saturn requires an understanding of the essential nature of the Saturn influences. A full elucidation of this matter is beyond

---

[153] In, Die Sybillinischen Weissagen, book 2, {Sibylline Oracles} J. Friedlibe, edit/trans. Leipzig, 1852.

148

the scope of this book. Although Uriel is a sun spirit, he does have a connection with the Saturn forces. This connection is indicated in a Rudolf Steiner notebook entry, in the notes for the final lecture of *The Four Seasons and the Archangels* lecture cycle, wherein Uriel's name is placed next to the word "Saturn". This is a difficult subject, as the Saturn forces are active in subconscious processes in the human being. For example, one Saturn influence is that of guiding our footsteps through life, so that those events and encounters required by karma do actually occur.

The striving, as a conscious ego-endowed being, to become conscious of the purpose or significance of such events is highly significant. It shows a major aspect of our ego; namely, its inner need to bring up to consciousness the major dynamics in our subconscious will. For example, when a person strives to consciously understand the significance of a recurring illness or obstacle in his or her life, this is, in effect, the striving to integrate the Saturn influences into the personality, the normal ego, into that part of our being that derives from the sun.

Our ego is cosmically, or astrologically, regarded as sun-born. In the words of Rudolf Steiner, "the sun forces have for mankind, in fact, the significance that they draw its will-nature toward the sun, so to speak".[154] These words, spoken in a midsummer lecture, define the essence of Uriel's activity. Uriel is, then, a mediator between the Saturn will influences of humanity, in that they have had a definite impact on the substratum of the Earth's own being, and the sun forces in the summertime. In summer, Uriel draws up, toward the sun, the will forces of the Earth and humanity.

[154] Lect. 30th Jun. 1922, in *Human Questions and Cosmic Answers.*

CHAPTER SIX

MICHAELMAS

As summer passes over into the autumn, the days become mellow and subdued. The sun's influence on the hemisphere weakens, the light assumes a soft, almost yellow quality, temperatures on the ground and in the warmth-ether layer above that hemisphere, fall. Gradually growth processes slow down, and the plant life withers and then, except for the evergreens, decays. As the sun withdraws from the hemisphere, the Earth-spirit begins to inhale its soul forces, bringing the many beings, including the dreaming elementals, back into its physical body.

The hemisphere begins to awaken; the elemental beings who were coalesced in a sleep state high in the sky now become separate, conscious beings again, and the higher beings of the earth-soul pervade the human environment with their consciousness.

This inner awakening is not obvious to our normal perceptions. On the contrary, humanity is aware of the fading and withering process, and feels as if nature is drifting into a sleep. This sense is not entirely wrong, for obviously those elemental forces responsible for the new growth and life of springtime are no longer needed; their work has culminated in the bountiful harvests now being gathered.

The old custom of a 'harvest home' festivity, wherein the last wagonload of the crop was ceremoniously ushered into the yard, was and still is, a fitting way for humankind to show a spontaneous gratitude for the life-sustaining gifts of Mother-earth.

This gratitude is probably the origin of the "corn dolly" or "spirit of the corn", which was given a place of honour in the harvest home festivities. The corn spirit (the word 'corn' here still has the correct meaning of 'a grain'; it does not refer to maize) is an echo of the reverence offered to the Earth-mother and to the great beings of the Earth-soul who through the dwellers of the middle kingdom maintain the fructifying forces of nature.

But once the last crops are in and the days are colder and bare, then a melancholy mood can develop, a mood of slight unease or depression. As a sensitive observer of the last century, R. Chambers, wrote,

> The face of nature is changing...the very sound of the falling leaves causes us to feel thoughtful, and many a solemn passage of the Holy Bible passes through the mind, telling us the time will come when we also `shall fade as leaf, {which} the wind has taken away. And all that thou hast shall fade away, as the leaf falleth from the vine.' At no other season of the year do these solemn truths strike us so forcibly as in autumn.[155]

Such an attitude as this must arise if, what I have called a simplistic nature consciousness, is allowed to dominate the soul; it is simply the counterpart to the springtime mood of 'feeling at home' in the rejuvenating world. Just as we must overcome this naive springtime mood in order to align our soul with the significant forces active at that time, so can we only locate the leitmotifs of the autumn festival when we have developed an understanding of the inner dynamics of that season.

The Earth-soul and humanity experience an inner awakening in autumn. Thinking becomes easier and stronger, and we are more centered. This process creates a source of inner light, an intensified consciousness in the soul. Verse 30 of the Soul Calendar (for late April in the southern hemisphere, late October in the northern hemisphere) speaks of this process:

> In the soul's sunlight are sprouting now
> the ripened fruits of thinking.
> In the assuredness of self-awareness
> all feelings transform.
> Joyously I can sense
> the autumn's spirit-awakening.
> The winter shall awaken in me
> the summer of the soul.

---

[155] R. Chambers, *The Book of Days*, W & R Chambers, London, 1868.

Autumn and the cult of the dead

Special observances and rituals designed to help the dead have been a major element of autumn festivals throughout the world. Such rituals have often involved leaving a candle alight all night, and a 'soul cake' or food offering for the dead in the kitchen. The dead were thought to draw near to their former surroundings, in need of some food. Such activity was common in non-Christian Europe.

The Christian churches also had a special festival day for the dead, for the martyrs and departed saints of Christianity. This festival, called All Saints Day, is celebrated on May 13th; it was created in the sixth century when the church rededicated the Pantheon, the Roman pagan temple, to St. Mary. In A.D. 835 the date for the festival was changed to November 1st, in order to bring a major pagan festival, Samhain, which marked the beginning of winter, into Christianity.

The Samhain festival was also part of the cult of the dead in old Europe. This festival began on the evening before November 1st, that is on October 31st; this evening gradually became known as Halloween, the evening of All Hallowed's Day, an alternative name for All Saints Day. The church was unable to suppress entirely the customs of Samhain, and these have survived into the twentieth century as Halloween pranks.

For centuries the evening of All Hallowed's Day remained an occasion for various rites connected with the elemental beings and the approaching winter. For example, protective rites against the demonic gnomes were enacted; and divination techniques were used by young people wishing to know something of their future spouses. The present-day Hallowe'en customs are a distorted remnant of the protective rites of the old Celtic festival.

In the thirteenth century, an additional church festival was placed in the late autumn; All Souls Day, on November 2nd. This festival originally had been celebrated around Easter time; it was transferred to its present date by the Benedictines. The pagan cult of the dead was thereby given once again Christian form. Singers went through the streets reminding people to pray for those departed souls who were in purgatory, candles were lit on gravestones, and special masses were held.

There were probably several reasons for the cult of the dead being celebrated in autumn. The theme of death can come to mind in the withering autumnal world, as Chambers points out: "As the fallen leaves career before us – crumbling ruins of summer's beautiful halls – we cannot help thinking of those who have perished". It is also the case that in autumn the physical and ethereal worlds are less manifest, and that the intensifying consciousness of humanity thus more readily confronts, even if unconsciously, the soul or astral realm of the earth, where the so-called dead exist. These and other factors have resulted in the placing in the modern church calendar of two consecutive days connected to the themes of death and life after death.

All Saints Day commemorates the blessed existence, in high spiritual realms, of evolved individuals, for whom death was in effect a rebirth or resurrection of their souls out of earthly life into Devachan, or the 'kingdom of the heavens'. In part, this festival celebrates a triumph over death. All Soul's Day also evokes a nuance of triumph over the forces of decline and darkness, in that through the prayers of the living, souls in lower realms of the soul world are believed to arise into the spiritual worlds.

That is, the teaching of the church that souls are in purgatory and need to be helped does not mean that they are in hell, the place of 'eternal damnation'. Purgatory, in church doctrine, is the lower astral or soul world, not Hell. In the words of one of the ninth century founders of All Soul's Day: "After the office {that is, festival} of the saints I have inserted the office for the dead, because many people pass out of this {earthly} world without being given entrance, at once, into the 'Company of the Blessed'."[156]

There are grounds for regarding such autumn traditions about death as incomplete fragments of ancient esoteric autumn festivals which were formed around the theme of spiritual regeneration or rebirth. Such festivals, created by the initiated priesthood of the ancient cultures, consisted of certain dramatic scenes portraying the resurrection of the individual out of earthly blindness; that is, out of egotism, into enlightenment, into a consciousness of the spiritual world and the higher self.

The discovery of such a leitmotif is another example of our principle of creating a contrast to 'nature consciousness'. In such sacred dramas it was not simply the

---

[156] Amalar of Metz, De Ordine Antiphonarii, quoted in Butler's Lives of the Saints, Burns & Oats, London, 1981.

enhanced alertness or inner centeredness of the individual that was contemplated but rather the fact that the human being has a spiritual potential which can be brought to life in the personality, leading to initiation. These festivals, known as the Rites of Adonis or Tammuz, will be considered again, later.

The horse cult of autumn.

Another old autumn festival leitmotif is of help in clarifying the effect of the autumn in-breath on the soul-namely, the horse. Horses played a prominent role in autumn festivals of earlier cultures. In the Grecian, Roman, North African, and European civilizations, horses were part of the autumn processions and rituals. The western seaboard of Scotland and the Hebridean Islands retained the ancient Celtic festival customs longer than many parts of Europe, and records exist of the horse races and processions on horseback that took place at the autumn festivals in these areas.

The date of this festival was September 29th, the day of the archangel Michael in the church calendar. On the island of Iona, the people would at this time make a journey on horseback around a small hill with an ancient cairn and stone circle on it.[157] On other islands, the menfolk engaged in horse-racing without saddle or bridles, and a common ritual was for the entire community to go on horseback to the burial grounds and, led by the priests, make the circuit around it. That such a ritual, which died out about 1830 in the Hebrides, was originally pre-Christian is very likely.

Indeed, it is clear from archaeological research that the horse was a significant animal to earlier peoples. And that the horse became a part of the autumn festival can be understood through the spiritual research of Rudolf Steiner concerning the significance of the animal realm. There is a connection between warm-blooded animals and the human psyche or soul forces. Animal species are of vital importance to humanity. Through some species, certain qualities that are inappropriate for the human soul are prevented from becoming part of our soul forces. Whereas other animal species, through their existence on earth, alter the elemental forces of the earth in such a way that particular faculties can develop in the human soul.

---

[157] F. Marian McNeil, *The Silver Bough*, (MacLellan, 1961, Glasgow, vol. 2.

The horse species, for example, which did not always exist on Earth but came into existence in Atlantean times, has enabled humanity to develop the thinking faculty, the faculty of personal intelligence and cleverness, rather than the ancient instinctive wisdom. In autumn, the enhanced alertness, which a sensitive observer can experience, enables our faculty of thinking to blossom. It seems easier in autumn to contemplate the deeper questions of life, to attain an understanding of the deeper riddles of existence.

Our intelligence is inwardly vivified in autumn, as verse 29 of the *Soul Calendar* (for late October in the north, late April in the south) describes:

> The radiance of thinking myself
> To enkindle powerfully within,
> From the Cosmos Spirit's fountain of strength,
> Disclosing the meaning of life's experiences,
> Is now for me summer's heritage,
> Is autumn's peace and also winter's hope.

Apart from the harvest festival, which is really more a festivity than a spiritual festival, there is virtually no autumn festival in the modern Christian cultures. Whereas the Easter and Holy Nights festivals have given to the spring and winter a significant spiritual nuance (even though little understanding exists as to just what the connection is), the summer and autumn have remained somewhat bare. In autumn, on September 29th, there is in the church calendar the day of the archangel Michael, when customs that were the remnants of the old Celtic autumn festival were celebrated, because the church wished to integrate such activity into the Christian festival cycle.

Through the efforts of the church, worship of this archangel became a part of the rites. When the people rode around an ancient site, for example, they would sing praises to the archangel Michael. But as these old festivals died out, this day became devoid of any significant activity. The day is known in a few countries as Michaelmas day, but it is no longer understood just why this particular archangel is connected to an autumn festival.

Autumn: the time of ingathering

As autumn approaches, the hemisphere draws its forces back down into itself, there is less activity in its ether body.

The intense growth and fruiting activity of spring and summer are over. Plants begin to wither and some wild animals go into hibernation. In the Earth-soul, however, processes develop during the autumn in-breath that lead to more activity for some of the inhabitants of the middle kingdom. Elemental beings, who in summer were drifting in a sleep state high above the earth, now descend to the ground, where they have tasks.

In particular, it is the sylphs who have tasks brought about by the withering and decaying of their plants. They must ensure that this process occurs in such a way that next spring, with the help of the gnomes, the plants can again grow up out of the soil: "They descend over the flora and satiate themselves with the plant world".[158] Because most of the inner activity of autumn is like this, it has no accompanying outer indication; this situation creates difficulties for the forming of a new autumn festival.

Only with a living, sensitive understanding of the inner side of autumn can a new autumn festival arise. The more it is possible for us to think our way through, in a clear and imaginative way, to the spiritual activity occurring in the Earth's aura, the more likely it is that we can create such a festival. With effort, we can begin to develop a perception of the elemental forces active in the Earth.

What processes occur in autumn? There are, in effect, two intensely contrasting dynamics, one malignant, the other offering a source of spiritual strength. The Hallowe'en festivities are the remnant of old Celtic rites for the late autumn, which arose through the response of earlier peoples to the lowly or even demonic elemental beings of autumn. As the separation between the sun and the hemisphere develops during autumn, then the lowly entities embodying the Earth egotism, the lower self of humanity, become more active.

These beings, particularly free in the winter, became known in earlier times as "the Wild Hunt". Thus in the ancient mystery centres, a meditation for winter was "guard yourself from evil". In autumn, this presence of demonic forces is not as strong as in winter, but it is growing. For in addition to that influence which has remained from summer, malignant forces from the Earth's interior are also

---

[158] GA 136, lect. 4th April 1912, in *Spiritual Beings in the heavenly Bodies and in the Kingdom of Nature.*

present, not so strongly yet, but still beginning to assert themselves. A sensitive person can detect something of this process when walking through the dense, swirling fogs of autumn, but it is especially the withering and decay that invokes an unpleasant influence:

> When toward autumn the plants wither and their leaves fall away, then, everywhere, the elemental beings appear which Ahriman sends {up} to the Earth's surface. There, he 'gathers in' all that which is dying away. He gathers this through his elemental beings. When one goes through the fields in autumn and gazes clairvoyantly at nature, then one sees that everywhere Ahriman stretches forth his forces, and everywhere he has his elemental beings, who bear to him that physical and ethereal substantiality which is withering.[159]

Another autumn process enabling ahrimanic powers to manifest, has to do with the intensified condition of the semi-etherized sulphur. We have considered how in summer this substance is animated to become a significant influence in the earth's elemental forces. High in the atmosphere, albeit in diluted form, sulphur exists in clouds. In the summer, this sulphur vapour becomes animated or fiery, because of the increased warmth and light. Sulphur is, in effect, a substance that has condensed from these forces – of warmth and light – and so every summer, it is as if the elemental forces that created sulphur in the remote past, when the Earth became a dense material planet, are once again strongly present, and the sulphur becomes inwardly intensified.

In Chapter Five we noted that through the presence of the elemental forces within sulphur, humanity in the summertime becomes radiant to the clairvoyant gaze of a being observing the planet from a distance. For sulphur also exists in the human organism, it is in fact essential for our earthly existence; it is a constituent of protein and of a vitamin B. Sulphur is part of our hair, our nails, and our skin. So in the human being, in late summer and early autumn, this intensified state of sulphur also exists. This is an especially significant process, for sulphur is a substance

---

[159] GA 150, lect. 14th Mar. 1913.

closely connected to Ahriman. The demonic forces in the astral world that emanate from Ahriman can manifest in the world through sulphur.

Although this is at first a strange concept, we need to bear in mind that the inner qualities of substances, which derive from the elemental forces that create them, are no longer perceptible to us. But a study of the living biochemistry of earlier times confirms the results of Rudolf Steiner's research, which he had the courage to report for the benefit of posterity. Some centuries ago, the European peoples said that the devil is to be found on midsummer nights near a mustard tree;[160] a statement which seems, to the non-holistic, non-perceptive mindset, quite absurd.

But it is very reasonable to conclude that the mustard seed is the product of the warmth-ether, and hence in this tree is one place where the sulphurous warmth is very intense in the plant world. The connection of sulphur with evil is a fundamental truth in the sacred scriptures of Judaism and Christianity. The term 'brimstone' (that is, 'burning stone') refers to sulphur. Brimstone is always indicated in the Bible as a substance that will be present in the future age when a fallen, evil section of humanity is on the earth:

> The light of the wicked shall be put out. Brimstone shall be scattered over his dwelling. (Psalm 18)
> Edom's streams shall be turned into pitch, the dust thereof into brimstone, and the land thereof shall become burning pitch...and it shall be a habitation of dragons and the satyr shall cry to his fellow. (Isaiah 3:9-14.)

The mention of dragons and satyrs in this connection is significant. The Book of Revelations also connects sulphur to evil powers, describing the future karma of a demonic, fallen portion of humankind as causing them to encounter destruction through their own self-created environment, portrayed as a sulphurous burning lake, Revelation 21:17. The lake represents the astral forces. Through the presence in summer of this activated sulphur, the ahrimanic powers become especially strong:

---

[160] Reported by Sir J. Frazer, in the 13 vol. *Golden Bough*, MacMillan, London 1976.

One sees how, on the one hand, human beings are shining out into the cosmos in the 'St. John's light', and on the other hand, how the dragon-like, serpentine form of Ahriman winds its way among the human beings, who are shining in the astral light.[161]

The dragon of autumn

Although in modern times such beings as dragons and unicorns are regarded as non-existent creatures of fables, or at most "archetypes from the subconscious", they are quite real, but not on a material level. Rather they are real on an astral level, in the soul world. There the demonic beings under the control of Ahriman can appear in the form of a dragon, or flying serpent. Although such entities are normally associated with darkness and the subterranean realms, it is also true that they manifest in the atmosphere, 'behind' the ethereal clouds of sulphurous vapours, and that they are then of a bright appearance.

Old legends refer to the sulphurous breath of dragons and to their existence in the late summer and autumn skies. In Chinese lore, dragons are regarded as especially prevalent in the summer, shining creatures dividing up the sky into territories for themselves. An old Chinese legend recounts that dragon skin glows in the dark, like the St. John's beetles.[162] This association of dragons with light and fire is a common experience of earlier humanity. Witness a poem by the first century Roman poet, Lucan: "You dragons... shining with golden brightness, scorching Africa renders you deadly".[163] The Old Testament also mentions radiant, fiery flying serpents. In the Greek language of the New Testament, the word used for dragon is very probably derived, as the brothers Grimm suggested, from the word for 'shining' or 'scintillating' (derchein).

As Rudolf Steiner taught, in summer then, the sulphur forces enable a strong ahrimanic influence to develop, similar in nature to the lower self of the human being. This ahrimanic influence also permeates the elemental beings who are in the heights during summer, and these then draw down near to us, as autumn approaches. Through this

---

[161] Lect. 5th Oct. 1923, in *The Four Seasons and the Archangels.*
[162] *Dragons*, P. Hogarth and V. Clery, Allen Lane, London,1979.
[163] ibid.

process, humanity is exposed to the ahrimanic forces connected to the lower impulses or lower self:

> Anyone who has the faculty for seeing, for feeling such things, knows that the nature sprites up there, above in the heights during summer, live in an element which is as much saturated with desire as is the desire life of humanity, which is connected to the animal nature of the human being.[164]

Indeed, the lower self of the human being manifests not only as dark muddy-red patches in the aura, but also, on an ethereal level, as sulphurous 'clouds' in the lower half of the aura. Therefore, in late summer, this aspect of human nature is stronger, both because of the presence of a sulphurous force in the aura and through the descent of elemental beings from the sulphurous heights of summer down to the Earth's surface.

The autumn festival of the Hebraic culture reflects the awareness by the priesthood in Old Testament times of these secrets of the season. Their autumn festival activities began with the festival of atonement, about the time of the autumn equinox. This was a solemn one-day festival, consisting of rituals by the priests, especially the high priest, designed to cleanse the temples, and thus the community of, sin and thereby ensure that God would continue to nurture and inspire the community with spiritual forces.

But it was not only an inner cleansing which was sought, through the sacrifices and prayers and fasting; it was also an objective atonement for the accumulated sins of the people. These sins were perceived as having an objective reality. The desires, thoughts, and deeds deriving from the lower self had invoked malignant elemental forces into the environment. It was the intention of the priesthood to deal with these forces, which by the autumn had accumulated, in an objective way, by gaining atonement for them. However, the term 'atonement', which suggests an 'at-one-ment' or unity in relationship, only refers to the final outcome or aim of the rituals for this festival.

The Hebrew word that is translated as 'atonement' derives from a word meaning 'to cover over', to thereby 'remove or nullify'. This festival sought to establish an 'at-one-ment'

---

[164] In *The Four Seasons & the Archangels*, lect. 15th Oct. 1923.

with the deity through covering over, or nullifying, lower astral influences. On this day, a bull was ritually sacrificed, indicating a link between the bull and the lower astral forces of humanity; its blood was sprinkled inside the Holy of Holies. Also, the remarkable scapegoat ritual was performed, wherein a goat, 'laden' with the malignant forces that had accumulated in the area, from the sins of the community, was sent away far into the desert. The point is that these rituals were more than simply symbolic.

The rituals of this day were designed to counteract the ahrimanic influences which become more obvious in the autumn. It was in this way that the unity between the community and their deity could be restored. In earlier times, the presence of ahrimanic forces was a perceived reality, and hence the need for some form of spiritual purification was self-evident. The esoteric commentary states that:

> The wicked cause 'imperfection' above and arouse 'judgement' {the necessary unpleasant consequences}, and bring defilement on the sanctuary, so that the mighty serpent shows itself.[165]

Hence, on the day of Atonement, and this day only, the high priest was allowed to enter into the innermost part of the temple, the Holy of Holies, wherein he could enter into communion with the deity and invoke the continuing presence of God in the community.

Then, a few days later, there followed a joyous week-long festival, the "festival of booths". This was both a merry harvest festival and a joyous festival of spiritual triumph. The term 'booths' referred to the requirement stipulating that when the menfolk (usually accompanied by the family) came to Jerusalem for the week, they had to make for themselves booths or temporary dwellings from branches of trees.

Thus during this autumn festival the community resided inside living houses, made from the leaves and branches "of splendid trees", including the myrtle tree, the foliage of which is fragrant. The theme of the temple services concerned the many blessings God had bestowed on the Israelites, and especially his triumphant powers which, for

---

[165] *The Zohar,* vol. 5, Soncino Press, 1970.

example, had guided the Israelites out of Egypt and safely across the desert, with its poisonous serpents and other dangers.

In the course of time, another significant symbolic ritual, involving water, was added to this festival. On the second day of the festival four oil lamps, in large golden lamp stands in an outer section of the temple, called the Court of the Women, were ignited. Then in this court, dancers, holding flaming torches, danced to the accompaniment of music. The next morning and for the remaining mornings of the week, a priest brought water in a golden pitcher and poured it into the hollow altar, while the congregation, accompanied by flute music, sang triumphant songs. This music was in fact The Hallel, that is, Psalms 113 to 118. Water is a symbol of the feeling life, and hence of the astral body (or soul). The soul is also symbolized by a woman, in contrast to the ego, which is represented by a man, often a king.

The intention of this festival was to direct the community's awareness toward the potential in the soul for spiritual triumph, spiritual renewal. The people stayed in "living houses", symbolic of an enveloping aura, filled with vitality ! And in "the place of the soul", in the Court of Women, a golden light arose, then streams of living water, or high, pure astral forces poured into the heart. The focus of this festival, was in short, the soul or astral body. This conclusion is in harmony with Steiner's presentation of the correlation between the four seasons and the four aspects of the human organism (see Chapter Four).

According to Steiner's research, the astral body is primarily affected by the elemental dynamics of autumn and should therefore be the focus of the new autumn seasonal festival. In autumn, Steiner noted,

> These impulses {of the summer, the spiritual light of the sun beings} are taken up into the soul life, and there they are permeated by human wishes: astral body.[166]

What was the message of the old Hebraic autumn festival? This festival presented images of what can be achieved in

---

[166] In Beitrag 19 to the Complete Works, p. 2.

the autumn by the soul when it strives, with the enhanced awareness that autumn brings, to attune itself to accessible spiritual forces, despite the presence of 'the dragon'. But any such process of spiritualization can only succeed on the basis of a striving to cleanse the soul of ahrimanic influences. The atonement stage had first to be achieved, by covering or removing the influences of the lower self. Once the dragon was overcome, then a spiritual victory could be attained, spiritual rebirth achieved.

Such leitmotifs counteract powerfully the simplistic autumnal mood ! Since the Holy Nights follow soon after autumn, this is an especially important part of the yearly festival cycle. The extent to which the soul may receive the divine Life-spirit forces during the Holy Nights is dependent upon the preparation that has been made, during the preceding autumn months and during the preceding years of our life. In the autumn, then, the striving toward the Spirit-self is particularly significant for the development of the Life-spirit forces from the Christ at winter.

Spiritual resurrection or rebirth in the ancient autumn festivals

It was not only the old Hebraic autumn festival that proclaimed the possibility of spiritual triumph or initiation. This theme was common to the autumn festivals of many cultures, festivals that were widespread in earlier times. Examples are the rites of Adonis in Greece and Phoenicia, of Tammuz in Babylonia, and of Attis in Syria. From the few extant descriptions of these festivals, it is known that in the autumn, a three-day period was set aside for the enactment of the death and rebirth of the god. An image of the god (for example, Adonis) was wrapped in burial clothes and then, amidst a great procession of priests and mourning worshippers, it was taken to a lake or to the sea and 'buried'.

For the next two days or so, the community was required to mourn the death of its god. Some of the dirges sung during this time have survived from the ancient Babylonian culture. Indeed, in the Old Testament there is an account of the mourning by women over the death of Tammuz. In Ezekiel 8:14, it is mentioned that women at the north gate of the temple were weeping as part of a ritual mourning for the 'death' of Tammuz, a Sumerian-Babylonian deity. Then on the third day, the priests led the people to the lakeside, and amidst intense jubilation, brought the statue of the god back up 'to life', proclaiming that he had returned to life, overcoming death. At this event the entire community celebrated the triumph of their god, singing songs of joy.

This ritual expressed themes that truly belong to the autumn festival; it portrayed the fact that the human soul is not extinguished by death, but rather, after three days of separation from the body, it is resurrected. The soul becomes conscious in the soul realm, and can begin its journey toward the spiritual realms. The autumn ritual linked this possibility to the spiritual powers of the community's deity. What for the wider community was portrayed as drama became existential fact for the aspirants of these early religions. For at this festival, they were initiated; that is, they were placed in a trancelike sleep and were led out of their bodies, in order to experience for themselves the reality of the higher worlds.[167]

These events were enacted over many centuries, but by about the time of Christ, as the old (pre-Christian) mysteries were dying out, this resurrection drama was (as we have noted in Chapter Five) transferred to the springtime, so that the outer, material 'resurrection' by nature could support the faith of the people in this reality. The god also became then a god of the vegetation; and especially with the rites of Attis, a decadent, even malignant, quality developed.

There is evidence that the Celtic peoples also celebrated a festival of spirit triumph in the autumn. In the remote western islands of Scotland, fragments of their festival traditions remained until early in the twentieth century. One such tradition is a dance ritual, performed at Michaelmas, shortly after the autumn equinox, called The Carlin of the Mill Dust. The ritual involves two dancers, a man and a woman, the man with a druidic magic wand in his hand,

> They gesticulate and attitudinize before one another, dancing around and around, in and out, crossing and recrossing, changing and exchanging places. The man flourishes the wand over his own head and over the head of the woman, whom he touches with the wand, and who falls down, as if dead, at his feet. He bemoans his dead 'carlin', and dances and gesticulates around her body. He then lifts up her left hand, and looking into the palm, breathes upon

---

[167] GA 306, lect. 19th April 1923.

it, and touches it with the wand. Immediately the limp hand comes alive and moves from side to side and up and down.

The man rejoices and dances around the figure on the floor. He does the same for her right hand, and then the left foot and the right foot in succession - they also come alive and start moving. But although the limbs are living, the rest of the body remains inert. The man kneels over the woman, breathes into her mouth, and touches her heart with the wand. Now the woman comes to life and springs up, facing the man. The tune varies with the varying phases of the dance. It is played by a piper or fiddler, or it is sung. The melody is quaint and irregular, and the words are curious and archaic.[168]

This resurrection dance is surely the last remnant of what was once an initiation ritual through which the acolyte achieved a spiritual rebirth. The normal soul qualities, in which Lucifer and Ahriman have an influence, would die away. The acolyte would relinquish his or her hold on the egoistical nature, and like the phoenix arising out of the ashes, the Spirit-self could become manifest. The word carlin is Gaelic, and appears to refer to a lowly woman with witchlike powers.[169] Thus the dance ritual focused on the death (that is, the overcoming) of the lower soul or astral qualities, with their unpleasant elemental forces, which are earthbound, come from 'mill dust'. Then the ritual portrayed the rebirth of the soul. Presumably the original rite would have shown that the reborn soul was now a vessel of the divine feminine or the Spirit-self.

The value socially, of an autumn festival with such a theme is obvious given the perspective I have been presenting. The partially conscious attitudes that develop in the soul in a particular season need to be counteracted, because such materialistic or 'maya-bound' thoughts are harmful to both humanity and the elemental beings. In autumn, the festivals of spirit triumph counteract the subtle inner ego weakening that can develop, giving rise to

---

[168] McNeill, *The Silver Bough*, vol. 2.
[169] It is a form of the German word 'Kerl" (or 'Kerl-in'); in English this became churl or rather 'churl-ess', but with an additional, magical witch-like quality.

anxieties and depression. Our consideration of the sulphur process of late summer has indicated that indeed there are strong negative influences active in autumn.

The 'dragon forces' of Ahriman are especially active. These demonic entities seek to strengthen in summertime their influence on humanity; as Rudolf Steiner taught they,

> ...try to ensnare and embrace humanity, to draw them down into the realm of half-conscious sleep and dreams. Then, caught in this play of illusion, which Ahriman...makes, people would become 'world dreamers', and in this condition become a prey to ahrimanic powers...[170]

Then, in the autumn especially, those ahrimanic powers seek to intensify the tendency to hate, anxiety, and fear.

Shooting stars and meteorites

Counteracting the ahrimanic influence is a cosmic force, active in autumn, connected with the role of iron in the human organism. Iron is especially important for our existence. It is an essential element in the bloodstream. Iron insufficiency affects our consciousness as well as the chemical-physical body, the well-known symptoms of anaemia being listlessness, tiredness, and general lack of will.

Because the bloodstream is the vessel of our ego consciousness, with iron insufficiency comes an inner weakening of consciousness conducive to the development of such negative states as anxiety and fear. Consequently the intake of additional iron would counteract, biochemically, the autumnal development of anxieties and general ego weakness that is enhanced by the ahrimanic influences of summer. With the additional iron we could 'take hold of' the body more effectively and manifest a greater inner strength.

Such a dynamic is more readily understood when we reflect upon the fact that iron is that one of the seven planetary metals that is essential for the development and maintenance of our ego-hood. It is through the iron in our

---

[170] *The Four Seasons & Archangels*, lect. 5th Oct. 1923.

bloodstream that we have the capacity to express our self, our personality.[171]

Indeed, we know through anthroposophical cosmology, that there was a time when iron did not exist on the Earth. Iron, like the other planetary metals, derives from the condensation of ether forces from one of the other planets; it developed on earth at the time of the creation of the human.

Without the presence of iron in the blood, incarnating human beings would not have been able to manifest the independent sense of self. Ever since the introduction of iron in preparation for the creation of the human, the Earth has been able to draw on this iron, and other minerals, so that there is sufficient of these for each new generation of living creatures.

The continual nourishing of the planet is a cosmic process, particles of minerals from space entering the Earth's atmosphere. The process is evident in the case of comets, which appear unpredictably in the night sky and pour out a finely diluted trail of essential trace elements into interplanetary space. These substances are then absorbed by the Earth, if the comet has approached close enough, or if the Earth, in its orbit around the sun, moves through the area in space where the comet has been. We do not usually perceive this absorption of cometary 'dust', as the particles are too small to cause any perceptible luminosity, except in some cases, when the particles do become visible, as meteors.

The cosmic nourishing process is quite conspicuous in the case of shooting stars and meteorites. Shooting stars create a bright streak of light across the night sky, as they speed through the upper atmosphere, vaporizing. They are known scientifically as 'meteors' or 'meteoroids'. Modern scientific research has uncovered a number of facts about them, but questions remain concerning their origin and nature. The shooting star's wonderful trail of light, usually between 70 and 110 kilometres above the ground, will be seen by observers up to 500 kilometres apart. Yet the material object that causes this visual phenomenon has a weight of about one hundredth of a gram (or at the most, in some cases, just one gram) !

---

[171] Two lectures are relevant here; 24th Oct. 1923 in GA 351 and 31st Mar. 1907.

And mathematical calculations indicate that the density of this tiny particle is about that of water. The radiance produced by such a tiny, semi-soft object is explained by contemporary science as the result of the speed with which it enters the atmosphere, about 45 kilometres per second, many times faster than a bullet. But the question arises for us whether the radiance of the shooting star might be caused by an ether force.

A powerful frictional effect of the ethereal energy of the shooting star on the Earth's ether layers would produce this extraordinarily brilliant light. This would then be the same phenomenon as that which, according to Rudolf Steiner creates the brilliant radiance of a comet's tail. This possibility gains when we consider that no solid rock has ever been produced by a shower of meteors. As we noted in Chapter One, a shooting star is not a solid object !

Even during prolific meteor showers – for example, the Geminids which produce about fifty shooting stars per hour – no tangible, solid rock ever descends to earth. Rocks that descend to the ground after hurtling through the sky, called 'meteorites' or 'bolides', are a separate phenomenon, quite distinct from meteors. Of the thousands of meteorites that have been collected, "not a single meteorite has been clearly identified with any particular shower {of meteors}".[172]

Meteorites are entirely solid objects, even weighing many tons. Like the shooting stars, they are highly visible, causing a brilliant streak of light; and like the shooting stars, their minerals are vaporized into the Earth's atmosphere. Advanced scientific research indicates that shooting stars contain iron, that every shower of meteors is contributing finely vaporized iron into the atmosphere. Meteorites likewise add iron to the Earth. Indeed, iron is a main element in meteorites. Chemical analysis of samples found on the ground indicate that there are two kinds of meteorites, one with about 25 percent iron, the other with about 90 percent iron.

Our questions about the origin of shooting stars and meteorites cannot be answered fully until more scientific research has been conducted and further effort has been made to integrate such research with the results of Rudolf Steiner's spiritual-scientific research. It is possible to identify the origin of about ten meteor showers that recur

---

[172] Encyclopaedia Britannica, (1983) vol. 12, p.361.

regularly each year. Mathematical calculations establish that these showers take place in a definite area in space, corresponding to the orbital path of a known comet. The shower of meteors occurs when the Earth crosses the orbital path of the comets.

For reasons still unknown, when the Earth encounters the orbital paths of other comets, no meteors are produced. Nevertheless, although we do not yet comprehend the full situation regarding the origin of meteors and meteorites, we may say that they derive from the same processes in the cosmos that have created comets.

Although such processes may be considered as having occurred long ago, when the solar system was entering its material phase, there are also comets that have been created recently. Indeed they are still being formed. Rudolf Steiner described how the sun creates new comets. He found that the sun ejects the substance of comets from itself, via the sunspots, obviously in a semi-ethereal, nonmaterial state.

Then this stream of energy condenses, later, into comets; and from these comets, some of the shooting star showers derive. The sun creates shooting stars and meteorites in the same way.[173] Modern astronomical research has discovered that the same minerals contained in meteorites are present in the sun; that is, in a semi-ethereal state, at the edges of sunspots and in the corona, the sun's outer atmosphere.

Hence some meteorites and shooting stars derive ultimately from the sun ! They derive directly from the sun in an ethereal state, from which they then condense into matter. They derive indirectly from the sun when they are the by-products of comets, whether recently formed or older. During the condensation process, creating the meteor, the absorption of ether forces from Mars contributes to the high percentage of iron.[174]

Rudolf Steiner discovered the deep significance of the shooting stars, of the wonderful iron forces they give to our planet. The finely vaporized iron gradually descends through the atmosphere, to be absorbed by humankind. In the human body, it finds its way into the bloodstream. The process that occurs in us, when iron unites with our blood, is parallel to the process whereby the shooting stars merge

[173] GA 231, lect. 17th Nov. 1923.
[174] Lect. 27th Oct. 1923 & 5th Oct. 1923

their iron into the atmosphere. Through the shooting stars, our iron-absorption processes are strengthened.

Throughout the year, shooting stars are yielding iron, and our blood is absorbing iron. During most of the year, meanwhile, the sulphur force is present only within humanity. But as we have noted, this force develops its maximum strength in summer, and by late summer the ahrimanic influences in sulphur vapour are present up in the atmosphere. As sources of counteracting iron, the late summer and autumn shooting stars and meteorites are thus of especial importance. As Rudolf Steiner suggested in a lecture from the Four Seasons and the Archangels cycle, one may say to oneself;

> There {above} are the shooting stars, whilst in every one of my blood corpuscles iron is taking form; my life is full of shooting stars...and this 'inner fall' of shooting stars...is especially important when autumn approaches, when the sulphur process is at its peak... for then the counterforce is present also.[175]

Steiner continued in another lecture from the same cycle saying,

> {This counterforce}, is to be seen in those remarkable products that from time to time fall onto the earth... and contain meteoric iron. When you look at a piece of meteoric iron, you have in it a remarkable witness of the iron dispersed in the cosmos. {And} in the shooting stars which come so frequently in August, bringing iron into special activity in the cosmos, as it were, we see revealed this counter force of nature... through this 'shooting in' of the meteoric 'arrows' from the cosmos, the {ahrimanic} desire element of high summer is purified.
>
> And what takes place in majesty and grandeur out there in the great cosmos, goes on continually also in us. We produce tiny iron particles in our blood, in combination with other substances, and while, on the one hand, there pulses through our blood the sulphurizing process, there works inwardly against it, meteorically, as the other pole, the iron inside us,

---

[175] Lect. 5th Oct. 1923.

bringing about the same process as is effected outside in the cosmos by the meteoric iron.[176]

In the same lectures, Steiner referred to the Perseids meteor shower, which recurs regularly in August in the northern hemisphere. He indicated that the timing of this shower is not accidental but rather the expression of the conscious spiritual guidance of the world:

> And when in high summer, from a particular constellation {Perseus}, meteors fall in great showers of cosmic iron, then this cosmic iron, which carries an enormously strong healing force, is the weapon which the gods bring to bear against Ahriman, as, dragon-like, he tries to coil around the shining forms of men. The force which falls on the Earth in the meteoric iron is indeed a cosmic force whereby the higher gods endeavour to gain a victory over the ahrimanic powers; when autumn comes...{thus} the blood...is rayed through by a force which is carried as iron into the blood, and wages war there on anxiety, fear, and hate. And so the gods with their meteors wage war on that spirit who would like to radiate fear over all the Earth.   (lecture of 5th October)

The autumnal shooting stars in the north and south

The northern hemisphere has its most extensive meteor showers in late summer and autumn. But what is the reality of the shooting star influence during the cycle of the year in the southern hemisphere, indeed over the entire globe? Shooting stars can occur singly at any time of the night (or day, when they are of course invisible). But they also occur in 'showers'; that is, many appear over a period of several days or even weeks, in a specific part of the sky. The particular section of the night sky from which they seem to ray down is called the 'radiant'. And a radiant is usually named after a constellation in its vicinity.

Astronomers know of about 200 such specific meteor showers; that is, they are recurring showers, taking place regularly each year at about the same time. The regularity as well as the size of these meteor showers, we know, is due to

---

[176] Lect. 15th Oct. 1923.

the fact that the Earth, as it journeys around the sun, passes across the fixed pathways of comets. The pathway of a comet is littered with fragments, from which derive the shooting stars. Of course not all meteor showers can be identified with the path of a comet. Perhaps the unidentified showers derive from the primarily ethereal comet-substance recently cast out by the sun.

Since the shooting-star showers emanate from fixed areas of the firmament, it is entirely accurate to identify some as northern hemisphere showers and others as southern hemisphere showers. A shower radiating from a part of the sky above the northern hemisphere, for example, the Quadrantids, near the Big Dipper, which is never seen (or only just seen) in the southern hemisphere, enriches the atmosphere of the north, but not that of the south. Another such shower, which we have mentioned, is the Perseid shower, from the northern constellation of Perseus. This name does not mean that they come all the way from the remote stars of that constellation, it means that this is the sector in the heavens from where they appear to originate.

This shower occurs in late July to mid-August, that is, in the northern summer, and it is the one that Rudolf Steiner refers to as being used especially by Michael, in the battle against the ahrimanic sulphur forces of the northern hemisphere's summer,

> And it is then, in midsummer, when from {the direction of} a particular constellation, the meteor-stones fall in mighty showers of shooting stars, in which such an immensely strong weapon of the gods is contained...this that cosmic power through which the higher gods seek to conquer the ahrimanic powers...that which in majestic greatness occurs in the cosmos, as the August showers of shooting stars shine into the human {astral} radiance in the astral light....

The shooting-star showers he is referring to are 'the Perseids', named after the radiant point, Perseus. Of all the meteor showers occurring throughout the year over both hemispheres, the Perseid shower may be strongest of all, producing about 68 meteors per hour, at maximum, during its three weeks of activity.

172

For the Christian Community church, the new festival cycle is not acceptable, as all festivals must have a global nature. So a problem arises when an autumnal, that is hemispherical, phenomenon is pointed out by Rudolf Steiner as the basis of the festival. To the church, the cause of Michaelmas must not be found in the seasonal phenomena; consequently Rudolf Steiner's teaching, that these Perseids meteors are the primary 'Michaelic' autumnal phenomenon, is portrayed as incorrect; "*...one should not assume that the cosmic iron {of shooting stars} is the same as the arising cosmic Imagination of Michael fighting the dragon* {with his sword}" (M. Samson). Bearing in mind the words of Rudolf Steiner on the previous page, let's read again a part of the quote we gave two pages back,

> And when in high summer, from a particular constellation {Perseus}, meteors fall in great showers of cosmic iron, **then this cosmic iron**, which carries an enormously strong healing force, is the **weapon** which the gods **bring to bear against Ahriman**, as, dragon-like, he tries to coil around the shining forms of men. (emphasis mine. AA)

It is quite clear that the Michaelmas festival, for either hemisphere, derives from the cosmic iron from shooting stars, being permeated by the archangel. But the church view denies that the Perseids shooting stars dynamic, referred to here by Steiner, is that which, permeated by the archangel Michael, creates the Michael-ic autumn dynamic.

The reason given is, the constellation of Perseus is also visible in the southern skies, so "*the 'Perseid' meteorites are also seen in the southern hemisphere at night ! *"[177]. And therefore, we are told, those meteors can **not** be thought of as a northern hemisphere {Michaelmas} phenomenon. It is on this basis, that the distant stars are then offered as the cause of Michaelmas (and of the other festivals).

But these objections are without a basis, as Perseus is visible for only a few weeks in the south, and this is when the southern hemisphere **has its springtime** (September-October), which is when the Perseids shooting stars are **not happening**. So the objection is irrelevant to the topic, since it is springtime in the south at that time, so there is no

---

[177] M Samson, *Festivals in the southern* ... p.114

autumn in-breath to draw the etheric-homeopathic cosmic iron down towards the ground.[178]

It is a core concept of the Michael festival, that this festival dynamic occurs in autumn, because it is then that the hemisphere's ethers are moving downwards, bringing the etheric iron energies down into our bodies. So the Perseids shooting stars of autumn do create the Michaelic basis of the festival, In the words of Rudolf Steiner,

> We visualize this {Archangel) Michael correctly, when we find his outstretched arm enveloped as if in flames from the sparkling meteors, which have melted together to form his sword....[179]

So the brief appearance of this constellation, low in the northern skies of the southern hemisphere, during the springtime is not relevant to our theme. Autumn shooting stars in the autumn, as well as the summer showers, are of value for Michael; and during the northern autumn, there are some quite strong showers, especially the Orionids, which in late October produce about 30 meteors per hour, at maximum. In addition there are invisible showers, that is, those that occur only during the daytime, discovered by radar, some of which are very strong.

In the southern hemisphere there is no shower parallel to the Perseids, no shower so exceptionally strong in the summer, in comparison with those at other months. The strongest shower in the southern hemisphere appears to be an autumn shower, the Eta Aquarids in early May, which has about 20 meteors per hour. Although Aquarius, being a zodiac constellation, is not exclusively a southern star group, but its meteor shower, coming from that general direction, is a strong influence in the southern skies; it is the brightest of all southern showers.[180]

There are also summer meteor showers in the south coming from entirely southern sectors of the sky, from the Southern Cross and Centaurus, in January and February. There is also a very strong shower at early summer, two weeks before St. John's Tide, that is, in early December. This is the Geminid shower, from the direction of the zodiac

---

[178] Perseus is also visible, but very low in the northern skies, for just 2 weeks in May, in the southern hemisphere.
[179] GA 229, lect.15th Oct.1923.
[180] The Carter Observatory Handbook, Wellington, New Zealand.

constellation of Gemini, which lasts for about one week, and is nearly as strong as the Perseus shower. But this is not exclusively a southern hemisphere star group, and its influence, although strong, appears to be less strong than that of the autumn Aquarid shower.

When we consider the strength of meteoric iron processes in the yearly cycle of the two hemispheres, we should take into account the different populations of the two hemispheres. The southern hemisphere has only about seven percent of the world's population; hence its much lesser quantity of summer meteoric iron is proportionately quite substantial, even if its summer meteor showers are smaller than its autumn showers. In the southern autumn there is also considerable meteoric activity, in March and April, from radiants in the southern sector of the heavens, from the direction of Corona Australus, Lyra, and Corvus.

It is, then, the celestial iron from these southern summer and autumn radiants that is especially imbued with forces from the archangel Michael, who is the guiding archangel of the elemental processes of autumn (for both hemispheres). It is the iron from these meteors that permeates the sulphurous presence in the hot summer skies above Australia, New Zealand, South America, South Africa, New Guinea, and southern Indonesia.

This meteoric process is then, the second dynamic of the autumn, counteracting the dynamic first mentioned in this chapter, that of the ahrimanic influences in the sulphur and decay processes. These two processes, developing in each hemisphere during its late summer and autumn, are the concomitant of the summer out-breath (although I omitted these aspects of the summertime from the chapter on St. John's Tide, in order to prevent the subject matter from becoming excessively complex). The following passage, again from Steiner's lecture on *The Four Seasons and the Archangels,* summarizes these two processes of autumn:

> And then we can see how, especially when autumn is approaching, there is a great raying out of sulphur from the nerve system toward the brain; the entire person can then be seen as a sulphur-illuminated phantom, so to speak. But raying into this bluish-yellow sulphur atmosphere come the meteor swarms from the blood. That is the other 'phantom'. While the sulphur phantom rises in clouds from the lower

part of the human being toward the head, the iron-forming process rays out from the head and pours itself like a stream of meteors into the life of the blood. Such is the human being, when Michaelmas draws near. (5th October, 1923)

This, then, is the inner reality of the southern hemisphere in February and March and of the northern hemisphere in August and September. And the situation is the result of the St. John's Tide, which (as we noted in Chapter Five) occurs in December and January in the southern hemisphere. In the Steiner passage I have just quoted, we encounter the term 'Michaelmas'. I mentioned this term earlier, as the name given to the days around the autumn equinox when the harvest festival was celebrated. I noted at that point that this term may have been used because in the church calendar a day in late September was set aside for the commemoration of the Archangel Michael.

We must ask whether the term 'Michaelmas' is still relevant for an autumn festival? This is because it refers to a date in the ecclesiastical calendar, and has been extended to refer to various old autumn traditions, some derived from the day of archangel Michael, but some non-Christian seasonal traditions. Most of the old traditions have now died out. One of the last to go, in England, was the custom of eating a goose at Michaelmas. This custom, of course, has nothing to do with the archangel Michael, or with the major dynamics in the hemisphere's aura at autumn.

It is probably the distorted remnant of a 'soul cake' ritual, wherein some food was especially prepared for the souls of the dead. But we have discovered that the day set aside in the church calendar for a major Christian festival – although it was approached through the church in a historical, non-seasonal way – does still have a hidden connection to the season. So St. John's Tide is rightly celebrated on December 25th in the southern hemisphere, and on June 24th in the north, because of the especial nearness of the sun gods, of those beings who in effect overshadowed John the Baptist, to the hemispheres at those times. And so it must be, too, with the placing of a day for the archangel Michael at the time of the northern hemisphere's autumn equinox. For there is a connection between this archangel and the autumn processes.

Michael – the archangel of the autumn

It is not possible to ascertain, from historical documents, why the church placed a commemorative day for this archangel in the autumn, on the September 29th. This date is given as the day when this archangel was seen, for the third time, at Mount Gargano, a major esoteric Christian mystery centre in Italy, in A.D. 492. Since the Mt. Gargano centre was a renowned holy place in early European Christian life, we may assume that this date became connected with the archangel thereafter.

Just a few years after this date, for the first time in Rome, a church (on the Via Salaria) was dedicated to the archangel Michael. The date for this dedication, also September 29th, may have been chosen in response to the visitation at Mt. Gargano. In the eighth century, the cult of this archangel developed strongly, and September 29th was the date used for the dedication of more churches to this being.

One reason for choosing an autumn date as the day of this archangel may well have been to connect this great being with the powerful meteoric process, which in autumn is specifically brought about in order to counteract the negative heritage of the summer, the sulphur 'dragon forces'. This connection would have been entirely appropriate in those times, for humanity still had an awareness of the reality of the spiritual worlds, and of the hierarchical beings, including the archangels. And, as we now know, the archangel Michael was portrayed then as the slayer of the dragon Ahriman.

Today, on the other hand, humanity is scarcely aware of the reality behind this legendary portrayal. Rudolf Steiner described how real actually is the background to this legendary motif. His spiritual knowledge and research showed that the widespread earnest reverence for this being in earlier times is entirely valid. It is precisely this archangel who has been granted the might to restrain the ahrimanic powers, so that they do not gain full control of humanity's soul forces. And this activity of the archangel Michael did not start with the Christian or Judaic religion; rather, it has been undertaken since remote times. The initiates of earlier cultures perceived this truth, and in their myths they portrayed for the wider community what they experienced of this great being.

In ancient Babylonian clay tablets, he is known as Marduk, who leads the gods in the battle against the dragon, Tiamat.

The archangel Michael is then the very quintessence of spiritual triumph, of conquering the dragon within. This means not only in a general sense of overseeing and protecting the evolution of humankind on Earth, but also in a direct, individual sense. A study of initiation texts of earlier times reveals that when the initiate succeeds in 'crossing the threshold' into the spiritual worlds, he is helped and accompanied by the archangel Michael. According to an ancient Hebrew text,

> When we were at prayer, there came to me Michael, the messenger of God. And I saw a chariot like the wind, its wheels were fiery, and I was taken up into the Paradise of Righteousness, and I saw the Lord... his face was flaming fire which could not be endured.[181]

Another such text reads:

> And the angel took me and led me thence to a fifth heaven. But the gate was closed. I said, "May we not enter?" He answered: "We cannot enter until Michael comes, who holds the keys to the Kingdom of Heaven"...and there came a great sound, as of thunder, and behold, a voice came, saying: "Let the gates be opened"...they opened, and there was a roar as of thunder. And Michael came, and the angel who was with me approached him, face to face.[182]

Such initiations were achieved only after the individuals had first overcome the dragon, the lower self, and had begun to manifest the spirit self. It was, therefore, particularly appropriate to link together the autumn dynamics with the archangel Michael, because the inner challenge brought by the autumn is so similar to that of the spiritual development nurtured by archangel Michael.

Following the initiates of earlier cultures, who had perceived the activity of Michael against Ahriman, the early Christian initiates, knowing that in the future this archangel would become especially active within the autumn, within

---

[181] In the Book of Adam & Eve, chapter 5, 1-4.
[182] The Third Book of Baruch, chapt. 1, in *Old Testament Pseudepigrapha*, London, OUP, 1979.

the autumnal meteoric iron process, had good reason for linking Michael to the autumn.

There was no doubt that he would be amongst what Rudolf Steiner describes as "the higher gods {who} endeavour to gain a victory over the ahrimanic powers, when autumn comes". Of course, it is also the case that Michael was, and is, active in the meteoric process generally, not only in the autumn, but whenever during the year shooting stars and meteorites appear.

The involvement of Michael with the meteoric iron process is indicated by references in the Zarathustrian religious texts from ancient Persia. In these texts, the archangel Michael is known as Mithra. The following extract obviously refers to the meteoric process and the activity of the archangel Michael within it,

> With his arms lifted up toward the abode of the immortals, Mithra, 'the Lord of wide pastures', drives forth from Paradise, in a beautiful chariot, that drives on, ever-swift...made of gold. On a side of the chariot of Mithra.... stand a thousand spears, well made and sharp-piercing. They go through the heavenly space, they fall upon the skulls of the Daevas {demons}. On a side of the chariot of Mithra, the Lord of wide pastures, are a thousand steel hammers, two-edged, well made. They go through the heavenly space, they fall upon the skulls of the Daevas. On a side of the chariot of Mithra...are a thousand iron maces, well made. They go through heavenly space, they fall through the heavenly space, upon the skulls of the Daevas.[183]

A major reason, then, for the association of the archangel Michael with the autumn is the fact that then the meteoric process within which he is active becomes especially important, in connection with the prominent sulphur-iron dynamic, autumn's heritage from the summertime. Strengthening the connection of Michael with the autumn is his close association with the sun beings in religious and esoteric texts. Indeed the name Micha-el is Hebrew for "Who is like God?" Now the term 'God' in the Old Testament often

---

[183] In the Mihir Yast, in the *Zend Avesta*, chapt. 31, Motilal Banarsidas, New Delhi, 1981.

refers to Jehovah, one of the Elohim. And the Elohim are the sun gods or 'Powers', the gods who are active in the (spiritual) sun, according to medieval theology. This viewpoint was confirmed by Rudolf Steiner.[184]

We have seen that one of the especial qualities of meteoric iron is that it derives from the sun ! We need to realize that there are in effect two kinds of iron on our planet. The one kind streamed into the planet long ago in an ether state, at the time of the fall of humanity, from Mars. This iron became part of the newly developing warm bloodstream of human beings, and enabled the ego to have a foothold in the physical body.

Through the presence of this iron in the bloodstream, the mind, the independent individual consciousness of human beings, could manifest. Through this iron, the heart and mind could begin to come to expression. But this cosmic process, through which the human being is evolving, was also used by luciferic spirits. They were able to influence human evolution through the inner fire arising in the human soul life via the inner fire of the Mars iron forces.

The second kind of iron, the kind that descends to the Earth via shooting stars, is truly sun-born iron, deriving from the inner, elemental forces of the sun. It is inwardly different from the old Mars iron; in it Michael and the normal hierarchical gods, rather than the luciferic beings, may offer humanity forces that strengthen the will, that allow the higher ego to manifest more strongly in us.

Modern humanity need not be condescending toward those earlier cultures which treated a piece of meteoric rock as sacred. When one livingly visualizes that a large meteorite (or 'bolide') weighing perhaps half a ton, is the material condensation of a stream of ethereal iron and other minerals, which has been poured out of the sun's ether body, in order to nourish the inner being of humanity, then indeed awe and wonder are fully valid feelings !

As I have mentioned, the early Christian initiates were aware that in the future Michael would become even more deeply connected with the meteoric process, during the autumn of each hemisphere:

> Those who had a spiritual understanding of the cycle of the year in the ancient mysteries...knew that

---

[184] In the Gospel of St. John cycle, lect. 20th May 1908.

during their own age, the mysterious event of the powers of Michael coming to the aid of the 'descending' human soul {that is, the soul during autumn} had not as yet taken place...but they also knew that this Michael power would eventually come to the aid {in a more direct way} of humankind on Earth...ancient wisdom therefore entered the day of Michael in the calendar on the 29th of September, a few days after the autumn equinox.[185]

That future time, which was prophetically foreseen in the fixing of an autumn date for the Michael festival, has now arrived. All these spiritual truths concerning the sun-born nature of the wonderful celestial iron in the meteors, and the activity of Michael in this process, over the ages, is summed up in the following quotation from Rudolf Steiner:

> And what is thus hurled out into the cosmos as 'sun substance' {via the sunspots}, that appears then within our solar system as comets and meteorites, {and} also the well-known phenomenon of shooting stars. Those beings, which govern the solar system {from} within the sun, they hurl these things out, especially in our age. They have already done this in earlier times, these things are not appearing only now, but they receive another significance now, than they had in earlier times.....
>
> Now those 'impulses' which exist in the iron which is hurled out, begin to have an especial significance for humanity. It is these impulses...which now...an especial spiritual being, who develops herewith his especial significance, and whom we call the 'Michael spirit' utilizes...in the cosmos. Thus for our age that element has entered into the cosmos, which was not present to the same degree in earlier times: that is, that the cosmic iron gives, through its spiritual significance to the 'Michael spirit'... the possibility to mediate between the spiritual {reality} and the material reality of the earth.[186]

---

[185] Lect. of 31st Mar. 1923, in The Cycle of the Year as Breathing process of the Earth.
[186] GA 231, lect. 17th Nov.1923.

With our recognition that the archangel Michael is now becoming more intimately present in the astral dynamics of each hemisphere's autumn we have uncovered the major leitmotif of the new autumn festival. But since the new festivals are also esoterically Christian, we must locate a connection between the activity of the cosmic Christ during autumn and that of the archangel Michael.

It is clear from the veiled reference to Michael in the Old Testament, and in other Hebraic religious-esoteric texts, that this archangel is extremely significant, that he is and has been active in human evolution, assisting the hierarchies as an intermediary between the sun gods and humanity. In these texts, he is in effect the instrument of God, that is, of the sun spirits. The Old Testament Judaic folk were the vessel for this great being's tasks in the evolution of humanity. The task of the Judaic culture then was, of course, to prepare for the coming to Earth of the foremost of the Powers, the cosmic Christ.

The archangel Michael was therefore especially closely linked to Israel in Old Testament times, as the Book of Daniel indicates (Dan. 10:13 and 12:1). Indeed, Rudolf Steiner's research showed that Michael was the vessel of the Christ being already in remote ages, long even before the development of the Old Testament Judaic mission. After the cosmic Christ united his being, spiritually, to the earth, Michael undertook to remain his servant, entering more deeply into the drama of humanity's earthly existence.

The profound connection between Michael and the cosmic Christ is beautifully indicated in an early Christian apocryphal text portraying a dialogue between the risen Christ and the disciple Bartholomew:

> And Bartholomew said: "Lord, when Thou went to be hung upon the cross, I followed Thee afar off, and saw Thee hung on the cross, and I saw the Angels coming down from Heaven and worshipping Thee. And then there came darkness; I beheld, and I saw that thou wast vanished away under the cross, and I heard only a voice in the Earth's interior....Tell me, Lord, whither wentest thou from the cross?"
>
> And Jesus answered and said: "Blessed art thou Bartholomew my beloved, because thou sawest this Mystery... when I vanished away from the cross, then I went down into Hades that I might bring up Adam

and all that were with him, according to the plea of Archangel Michael". Then, the ascent of Adam up out of Hades is seen, he was borne aloft by Angels.... Again Bartholomew said: "Lord, I saw the Angels ascending before Adam and singing praises. But one of the Angels, which was {a} very great {being}, superior to the rest of the Angels, would not ascend up with them; and there was in his hand, a sword of fire, and he was gazing steadfastly at Thee only. And all the Angels besought him to arise with him, but he would not".

We understand that St. Bartholomew is referring to the archangel Michael. In our present age of the sun-archangel, which will last for several centuries, it is possible for this great archangel to interweave his own powerful spiritual forces into the high astral substance that the shooting stars release into the atmosphere, as iron vapour, during the autumn. The following quotation describes the activity of Michael in the hemisphere's autumn:

When one feels all this in true earnestness, then from this feeling, there takes form a 'cosmic imagination'...and from this experience there arises, coming before the soul in living actuality, the being and form of Michael. Out of that, which I have described to you, there manifests the figure of Michael in his battle with the Dragon, with the animal nature of humankind, that is, with the sulphurizing process. And when one understands what is actually going on there, then the soul, which takes its own form and origin from the interweaving life of the cosmos, cannot but bring forth {as an imaginative image} that of the fight of Michael with the Dragon. But he appears with a pointing sword, pointing it toward the higher nature of the human being...and the arm of Michael appears to us in the midst of a sparkling shower of meteoric iron. These showers take form from the power that streams out from Michael's heart.[187]

---

[187] GA 229, lects. 5th & 15th Oct. 1923, (*Four seasons & the Archangels*).

This autumnal activity of Michael is essential for the spiritualization of the hemisphere's life forces in winter, for the development of certain spiritual forces, deep in the core of the planet. The joyous Holy Nights process could not be fully achieved without the power of Michael first clearing a pathway for the descent during autumn of the cosmic Christ and the spiritual sun forces that were absorbed during the summer. The hemisphere's astral aura must be brought to a high state of purity, in order to enable the 'birth' of the Chrestos radiance in winter. And precisely the same process has to be followed by any person who wishes to partake fully in the Holy Nights (see next chapters).

This is, then, the twice-yearly task of the archangel Michael, a task which is undertaken for each hemisphere:

> Before the yearly cycle is again completed and December {**that is, June in the south**} approaches, when the Christ impulse may be born in the quickened earth, the earth {hemisphere} must be cleansed, of the dragon, of the forces of Ahriman, by spiritual powers. The Michael power must unite with all that flows into the earth {hemisphere} as it inhales between September and December {between March and June in the south}.
>
> The purifying powers of Michael, conquering evil ahrimanic forces, must unite with this in-streaming breath, in preparation for the Christmas {Hallowed Night} festival that it may draw near in the right way, and so that the birth of the Christ impulse can be accomplished. Then the Christ impulse ripens and matures until the out-breathing at Easter {that is, spring}.[188]

Once the hemisphere has its springtime, it is necessary for this great archangel to absorb spiritual forces from the cosmos.

> Then the out-breathing into the cosmos begins again, then the Christ takes Michael with him, amidst this flowing out {of the earth's soul}, so that Michael may once again appropriate to himself from the cosmos

---

[188] From lect. 31st Mar. 1923 in *The Cycle of the Year as ...*

184

those forces which he had exhausted through his fight against the earthly ahrimanic realm.[189]

In Chapter Nine we will consider how an archangel is active in a minor dynamic in the opposite hemisphere to the one where he is the majestic regent of the season.

The Michael festival

The new Michael festival is not connected to the historical life of Christ. It cannot be fully expressed in the ecclesiastical festival cycle, when it is understood as an esoteric festival, for it can only arise through a striving toward an awareness of and a harmonizing with those processes in the hemisphere's aura that I have described. As Steiner taught, the new Michael festival can be created only when "the human being feels the resurrection of the soul within the 'burial of nature', in order to rightly counter the 'earthly burial {process}'."[190]

That is, perception of the powerful meteoric and Michaelic powers of autumn, which can enable humanity to achieve a spiritual victory over the earthly realm, with its power to 'bury' the spirit, and eventually to bring physical death, is an essential element in the creation of a Michael festival: "There, where nature is in decline, there the human being should commemorate his ascent, his resurrection in the spirit."[191]

This attitude, which is the basis of a Michael festival, is inspired by the second half of the historical Easter events, the resurrection of Christ, and proceeds into the present reality of the season of autumn: "The human being has arisen {through the fact of the resurrection of Christ}, and therefore can confidently be laid in the grave {because he will be able to arise out of death}."[192] Such a basis is exactly the opposite of that for the new Christian spring festival, as we described it in Chapter Four, where the blossoming springtime calls forth awareness that the Christ-being descended via death into the material world, in order that

---

[189] ibid.
[190] Lect. 21st May 1923 in *Man's Being, Destiny and World-evolution.*
[191] GA 306, lect. 19th April 1924.
[192] Lect. 1st April 1923 in *The Cycle of the Year as....*

humanity, although descended into matter, may continue on the pathway toward the final goal of earth existence.

Rudolf Steiner defines the festival we have been describing as a Michael festival, "this festival, the one which heralds the autumn".[193]

> The festival, which contains the thought: "he has risen and can {therefore} be tranquilly laid in the grave" must occur in the time when the leaves begin to turn yellow and fall from the trees… when {through} withering the plants incline to the earth, and all that develops on earth begins to be a symbol of the grave.[194]

The festival must occur at this time because then the archangel Michael is the regent of the hemisphere's elemental processes, as servant of the cosmic Christ in the life processes of the hemisphere. A festival that seeks to link humanity to an archangel must occur during the time that the archangel is the governing being in the hemisphere:

> The Michael festival – it will be a festival {placed} in the last days of September (*or March in the southern hemisphere*), when autumn approaches, the leaves wither, the branches grow bare and nature approaches its death, just as it faces a new budding life at Easter, and when we experience in nature's fading life how the soul of the Earth {in that hemisphere} is then united with the earth {hemisphere} and brings with it Michael, out of the clouds.[195]

It is so important to note that here the word 'September' is spoken because Rudolf Steiner, and his audience, were both situated in the northern hemisphere ! That is why I have inserted 'March' into the quote given above. This brings in another very significant point about language, about understanding the context of Rudolf Steiner's words.

As I briefly noted earlier, when he says the phrase, "the earth" in lectures on festivals, he actually means "hemisphere" – in most cases. For example, in the lecture

---

[193] Lect. 8th April 1923.
[194] Lect. 1st April 1923.
[195] GA 224, lect. 23rd May 1923.

above, "...the soul of the Earth {in that hemisphere} is then united with the earth", I have made a faithful translation by spelling the first word 'earth' with a capital, but the second use of the word has no capital. This is because the first occurrence is about the Earth-soul or combination of spirit beings who make up the astral body or soul of planet Earth; whereas the second occurrence is about the hemisphere in its seasonal cycle.

Actually, Rudolf Steiner could have avoided saying, "*the soul of the Earth {in that hemisphere}*" because he is referring to only that part of the Earth-soul which is in one hemisphere. But he prefers to address this one part of the Earth-soul as "the Earth-soul". If he had used the expression, "*the one half of the Earth-soul {in that hemisphere} is then united with the earth {hemisphere}...*" then his listeners would have been impelled to confront the two hemisphere situation; but as we already noted, this is a truth for which his audiences, in general, were not ready.

Hence Rudolf Steiner also states in the same lecture,

> now with us {*people in Germany i.e., the northern hemisphere,*} it is winter, the Holy Nights, the winter solstice time; thus, this is the time when the Earth-soul is entirely united with the earth. For then the covering of snow blankets the earth ...

Note two very important things here. Firstly the term 'earth' here actually means the hemisphere; and this is the case in all the verses of the Soul Calendar. Secondly, it is implied here (but not fully spelled out) that the Holy Nights are the same thing as the wintertime. However this implication is exactly spelled out, in many other lectures, as will be shown in the chapters on the winter season.

But, it is precisely the cultural problem for some people, especially those affected by the European religious-cultural background, that the hemispherical aspect is hard to grasp. And from this problem there arises a rejection of this very significant research of Rudolf Steiner. In the lecture given before the one we have quoted above, concerning the Michael festival, he tells his audience that, the 'Michael-Idea' will become living pre-eminently through an autumn festival.[196]

Hence the idea of creating a Michael festival in the southern hemisphere in September, so not placed in the autumn but in its springtime, can not be a festival through which the influence of Michael as the regent of the season is activated; for this to occur, this archangel needs to be this regent in the aura. This archangel is not there as the dynamically powerful Regent, in springtime, up above, in the astral aura of the southern hemisphere, monitoring the elemental beings as the meteoritic iron streams in.

Hence Rudolf Steiner taught that a Michael festival must be celebrated in autumn. We can see that this is indeed the case, because in the lectures on the Michaelmas festival, before commencing to tell the audience what happens in the autumn (and other seasons) he makes a very clear statement about with the southern hemisphere. In this lecture for example, he has such passages as,

> As autumn approaches the soul-aspect of the earth {hemisphere} has drawn itself back into the earthly element, with the drawn-in 'breath-power', until the Holy Nights time occurs...Michael had cleansed the earth {during the autumn} in that hemisphere} is then united with the earth {hemisphere} so that the Holy Nights the birth of the Christ-impulse can take place in the right way..."

Now at first this looks like a statement which is about a global phenomenon, but before describing these deeply spiritual dynamics, and bearing in mind that this teaching is intimately interwoven with our planet having two hemispheres, he tells his audience this,

> In regard to this breathing process, we can only look **at one part of the Earth** {at a time}. We are now considering that part which we ourselves {*in Germany, hence northern hemisphere*} are living on: in the other, **the opposite, side of the Earth,** the conditions {in the spiritual forces of the atmosphere} **are the opposite.**[197]

---

[196] GA 224, lect. 13th April 1923.
[197] GA 223, lect. of 31st Mar. 1923, *The Cycle of the Year as a..* p.12.

The words in italics are added by me; and I have used bold fonts to emphasize the key words. The phrase, "*the opposite side of the Earth*" **means the southern hemisphere.** So we are being told here that what Rudolf Steiner teaches about the autumn in the northern hemisphere, with its inherent influence of Michael, applies to the southern hemisphere **in its autumn,** which is in March-April. This insistence from Rudolf Steiner that a Michael festival has to occur in the autumn, does not come from an abstract attitudinal principle. It is due to the possibility that **only then can people become experientially aware of the spiritual activity behind the process involving meteoric iron versus the sulphur influence.** It is in the autumn that this process is maximal and permeated by forces from the great archangel, Michael:

> The Michael festival must be linked with a great and sustaining inner experience of the human being, with that inner force which summons us to develop self-consciousness out of nature consciousness through the strength of our thoughts, the strength of our will, so that we may be able to master the meteoric iron process in the blood, which is the opponent of the sulphurizing process. To be sure, sulphur and iron have flowed in human blood ever since there was a human race. What takes its course there between sulphur and iron determines the unconscious nature of the human being. It must be lifted into consciousness. We must learn to know this process as the expression of the inner conflict of Michael with the dragon; we must learn to raise this process into consciousness.[198]

The new Michael festival will occur in late March in the southern hemisphere, and in late September in the north. It is a festival for,

> the conquest of anxiety and fear; a festival of inner strength and initiative; the commemoration of selfless self-consciousness...at this autumn festival of Michael there should grow...everything which opposes love of ease and anxiety; and which should

---

[198] Lect. 13th Oct, 1923, in the *Four Seasons and the Archangels* cycle.

develop towards inner initiative and free, strong will.[199]

The Michael festival has a unique aspect, namely that it requires, and brings the participants into, a relationship with this archangel who is the helper or inspiring companion to every person who today seeks spiritual development. True spiritual knowledge is inspired by this very archangel, who enables modern intellectual humanity to grasp spiritual truths in a clear, conscious manner. The full significance of this archangel is not, however, the task of this book. The reader may turn to Rudolf Steiner's works for further study of the extraordinary importance of this being.

To strive toward spiritual consciousness by strengthening and also spiritualizing the ego, rather than by sinking it into a semi-conscious state is what Rudolf Steiner described as a "Michael-ic" striving. Through such a striving, one may develop perception of the changing spiritual reality behind the changing seasons of the year. And since there is virtually no historical content about the theme of the Michael festival, it has to be formed through becoming attuned to the actual elemental and spiritual dynamics of the autumn. The creation of a 'Michael' festival has to be a Michaelic deed !

This is why Rudolf Steiner emphasized that it would not be right to simply 'formulate' a Michael festival; in this respect the seasonal festivals are different from the historical-ecclesiastical festivals. In fact, all four new Christian seasonal festivals have this Michaelic quality.

The kind of attitude toward nature that Michael seeks from humanity is not one that declares we have no inner connection to the cycle of the year, but rather one that acknowledges that, unaware as we may be in our normal consciousness of the cosmic spiritual reality manifesting 'behind' the cycle of the year, we are nevertheless deeply connected to it. And the great Archangel seeks also the acknowledgement that the time is now at hand for us to redevelop our connection to the spirit manifesting in the seasons. In Steiner's words,

> Precisely through that which is our innermost being, we are most intimately united with the inner reality

---

[199] Lect. 5th Oct, 1923, in the *Four Seasons and the Archangels* cycle

of nature, we are not beings who only stand at nature's doors and knock. [200]

The attainment of such a perception requires initiative and also cognitional courage. There is a hidden fear placed in the soul, which seeks to prevent the conscious quest toward the spiritual renewal:

> The Michael forces do not let themselves be attained through any kind of passivity....They allow themselves to be attained solely and only through the human being, with a loving will, making himself {or herself} an instrument of the divine-spiritual powers.[201]

In this sense, Rudolf Steiner described the Michael festival as a festival of courage.[202] It is precisely through the exceptionally close relationship of the archangel Michael to spiritually questing souls that the Michael festival will be so significant. For Michael wills to assist humanity to develop a spiritual consciousness; whereas Uriel and Gabriel and Raphael are working with aspects of our being less responsive to our volition. (In Chapter Nine we will consider all four archangels and their interweaving with each other.) The devotion of Michael to the spiritualization of our consciousness is wonderfully indicated in a Christian apocryphal text portraying a dialogue between Michael and departed souls in the lower soul world:

> And Michael answered and said: 'Harken when Michael speaketh; I am he that stands in the presence of God always. As the Lord liveth, before whose countenance I stand, I cease not for one day nor night to pray continually for the race of man...And I say that if any man doeth but a little good, I will strive for him and protect him'.[203]

There is an additional aspect of autumn that is deeply connected to the theme of spiritual rejuvenation and the battle against the dragon. When in autumn a plant's

---

[200] Lect. 25th Nov. 1923 in the cycle, *Mystery Centres.*
[201] Lect. 28th Sept, 1923 in *Michaelmas & the soul-forces of Man.*
[202] Lect. 8th April, 1923, in *The Cycle of the Year.*
[203] In *The Apocalypse of St. Paul,* in the Apocryphal New Testament.

blossoms wither and die away, then the nature sprites living with that plant are freed, and they seek to arise into the soul world. This freeing of forces creates a living elemental reality that contrasts with the fading, dying material world. Awareness of this 'living water' or astral vitality is part of the Michael festival.

As Rudolf Steiner stressed, "one of the spiritual elements of the autumn is this ascending spiritual element which is becoming free, arising out of the withering material world".[204] The reader will note that this discovery of ascending spiritual substantiality in autumn contrasts with the perspective expressed many times in these pages, namely that in autumn, there is an in-breathing process. These two dynamics are not contradictory.

The in-breath process refers to an over-all 'inhaling' by the Earth-soul of its forces in the autumn hemisphere, whereas the ascent mentioned above refers to specific beings (plant and blossom sprites) who are released from their tasks at this time of the year. Similarly, in the springtime, although there is an overall ascent of forces and beings from the spring hemisphere, a contrasting phenomenon occurs,

> Certain beings, who are not united to the earth {hemisphere} in winter – but who are present in the cosmic environs of the earth – descend to the ground in spring. They unite themselves with the plant life. There they enjoy a kind of rest, in that they unite themselves to the earth {hemisphere}. The hemisphere's own life is itself stimulated through this union of spiritual substantiality to the earth, which arises through the peace which these beings experience here. The spiritual eye sees life, rich and abundant, stream into the earth {hemisphere} from above, in its atmospheric environs.[205]

People can assist the establishment of the new autumn Michael festival by developing our perception of such realities,

---

[204] Lect. 1st April, 1923, in *The Cycle of the Year....*
[205] Lect. 16th Oct. 1916

The human being may feel the resurrection of the soul at that time when nature is 'lying in the grave', in order to rightly counter the earthly death reality. If in so doing we create that festival which is related to the Easter {*that is, spring*} festival as the autumn sun is related to the springtime sun, then will humanity have gained the strength to give to itself a {true, seasonal} festival.[206]

This activity itself is precisely the Michaelic path;

The spiritual life of the human being on earth is connected with the dying and declining physical life. For in the act of thinking, the physical matter in our nerves is destroyed. Thought wrests itself forth from dying matter... we thus learn to feel the kinship of humanity's spirituality with the spirituality of nature. And this can again give us the impulse to strengthen our human will; it can inspire us to permeate our will with spirituality. When we permeate the will with spirituality, we become associates in Michael's activity on earth.[207]

Until those people who find the will to assist Michael by taking up the challenge of the new festivals, which derive from the hemispheric seasonal cycle, the tasks of the Michael school will remain uncompleted.[208] As Rudolf Steiner told one audience, "When one can once again spiritually experience the seasons of the year, that is the 'Michael consciousness'"[209] But should the dragon forces in humankind be un-resisted in autumn, then, as the nature sprites seek to ascend into the soul world, to withdraw from the material processes, they can be ensnared by the dragon, by ahrimanic beings.[210] This was explained in another lecture,

In accordance with the extent to which we human beings have permeated ourselves with the strong

[206] Lect. 21st May 1923.
[207] Lect. 2nd April, 1923.
[208] The term, The Michael School, refers to all those souls who received, some centuries ago, in the spiritual world prior to returning to the Earth , inspiration, from this archangel, about achieving spiritual renewal today.
[209] Lects. 29th & 30th Nov. 1923.
[210] Lect. 28th Sept, 1923.

Michael power, it will be we who 'lead' the elemental beings upward, into the spirit, toward which they are striving.[211]

The future state of the Earth will be determined by the extent to which this 'leading up' is achieved:

> The human being will not only have breathed physical oxygen in and out, the human being will also have participated in the development of nature, will have participated in casting a spell over spirit beings in nature and also releasing them from such spells.[212]

He continues, telling his audience that, the extent to which we have or have not doomed such elementals to the control of Ahriman determines the degree to which we can really achieve the high ideals we have theoretically laid claim to. The elusive factor that lames our will, preventing initiative, is directly influenced by the quality of our own influence on the nature sprites. We can help ourselves by striving to view nature as an expression of spiritual and elemental processes. Through the Michael festival, through the striving to participate in the autumn processes, so as to manifest our own initiative for spiritual development in a free and courageous manner, this unfree laming influence can be overcome. We can release the nature sprites.

The attainment of inner freedom through development of the forces needed to overcome the dragon, this is offered to humanity in the meteoric iron process. Rudolf Steiner presented an invaluable description of this opportunity in a lecture on 16th Nov. 1923;

> If we were beings who had no iron in our blood, then in our souls the feeling for freedom, the impulse for freedom could manifest quite well, but we would never have a body which we could use, in order to carry out these impulses to freedom. The fact that we can not only grasp the concept of {inner} freedom, but also sense in our body the power to make this body the vessel of the impulse to freedom, derives from this: that in our age we can learn how

---

[211] Ibid.
[212] Lect. 17th Nov. 1923 (in the afternoon).

...Michael is able to place the cosmic iron in his service. And that we can learn, if we ever more and more understand the Michael impulse, to place the 'inner iron' in us at the service of the impulse to freedom.[213]

With the study of such mysteries comes understanding of the maxim which the great initiates of ancient times gave to their students, for the season of autumn. "Look around you", they said, and this was, as Rudolf Steiner indicated, "an exhortation to that which should be striven toward, by the soul".[214] The proper focus of the autumn festival, as we have noted, is the soul, the astral body. The acolytes were advised to consider the stark polarity in the elemental influences of the earth's aura at autumn; to consider the polarity and to form a conscious relationship to it.

Summing up the nature of the new autumn festival, Steiner explained:

> Despite the withering, decaying world of nature, the eternal lives in the human being. This we should focus on, spiritually, now; that is, that spiritual essence which, in life after death {and while we are still on Earth, through initiation}, brings us resurrection ! [215]

As we contemplate the forming of a Michael festival, some guiding thoughts arise in the soul. A world of autumnal decay and bareness lies around us. And yet in the fiery radiance of orange-red leaves now meeting our gaze, it is as if a sign is given to us; a sun-born power strong and triumphant is drawing near.

For to spirit vision, there lives amidst autumn's subdued and mellow world, surging cascades of radiant spiritual forces, forces that push away fear from human hearts, that subdue the shadow self of the seeker. High overhead, shooting stars hurtle through the night, dispersing sun-born celestial iron through the skies. Vivified by the presence of Michael, this iron now becomes a sword in the hand of the archangel of autumn.

---

[213] Lect. 16th Nov. 1923.
[214] Lect. 8th April, 1923.
[215] Ibid.

When Rudolf Steiner revealed the inner significance of iron within the human organism, and its connection to the autumnal activity of Michael, he gave us a simple, expressive meditation:

> O human being, you mould it to servicing {in} many of your works, you manifest it, in accordance with the value of its substance. Yet, it will bring you healing only when it reveals to you the lofty power of its spirit.[216]

Themes of Michaelmas

We remember: the mission of archangel Michael; his unceasing work on behalf of humankind since remote ages and his will to serve the intentions of the cosmic Christ.

We contemplate: the autumn; from the summertime, a sulphur vapour permeates the hemisphere's atmosphere, providing a vehicle for the dragon. The in-breath brings this sulphur down to the earth, with the descending elemental beings; plant life begins to wither and fade, releasing multitudes of nature sprites. As the Earth-soul, through the in-breath, is quickened, our thought life is enhanced; ahrimanic forces seek to influence the lower self, where an enhanced sulphur presence exists, to incite fear, hate, and anxiety, and to ensnare the released elementals.

But celestial iron forces from meteors permeate the air we inhale; this iron, in which the power of Michael is active, then permeates our bloodstream; above, archangel Michael guides this process.

We realize and seek to experience: spiritual development and the rise of inner strength, which are especially possible now, and necessary to prevent further imprisonment of elemental beings. In our being, the iron forces are raying into the blood, weakening the power the ahrimanic sulphur has with us. In our being and in the hemisphere's aura, Michael battles to cleanse the earth, so that the seeker may develop in winter, the Life-spirit, so that the cosmic Christ forces, now descending into the hemisphere, may unite the cosmic Life-spirit to the Earth's ether body.

---

[216] Lect. 5th Oct, 1923 in *The Four Seasons*

We seek to achieve: a closer connection to the archangel, who is the way to the mysteries, and the Spirit of our Age. And we seek to achieve further courage and insight for the tasks of our age. And an ever clearer awareness of the meteoric iron, of its presence and power in us. And we seek to strive thereby to develop the Spirit-self qualities so that during the Holy Nights of winter we may be attuned to, and receive, a gift of Life-spirit from Christ Jesus.

The difficulty of grasping the idea of the new seasonal festivals is high-lighted also by a New Age writer, who in commenting on Rudolf Steiner's lectures about Michaelmas stated, that the autumn equinox of course occurs twice each year as there are two hemispheres, but Rudolf Steiner was not concerned with this, "he was referring to the autumn equinox as an abstract geophysical concept."[217] Nothing could be further from the nature of how Rudolf Steiner thought. He was referring to the actual reality of the Middle Kingdom and all of its fascinating beings, and especially how the great Archangel Michael, closely assisting the cosmic Christ, worked with their activities amidst the etheric and astral influences created by the autumn.

---

[217] Corinne Heline, in *Star Gates*, (Rosicrucian Fellowship publications),1975.

CHAPTER SEVEN

MIDWINTER-HOLY NIGHTS AND THE CHRIST CHILD

As the winter draws near, the in-breath of that hemisphere is completed; the Earth-soul has drawn its forces down beneath the soil. Its powers weakened, the sun journeys low across the sky, creating less light and heat in the atmosphere. No longer do shimmering currents of ether energies spiral upward, carrying the elemental beings. Elemental beings and ethers are now concentrated below, in the ground. The gnomes have become intensely active underground, moving at will through the layers of rock and minerals. The many spiritual beings that form the soul of the Earth are now incarnate, so to speak, and thus the hemisphere is intensely awake.

In the winter nights, the moon rises high in the sky, staying for about fifteen hours above the horizon, while the daytime sun is gone after perhaps only nine hours. The moon, which regulates the ether body of the Earth, now has a greater influence in the winter hemisphere, than the sun. This predominance of the lunar forces is revealed by a beautiful winter phenomenon – snowflakes !

The influence of the moon, numerologically, is associated with the number 6. For example, the moon's nodal regression cycle, the time it takes to return in its orbit to the point where it intersects the apparent orbit of the sun, is 18.6 years; its 'naros' which is connected to its nodal cycle. This is the time before a new moon will again occur on the same day in the calendar, at the same time of day, and in the same position in the heavens as the current instance, and takes 600 years.

This keynote rhythm of six was perceived by ancient peoples and reflected in the rituals of their moon rites. The principal rituals of the Druids were held on the sixth day of the new moon; in bands of six they would set out to gather the mistletoe, a moon-governed plant, which flowers in winter.

When in winter the raindrops turn into snow, each snowflake is a hexagram, formed on the structure of a six-pointed star. As Eskimo folklore tells, the moon is the 'sender of the snow'. Moisture is formed from the intermingling of the chemical-ether forces of the Earth with those that ray down from the moon. If the precipitation forms when the earth's light-ether is receiving minimal solar ethers, then the lunar ether rays encounter mainly the old, decaying light-ether which is electrical energy. From the combined activity of these two forces, that is, the electrical energy produced by decaying light-ether and the moisture generated by the chemical-ethers, the hexagram pattern emerges.[218]

In winter too, the weather becomes stormier, wilder. We sometimes say, "the elements are battling each other". Behind this expression there lives a reality. When the unpredictable, energized condition develops in wind and rain, creating blizzards or driving storms, then malignant, ahrimanic elemental beings are manifesting. For they experience an intensification of their consciousness in winter. During the summer they had to accept being controlled by the divine spirits manifesting within the sun's forces. Nevertheless, in bringing to completion the summer growth, they have experienced a kind of ecstasy, for they were unfolding their strongest creative forces in that activity. But now, in the winter, they are freed of this control.[219]

Through their disharmonious, destructive nature the storms and heavy fogs and blizzards arise. The 'frost giants' of fairy lore are the ahrimanic gnomes, whose urge is to create excessive cold and frosts; the 'water giants' are likewise ahrimanic undines, through whom floods and thick fogs derive. When violent storms develop, such as hurricanes, then the storm giants, or demonic sylphs, are active. Demonic pyrausta become 'fire giants', who, in summer, fan the flames of bushfires, as well as causing searing heat waves.[220]

The influence of these lowly elemental beings in the 'middle kingdom' of faery, and thus in nature, is similar to that of human egotism in social interaction; Rudolf Steiner called them "the servants of earth egotism". Their power is connected to the strength of the so-called lower self in humankind. Hence initiates of the Judaic and Christian

---

[218] Lect. 13th Oct. 1923.
[219] GA 218, lect. 16th Nov. 1922.
[220] ibid.

cultures, in their apocalyptic texts, always describe weather catastrophes as linked to future times when decadent or evil thoughts and feelings are given free expression by humanity.

So a fundamental dynamic of the wintertime is the strengthening of malignant elementals.

> Winter, however, is the time in which the earth {hemisphere} develops that which is in its egotistical atmosphere; it is the time when that which is in it triumphs over that which, coming from the cosmos in the summer, works into the earth, bestowing its blessing...Our soul has the same forces in it, even if only in embryonic form, as those which are active outside us in the wind and weather and in the elemental powers; they are active within us as forces of thinking, feeling, and willing. When the winter comes, enabling the egotism of the earth with its elemental powers to become more potent...then one feels that all this is related to the human being's own inner world.[221]

Thus the outer phenomenon of increased hours of darkness and a weaker, paler sun has a corresponding inner reality, the increase of malignant astral influences in the hemisphere's astral and ether organism. This correspondence, this inner reality, was known to people in earlier times. Take the legend of 'the Wild Hunt'. A band of demonic, ghostly fiends and jet-black hounds led by a terrifying huntsman, rage through the sky on dark stormy nights around the winter solstice, their shrieking and howling heard above the tops of the windswept snow-clad trees. In the Shetland Islands, these were known as "the Yuletide host", in Germany as "das Wüthende Heer" (the raging hosts).

In olden times in Europe, the community practised various customs to protect itself from such malignant influences. For example, pine resin was burnt during the nights and, as in parts of Asia, processions of people making as loud a noise as possible made their way through the villages and towns. In the Shetland Islands, the belief persists that around the winter solstice, the Yuletime, the

---

[221] Lect. 8th April 1923 from *Cycle of the Year as Breathing-process*.

"trows" (trolls or ahrimanic gnomes) are released from the subterranean depths of the earth and thus have access to its surface, where they seek to harm human beings. The present-day children's festival of Hallowe'en, with its demon masks and lights, is the remnant of the ancient Celtic winter protection rites.

Hence, as I have already mentioned, a meditation for wintertime in the ancient initiation centres was "guard thyself from evil".[222] In earlier times, people experienced how the earth is "on its own" in winter, how the interaction between the telluric middle kingdom and the sun beings virtually ceases. The in-breath of winter is not only an ether process, it is also an astral or soul process:

> At wintertime, the astral body of the earth {hemisphere}, which is interrelated with that of the sun, draws back from the sun; it is left to its own resources, it withdraws into the centre of the earth.[223]

We need to grasp the truth that the spiritual reality behind the sense world and its life processes is as real as these words indicate. For an anthroposophical worldview that accepts this concept generally, but blocks it in regard to the seasons, will hinder the development of the new festivals, which could bring humankind into a living relationship with the cosmic Christ. Rudolf Steiner's words refer to a hemispherical phenomenon; each hemisphere undergoes this process during its wintertime. As Steiner indicated,

> The astral body of the earth undergoes transformations throughout the course of the year; these transformations are opposite **in the two hemispheres** of the Earth.[224]

In other words, during winter the Earth-soul in the winter hemisphere, awakens, or draws back down into the earth, and the aura of the winter hemisphere separates from the sun's aura. But since this is a hemispherical process, the Earth-soul in the other hemisphere passes over into a sleep or 'excarnate' condition. Hence Rudolf Steiner taught that,

---

[222] GA 100, lect. 22nd Nov. 1907.
[223] Lect. 27th Nov. 1907.
[224] GA 98, lect. 13th Dec. 1907.

> The Earth-soul is never really in sleep {completely}; rather, when it lets its waking phase pass over into sleep for one hemisphere, it then transfers its waking activity **to the other hemisphere**.[225]

The separation of the Earth and sun that occurs each year; in fact, twice a year, once for each hemisphere, is a repetition, so to speak, of the cosmic event wherein the Earth, which had been part of the sun, was cast out into space and then gradually condensed and began to orbit around the sun. This event took place in the Hyperborean age, which preceded the Lemurian age. While still within the sun, the Earth was of course not yet a solid material globe, it existed as an ether and astral (soul) organism.

And of course when the Earth was within the sun, the sunlight could not shine upon the planet from outside; the sun's forces were an inherent part of that primeval predecessor of the Earth. Once cast out of the sun, now isolated from the radiant solar forces, from the sun beings, receiving their influence from afar, the Earth became more and more dense, less and less permeable to the forces of the sun, less permeated by solar ether rays.

A deep purpose has been active behind the process that has led to the earth's experiencing now the ongoing 'cosmic winter' phase; its existence as a satellite, orbiting around the sun. This purpose is that the Earth, through its and humanity's striving, shall develop in itself the spiritual light or state of consciousness that the sun already has. Only through being placed in a state of isolation is it possible for the planet to develop its own existence and to then evolve further. Only in this way could the human life wave develop into individual spirits, with individual physical, ethereal, and astral (soul) bodies. The spiritual potential of the individual can emerge, through life after life. Indeed, the spiritualization of the earth depends upon humanity developing its spiritual potential.

It is in this way that the transformation of the Earth into a star, a sun, in the far distant future is possible. The new festivals that we seek to create will play an important role in this spiritualizing process. Through the cosmic wintertime humanity has evolved individual souls in which individual egos can now manifest and maintain consciousness-except,

---

[225] Lect. 23rd Mar. 1913.

that is, at night when in the absence of the sun, we tend toward a sleep state.

In the winter, when the inner separation of hemisphere and sun reoccurs, a tendency toward sleep arises in a portion of the Earth-soul in that wintertime hemisphere. Animals and certain kinds of elemental beings, which are so active in spring and early summer, now having been drawn down into the ground, become quiescent; "at rest and still, they remain there".[226] Otherwise, the winter brings an intensified consciousness to the various beings that constitute the earth soul.

Our own consciousness is also intensified in the winter. Our thinking life, which is connected to the gnomes, becomes intensely active in winter. It is especially in the activity of thinking that our ego manifests itself. Our personality does not have access to much that belongs to our feelings and our will. Thus each winter is a testament to the divine goal behind the separation of the Earth from the sun: the development of conscious (ego-ic) human beings.

But this purpose is not simply fulfilled through the attainment of ego-hood, for humanity's ego consciousness needs to be lifted up beyond egotism into awareness of the spiritual reality of life. In winter, the interest in transcending our personal self manifests in the feeling for community, the social urge that leads to gift giving and communal meals and games, for example.

In the darkness of winter, the human ego feels its inner strengthening, and in seeking to transcend itself, strives for community with others. We may say that the ego becomes more radiant, more illumined by the spirit, as a result of this inner urge. A winter verse in the Soul Calendar (verse 43), when rightly understood, indicates this dynamic.

> In the wintry depths grows warm
> true being of the spirit;
> It gives to World-maya,
> Through forces of the heart, real inner being.[227]
> The coldness all around* is defied in humankind,
> whose fire-of-soul grows stronger. (* literally, 'world's')

---

[226] Lect. 5th Oct. 1923.
[227] The expression, 'real inner being' is literally 'powers of existence' (Daseinsmächte).

203

The hemisphere also develops a strong inner striving in winter; it is impelled to develop a definite activity in its ether body, or else the springtime renewal of life could not occur. The intense activity and power of the ether processes of spring are indirectly visible to us; in winter, we see little sign of the hemisphere's ether forces, but they are active then too, inwardly, as it were. In the winter soil are countless seeds, which developed in plants during the summer and autumn, and since have fallen to the ground. Received into the dark soil of Mother-earth, they are exposed to the winter's moisture and coldness, inducing the chemical changes that make germination possible.

This is a powerful process, the fertilization of the plant realm, affecting the buds and roots of perennials as well as the seeds of new plants. These physical processes derive from the gnomes' activity using the life-ether. As Rudolf Steiner put it, "now we find that the gnomes are rapidly 'weaving' around, whirring around the roots of the plants".[228] The life-ether activity undertaken by the gnomes, which stimulates the root systems of plants, also affects the corresponding part of the human ether body-the head area, including the brain.

In earlier times, people were aware of the intense activity undertaken in winter to maintain the fertility of the earth. This awareness was the origin of ritual dances that took place around the winter solstice; these dances still survived (no doubt in corrupted form) in many parts of Europe until the 1930s. They were sword or stick dances, wherein the earth was briskly tapped or star formations formed by holding the swords up in the air. When the dancers were asked why they carried out this dance, they would answer that the crops would fail if the dances were not performed and also that they wanted to awaken the 'earth spirits'.

In addition to the gnomes, certain nature sprites that would prefer to follow the sun-beings, and who find the winter a dismal prison, must be present in the wintertime in order that later the spring and summer may successfully unfold their fertility. In the wintertime, the Earth-soul in that hemisphere awakens, which includes not only the gnomes but many great, divine hierarchical beings. And the people of earlier times felt this awakening:

---

[228] Lect. 2nd Nov. 1923 in *Man as a symphony of the creative Word*.

The human being felt as it were alone with the earth in the cosmos at the winter solstice, and actually sensed the descent, again, of a divine spiritual reality into the earthly realm. Then the Earth-soul creates out of its own being what it can so make, at a time when the cosmic influences are minimal.[229]

The isolation of the hemisphere in winter is also an important factor for its ether forces:

At this time, for each hemisphere, the solar ether rays coming to the earth are withdrawn; something happens then which is similar to when the sun went away {that is, in Hyperborean times}.[230]

The creative striving by the earth in the winter hemisphere is, again, part of the spiritualization process, the Earth developing its own inner creative forces in anticipation of its future 'sun' existence. How will a solar power or force develop through this winter process? What kind of creative energy is accessible to the winter hemisphere, to stimulate its own ether body, its own ether and astral auras, when they have been separated from the sun? The source of the needed energy is the 'inner sunlight', the sunlight that was absorbed into the earth soul during the spring and summer and that is now, in winter, present beneath the ground !

From its own forces, which it has retained from the summer and autumn days, the earth produces, when the sun has its least influence, its own especial 'raiment' for the shortest days of the year.[231]

Such inner changes as these were perceived by people in earlier ages. Rudolf Steiner describes it like this,

At the time of the winter solstice they felt themselves to be intimately united with the earth, with all that which the earth {hemisphere} had preserved from the time of the warming, brightening summer. [232]

---

[229] Lect. 25th Dec. 1921 and 26th Dec. 1921
[230] From an archive lecture of 1905.
[231] Lect. 25th Dec. 1921.

[232] Lect. 26th Dec. 1921.

In discussing the summer festival, we saw how the out-breathed soul forces were then permeated by the sun's ether and its inner, spiritual light. These sun forces are united to the hemisphere's aura as it descends during the autumn. In the springtime, it is the solar life-ether that is absorbed into the Earth's ether body; around the summer solstice the actual devachanic inner sunlight is brought into union with the Earth's astral aura. These processes are of especial interest here for they have a connection to some aspects of the present-day Christmas festival. When the hemisphere 'holds its breath' at winter,

> ...its soul and spirit nature is completely absorbed. Deep in the interior of the earth rests all that which the Earth {hemisphere} had unfolded during the summertime, so as to be activated by the cosmos. Everything which had opened up, surrendering itself to cosmic forces during the summer, has been absorbed by the earth, and rests in the depths of the Earth.[233]

Rudolf Steiner pointed out that it is the presence of these solar ether forces that enables root vegetables to be stored over winter, if they are placed in the ground, not just in the cellar.[234] But the solar forces that permeate the Earth's interior in winter are not only from the sun's ether rays; the innermost spiritual sun radiance is there, too. It is in this special, sun-permeated state that the Earth-soul awakens, or incarnates, as it were. It is the return of the multitude of spiritual beings, beings as evolved as the dominions, back into the earth that causes the awakening in winter.

What happens, then, beneath our feet in winter? As the plants die away in autumn and early winter, their seeds fall to the ground and seek to take root in the soil. The gnomes perceive the complex geometrical forms of the different plants, the ideas, the archetypal thoughts, the cosmic forces lying behind their structure.[235] These insights flow into the gnomes; they do not have to make any analytical deductions.

They possess a kind of 'automatic' intelligence, a universal intelligence, which does not depend on logical

---

[233] Lect. 31st Mar. 1923.
[234] Lect. 23rd Dec. 1922.
[235] Lect. 2nd Nov. 1923.

processes. The other elemental beings involved in plant growth, having been drawn down into the ground, develop a receptive, quiescent state. The plant and mineral kingdoms become interwoven, or their nature beings do, that is. "In winter", as Rudolf Steiner noted, "the elemental beings of the plant realm meet in the earth those of the mineral realm".[236]

Around the time of the winter solstice, this intermingling intensifies, and the plant elementals, the undines and sylphs, experience a deepening of consciousness. For the consciousness of the Earth-soul, when it is centred within its physical-mineral body, via the activity of the gnomes, is profound. When we are awake and perceiving the world through our senses, we are aware of the things in the surrounding environment. So too, the Earth-soul in the wintertime. The gaze of the beings in that hemisphere extends far out into cosmic space.

The Earth-soul contemplates all that is happening amongst the stars and planets, its consciousness becoming imbued with the cosmic processes; and it comprehends the effect of these processes on the earth, on plant life for example.[237] This profound intelligence in the Earth-soul is only possible in the wintertime, when there is "the least amount of influences affecting the Earth-spirit, so that it can concentrate upon its own inner being"; that is, upon what is permeating its inner being as a result of its cosmic sensing activity.

Much of this cosmic sensing is reflected in the consciousness of the gnomes who work with the minerals. In the wintertime, the plant elementals gain access to this profound consciousness. Again, in the winter, the hemisphere's own intelligence is most intense, when "that which one can call the 'intellect' of the earth is in its most active state".[238]

In this way it becomes possible for the gnomes, undines, and sylphs to bring about, in due course, the new spring growth in harmony with the cosmic forces from which the different species derive. The creative activity of the elemental beings in the Earth, arises in response to the archetypal ideas or patterns for the plant kingdom that the

---

[236] Noted in Supplement 19 to the Complete Works, p.1.
[237] GA 165, lect. 5th July 1908.
[238] Lect. 26th Dec. 1917.

earth soul perceives in winter. These living archetypes of the plants, their spiritual essence, manifesting as the zodiacal and planetary forces of each species, exist on the devachanic plane, the realm (chan) of the resplendent gods (devas). Now they illumine the consciousness of the Earth-soul. A Steiner notebook entry reads,

> The earth's own nature matures/ripens at Christmas, then the earth imprints this cosmic content into the roots of the plants, then opens itself {in spring} again to the cosmos.[239]

The term 'Christmas' in this context refers to the winter's Yuletide-Holy Nights season, in the winter hemisphere; this will become self-evident later in this chapter. In earlier times, people experienced how the awakened presence, in the Earth-soul, of the spiritual beings who guide the life processes of the planet made the winter a holy time, a time when they could be nearer to high spiritual beings. An indication of this experience is found in the remarkable procedure that existed amongst native Amerindians in British Columbia. The tribal nobles had two sets of names, summer names and winter names. The initiation of the chosen men took place in winter, for only then could the guardian spirits of the human beings be contacted.

These deities then bestowed 'inner' names on the initiated. The very structure, the social structure, of the community was changed in winter; extended family groups, common during the rest of the year, were dissolved in winter and all initiated men who received their initiation from the same spirit lived together.[240]

Earlier people were also aware of how the consciousness of the Earth-soul in winter is uplifted or illumined by its perception of the divine cosmic forces coming to expression through its ether body. In northern parts of Europe, where the old clairvoyance has lingered on, there still exist old legends and tales about such interweaving of divine and elemental powers. In Iceland, the legend of the sacred rowan tree tells of how, around the winter solstice, a rowan tree

---

[239] Noted in Supplement 19 to the Complete Works, p.1. The German reads: „aber das Eigene der Erde reift Weihnacht – da prägt die Erde ihr Kosmisches der Pflanze ein – dann öffnet sie sich wieder dem Kosmos."
[240] Frazer, the Golden Bough, vol. 3. chapter 6.

becomes radiant, every branch glowing with an unearthly light, which no stormy wind can extinguish.[241]

Rudolf Steiner described the sacred nature of the spiritual forces that come into being in wintertime, and the contrast of winter with summer, in this verse, part of which was quoted in chapter 5:

> Asleep is the soul of the earth
> In summer's heat;
> Then, the mirror of the sun
> Brightly shines
> In external space.
>
> Awake is the soul of the earth
> In winter's cold;
> Then, the sun's true being
> Is spiritually glowing
> In the earth's inner being.
>
> Summer's joyous day
> For earth is sleep;
> Winter's hallowed night
> For earth is day.

The "mirror of the sun" may be regarded as referring to the sun, but in view of the summertime mirroring phenomenon, this term is no doubt more accurately understood as a reference to the summer hemisphere.

There is, then, a hallowed, or holy, quality in winter (around June in the south, around December in the north) coming from the presence of "the sun's true being". What spiritual power is indicated? What is the unearthly radiance that illumines the plant world in winter, as indicated in the legend of the rowan tree? Does this spiritual power have a connection to the twelve days of Christmas? Why did the Church justify the placing of Jesus' birth on December 25th by declaring that day to be the "birthday of the sun of righteousness" (St. John Chrysostom).

Astronomically, this is correct, for on the 25th of December, the days do begin to become longer. Thus in Mithraism, December 25th is the day of the rebirth or reascent of the sun. And in such religions this day is

---

[241] In the article, 'Heilige Nacht' in Meyers KonversAtion Lexikon (1897)

likewise the birthday of the demigod or sun hero, Mithra for example.

If we reflect on that special joy, that mood of delight and enchantment, that belongs to Christmas, we can ask whether it derives solely from commemoration of the birth of Jesus. Is there present in this mood the influence of winter? Those who have grown up in the southern hemisphere and therefore have had Christmas in summer, often find when they experience Christmas in the north, when it is then winter, that the festival has much more of a spiritual ambience.

We know that in the northern hemisphere a period of about two weeks after the winter solstice has been regarded as especially sacred. Pre-Christian religions in remote antiquity held this view, as did the more recent Celtic peoples, for whom this period was part of the Yuletide festive season which began in November and lasted about two months.

It is also interesting to note that in Old Testament times and on into the Christian era, the Hebrews began their Festival of Lights, also called the festival of dedicating (hallowing) the temple, on the evening of December 24th. This festival lasted eight days, during which all houses and the temples were aglow from lighted candles. It was also on the night of 24th of December that Jesus of Nazareth was born, as well as Krishna, Dionysos, Horus, Tammuz, Mithra, and other part-god, part-human individuals of antiquity. Likewise, in ancient times the winter festival of the Greeks was called the Feast of Lights.

In recent decades the question arose amongst anthroposophists in the southern hemisphere whether in the southern hemisphere the Yuletide or "the twelve days of Christmas", as the festival became known in the Middle Ages, really occurs in June and July. In other words, whether it is a winter, seasonal phenomenon. Does Christmas occur in June and July in the southern hemisphere, or is it related to the calendar days of December 25th to January 6th? We need to restructure this question before we can answer it. We need to gain a clearer knowledge what the twelve days of Christmas really are, and then we need to locate their connection to the birth of Jesus.

Initiates of the sixth degree

The relationship of the twelve-day Yuletide to winter and to Christmas is especially important, for a renewed understanding of the twelve days of Christmas is one of the most important tasks in life for those who want to work toward a spiritual renewal of civilization. An understanding of the systematic approach to spiritual development, that is, the process of initiation as it was carried out in various great religions of the past, is particularly helpful in the task of understanding the Holy Nights.

These procedures, involving seven stages or degrees, are referred to in esoteric texts, especially those from the Mithraic religion. From the first stage or degree to the fourth stage, those seeking spirituality were led through trials and soul exercises which assisted the attainment of higher consciousness. This consciousness developed as the moral-ethical nature was strengthened through the struggle against the lower self. The fifth degree was reached when the higher self not only inspired the initiate, bringing the capacity to behold the soul world and at times to become conscious in the spiritual world, but also permeated the personality.

The personality became so transformed through the purification processes that the human spirit could manifest in the person. Anthroposophy calls this process the transformation of the soul, of the astral organism, into the Spirit-self. The Spirit-self was known as 'Sophia' in early Christian initiation centres (it did not refer to a goddess). This state of spirituality is generally regarded as the highest achievement possible for humankind-indeed, as the very purpose of the spiritual quest.

After this state is achieved, the three soul powers are divinized, they become the vessel of the higher self: thinking transcends abstract, materialistic thoughts; the emotions reject the yearnings of personal desires; and in the will, selfless service to the world holds sway. In earlier times a person who attained this state was known as wise. Wisdom was understood to arise when both head and heart are illumined by the light of the spirit.

Such initiates can comprehend the mystery of the human as a microcosm within the macrocosm; they perceive the cosmic forces behind specific organs or soul powers. They perceive, for example, the connection between Venus and the function of the kidneys, or between Saturn and the destiny-guiding power that works below the threshold of consciousness. And they can follow the pathway of a soul whose earthly life has ended; they can behold its journey in the spiritual worlds and its descent to a new life. Further, a fifth degree initiate has achieved the capacity to commune with, to serve, the folk soul of the nation. The guidance this initiates gives to the folk is in harmony with the intentions of the archangel guiding the destiny of the nation.

One may ask, what higher spiritual achievements are possible? Since by the fifth stage, the soul has become divine-since it has achieved what Christians term 'sainthood', what further goals can there be? Has not such a person brought the Christ consciousness to birth within? Does not the Christmas festival, through the image of the Christ child, present this goal to us? No, for the Christ child image, although encompassing this state of spiritual achievement, extends beyond it.

When the fifth degree of initiation was attained, then the consciousness became literally angelic. The hierarchy of the angels is composed of those beings whose are already spiritualized, who have attained the Spirit-self. The initiate of the fifth degree was 'reborn' through the Holy Spirit, for the transformation of the initiate's soul was attained with the help of the foremost, the leader of the angelic hierarchy. In this being, the Holy Spirit, part of the great primal Trinity, comes to manifestation.

For this reason the foremost of the angels was known as the Holy Spirit, too. Through the coming of Christ to the Earth, it has become possible for all humanity to attain the Spirit-self. As a result of the resurrection of Christ, the Holy Spirit (or 'the Comforter') can now draw near to all humankind, whereas previously only a few individuals could become permeated by the Holy Spirit. In a sense, we can regard the spiritual forces that the Holy Spirit brings to the striving soul as coming from the Christ.

But there is a further stage in spiritual development wherein spiritual forces, directly from the Christ, permeate the human being. When this further state is achieved, then one becomes an initiate of the sixth degree. This sublime state of spiritual consciousness was achieved in the past, although the way in which the Christ forces streamed into the initiates then was different to the way in which the streaming happens today, since the union of the Christ to the earth. In the fifth stage of spiritual development, the soul body is transformed or spiritualized; the sixth degree is attained when the ether body is spiritualized. What does this mean? What is the nature of our ether body normally?

We work during the day then at night become weary. During sleep our life forces are renewed; the ether body absorbs forces from the world ether. The tasks of maintaining our life processes, and of procreating, make demands on the ether body. Illnesses place further demands on its restorative powers; and waves of strong emotion, when they flare up in the soul, impair the harmonious rhythmical processes within the ether body. But just as our soul powers of thinking, feeling, and willing have behind them a spiritual, archetypal essence or potential, so too behind the ether body is a divine, immensely creative spiritual essence. This archetypal essence exists in the spiritual world, or Devachan.

The sixth degree initiate can so transform the ether body that this powerful spiritual potential within it comes to manifestation. The ether body no longer just absorbs life forces from the cosmos; it now can stream life forces out of itself; life-bestowing, living ether forces. This stage of development will be attained by humanity in general, in the far future.

But it manifests even now in exceptional creative activity; the flash of creative insight wherein the artist perceives the idea of a work of art is due to this union of wisdom and the divine creative life forces. The wisdom, the selfless understanding of life, which the Spirit-self brings, can become so strong that the initiate develops a love which is a creative power. For then the divine forces in the ether body become accessible, and when used, change the very elemental substance of the world,

> Imagine an utterly giving, outpouring love that unites with the creative generative power {of the ether body}; that is the Life-spirit.[242]

Life-spirit is the term Rudolf Steiner gave us for the transformed ether body. The Life-spirit can come to birth only in the divine feminine, the purified soul or 'Sophia' soul. The ether body is continually affected by all desires, feelings, and emotions in the soul, via, for example, the 'ductless glands'. These glands become active, forming

---

[242] Lect. 9th June 1906.

secretions in direct response to the impulses arising in the feelings; the ether body manifests in the physical body through these glands. When the soul life has become free of yearnings and cravings that arise like disruptive storms, then the ether body's functions become ever more harmonious and rhythmical. The divine creative powers from which the ethers derive can begin to manifest in the initiate's ether body. The spiritual, creative powers within the ether forces can then begin to function.

In describing the deep inner harmony that arises in the soul and ether body of the sixth degree initiate, Rudolf Steiner used a very significant image; that of the 'motion' of the sun 'through' the Earth:

> If you could look back to the primeval past of our solar system, you would then see that this solar system has emerged out of the struggle of the 'warmth chaos', and that the harmony in our world-order has created itself out of the disharmony. That is, the peaceful harmony and order have developed out of disharmony and chaos. But how have these come into being? In this way: {through the fact that} the sun has such a regular, ordered motion that we could not even think that the sun might deviate from its pathway, even for a moment. Harmony is so deeply established in the being of our cosmos, and the sun in its movement *through* the cosmos is so unshakeably fixed to its course, that nothing can move it from its path.[243]   {emphasis mine}

The harmony that Rudolf Steiner referred to here produces the awesome, complex patterns of the planets in their movements 'around' the earth.

> In this journey of the sun across the sky, the old Persian {or Greek, or other} initiate of the sixth degree saw his own inner destiny. So unshakeably must the sun within his being illumine him, the 'sun of his spirit', that it would be just as impossible for him to deviate from the path of goodness and

---

[243] From an archive lect. 19th Dec. 1904.

214

wisdom, as it is for the sun to deviate from its pathway.[244]

Such initiates were called sun heroes: Hercules, Zarathustra, Cuchulainn were all sixth-degree initiates. So too was Joseph, the son of Jacob-Israel; the story of his coat and his jealous brothers portrays aspects of the achievement of this high stage of development.[245] There is a deeper reason for the use of the expression "sun hero" to describe these initiates. They achieved more than harmony of their ether bodies with that of the sun.

They developed a profound inner connection to the life forces of the spiritual sun. Further, the consciousness of the sixth degree initiate can rise from perception of the correspondence between the macrocosm and humanity to a union with the greater world. The initiate's own being merges with that of the macrocosm.

This stage of spiritual development is of course still possible today; the seven degrees of the initiation are attainable through a Christ-centred path of development. In particular the anthroposophical path of self-development offers this possibility in a form suited to modern times. Such a sun hero, a solar initiate, also attains to communion with or resonance with, the Earth-spirit.[246] A new capacity of clairvoyance arose in the sixth degree initiate. He or she had to learn to encompass in vision not just that which has taken place during the past millennia; rather he had to know the entire evolutionary journey of humanity. In such initiation activity he gazed back over millions of years.[247]

That is, this person attained the state of clairvoyant consciousness that Rudolf Steiner called 'Inspiration'. Whereas most psychic experiences are connected with the soul world, Inspiration or 'Cosmic spiritual consciousness' brings conscious perception of Devachan; that is the spiritual world itself. Inspiration reveals what takes place during the evolution of humanity on earth, that is, the series of phases or 'globes' which together constitute a great cycle of evolution. The actual initiation process for the sixth

---

[244] Ibid.
[245] Ibid.
[246] Lect. 19th Sept. 1906 in GA 97.
[247] Lect. 17th Dec. 1906.

degree was undertaken at a very definite time. It had to occur in harmony with the cycle of the year.

This further stage in the spiritualization of the soul took place in winter, three days after the winter solstice.[248] Rudolf Steiner described a preliminary ritual for the attainment of the Life-spirit. This ritual also took place on the third day after the winter solstice; on the 25th of December in the north, which corresponds to the 25th of June in the south,

> They gathered together already early in the evening of the 24th. They sat in deep silence together in the darkness. Thoughts about eternity filled their minds. Then toward midnight mysterious tones arose, flowing through the chamber, now louder, now softer. The acolytes who heard these tones knew: "This is the music of the spheres". Profound, hallowed reverence filled their hearts. Then a faint glow developed; it came from a faintly illumined disc. They knew: "This is the earth".
>
> The illumined disc became darker and darker, until it was entirely black. The chamber, at the same time, became brighter. Those who saw this knew that the dark oval was the earth; the sun, which normally illumined it, was now covered {by the earth}. The earth can no longer see the sun {that is, at midnight the sun is behind the Earth}. Then around the disc of the earth, ring upon ring of rainbow colours formed, flowing outwards.
>
> They thought: "Thus did {the spiritual counterpart of} the sun appear to Atlantean humanity". Then, around midnight, in place of the black earth disc, there arose a magenta glowing sphere. On this was a word, which varied according to {the language of} the people. In our present-day language this word would be 'Christos'. Those who saw this glowing magenta disk knew: "This is the sun". The sun appeared to them at the midnight hour, when the world around them rested in deepest darkness. They had experienced, in images, that which in the mysteries one called: seeing the sun at the midnight hour.[249]

---

[248] Ibid.
[249] Ibid.

The word "Christos" here, has a meaning far beyond ecclesiastical views; it is about the Life-spirit forces in the sun. We can just note it is very likely that in ancient Greek pre-Christian Mystery Centres, the word which appeared on the disc representing the inner sun, "Chrestos". We will consider the meaning of this word later, when we explore the theme of the sun at midnight. For now, it is important to note that the dramatic scene enacted for those aspiring to the sixth degree actually took place within other persons who that night attained the sixth degree, in whom the Life-spirit was born.

At this point, we may glimpse the deep validity of the designation "sun hero" for one who develops the Life-spirit; for where is it possible to behold a being whose life forces are permeated by the creative, life-bestowing life spirit powers? Within the sun ! Every star pours out measureless amounts of ether forces, bestowing life and light on all living beings on its planets. The connection between this sixth degree initiation and the sun becomes clearer when we recall that the inner solar forces permeating the out-breathed summer aura, are drawn down into the hemisphere at winter,

> The sun gold that during the peak of summer forms in the heights draws into the depths of the earth where, on a spiritual level, it weaves and surges through the depths of the earth. There it vivifies that which in the midst of winter is seeking {a source of} life for the following year.[250]

Steiner described this presence of inner sun forces in winter as a phenomenon contrasting with the summer dynamic:

> The external power of the sun is fully outpoured in the spring and summer sun. In that the physical power of the sun ever more declines, its spiritual power intensifies and becomes stronger and stronger toward Christmas-Holy Nights.[251]

It is now clear that the term 'winter' could have been used here; as the term 'Christmas' is obviously synonymous with

---

[250] Lect. 12th Oct. 1923.
[251] Lect. 25th Dec 1907.

the winter-time in this context. In the same lecture, Steiner comments,

> When the days become shorter, when the autumn and winter approach, the sun withdraws its forces more and more. In the same degree, however, in that the physical force of the sun is withdrawn, the spiritual force grows. And it is conferred on the earth most strongly when those days come when the shortest days arrive, and when the nights are longest.

In the wintertime the ethereal and astral auras of the hemisphere become permeated by sacred spiritual powers. This transcendental spiritual presence, however, is primarily to be found under the ground, in the depths of the earth. Thus the winter solstice initiation gave one an experience "like a descent into the depths of the earth element".[252] The question arises, since the interior of the earth is an intensely dark realm, whether the presence of the sublime inner sun forces there may have a connection to the Christmas leitmotif of 'light in the darkness'.

Before considering this point further, we should again recall that midwinter was in the past regarded as a holy time. People felt that amidst the malignant influences, a sacred spiritual presence exists. On the Shetland Islands, where the old traditions were maintained until very recently, the Yuletide began somewhat later than in other areas, it began on the evening of December 19th, which was called Tulya's E'en (that is, 'Yule's evening'), and lasted about a month.

The evening before the solstice, December 20th, was called Tunderman's Night (Tunderman = 'thunder-man', that is, the god Thor), and this night was especially sacred. Neither work nor amusements were permitted; great misfortune would befall a household which broke this rule:

> The very babe unborn cries, 'O dule ! O dule !' For the breakin o Tunderman's Night five nights afore Yule.[253]

This hallowed quality, which the winter in-breath causes, is mentioned in Shakespeare's *Hamlet*:

---

[252] Lect. 1st April, 1923, in *Cycle of the Year*.
[253] 'F.M.McNeil, *The Silver Bough*, vol. 3. MacLellan, Glasgow, 1961.

Some say that ever 'gainst that season comes
Wherein our Saviour's birth is celebrated,
The bird of dawning singeth all night long;
And then, they say, no spirit dares stir abroad;
The nights are wholesome; then no planets strike,
No fairy takes, nor witch hath power to charm,
So hallow'd and so gracious is the time.

(1.1.158-64)

The Holy Nights

With exposure to the work of Rudolf Steiner many people have become aware that the twelve or thirteen days that make up the Holy Nights are a time of deep spiritual significance. An important question for people in both hemispheres is this: are the Holy Nights an integral part of the season of winter, or are they a unique non-seasonal period of time encompassing all of the globe? Until this question is resolved, neither hemisphere will be able to achieve a true Holy Nights festival, nor will humanity be able to understand the relationship of this festival to the Christmas festival.

We began to answer this question by considering the nature of the winter solstice initiation, the sixth degree of spiritual development. Whether this process, in a metamorphosed modern form, is part of the Holy Nights, we have yet to decide. But it is certainly a midwinter process; that is, it would occur in the southern hemisphere in late June.

What processes do occur during the Holy Nights? Apart from the research of Rudolf Steiner, modern humanity has no definite knowledge of the significance of the days around the winter solstice (in the northern hemisphere, where now the Holy Nights coincide with the winter solstice). The so-called twelve days of Christmas no longer have any experiential meaning for us.

Thus, in the English-speaking world, Christmas tends to be a one-day festival, with a prologue on the 24th, and an epilogue on the 26th for rest and for recovery from the festivities. In the time of Shakespeare, however, the Christmas-Yuletide festival still lasted for twelve days. The term 'Christmas' (Christ-mass) came into being in the twelfth century, and refers to the special Mass centring on the birth of Jesus.

In Europe, for example, in the German speaking lands, the term 'Hallowed Nights' (Weihnacht) is used; this time around the solstice is thought of more in terms of nights. Steiner also placed the emphasis quite specifically on the nights of this time. Until now, in anthroposophical communities, the Holy Nights were considered to have their importance because of zodiacal influences, the exact nature of which the earlier anthroposophists could not determine.

In addition, a profound process connected with the Christ-being is thought of as also connected with the Holy Nights. We will consider this process later. We now need to examine why the nights are emphasized more than the days during this time and, again, whether the phenomena of the Holy Nights, which we have yet to identify, occur for the whole Earth during the time from December 24th to January 6th or whether they are in fact created by the winter in-breath.

During the time of the Holy Nights in the northern hemisphere the consciousness of the plant realm merges with that of the mineral realm.[254] Both these realms are, of course, experiencing degrees of unconsciousness; but the elemental beings of the plant realm do commune during the Holy Nights with those of the mineral realm, the gnomes. In the gnomes there lives a consciousness of the devachanic, archetypal, spiritual ideas that have formed the mineral-physical world. As we have seen, it is precisely during wintertime that this informing phenomenon occurs. Indeed, the process is described as not being restricted to the time of the Holy Nights but rather as occurring during the depths of the winter in-breath.

When speaking of this intimate dialogue that the cosmos and the earth {hemisphere} have in winter, Rudolf Steiner taught that in earlier times, when the initiated priests wished to 'listen in' on this dialogue, specially prepared priestesses were given the task. And this process, according to Steiner, was not objectively limited to twelve days. "In earlier times", he said, "our present Christmas-Yuletide period {that is, the twelve days} was not precisely the decisive time; rather, it was a period lying more or less around this time".[255] The number twelve has been given for cultic or symbolic-sacramental reasons.

---

[254] Lect. 31st. Dec. 1915.
[255] Lect. 17th Mar. 1917, in *Human and Cosmic Metamorphoses*.

During the time of the Holy Nights in the northern hemisphere our consciousness can experience, to some extent, the sublime state of inspiration. The *Dream Song of Olaf Åsteson,* a fifth-century Norwegian saga of which only fragments exist today, describes the spiritual experiences during the Holy Nights of a Celtic-Christian initiate. Part of Olaf Åsteson's experience was to behold the "sun at midnight", as recorded in the collected fragments of this epic saga. As we have noted, this experience occurs when the sixth degree of initiation is achieved, and this stage of spiritual development is consummated when the spiritual forces active in winter are able to work upon the soul. Rudolf Steiner taught that such deep visions are possible in wintertime for more evolved souls:

> Especially gifted people become 'graced' with inspirations from the spiritual world, becoming inspired in the nights between Christmas Eve and the Three Kings Day {that is, January 6th}. A beautiful legend exists of *The Dream Song of Olaf Åsteson,* who 'went to sleep' on Christmas Eve. There have in fact always been 'graced' people who have gone through a nature initiation, so to speak, because of the elemental forces active in them. This, a person can undergo, if he carries out faithfully the requirements of the way of initiation.[256]

The use of the term 'graced' in this context is especially significant; we have noted how people in the past regarded this midwinter time, in which such experiences as Olaf Åsteson's took place, as holy. That Olaf Åsteson's experiences are referred to as 'dreams' is quite understandable, in that the seer attains to the same realm as the dreamer. Steiner reported that in earlier times Scandinavian peoples in general entered a kind of dreamy state around the winter solstice, that psychic experiences could then occur.[257]

Historians confirm that people in old Europe found that the most significant time of the year for dreams, that is, psychic dreams, was the solstice, either the winter or the

---

[256] Lect. 7th May 1915.
[257] From an essay by Rudolf Steiner, found in the Archives, and published in GA 158.

summer solstice. As is evident from these pages, the winter solstice psychic dream experiences have a deeper potential than those of the enchanted summer nights.

Olaf Åsteson's experiences, including the beholding of the sun at the midnight hour, certainly came about because it was wintertime. Our look at the seasonal connection with the sixth degree initiation should make this point clear. If he had lived in the southern hemisphere, he would have had the experience in late June. Steiner's placing of Olaf Åsteson's experience 'in the nights between Christmas Eve and the Three Kings Day', we may see as pointing us toward the conclusion that the Holy Nights are an integral part of the season of winter.

The Dream Song of Olaf Åsteson records, further, a powerful vision of the destiny of humankind. In effect, Olaf Åsteson saw the fall of humanity and its consequences, the dark lower astral realms where souls must struggle through the effects of the fall. During the sixth degree initiation, on December 25th (or June 25th in the south), the initiate beholds the great vista of humanity's evolution, from the fall in old Lemuria through to the coming of Christ to the Earth. In profound visions, the initiate sees the disharmony in the soul and the ether body caused by the fall.[258]

The initiate's vision thus extends back over millions of year, across the phases (or 'globes') of evolutionary processes that lie between this time cycle and the Lemurian age.[259] And as part of this experience, the relationship of the Christ being to the fall, or rather, to the renewal of the human soul, is comprehended,

> In the time of the thirteen nights, in the actual winter solstice time, the soul {of the seer, that is} can see all that which the human being has to undergo because of its separation from the Christ spirit, everything which has to come over a person, because this human being has gone through those incarnations which are as they are, through the forces of Lucifer from the beginning of the development of the Earth.[260]

---

[258] Lect. 26th Dec. 1911.
[259] Lect. 17th Dec. 1906.
[260] Ibid.

This vision encompasses a vista of millions of years, spanning the various phases of evolution since the fall in Lemurian times. Such an experience is possible only when the faculty of 'Inspiration' is developing. The attainment of such cosmic consciousness as Inspiration is precisely the result of attaining the sixth degree or sun initiate stage. The faculty of inspiration develops only as the ether body itself is beginning to undergo the transformation into Life-spirit. Indeed the reason for enacting this initiation process at the winter solstice is that,

> at this time of the year, forces are moving through the environs around one, which are favourable for this awakening {this inspiration}.[261]

Here Rudolf Steiner is using the expression, "Weltenraum" referring to the divine Life-Spirit radiance which, due to the winter in-breath, is active in the environment of the wintry hemisphere. But a Christian Community church writer (M.Samson) presents this word as meaning "cosmic space", despite the context plainly showing that this is not the meaning. Samson tells his readers that Rudolf Steiner here is referring to forces streaming through 'cosmic space'; and therefore the distant stars are creating the Holy Nights, (for the entire globe).[262] But as we noted carefully earlier, the term 'world' in Rudolf Steiner's usage can mean either the cosmos, or our planet, or the local environs.

Here he actually means, beyond all argument, the local wintry environs. For, as he told his audience just a few minutes earlier, at this Holy Nights-Yuletide time, the initiate was able,

> to perceive the active forces {of the spiritual sun}, in colour-filled glory; he could see the **environs all around him** crowded with spiritual qualities, with spiritual beings; he was able to behold the spirit realm **all around about him**, where he experienced the greatest {realities} that a person can experience.[263]

---

[261] GA 96, lect. 17th Dec. 1906.
[262] M.Samson, *Festivals in the southern hemi...*, p. 162.
[263] In Steiner's words, "die Welt um sich her....die Geisterwelt um sich herum, wo erlebte das Größte, das ein Mensch erleben kann."

Rudolf Steiner's new festival concept is obscured by these semantic devices, and a significance of the stars for seasonal dynamics is invented, to be a basis for new festivals which thereby would remain global, not being caused by the seasonal cycle. Among his last teachings were letters to Members from his sick-bed; at the end of one letter he wrote that a true celebration of the traditional Christmas Day event should make current and vivid in the soul how,

> "the glory of the divine-spiritual beings who manifest their likeness {or image} in **the star-expanses** proclaim themselves to human beings, (and how the liberating of human beings occurs in the earthly places from the Powers who seek to remove human beings away from their origin). [264]   (emphasis mine AA)

But the key phrase in this passage *(in Sternenweiten)* is again translated incorrectly, instead of 'the star-expanses', or 'starry-expanses', it is presented (by Samson) as "their images are manifested in **the stars**", a nuance which again transfers the essence of the Christmas event up to the stars in galactic space.[265] But, as this letter is about the one-day Christmas Day event, it is not a relevant argument. However such a translation obscures the focus of the letter, which is about how, when Jesus was born, divine beings were filling the wintry firmament around Bethlehem, amidst its bright starry ambience, with their spiritual presence.

This kind of argument from church persons is particularly disconcerting, as Rudolf Steiner clearly told the priests themselves in the 'Autumn Course', that the Holy Nights festival is directly caused by the winter in-breath condition of the hemisphere,

> The Holy Nights-Christmas ({Yuletide} festival is placed from an old consciousness, in that time in which the sun draws its forces away most strongly from the earth {hemisphere}; in that time {season} when the earth, with all of its capacity, including what all this can signify for human beings; and is most especially in charge of itself. With the Holy Nights-Christmas time, we have to do with an earth

---

[264] Leading Thought, 28th Dec. 1924.
[265] M.Samson, *Festivals in the southern hemi...*,p. 67

{hemisphere} which is forsaken by the heavens...so we have the Holy Nights-Christmas festival firmly placed in the calendar entirely according to earthly circumstances.[266]

It is important to note the there are no teachings from Rudolf Steiner to the effect that spiritual essence of the new seasonal festivals is created by the stars.

It is then very clear with this festival that, any attempt to place the stars as the cause of spiritual conditions which become the basis of this festival, does not have a basis in the works of Rudolf Steiner. We shall encounter in this chapter, many other statements from Rudolf Steiner which teach this same truth.

However, Steiner did refer to how vivid and intense the stars are to us at Yuletide. This has two causes; in natural terms, it is due to the clarity of the air in the winter nights; in subtle spiritual terms, it would be the result of a discrete sensing, of how strong is the focus of the earth-soul, in the winter hemisphere, on the zodiac forces above it. None of these references, nor other similar ones, seek to declare that the stars (including the non-zodiac groupings) are in any way the cause of a seasonal festival.

This wonderful phenomenon is a wintertime process, and the development of this high clairvoyance in a brief, small measure during the Holy Nights, by especially gifted souls, is also possible, as a winter process,

> Thus we may say, in the epoch of materialism {which is now ending}, there could always be people who could, when the spirit of the Earth is most awakened, in the middle of winter, then unite with the spirit of the Earth, and receive Inspirations.[267]

So we may say that this 'signature' or feature of the Holy Nights, this looking back to the Fall of humanity and to our relationship with the Christ, this beholding through the faculty of Inspiration of the evolution of humanity, is also a winter phenomenon.

---

[266] GA 343, Autumn Course to Priests, lect. 5th Oct. 1921, am, p. 383 (German version).
[267] Lect. 7th May 1915.

Descending deep inside the earth

In our exploration of the phenomena that occur during the Holy Nights, we will eventually turn our attention to the role of the zodiac. Though Steiner only mentioned the zodiac on four of the ten occasions when he discussed the Holy Nights, the zodiac forces do have an important connection to this time, albeit not in the sense that a spiritual journey through the zodiac is undertaken, nor in the sense that a specific zodiac sign correlates with a specific night of the twelve or thirteen. The nature of the connection will become clear, later in this chapter, after we have considered certain secrets of the winter in-breath.

Because we can see it happening, we do believe that the seeds have to descend down into the earth once they have been formed each year by the out-breath of summer. We know that in this way the seeds can sprout and grow. But without developing spiritual perception, we cannot notice that,

> such a cycle also exists, continuously, for the human soul. A person first realizes this once he {or she} is initiated into the great mysteries of existence. The inmost being of our soul is united to the spiritual forces of the earth, just as the force within every plant seed is united to physical forces of the earth.[268]

The nature of the Earth's interior, and its involvement in cosmic processes, belongs to these great mysteries. An understanding of the Holy Nights and their connection to wintertime arises when the light of these 'great mysteries' illumines our efforts to renew the festivals. In the Holy Nights, then,

> just as the plant seed descends into the depths of the earth in the time that we call Christmas, so also does the human soul descend into deep, deep spiritual regions, gathering strength from deep regions, as does the plant for its blossoming in spring.[269]

We need to remind ourselves again that the German term translated as 'Christmas' in this passage is the usual German

---

[268] Lect. 26th Dec.1911.
[269] GA 96, Lect. 17th Dec. 1906

226

expression, "Weihnachtszeit", which means the time of the 'hallowed or sacred nights'. This is, in its origins, a non-Christian, non-ecclesiastical term, referring to the period of the winter solstice festival in pagan Europe.[270] Of course, this term now has all the orthodox religious connotations in modern German that the word 'Christmas' has for the English-speaking world.

Still, Steiner could have decided to replace the word with the more strictly ecclesiastical German equivalent, 'Christfest'. But on the contrary, Steiner used the term 'Weihnachtszeit' very gladly and even emphasized its seasonal or winter nuance, speaking of the "winter-Weihnacht" (winter-Holy Nights-time).[271]

Let us consider the significance of this remarkable indication, that the wintertime brings us into some kind of relationship with the interior of the Earth. The winter solstice initiation was described as being "like a descent into the depths of the earth element." This wintertime dynamic is confirmed by further Steiner indications, about the summer and winter mysteries, in a lecture he gave on December 23rd, 1922:

> In winter the human being does not unite with that which is out there in the atmosphere; rather we incline toward the interior of the Earth. We turn toward the 'gods below'.

In an earlier lecture, in December 1909, Steiner had also described this descent of human beings, during the night, as specifically a wintertime process:

> We see, then, as the layer of plants in the autumn disappears, the outer power of the sun reduces, and the awakening spirit becomes our guide to the depths, into which the spiritual life withdraws, into {the place} there where we deliver over to the spirit the "sprouting seeds" for the coming springtime. Thus, we live, together with the power of the plant seed, quite literally inside the earth, we penetrate the earth.[272]

---

[270] The article "Heilige Nacht" in Meyers Konversations Lexikon, 1897.
[271] Lect. 13th Mar. 1917.
[272] Lect. 12st Dec. 1909.

Let us really try to visualize this reality, as seen by the clairvoyant. A seer, observing the journey of the people at night-time, during most nights of the year, would see them leave their sleeping physical body at night and rise up into the heavens in their astral body; their silver cord trailing behind them as they ascend, keeping the vital link to the physical body.[273]

But, in late June to early July in the southern hemisphere, in late December to early January in the north, the seer would first see, three days after the winter solstice, for the 12 or so days of the Yuletide, these souls descending deep into the earth. Only later, would the seer see these souls then arising up above the ground and ascending into cosmic heights.

Why the descent into the Earth? And what connection does it have with Christmas? The interior of the Earth, on the astral level, contains powerful, elemental forces, and often these are of a malignant nature. But as Steiner taught, in a text I have already quoted, the force of the spiritual sun that permeates the out-breathed summer aura, in autumn and winter is drawn down "into the depths of the earth, where it, on a spiritual level, weaves and surges through the depths of the Earth".[274]

Thus, although the spiritual reality of the interior of the earth is quite malignant (Kamaloca, the lowest, most malignant of the astral realms, and also Ahriman, have their location in the interior of the Earth), there is present during the depths of winter a holy spiritual power from the sun sphere. The secret of the Holy Nights of winter is indicated, although in a veiled manner, in the meditation used by those seeking the winter initiation into the sixth degree. This ancient verse was revealed by Steiner:

> Behold the sun
> At the midnight hour
> Build with rocks
> In the lifeless ground.
>
> So, in the declining world

---

[273] The silver cord is mentioned in the Bible in Ecclesiastes 12:6, and spoken about by Rudolf Steiner in an archive document from 1903.
[274] Lect. 12th Oct. 1923.

And in death's dark night
Find creation's new beginning
And morning's young might.
The heights reveal
The gods' eternal word
The deeps should guard
The peaceful treasure hoard.

In darkness living,
Create a sun !
In matter weaving,
Know spirit-bliss begun !

The beholding of the sun at midnight (on December 25th in the north or June 25th in the south) is an extraordinary concept. Rudolf Steiner explains that the experience is possible when the faculty of Inspiration arises. Then, at midnight, the seer can pierce through the material substance of the Earth to see the sun on the other side of the planet. But the concept has a second meaning; a more esoteric meaning is present in that initiation meditation, unveiling the sublime secret of the Holy Nights.

We noted earlier that when the acolytes inside the darkened crypt beheld a disc representing the sun, a word appeared on this disc. And I mentioned that in the Greek Mystery centres, that this word was very likely 'Chrestos', not 'Christos'. The reason for this conclusion is that Rudolf Steiner reveals that it was chosen as the Greek term for the Life-spirit.[275] The fundamental meaning of this word Chrestos is 'useful', but it can also mean 'good', in the sense of virtuous; that is, it points to an **active** goodness.

And the Life-spirit allows loving kindness to become an actively healing and beautifying force. Thus a sun hero or sixth degree initiate, in whom the Life-spirit or inner, spiritual sun forces are active, would be defined as a 'Chrestos' person. The symbol for the Life-spirit or Chrestos was the mysterious Chi-rho, which Christian theologians from, earliest times have portrayed as an abbreviation of the word 'Christos'.

That 'Chi-rho' represents the Chrestos or Life-Spirit is indicated by an early fourth-century church in Syria which has the inscription: "***The Lord and Saviour Jesus, the***

---

[275] Lecture of 24th Dec. 1905.

Virtuous {Chrestos}"; instead of "....*Jesus the Anointed One (Christos)*"[276]; and also that Rudolf Steiner taught that in the early centuries of Christianity, Jesus Christ was understood to be such a sixth degree initiate, a solar initiate.

The Chi-rho symbol

It is said that the Chi-rho was first used in connection with Christ by the Emperor Constantine in A.D. 312. But it has been found in Christian-Gnostic graphic art from the second century ! This symbol is also found in non-Christian sacred (initiatory) art, see Illustration 7; and on an ancient bread-baking mould, which is dated to the fourth century AD but is probably much older than that, see Illustration 8. This pre-Christian 'Christian' symbol of the Life-spirit was later designated as the symbol of the word 'Christos', which refers to an anointed person; in effect, that man in whom Deity is present. In this connection it is interesting that Pitt-Rivers has confirmed that in the standard Greek lexicon of Scott and Liddell, the reference to the word 'Chrestomathies', a term which indicates the more esoteric nuance of the word Chrestos, was deleted from the text after 1929.[277]

Rudolf Steiner taught that the mission of the Earth is the development of love in humanity; that is, the development of the ego and therewith the potential to rise above egotism to selfless love. The Life-spirit is a major part of this capacity for love. For this reason, in the first centuries of Christianity, when there was still an esoteric understanding of the Christ reality, the Chi-rho symbol was used to express the sublime significance of the coming of the cosmic Christ. It was also used as a symbol of the human 'vessel' of the Christ, that is, Jesus of Nazareth. There is a deep reason for this association of Jesus with the Life-spirit, and we shall consider this shortly.

We have seen that when the Spirit-self is attained, the initiate has achieved in a sense, the spirituality that exists in the angelic hierarchy. When the sublime sixth degree is

---

[276] From G.R.S. Mead, *Fragments of Faith Forgotten*, p. 249, University Books, N.Y. 1966. In the ancient Greek: Ἰησοῦς Χρηστός (instead of Ἰησοῦς Χριστός)

[277] G. Pitt-Rivers, *The Labarum*, Allen & Unwin, London 1966.

230

attained, and the loving understanding becomes an active love wherein the spiritual forces of the ether body are activated, then the divine creative forces of the archangelic hierarchy are present in the initiate. It is the task of the archangels to help humanity reach the Life-spirit stage. It is not surprising that, as Steiner reported, "a shudder {of awe} ran through the soul of an acolyte who glimpsed such a sun hero".[278]

For when the Life-spirit is being developed, the Christ reality draws near, in someone who was a 'sun hero', who attained the sixth stage, as Steiner said later in his lecture, "in him the Christ is inwardly born". He who descended to Earth, the leader of the sun gods, the leader of those divine hierarchical beings whose outer expression is the sun, makes possible the attainment of the Life-spirit. With the preceding quotation we encounter the same expression as that used to describe the essence of Christmas, the birth of Christ in the human. Is this the origin of the term "Christ child"?

We have considered how, through the coming to Earth of the Christ being, the influence of Lucifer was overcome and the way to spirituality, to the Spirit-self, was opened. The Holy Spirit can assist the efforts made to transform the soul. But in addition, the mystery of Golgotha enables all mankind, not just the selected few, to achieve the Life-spirit, that is, selfless love as a creative power. The Christ is actually that being through whom the first spark of Buddhi {Life-spirit} was initially awakened.[279]

In winter, as the inner sun force, especially its Life-spirit, the spiritual essence behind its rays, permeates the subterranean depths of the hemisphere, then the possibility is strongest that humanity will develop its own Life-spirit potential. Thus, within our own ether body, the 'sun of Christ' may arise in us. Such living spiritual development processes do not proceed in a regimented, set manner; the Life-spirit (or Buddhi) can start to develop during the time that the Spirit-self is striven for. This spiritual dynamic of the wintertime arises in both humanity and the Earth. Not only humanity, but the Earth, too, will bring to expression the divine creative forces in the ether body. In the hallowed nights of winter, the interweaving of humanity's

---

[278] Lect. 15th Dec. 1906, in GA 97.
[279] Spoken to Marie Steiner, reported in GA 262, p. 90.

7 Mithraic mosaic of an initiate with the Chi-rho symbol.

The Chi-rho and pomegranates represents the Chrestos or Life-Spirit. From an ancient Roman Mithras centre. Found in the village of Mary St. Hinton, UK. Dated to ca. AD 350, but very probably comes from an earlier century.

8   A Teutonic bread mould found in Germany, near Ulm.

Since it has the Chi-rho symbol init, it is regarded as Christian, and dated to 4th century AD; that is after Emperor Constantine had his vision of this same symbol. But this is an pre-Christian initiatory symbol; and hence this artefact is probably several centuries older.

and the Earth's soul forces assists the development of the solar, life-bestowing radiance of the Life-spirit deep within the planet. During the winter of each hemisphere, the spiritual-sun forces intensify inside the Earth.

Every winter, that is twice in every year, this inner sun, called by Steiner "the Christ sun", increases. Eventually, in this way, the spiritualization process that began in the primeval Hyperborean age, wherein the Earth was cast out of the sun, will be fulfilled. Thus, because each winter our planet moves further toward this goal, the wintertime Christmas festival and the nights around the time of the winter solstice have their beautiful, enchanted magical quality. In Steiner's words:

> Then comes the autumn and the winter, and then in the depths of the soul, the human being should feel: with the diminishing of the outer physical sun forces, with the drawing near of winter, as everything outside dies away and it becomes darker and darker, then the highest divine-spiritual forces unite with that part of the earth on which we are living {that is, the hemisphere}, then we feel ourselves as if enveloped in these highest spiritual beings.
>
> We feel deep in the soul as if we belong to them. Thus we feel the deepest devotion, when we know that with the coming of winter, we may behold, as they manifest directly in our environment, spiritual forces which have the same origin as that of the human being. Anthroposophy has been called upon to learn to know these forces.[280]

In pre-Christian times, the sixth degree initiate beheld, at the midnight hour on December 25th, the sublime sun god Christ, within the sun, and also present indirectly in the earth, nurturing the Life-spirit process of midwinter. But after the events of Golgotha, the Christian initiate beheld the Christ as united to the Earth-soul. When we understand the interweaving of these divine ether forces and the indwelling Christ, then the new Christian winter festival can arise.

Again, Rudolf Steiner's words can provide a foundation for contemplation of this new festival:

---

[280] Lect. 26th June, 1908.

234

Through the mystery of Golgotha, the Christ ego, which otherwise could only be sought for in the sun, passed over into the Earth. It united with the Earth, and in the spirit of the Earth we find the Christ ego, the sun ego. And the initiate may now, in the new {post-Golgotha} age, equate the sun spirit with Christ, with the central spirit of the Earth, whereas, in olden {pre-Golgotha} times, the Sun-spirit was sought at midnight of "Hallowed Night" {that is, Christmas}, in the sun sphere.

In this feeling {of being} livingly united to the Christ spirit lies the Christian consciousness, not only the consciousness of the normal Christian, but of the Christian initiate. This is the process that occurs each year when the days become shorter and the natural earth passes into slumber. Then the process is this: that we can come into direct union with the spirit of the Earth. Therefore, the placing of the birth of the saviour in the time of the shortest days and longest nights was not a matter of random selection, but arose from the principle of initiation.[281]

It is, of course, entirely clear from these words, that the Christmas festival – when it is brought into relationship with the seasonal cycle of the year – is a winter festival for either hemisphere. Steiner's words again sum up for us the secrets of esoteric Christianity that we have uncovered concerning the Christmas and Holy Nights festival:

We need a new Christmas {festival}, a Christmas which does not only remember the birth of Jesus of Nazareth, but which brings a new birth, the birth of the Christ impulse.[282]

And again:

The Christmas-Holy Nights mystery, when it is understood as a mystery, belongs paramountly to winter.[283]

---

[281] Lect. 13th Dec. 1907.
[282] Lect. 26th Dec. 1921.
[283] Lect. 23rd Dec. 1922.

The expression, "the Christ should be born in us at Christmas", is often used, but without a clear understanding that it has a quite specific meaning; it refers to a quite definite process that arises in the Earth-soul at wintertime. That we descend while asleep, into the earth, during the wintertime, makes possible the wondrous mystery of the Holy Nights. We descend into the earth at this time, and this penetration is described as a process similar to that undergone by the plants. In what sense? We are not referring simply to the physical descent of plant seeds a few metres down into the ground.

We are referring most importantly to processes in the ether currents of the plant organism. For etherically, plants are connected to the subterranean depths of the earth, indeed to the very centre of the earth; the inner sunlight, which the plant blossoms absorb during summer, is transmitted, via an ether current originating in the plant's root system, down into the core of the earth.[284]

> The normal human consciousness beholds nothing of that which happens for the soul in the depths of the earth. For those whose spiritual eyes are opened, however, the time of the thirteen days and thirteen nights is a deep time of spiritual experience. Yes, parallel with the experience of the plant seed in the natural-physical depths of the earth, there occurs a spiritual event in the spiritual depths of the earth-this is parallel to the plant process. And the seer... can feel himself descending, penetrating into such spiritual depths. If the plant seed has its most important time down there, below, the human soul {also} has its deepest experiences in this time.[285]

Rather than journeying in some special way through the zodiac during the Holy Nights, as earlier anthroposophists theorized, we journey, on a spiritual level, in our soul body, into the crust of the Earth. And only after this, do we move up into the planetary spheres and the starry heavens, and through the zodiac, as we do every night. The current idea in anthroposophical circles, that the essence of the Holy Nights

---

[284] Lect. 6th Aug. 1908.
[285] Lect. 26th Dec. 1911.

is a night-time journey through the zodiac is erroneous, for that is a journey we undertake every night.

The descent into the Earth's interior is the secret of the Holy Nights, or rather, the main secret.[286] Still, although it does not represent a special journey through the zodiac, the winter in-breath does have a significant zodiacal aspect, which we will explore further later in this chapter.

Jesus of Nazareth – a new kind of sun hero

What is then, this important experience that we undergo during the Holy Nights of winter? To answer this question, we need to understand the unique nature of Jesus of Nazareth. One reason the early church had for establishing the birthday of Jesus as December 25th, which was the day for initiation into the sixth degree, was that people thought Jesus was (that is, became) a sixth degree initiate, in the classical sense. This view, however, was in error.

For Jesus, whose birth is described in the Gospel of St. Luke, was "the child of mankind", the primal human soul, that soul which, alone, was held back from incarnating on the earth when the rest of humanity began to incarnate in the Lemurian age. The ether body, as well as the astral body of this soul was holy; the primal, sacred ether forces that humanity had access to prior to the fall were, for the first time in history, incarnated to build the body of that child.[287]

It was because Jesus was of such a uniquely holy nature that he could become, in his thirtieth year, the vessel of the sun spirit, the Christ. Because of his especial nature, he was a sun hero in a sense, but not in the classical, initiated sense. But December 25th is nevertheless the correct date for his birth; for he who was to become the vessel of the Christ, from whom divine, self-sacrificing love was to arise in humanity, had to be born at that time in the northern hemisphere's wintertime when the inner sun force is so strongly present in the hemisphere (or, as Rudolf Steiner indicates, on a day very close to that).[288]

Jesus was a sun hero in an additional sense in that he became, through the baptism in the Jordan, the vessel of the

---

[286] There is a collection of sayings in the Steiner Archive, with a paragraph for each of the Holy Nights, but the editors there view these are written by someone else, not Rudolf Steiner.
[287] Lect. 26th Aug. 1911, in *Wonders of the World, Ordeals of the Soul....*
[288] *Cycle of the Year*, first lecture.

sun spirit, the cosmic Christ. Through this union of the Christ, the sun spirit, with Jesus, the Easter events became possible, through which in turn the Life-spirit forces of the cosmic Christ were brought to the Earth:

> Jesus was a 'global sun hero' in a really unique sense. When we grasp this idea, then we also understand that the earlier, old winter solstice festival had a significance different from the Christmas festival of today...for previously that which is holy was 'divine', it held sway in unattainable heights above humankind. But now {through Jesus of Nazareth} that which is 'divine' has descended to the human personality.
>
> That is the most important event of our epoch, that the Christmas festival, which had always portrayed the birth of an initiate, now portrays the birth of the greatest sun hero of all, Christ himself... What previously was never there, is now there, namely, the possibility that the human being can bring to birth the light in himself. He can do this, because the light was, for the first time ever, incarnate in a human being.[289]

We should note the extraordinary implication in Rudolf Steiner's words here; "the Christmas festival which had always portrayed the birth of an initiate", namely, that here Rudolf Steiner defined the festival on the third day after winter solstice, (December 25th) in the millennia preceding Christianity, as the "Christmas" festival ! When we realize that the German expression means 'hallowed nights', and that Steiner located this festival in the wintertime, this remarkable definition of Christmas takes on extreme significance.

Steiner's words instruct us to think of this festival in an unprejudiced, non-sectarian manner, in order that the final secret of the Holy Nights may be discovered. We are then enabled to overcome the abstract attitude toward Christmas, to find the way to become aware of the Christ-permeated seasonal processes, that is, the life cycles of both hemispheres.

---

[289] Archive lecture, 19th Dec. 1904.

This lecture extract also reveals a deep truth concerning the baptism in the Jordan (and we will explore this point further when we consider the Epiphany festival in Chapter Eight), that through the attainments of Jesus of Nazareth, through the union of his being with the cosmic Christ, at the baptism, each individual human being has been given the possibility of developing a close connection to the light and life of the cosmic Christ. The term Life-spirit refers to precisely this light and light.

What connection does the historical deed of the baptism have with the season of winter? In the lecture extract we have been discussing, Steiner indicated that this theme of humanity's access to the Life-spirit of the Christ-being belongs to the "Christmas festival". But this festival is defined as being intimately connected to the midwinter festival of antiquity. Thus, the historical baptism, wherein the cosmic Christ was 'born' in the earth, and the birth of Jesus both have a connection to the wintertime. What is then the relationship of winter to the Christ reality? When one understands the nature of the breathing process of the hemispheres, the answer becomes clear,

> So we see that one can say: at Christmas time {that is, in the winter hemisphere}, the earth {hemisphere} has absorbed its soul forces into itself; it has in the great annual breathing process absorbed its soul organism into itself. The Christ impulse is born in the earth's {hemisphere's} inbreathed soul forces, in the interior of the Earth. Deep in the earth's core, each winter, the Life-spirit forces of the Christ being increase.[290]

Earlier, I stated that although the phenomenon of beholding the sun at the midnight hour, on December 25th (June 25th in the south), has been explained as seeing through the Earth, and thereby seeing the sun on the other side of the planet, the mystery has a further aspect. Now we are ready to consider this hidden, deeper meaning. The "sun at midnight" is beheld not only by seeing all the way through the Earth to the other side of the planet, but also by contemplating the interior of the Earth itself, wherein,

---

[290] Lect. 31st Mar.1923, in *Cycle of the Year as ...*

amidst the dark elemental powers, a sublime radiance glows more brightly,

> We feel ourselves as it were, descending into the deep, frosty, apparently dead world under the earth; not only divining, but discerning that the spirit {there} awakens new life out of the death. Whatever stage of development we are at, we can understand what in all ages those who were initiated felt, who actually then, in the Christmas night, descended down at the midnight hour, in order to behold there the spiritual sun at the midnight hour of Christmas night.[291]

We have noted that during the wintertime, a powerful ether process, the wintertime permeation of the hemisphere by the inner solar ethers, brings about the fructification of the life-forces of nature,

> The spiritual sun of the Christmas night conjures forth in the first place, out of the apparently lifeless rock, the sprouting, germinating life, so that it may appear in the new spring[292].

In addition, the Life-spirit forces of the indwelling Christ increase, that the Earth may gradually transform,

> The {inner Christ sun} forces ray through the earth, vivifying and fructifying it, so that the Earth itself will be a bearer of the Christ power, of the Earth-spirit. Thus, that which is born to us in each Christmas, is each time born anew.[293]

This enlivening of the hemisphere's ether body by the assimilation at midwinter of the powerful, spiritual (inner) ether energy governs the life processes through which the springtime growth occurs. Such secrets of the earth's elemental life were known to the ancient initiates of old European mystery centres. Rudolf Steiner reports that millennia ago, in a certain northern tribe, the priesthood

---

[291] GA 117, Lect. 21st Dec. 1909.
[292] ibid.
[293] Lect. 25th Dec. (*The Mysteries - Goethe*).

arranged for the tribes people to restrict the act of conception to the days around the spring equinox.

Hence the women gave birth at approximately the winter solstice; the first child to be born immediately after the day which we now call "Christmas Day" was chosen to be the king of the tribe, until his 30th year. However, this precise coordinating of the propagation of humankind with the seasonal cycle had to cease in the interests of the freedom of the individual.[294]

The springtime growth of the plants is part of the yearly cycle; the midwinter strengthening of the ether forces of the hemisphere determines when the new growth in springtime will occur. But the wintertime Christmas impulse determines the timing of the springtime Easter event, thirty-three years later,

> The successive 'Hallowed Night' impulses are not at all of the same strength; rather, some are stronger, some are weaker. This is indicated thusly: that the time between Hallowed Night {that is, Christmas} and Easter is variable, that is longer or shorter.[295]

We have here confirmed, once again, the fact that Easter is a springtime festival as well as an ecclesiastical-historical festival. And it is also clear now that Christmas, apart from its commemoration of Jesus' birth (as a historical event, that is), is a winter festival. Just as the new spring Easter festival enables those celebrating it to develop a relationship to the Christ reality, as it now exists, amidst the dynamics in the Earth-soul, so too will the new winter Christmas festival,

> And so the Christmas festival itself should not only be a 'birth commemoration' festival; rather it should become, when it is experienced in the near future, year after year, a festival of a directly contemporaneous birth, the festival of a contemporary event.[296]

In other lectures besides the one I have just quoted, Rudolf Steiner indicated the need for a new concept of the birth of Christ, the need for an experience of the contemporary birth

---

[294] Lect. 24th Dec. 1916.
[295] Lect. 26th Dec. 1917.
[296] Lect. 25th Dec. 1917, in GA 209.

of Christ. However, when we recall the statement that through the achievements of Jesus of Nazareth, "the human being can bring to birth the light in himself", it becomes clear that in speaking of a contemporary birth, Steiner did not mean simply a general moral-ethical renewal. Rather, he referred to a definite spiritual force,

> ....that can arise into being from the depths of the human soul, namely, that which flowed into the aura of the Earth through the mystery of Golgotha. We want to quicken this {spiritual essence} in us, through such festivals {of that of the Holy Nights-Christmas}[297]

The Christ child

What is the "Christ child"? Since the cosmic Christ was never a child, never born in a manger, can this be a valid expression? The historical Christmas festival has the great task of commemorating the birth of the two Jesus children, but in the traditional northern hemisphere Christmas festival, the child Jesus is also referred to as the "Christ child". Of course this designation is not accurate. But the truth concerning this matter is deeply veiled. It was especially in smaller, more intimate groups, speaking to souls whose past lives had prepared them for such sacred knowledge, that Rudolf Steiner discussed these matters.

In one of his more intimate lectures, which I have already quoted in connection with the divine descent through the sun hero Jesus into the human personality, we find these words which may facilitate our understanding of the concept of the Christ child:

> The Christmas festival is not {concerned with} something transient and of the past, it is not a festival commemorative of something which is of the past; for the Christmas antiphon does not proclaim: Christ was born, or Christ has been born. Rather, it says: "Today, Christ is born". It always speaks of "today". That is significant and important. "Today" is spoken of, in the sense of Christ's own words; "I am with you, unto the end of time". This {contemporary birth} is something with which each year comes

---

[297] GA 150, Lect. 22nd June 1907.

before us, anew, and reveals the connection between humanity and heaven....

The human being must attain that inner harmony, that rhythmical nature, which is portrayed to him by the Christ, who was incarnate in Jesus. This is the connection between humankind and heaven. The sun should not only traverse the sky and attain **new strength at the winter solstice**; it should also beget in humanity a resurrection, a birth of light from out of the very depths of the human being, toward the {development of} **a culture of sun initiates**, in the present epoch of civilization.[298] {*bold fonts are mine AA*}

In other words, through the development of the new winter Christmas festival, the attainment of the Life-spirit or creative love, and the high clairvoyant consciousness which this brings, will be possible for humanity. To speak of "a culture of sun initiates" is to speak of a time when humanity will be graced with, and guided by, people who have brought to birth the divine Life-spirit forces in themselves. Is this the vista which so profoundly affects us when the traditional {that is, wintertime} Christmas festival is celebrated?

What period of time does Steiner refer to when he speaks of the "culture of sun initiates"? I have translated his text at this point freely, for the sake of clarity. Literally, it reads: "a 'sun hero-dom' of the fifth large cultural Epoch".[299] The term the "fifth large cultural Epoch" is a technical theosophical-anthroposophical expression for the large epoch (previously called a root race) which began after the end of Atlantis, about nine thousand years ago, and which will continue until about AD 8,000.

Thus Rudolf Steiner is indicating that during the next six thousand years, many people may develop this Christ impulse of the Life-spirit, through this process that is sustained and strengthened every winter. That is, again, in late June for people living in South Africa, South America, New Zealand, Australia, southern Indonesia; and in late December in the northern hemisphere.

---

[298] Lect. 19th Dec. 1904.
[299] In German, „Die Sonne soll auch im Menschen gebären ein Auferstehen, eine Geburt des Lichtes aus dem tiefsten Innern heraus, ein Sonnenheldentum der fünften Würzelrasse entgegen."

We see that the union of the human being to the Christ impulse, to the divine life forces of the Christ, occurs naturally each wintertime. This concept, which implies that the Holy Nights, or twelve days of Christmas, occur in each hemisphere in its winter, because of the inner, spiritual reality of winter, will be further considered in the Chapter Eight.

This truth was indirectly proclaimed by Rudolf Steiner in 1913,through his gift of to humanity of *The Soul Calendar*, which is, as we have already seen, a series of meditations revealing the spiritual significance for humanity of the cycle of the year. This book was published in 1913, the year of the founding of the Anthroposophical Society. Its verses establish the Holy Nights as a wintertime phenomenon and also, as we discovered in Chapter Four, the esoteric Easter festival as a springtime event for both hemispheres. In using this book, the reader in the southern hemisphere must take a starting point six months different from that taken by a reader from the north.[300]

The verses start at Easter with verse number 1, and proceed through the year, with verses 37 and 38 occurring around the winter solstice. Hence in the south, the 'Easter' verse is to be contemplated during that week which begins on the first Sunday after the first full moon after the spring equinox. My understanding of the inner reality of the cycle of the year has assisted me in comprehending and translating these verses. Verse 37 of The Calendar of the Soul (for roughly the period from the 15th to the 21st of December in the northern hemisphere and from the 15th to the 21st of June in the southern hemisphere) reads as follows:

verse 37: WINTER
To bear the spirit's light
within the hemisphere's winter night
Aspires blissfully my heart's desire
So that soul seeds, glowing bright,
Take root in cosmic depths
And that the Word of God in senses' darkness
Resounds, enkindling light within all being.

---

[300] As Rudolf Steiner confirmed to his students Fred Poeppig and Emil Bock.

The meaning of this verse will be, to some extent, clear from those mysteries that we have considered in this chapter; but the reference to the word of God which resounds through the earth (winter hemisphere) remains unclear until we understand the zodiac aspect of the Holy Nights. In this Soul Calendar verse I have changed 'Earth' to 'hemisphere', for the sake of clarity.

The zodiac and the Holy Nights
What is the relationship of the zodiac to the Holy Nights? During the Holy Nights of the wintertime, an intimate interweaving takes place of forces from the cosmos and our soul. The Earth is continuously within the out-streaming forces from the cosmos, from planets, from our sun, from other suns, other stars in our galaxy. However, those star groups lying behind the ecliptic, that is, the path of the sun across the heavens during a year, have a special influence on us. These are the zodiac star constellations. A study of their spatial position in our galaxy does not reveal any special significance in these star groups, with regard to the Earth. But it is significant that the sun and the planets ray out their forces to us against the background of these constellations.

The subtle forces rayed out by these zodiac stars become, through this connection to the solar system, of great importance to the Earth. We have already noted that the winter solstice initiation brings perception of the cosmos, through the faculty of Inspiration. This perception was symbolically portrayed for the acolytes during their time in the crypt through the production of mysterious musical tones; they then knew that "this is the music of the spheres". That is, through the faculty of Inspiration, the inner, living reality of the cosmos was clairvoyantly perceived.

It is characteristic of Inspirational clairvoyance that the perceived objects or forces seem to inwardly resound to the observer; it is a kind of inner listening. During the Holy Nights it is easier for the person developing clairvoyance to experience this consciousness. It is at this time, as we have seen, that the high spiritual force is present in the hemisphere which can consummate the spiritualization of the soul, so that it can begin to transform its ether body.

Truly, the Holy Nights of each hemisphere are a time of immense spiritual potency, for precisely during this time the Earth-soul in that hemisphere perceives the zodiac

245

influences. That is, the consciousness of the beings who constitute the Earth-soul is permeated by an awareness of the influences from sublime hierarchical beings who work through the zodiac into the Earth.

Therefore, when a person has an experience arising from clairvoyance at the level of Inspiration during the midwinter, whether in a faint manner through grace, or otherwise, an intense zodiacal element is present. For the person at this time perceives not only the living reality of the zodiac, in the heavens, but also the powerful presence of zodiac forces in the Earth-soul.

As I have mentioned (p. 203-4), in wintertime the gnomes are perceiving the transcendental Idea, that is, the spiritual or archetypal Idea behind the forms of the plant kingdom; the forms with which the sylphs were working until autumn. These archetypal Ideas are brought into manifestation on Earth via the zodiac and planetary forces. The nature of these cosmic forces also permeates the sylphs, as they quietly rest in the earth. Hence, Rudolf Steiner describes the Earth-soul as engaged in a dialogue with the cosmos (zodiac) during the wintertime.[301]

Here we need to note that in the lecture where he mentions this, he refers to it as happening at the time of New Year's Day, and of the 13 nights (of the Holy Nights-Christmas time). Consequently, his comments have been used, wherever understanding of the new festivals has not arisen, to argue that the Holy Nights are a global phenomenon, and this dialogue of the mineral realm (i.e, the gnomes) and the plant realms (.i.e, the nature sprites) is a once-a-year', global event.

To be clear about this point, we need to know that Rudolf Steiner in his lecture refers to the union of the "complete mineral consciousness" with the "complete planet consciousness" occurring at this time. This enabled the clergyman, Benesch, to state that,

> "this is a unitary process for the entire Earth, and only occurs when it is the northern hemisphere winter time..."[302]

---

[301] Lect. 13th Mar. 1917.
[302] F. Benesch "*Weihnachten im Sommer...*"p. 22

However, a careful analysis of the lecture reveals that the term "complete" and "complete planet" are used poetically, to mean the entire **hemisphere**, not the entire globe. So here Steiner means 'the earth/world around one", (not 'the Earth' as the planet). For in the lecture about the mineral and plant consciousness communing, Steiner refers constantly to the seasons, and places the phenomenon of the speaking of the two realms, as arising in "the winter-time".

But above all, as conclusive proof, we can conclude that Benesch and his colleagues are entirely incorrect, from other words of Rudolf Steiner, specifically about the Holy Nights. Namely that, "*this occurrence **is an integral aspect of the seasonal cycle of the year**...If it were not united to the seasonal cycle of the year, then the {impossible} result would be, that one person could celebrate a Christmas-Holy Nights in December, another person in March.*"

We shall be examining the full lecture extract that these unambiguous words come from, in detail later (p. 285). So, when he refers to a seasonal dynamic, Rudolf Steiner may in fact use the term, the "complete Earth" but meaning simply the hemisphere, or indeed just the local environs. We shall soon be exploring more of his statements about the meeting with cosmic Christ forces in the Holy Nights. In one of these he again emphasizes that this occurs, because of the wintertime, which is a hemispherical thing; however, his actual words are, "*the human being in fact, together with **the complete earth** is {now} inwardly surrendered to the spirit*".[303]   (emphasis mine AA)

It is obvious here, since he is taking about the winter, that he means, and can only mean, the hemisphere which is in its wintertime. Finally, as we briefly noted earlier (p. 204), when he was preparing for his great foundational lecture-cycle about the new seasonal festivals for both hemispheres, "***The Cycle of the Year as the Breathing-process of the Earth and the Four Great Festival Times***", he wrote in his private notebook,

> In winter the elemental beings of the plant realm meet in the earth those of the mineral realm"....deep wintertime, the plant spirits unite with the spirits of the minerals.[304]

---

[303] GA 175, 20th Feb. 1917, p. 59
[304] In Supplement to the GA, No. 19, p.1 and 3.

Rudolf Steiner provides further information about the winter in-breath and how it affects the nature spirits. He speaks of now the Earth's soul in the winter hemisphere perceives the inner nature of the forces that have created the minerals.[305] For there is consciousness behind the minerals, because there is an archetypal Idea from which the physical-material world has its origin. The forces that have produced the rocks and crystals exist in the spiritual realm, which we have called Devachan, from which the human spirit descends to a new life.

The consciousness behind the minerals is especially deep and transcendental, even though it cannot manifest directly in the world; it is related to the human being's subconscious will forces, which are equally unconscious in this world, and equally significant in the dense matter of the body.[306]

For our subconscious will activates our bones, our limbs, guiding us through life. In winter, the Earth-soul perceives the inner nature of the minerals, the archetypal spiritual forces behind them, these forces that ray into the Earth from the zodiac. Steiner called this particular raying in, which is via the zodiac, the 'cosmic Word'. These influences are not only seen by the faculty of inspiration, they are also heard, they resound,

> The winter solstice initiation experience enabled the person undergoing it to perceive the cosmic Word resounding through the cosmos, the cosmic Word which....proclaimed the being of the cosmos {"das Weltenwesen"} from the star constellations.[307]

And because the initiate also gains the capacity to commune with the Earth-soul via this higher consciousness, he perceives that the Earth-soul, in the winter hemisphere, withdrawn down into below the ground, is in deep communion with the zodiac forces.[308] The fundamental truth underlying the new festivals is that the Christ being has become united with the soul of the Earth, that he is present, as the guiding ego of the planet, in the life processes of both hemispheres. In the words of Rudolf Steiner, (with explanatory words in brackets added by me,

---

[305] Lect. 31st Dec. 1915.
[306] Lect. 1st Oct. 1921 in GA 207.
[307] Lect, 26th Dec. 1921.
[308] Lect. 22nd Nov.1907.

248

The Christ-being has, since the resurrection, united his 'soul' with that of the Earth. His astral body is in continuous union with that of the Earth; he has become the planetary spirit of the Earth. The Earth is his body, he leads Earth evolution".

Hence, in the wintertime, he is also withdrawn deep into the core of the earth. For the lecture continues,

"the astral body of the earth {that is, the hemisphere} withdraws {in winter} into the central core of the Earth...the seer can observe this with great exactitude.[309]

Hence all that which is present as zodiac awareness in the Earth-soul also lives in the consciousness of the Christ-being. Steiner's words express this cosmic nature of the Holy Nights:

The Earth-spirit, concentrating upon its own being, experiences the secrets of the infinite universe in the Earth's soul life and we human beings, when we give ourselves up to this experience....then experience the holiest secrets.[310]

Let us now recall that during the summertime, *devachanic* spirit light from the sun was absorbed into the hemisphere's aura. As we noted in Chapter Five, the cosmic Christ is also involved in this process, he receives these forces, too. But the Earth and Christ being are also permeated by zodiac forces,

The earth {hemisphere} has completely out-breathed. All its soul forces have poured forth into cosmic space and are permeated with the forces of the stars. The Christ, who is now united with these soul forces of the earth {hemisphere}, now unites his power also with the solar and star forces, which are flowing into the earth's soul {hemisphere}.[311]

---

[309] Ibid.
[310] Lect. 31st Dec. 1914 in GA 158.
[311] Lect. 31st Mar. 1923 in *The Cycle of the Year as...*

This spiritual essence from the zodiac, absorbed during the summer, is drawn down into the earth in winter time.

> The sun gold, directed by Uriel, draws into the depths of the earth, spiritually permeates the depths of the earth, vivifying there that which, during the wintertime, seeks life for the next year.[312]

The relationship of this process, guided by archangel Uriel, to the tasks of the archangel of winter, Gabriel, will be considered later. Thus, in the Holy Nights of winter the hemisphere is immersed in deep contemplation of the formative, causal forces of the zodiac, the 'divine Word'. One feels that now the gods that constitute the Earth-soul renew their inner attunement to the cosmic purpose regarding the future of the Earth, namely spiritualization until it becomes a star, a new sun.

This purpose is gradually coming to expression, through long cycles of time, by the interweaving between the cosmos and Earth of ether and astral forces regulated by the zodiac. The festival would have as one of its focus points, the contemplating by these divine beings, in the winter time, of such cosmic forces.

It is through this process that the future year, and indeed future zodiac ages, derive their special characteristics; the age of Pisces, for example, or the future age of Aquarius. Such secrets of the winter in-breath were perceived already in remote antiquity. An ancient Indian text, the Rig Veda, mentions twelve Holy Days that occurred about the time of the winter solstice. It is said that these days are an image of the coming year; that during these days the Ribhus are resting from their labours, in the home of the sun gods.

The Ribhus are elemental beings, referred to in multiples of three; together with a fourth such kind of being, Twashtri, connected with the element of fire, they constitute the living reality behind the four elements. The Ribhus are, therefore, the artisans of the gods; they dwell "in the region of the midair {probably the ether aura of the Earth}, they help make the grass and herbs grow". That they are said to be in a quiescent state, resting at the time of the winter solstice in-breath, corresponds with the research of Rudolf Steiner. He reports that, the elemental beings and other nature beings {that is, sprites} "come into contact with each other during

---

[312] Lect. 12. Oct 1923, in *The Four Seasons and the Archangels.*

250

this time, and, apart from the gnomes, quietly rest in the earth".[313]

These holy winter days are said to reflect, in miniature, the months that will follow. During the course of a year, the sun journeys in front of the entire zodiac, all twelve signs during the twelve months of the year. This interaction between the sun and the zodiac is of great significance for the Earth; for example, with regard to the astrological sun signs of incarnating people. During the weeks around the winter solstice, around the Holy Nights, the zodiac forces permeate the consciousness of the hemisphere and from the contemplation of this twelve-fold force, the hemisphere is able to prepare the growth and new life of the coming year.

From perception of this dynamic, the thought has arisen in many countries that the weather of each successive month of the coming year can be foretold by observing the weather of each succeeding day of the twelve days of Christmas. This belief, which exists in ancient folklore, is a symbolic expression of the significance for the Earth of the twelve-fold cosmic Word permeating its inmost being during the Holy Nights.

For the essence of this phenomenon, which occurs in the Holy Nights of midwinter, is obviously not limited simply to elemental or ether processes. Of course, the weather of the following twelve months cannot be the same as the weather of the twelve days around the winter solstice; there may be, for example, a driving snow storm for those twelve days.

During the winter in-breath the hemisphere draws the spiritual sunlight and other cosmic forces from the zodiac and the planets deep into the earth. In Chapter Eight we will explore further the significance of this Life-spirit radiance, including the Life-spirit forces of the Christ being, in the Earth. Now we will complete our consideration of the relevance for the Holy Nights of the zodiac forces.

We have seen that during the wintertime the Earth-soul, now intensely awake, becomes aware of the spiritual forces that stream into the earth from the zodiac throughout the year. These beings also now gaze far out into the cosmos, perceiving the zodiac amidst the starry world around it. And that spiritual essence of the mineral realm, which rays down from Devachan (Spirit-land), via the twelve-fold zodiac Word, is now perceived by the elemental beings.

---

[313] Lect. 5th Oct. 1923 in *The Four Seasons and the Archangels*

This is the situation in the hemisphere around the time of the winter solstice; as I have indicated, the process is not limited to twelve days and thirteen nights. Rather, the numbers 12 and 13 are surely intended to assist people in contemplating the formative, creative influence of the zodiac, on the earth,

> The time from Christmas until beyond New Year, approximately until the 6th of January, is indeed suitable for having experiences {like those of Olaf Åsteson}.[314]

When the new Christian seasonal festival of the winter is created, it will be possible for the participants to begin to approach the Christ being through contemplating such truths as these. For this contemplation and perception of the zodiac forces, by the earth in winter, is profoundly interwoven with the mystery of the Logos, of the high spiritual being-connected with the Trinity – which is represented in the sun god Christ (also called in these pages, the 'cosmic Christ'). Rudolf Steiner revealed that we must extend our understanding of the Christ reality beyond the sun god, sublime and glorious as that being is.

The cosmic Christ was himself a vessel for the still higher, more sublime aspect of the Christ mystery called **the Logos**. Steiner experienced the zodiac as an expression of the soul of the Logos, this higher aspect of the Christ being, the second part of the sublime Trinity. That is, the influence of the twelve-fold zodiac in its entirety derives from the creative powers of the Logos; all of the wisdom and creative potential within the zodiac, in its rhythmical interweaving with the life of the Earth, derives from the creative powers of the logos, from the divine word or Logos of St. John's Gospel.

A ray or aspect of this being is present in the great sun god Christ. Hence all that the Earth is to become, in future ages and aeons, via the formative influence of the zodiac, is contemplated by the Earth-soul in winter. The elemental beings, guided by Gabriel, are working to ensure that the new life of spring will be a true expression of the archetypal zodiac influences. And the cosmic Christ, contemplating the zodiac influences, imbued with zodiac forces absorbed in

---

[314] Lect. 31st Dec. 1914.

the peak of the summer, now unites this experience with that being from whom the zodiac itself originates, now again becomes the vessel of the Logos. This happens twice in a calendar year; once for each hemisphere.

Again, there is no special outer journey through the zodiac that we undertake at the time of the northern Holy Nights. Rather, the various phenomena of the Holy Nights of both hemispheres arise from the nature of the winter in-breath. This brings cosmic forces into the core of the Earth. Hence Rudolf Steiner, when speaking of the zodiac aspect of the Holy Nights, taught that these specific twelve days are there,

> ....as if to enable one to immerse oneself in the twelve universal forces of the cosmos...the soul should allow itself to be inspired by the wisdom which is symbolically portrayed in the twelve signs {of the zodiac}.[315]

The dynamic in earth evolution wherein the twelve zodiac forces carry its evolution forward, so that the Earth may in the future become the ethereal New Jerusalem, with its symbolic twelve-sided walls, will be strengthened when humanity, aware of this process, creates the new Holy Nights festival of winter. In the same lecture, Rudolf Steiner therefore indicated that our relationship to the zodiac at this time is one of striving to bring to expression the wisdom, the creative potential of these forces,

> If only humanity will have the will to allow itself to be inspired by that wisdom, which in the twelve forces, in the twelve holy forces, penetrates into the universe; this is symbolically portrayed in the twelve signs of the zodiac, which in truth just portray spiritual wisdom.

And in the same lecture Steiner adds a second characterization of these archetypal forces,

> if only humanity would have the will to allow itself to be inspired by thoughts concerning the holy *childlike* divine origin of mankind. {emphasis mine AA}.

---

[315] Lect. 21st Dec. 1911.

253

It is precisely in Devachan or the true spiritual world that we have our origin; and the primal 'soul of mankind' who incarnated as Jesus of Nazareth was the very embodiment of these divine qualities. Hence through his being the Christ could come to manifestation. Therefore, he went on to say in the same lecture,

> We feel the deepest devotion, when…with the coming of winter… we behold… spiritual forces which have the same origin as that of the human being.

In earlier times, people were aware that the earth soul was perceiving in winter the spiritual, archetypal forces in which the idea or essence of the realms of nature exists (and from which they condense into existence on Earth). It is therefore not surprising to learn that in old non-Christian Europe the evening of December 25th was called also "the night of the Mothers".[316]

Concerning the old term Modra-necht, Sir Edmund Chambers wrote, "Philologists say that it can only mean 'night of mothers', and we therefore must explain it as due to some cult of the 'Matres' or triad of mother goddesses".[317] This expression refers to the matrix forces, the archetypal ideas behind creation, ideas which are themselves nurtured by the hierarchies, specifically, by the goddesses. Rudolf Steiner taught that 'The Mothers' refers to,

> the Devachanic realm which is the primal fountain of all things…it designates the forces which crystallize the spiritual reality into the sense world, like a crystal out of the surrounding rock.[318]

As I have stressed, the interaction between the Earth and the zodiac is of an inner nature; it does not derive from an outer, spatial phenomenon. The idea, taught in England, by an Austrian anthroposophist in the 1930-60's, that the zodiac aspect of the Holy Nights is made possible through the earth making a loop in its orbital path, just during the twelve days (of the northern hemisphere only !) is obviously without any foundation.[319]

---

[316] Hastings *Encyclopaedia*, vol.5, p.891.
[317] Ibid.
[318] Lect. 26th Jan. 1905 and x/x/1909
[319] J.W. Stein is reported to have stated this.

Two levels of spiritual experience arise from the dynamic we have been exploring. First, we can perceive the wisdom of the hierarchies, the zodiac word through which the world is maintained; and this wisdom can be, thereby, further developed in us. The Spirit-self can therefore come to expression more strongly, for it is through the presence in us of wisdom that the Spirit-self develops in our soul. We draw near to the 'realm of the mothers'. And because the Spirit-self of the Christ now permeates the Earth-soul, the development in our soul, during winter, of the Spirit-self is further assisted. In other words, the Christ has united to the Earth, and during winter, a closer connection develops between the soul and the Earth-soul.

The second level of spiritual experience is the further progress toward the Life-spirit that is possible at this time. The Life-spirit is that special gift to the Earth of the cosmic Christ. When Rudolf Steiner indicates the realm that humankind should strive to enter, or to gain awareness of, during the Holy Nights, he mentions the 'realm of the universe', from which the cosmic Christ descended to earth. Steiner is not referring to a spatial journey but to the possibility of attaining consciousness of an even higher realm in the heavens than that of the Spirit-self.

For the Spirit-self has its existence in the fifth realm of spirit-land; there, as a living presence, is the divine wisdom that rays forth from the hierarchies and via the zodiac influence governs the development of the earth. But the 'realm of the universe', of the Christ, is still higher; it is the sixth realm of Spirit-land,

> Here one experiences the source of the origin of the universe...in which the origin of the world exists, that voice of which the sages speak as being of the Word from which all creation has emerged." [320]

This sixth realm of Heaven is also called by Rudolf Steiner "the realm of the sun and planets creating logos." [321] It is to this sublime realm that a person in whom the Life-spirit has been developed has access. During the hallowed nights of midwinter, it is possible for each human soul to progress further toward the sixth degree of spiritual development,

---

[320] Lect. 10th June 1906 & in an archive document of Jan. 1904.
[321] Ibid.

toward the spiritualization of the life forces, and thus to manifest the selfless joyous love which has a healing, creative power in the world. Rudolf Steiner revealed this deep mystery. Gradually, through the cycle of the year, through the spiritual dynamics behind the seasonal cycle, humanity achieves the birth of the Christ child.

Through the new winter festival, a doorway will open between forces of the high realm and the festival participants. During each hemisphere's Holy Nights, the zodiacal influences, as a manifestation of the wisdom of the hierarchies, may be contemplated. One may contemplate the significance of the Christ reality in the interweaving of human and zodiac influences, such as the spiritual-psychological influence of the twelve signs, which over many millennia have formed a twelve fold ego-hood for humanity, through the process of reincarnation.

For in the course of one Platonic year of about twenty-six thousand years, we incarnate twenty-four times, twice in each zodiac age. Although this is a general pattern, however is often broken by the demands of complex karmic forces. In the next chapter we will consider further the nature of the Christ child and of the Holy Nights in relation to the Epiphany festival.

CHAPTER EIGHT

EPIPHANY AND THE HOLY NIGHTS

We are not left on our own, during the descent into the Earth, during the winter nights, with the task of developing the Christ sun within. For perhaps the most sacred of the themes that the new Holy Nights festival will offer to humanity is that of the close connection which develops between humanity and the risen Jesus Christ, the vessel of the cosmic Christ, during the Holy Nights. Before considering the help we receive at this time from the risen Christ, we need a clearer understanding of the relationship of the Holy Nights and Epiphany to the Christ child.

Through the Spirit-self purity that Maria, the Madonna, had attained, it was possible for the primal, pristine Jesus soul, that soul in whom the creative love forces of the Life-spirit were in essence present, to incarnate. Although the birthday of this holy child is indeed worthy of commemoration, it has never really been celebrated, as the exoteric aspect of Christianity dominated in the churches, and the distinction between Jesus and the Christ was lost.

Hence when Christmas Day was inaugurated in the fourth century, it celebrated the birth of Christ, as a child, truly an invalid idea. However, December 25th was the great festival day of other competing religions, for they celebrated on that day the birth of their sun hero founders. Therefore the festival of 'Christmas' was of help to the church in that it directed the attention of the community toward the birth of Jesus.

Such pragmatic matters were important to the church. For the popularity of other religions, especially Mithraism, was strong and growing stronger. During the third century A.D. the midwinter festival of the Mithraic religion, called "The Birth of the Invincible Sun", was strengthened through the official decision of the Emperor Aurelian to institute this festival in Rome. He had already caused a great temple to the sun to be built in Rome, on the Campus Martius. Furthermore, the cult of Sarapis, an Egyptian 'god of the winter sun' was becoming increasingly popular at this time, from Egypt across to Gaul. There were also the Roman

Saturnalia and Kalends, two folk festivals, in the wintertime, celebrated with much merriment. Of course, insofar as Jesus was regarded as a sun hero, this was in fact an appropriate date. As I have already noted, this date is confirmed as accurate by Rudolf Steiner.

However, long before Christmas was established as the festival commemorating Jesus' birth, the Epiphany festival was celebrated. The word epiphany, of Greek derivation, means 'manifestation'. To the early Christians the real manifestation of the cosmic Christ to the Earth occurred, for the first time, at the baptism in the Jordan when the Christ forces descended to Jesus. For it was then that the 'light divine' and the Life-spirit or inner sun forces of Christ entered the earth sphere, to be fully united to the Earth later, through the Easter events.

Thus the original Epiphany festival was, and is, more important than the festival celebrating the birth of Jesus. The Epiphany event signified to the early esoteric Christians the birth of the radiant glory of the Christ reality in the fallen or impure soul body of the earth. It is important to note that the date for the commemoration of this event is January 6th, which marks the end or culmination of the Holy Nights !

On this date, January 6th, as the early Christian initiates would have known, the mystery religions enacted a profound ritual. This festival celebrated the birth of a mystical child by a virgin. In the Greek mysteries, her name was Kore. She represented the interweaving of higher astral forces between the human soul and the Earth.[322] This festival derived from perception of the winter Holy Nights process, wherein those spiritual forces which we have considered in Chapter Seven become manifest in the Earth-soul. The essential secret of the Epiphany festival can only be understood when it is known that through the descent of the cosmic Christ to Earth, this process was given an immensely powerful renewal.

Hence, the central dynamic of the old mystery ritual can be transferred to this new festival, although metamorphosed so as to reflect the changes which have occurred to the earth through the descent of the Christ. When the difference between Jesus and Christ was no longer understood, this original Epiphany festival was actively suppressed, and the

---

[322] Lect. 22nd Aug. 1911, in *Wonders of the World, Ordeals of the Soul...*

Christmas festival was introduced. Then Epiphany became the festival of the Three Kings. That is, Jesus, by now called the "Christ child", 'manifested' to the three Magi. Rudolf Steiner taught that it is essential to re-establish the real Epiphany festival.[323] This is not to say that the Three Kings festival is devoid of value, but it and therefore Advent need to be reassessed.

To the early Christian esotericists, the Epiphany festival commemorated the entry of a divine spiritual force into the Earth's own soul, which permeated the darkened, tainted sea of harmful negative astrality which developed in the planet's aura through the influence upon humanity of luciferic spirits. The River Jordan symbolizes this lower astral aura of the Earth; the soul world is often symbolized as a mass of water.

Thus, in the recently discovered initiation teachings of the first Christian Gnostics, such contemplations as these occur regarding Epiphany: "Jesus manifested himself at the Jordan; this was the 'fullness of Heaven'. He, who was begotten before everything, was begotten anew". And also: "But the son of man came forth from imperishability, being alien to defilement. He came to the world by the River Jordan; and immediately the Jordan turned back. And John bore witness to the descent of {upon?} Jesus. For he is the one who saw the power which came down upon the Jordan river".[324]

An Epiphany ritual which reflects this earlier knowledge of the true significance of the baptism is celebrated in eastern churches. It is called "The Blessing of the Waters". On January 6th, an elaborate ritual is performed, wherein a body of water, for example, a river or pond, is blessed by a bishop, who invokes the power of Christ into the water. The leitmotif of this ritual has not only an historical relevance; it is also relevant to the contemporary, seasonal reality, to the reality of the Holy Nights.

Connected with this process, is the once widespread tradition of driving away evil beings on the twelfth night. On the last of the Holy Nights, it was the custom in Europe for the townsfolk to go in processions through the night, driving away demonic influences, purifying the environment

---

[323] Lect. 26th Dec. 1921.
[324] Nag Hammadi, *The Gospel of Philip*, and the Testimony of Truth, E.J. Brill, Leiden, 1966.

through various activities, especially creating a loud clamour of noises, and chanting protective verses.

In Russia, this rite was administered by the church, in a powerful ceremony: "On a frozen lake, a huge cross made of blocks of ice was constructed, a procession of people, led by church dignitaries, approached this cross, singing a strange melody. There were men holding banners, around which an empty space was left. In this space, and attached {that is, caught} to the banners were demonic sprites. A hole was carved deep in the ice, underneath the cross; and the priests then intoned the words whose power drove the malignant beings down into the hole, deep into the earth".[325]

Such malignant powers are connected to the lower self of the human being. Hence the removal of such powers from the earth is another aspect or leitmotif of the new Christmas winter festival; through such new festivals "the egotism of humanity will cease".

It is important that the original Epiphany festival be re-established, as an historical festival. But because it is placed on January 6th in the northern hemisphere, it can also become an essential part of the new twelve-day winter Christmas or Holy Nights festival, that is, through our also celebrating it in a metamorphosed, contemporary, seasonal form. We can bring this about through discovering the connection of the historical Epiphany events to the spiritual reality of winter.

It appears that the Epiphany festival was placed in the time of the Holy Nights so that its connection to this season could later be discovered, just as the historical Easter festival was placed in the springtime sun and moon dynamic so that it could later become – in a metamorphosed form, the basis of a Christian springtime festival. For the great theme of the original Epiphany can be, indeed must be, brought into relationship to the cycle of the year, not abstractly, but organically. Indeed, this theme, the birth in the Earth-soul of devachanic, spiritual forces from the Christ impulse, becomes reality, as we have seen, every wintertime. Again, historically,

> Epiphany commemorates the descent of the Christ
> from the spiritual heights and the immersion of

[325] C.Miles, *Customs and Traditions*, (Dover Books, N.Y. 1976)

Christ into the body of Jesus of Nazareth. This was originally the birth of Christ in Jesus.[326]

Rudolf Steiner clarifies this further in another lecture,

> The baptism in the Jordan signifies that the cosmic, transcendental being of Christ descended from the heights of heaven and united itself with the being of the man Jesus of Nazareth. The baptism by John in the Jordan thus signifies the fructifying of the earth from cosmic realms...it signifies a reciprocal interaction of heaven and Earth.[327]

Understanding this cosmic significance of Epiphany is vital to re-establishing the truth of the cosmic nature of the Christ-being in modern times. There is, first, a historical significance to this very important Christian festival. This has, however, been suppressed. However, as with the other historical festivals, its main theme, the vivifying of the earth by the descent of the sun god Christ, can be metamorphosed.

It would then be seen to have a connection to the cycle of the year; namely, to the wintertime, wherein Life-spirit forces are able to permeate the depths of the Earth. In Chapter Seven we saw that in the cycle of the year, the Christ force, which descended historically at the baptism, is absorbed into the aura of the Earth every winter. In winter, as we noted earlier, "the Christ impulse is born in the interior of the earth."

And, further, because the primal, archetypal man, Jesus of Nazareth could unite these forces to his own being, every human being can thereafter, during the winter nights, receive from the cosmic Christ, via Christ Jesus, these inner sun forces. As I have noted, it is because of the achievement by Jesus that,

> the possibility is now there...that the human being can bring to birth the light in himself {or herself}. He can do this, because the light was, for the very first time, incarnate in a human being.[328]

---

[326] Lect. 21st Dec. 1911.
[327] Lect. 25th Dec. 1921.
[328] Lect. 19th Dec. 1904.

Before considering further how these two themes of the historical Epiphany festival can be brought into a relationship to the wintertime life spirit process, it is necessary to consider again the meaning of the symbolic Christ child.

The Christ child
In the historical festival cycle, the commemoration of the birth of Jesus, as presented in the Gospel of St. Luke, will be important, for this primal soul has an immense significance to us. One aspect of his significance is that, through the fact that he could become the vessel of the Life-spirit forces of the Christ, he became, as it were, an archetype of the 'christed' human being.

For after the resurrection, Jesus of Nazareth, permeated by the Life-spirit glory of the sun god (or cosmic Christ) became the risen Christ, or "Christ Jesus". That is, the sacred, literally angelic spirituality (that is, Spirit-self) of Jesus could bring to expression the sublime archangelic creative, selfless love of the Life-spirit. United to this man, streaming into him, was the presence of the cosmic Christ.

Each winter, the indwelling cosmic Christ and the Earth-soul meet, as it were, deep in the Earth. Thus, twice a year, the earth may receive a little more of the inner sun forces, or Life-spirit. And likewise, twice each year, during the winter of each hemisphere, individual human souls, upon descending deep into the earth, on a spiritual level, participate in a similar process, assisted by Christ Jesus himself.

Rudolf Steiner revealed the intimate, sacred mystery of the 'meeting with Christ Jesus' which occurs in the season of winter. When, during winter, the hemisphere's astral forces are drawn down below the ground, they become imbued with the Life-spirit radiance from the cosmic Christ, and from the sun gods. Then Christ Jesus wills to let this radiance permeate human souls, so that in the future we may develop this power of creative love from our own inner sun. Indeed, as I have noted, there should arise, during the remainder of our present epoch of civilization, many sun initiates. (To find proof that the Gospels themselves view Christ as the sun-god, see my book, *The Hellenistic Mysteries and Christianity*.) How does Christ Jesus assist us to develop the Life-spirit? Steiner revealed this mystery in the following words, from two lectures of his 1917 cycle entitled *Human and Cosmic Metamorphoses*:

Every evening we go through a meeting with our angel, at about midnight. Even as this meeting is connected with the course of the day, a second meeting occurs which is connected with the course of the year. Human life does not run its course uniformly through the year. When the sun develops its greatest heat, each person is much more dependent on his own physical life, and thereby the physical life around him, than during the winter. In winter one has to struggle with the phenomena of the elements, one is thrown back upon oneself. But at that time our spiritual nature is freed; freed from itself, and from the earth, and we are then united to the spiritual world, to the entire spiritual environment.

Therefore, the special feeling which we connect with the Christmas mystery and its festival is in no way something arbitrary; rather, it is connected with the time of the year in which Christmas is placed. In those winter days, appointed to this festival, the human being is then, as is indeed the entire world around us {that is, the hemisphere} given over to the spirit. Then the human being passes through a realm, so to speak, in which the spirit is near. And the result of this is precisely that, at about Christmastime, and on to our present-day New Year, the human being goes through a meeting of the astral body with the Life-spirit.

In the same manner, the human being undergoes, in the first meeting {during each night}, an encounter of the ego with the Spirit-self. This meeting with the Life-spirit depends upon the nearness of Christ Jesus {to the individual}. For Christ Jesus manifests himself through an archangel. He is, of course, an immeasurably higher being than they, but that is not the matter with which we are concerned at the moment. What we need to consider is that he manifests himself through a being from the realm of the archangels. Thus through this meeting we draw especially near to Christ Jesus, in our present stage of evolution, which has existed since the mystery of Golgotha.

And in a certain sense, we may call this meeting with the Life-spirit, which occurs deep down in the depths of the human soul, the meeting with Christ Jesus. Now when a person has deepened and spiritualized his feelings, either through the development of a spiritual consciousness by way of religious exercises, or, to supplement these, has also accepted the concepts of spiritual science, then, just as the person can experience the after-effects, in waking life, of the meeting with the guiding angel, so too can the after-effects of the meeting with the Life-spirit be experienced...In a profound sense, and this should not be blotted out by the materialistic abstract culture of today, Christmastime is bound to processes in the earth. For the human being, together with the earth {that is, their hemisphere} undergoes the 'Christmas-Holy Nights alteration' of the hemisphere.[329]

It becomes apparent here that these remarkable words refer to both Jesus, and an archangelic aspect of the cosmic Christ. This is the case, because since the Resurrection, Jesus became united forever with the cosmic Christ. Hence the two beings can no longer be regarded as separate. We need also to note here the emphasis that Rudolf Steiner places on the Holy Nights being caused by the winter time. Later in the second of the two lectures I have just quoted, Steiner emphasizes again that this encounter with the Life-spirit occurs in the winter, and thus in either hemisphere:

This meeting the human being has with the spiritual world, in the cycle of the year, on any point of the earth, in that time in which it is, for that point of the earth {i.e., hemisphere}, in fact, the Christmas wintertime.

One could at first think, from the above quote, that this means anywhere on the globe, and not just in the winter hemisphere. But we shall shortly examine further sections in his lecture which specify that it only occurs it the winter.

---

[329] Lects. 20th & 27th Feb. 1917.

What is then the glorious, joyous secret of the Holy Nights? It is this, that the winter in-breath – **either in the southern or northern hemisphere** – draws the Life-spirit forces from the sun sphere and of the cosmic Christ down into the womb of mother earth. That divine light which is the inner essence of creative, healing love, is able to permeate the astral body (soul) of the earth. And through the activity of Christ Jesus this same divine power, which humanity is destined to consciously experience in the far distant future, is drawn into the soul of each individual. This occurs because of the spiritual dynamics which arise through the winter in-breath. But, as Steiner stated in the lecture I have been quoting, this depends upon the nearness of the individual to Christ Jesus.

And it depends upon the individual knowing about this process. That is, people in both northern and southern hemispheres need to be aware of this sacred mystery which unfolds during their winter. Awareness of this process is necessary for its fulfilment, just as with the spiritual processes which occur in other seasons. Only when the contemporary Christian festivals come into existence will it be possible for humanity to fully participate in the spiritual processes upon which the future of the earth depends. Without the conscious participation of humanity, these processes cannot be brought to completion.

This is clearly shown in the second of the two verses in the Soul Calendar for the Holy Nights, verse 38 (for 'Christmas', or the week from about the 22nd to the 28th of December in the north, of June in the south):

> I feel as from enchantment freed
> The spirit child in womb of soul:
> In radiance of the heart
> The holy cosmic Word has now begotten
> The heavens' fruit of hope
> Which jubilantly grows in distant realms
> From my own being's divine depths.

The future transformation of the Earth depends upon the degree to which humanity achieves the birth of the spirit child. The "spirit child" referred to here is the germinal beginnings of the Life-spirit. This is the esoteric meaning of the expression 'Christ child',

> That which grew out of the dying world as new
> fruits of life {in the earth and initiates} was
> experienced by the initiates as the birth of the Christ
> child in the spiritual world.[330]

It is precisely this process which is described in verse 38 of the *Soul Calendar*, which I have just quoted, a process which takes place twice each year, during each hemisphere's winter. The Soul Calendar provides the meditative tool through which the spiritual contents of the new festivals can be created.

Early esoteric Christian groups had a wonderfully artistic symbol of this development of the Life-spirit, or Christ child, from the striving towards the spiritualization of the soul, the black Madonna. In Illustration Nine such a carving is shown, which depicts the Jesus child actually not as an infant, but an alert, strong, adult-like child, with his hand raised in the gesture of peace.

Esoterically, peace is that quality which arises when the storms in the lower self have vanished, and the inner harmony brings the Life-spirit to manifestation. The Spirit-self which can begin to form the Life-spirit is also the source of peace, peace not only to the individual, but also to the environment.[331] So, the woman represents the purified astral body, and the child depicts the Life-spirit.

Hence the Christmas message of the angels is deeply true: "Divine revelation {is} in the heights, and upon earth, peace to people of goodwill". Now the profound wisdom in the winter solstice meditation of the ancient mysteries can be seen: "Behold the sun at the midnight hour...the heights reveal the gods' eternal {zodiac} Word...the deeps{the earth's interior} should guard the light that shines in its darkness", deep in the ahrimanic depths of the Earth, the gods must guard the ever increasing droplets of golden dew. And we can express the inner meaning of verses 37 and 38 of the Soul Calendar thus: Soul seeds take root in the spiritual-archetypal level of the Earth's inner being, depending on the degree to which human beings allow the Christ child to develop in their own soul forces.

---

[330] Lect. 15th Dec. 1906.
[331] Lect. 24th Oct. 1924.

VIRGINI PARITVRÆ

104. - Cathédrale de CHARTRES (E.-et-L.) - Notre-Dame de Sous Terre

A rare image of this black Madonna; it represents the Life-spirit emerging (as a child) from the maternal Spiritual-self. The inscription says "virgin who has given birth".

The difference between the new hemispherical winter-Christmas festival and the ecclesiastical Christmas festival has become very clear now. The latter has the task of strengthening the belief, the faith in the historical events of the life of Jesus Christ. The presentation of the 'Christ child' in this festival inspires the church community to a stronger reverence and interest in the events of the Gospels, so that the consciousness can be illuminated during daily life. This kind of spiritual working is valid and effective within the context of a global, simultaneous festival format.

But the new festival cycle, which enables humanity to develop a conscious relationship to the cosmic Christ, and to Christ Jesus, in their working within the life processes of the Earth, that is, of the hemispheres, places the participants within the cycle of the year, in the ongoing spiritual development processes of the earth and humanity.

Hence, of the **ecclesiastical** Christmas festival, it should be said, regarding the southern hemisphere, that the inner essence of the Christmas festival cannot be found in the workings of nature, or in the seasons. That is, there can be no question of the church festival being connected to the winter; therefore, this **historical** Christmas occurs for the southern hemisphere at the same time as for the north.

However, when a spiritually contemporary connection between the Christ reality and the life processes of the Earth is the basis of a festival, this reasoning does not apply. The inherent non-acceptance in the Christian Community church of the new festival concept, is reflected in the statements presented by various of its clergy; E. Capel, writing in the first publication from the church on the subject of the two hemispheres, stated, referring to Christmas "....the birth of the Spirit-Child...this will not be found in the workings of nature, or in the season."[332]

Similar errors are encountered wherever the ecclesiastical attitude prevails; and no doubt would be expressed by clergy in other churches, too.[333] But such attitudes are quite correct

---

[332] *Festivals in North & South*, Evelyn F. Capel, Floris Books, in 1979, p. 24.

[333] For example, M. Samson, 2016, states this same error; "Rudolf Steiner meant, as the conditions in the southern hemisphere are the opposite (to the north), we celebrate the same festival in opposite seasons." (p.21) And, p.59, "the new festivals {i.e., new **church** festivals} must find their source and content out of the spiritual understanding of the human being...we give the course of the year its new expression, that enables it to be a platform for revelation of Christ."

when applied to the old, traditional church festivals; for the two festival cycles have entirely different natures. In the ecclesiastical cycle, there is no Holy Nights or Yuletide; there is the celebration of the birth of Jesus, Christmas Day. It has no connection to the seasonal processes of the hemispheres; the festival is simply placed in the flow of the calendar days, that is, once a year for the whole planet.

But in the new festival cycle, born of Christian initiation wisdom, the Holy Nights or Yuletide are recognized as occurring twice each year, as a reality in the aura and interior of the Earth. Hence one may undergo two meetings with Christ Jesus during the year, if one travels to the other hemisphere and thereby undergoes its winter in-breath process also.

For those to whom the night-time phase of life is becoming a clearer, deeper reality, these two meetings are objectively real. However, it may well be that the full effect of the Holy Nights with regard to the transformation of the ether body is not experienced when the traveller enters abruptly into the winter dynamic, just shortly before the winter solstice. In the words of Rudolf Steiner,

> The Christmas {Holy Nights} festival has not merely symbolical meaning, it also has natural significance... at this time {of the yearly cycle}, a force recedes from humankind which otherwise comes to it. When the disciple is so far, he must heed this. The human being must develop the forces from within, which otherwise come from without. The source of this must be cultivated in wintertime...this is indicated in the placing of the festivals {in the yearly cycle}. Christmas {Holy Nights} is the vivifying of inner etheric forces, and is placed in the time {of the year} when the earth {hemisphere} gives out the least forces of all.[334]

And this process, from which in the future a culture of 'sun initiates' will arise, is that same process which anthroposophy offers to humankind, as these words from Rudolf Steiner indicate,

---

[334] Lect. 22nd June 1905.

Thus, what we have to aim toward is a kind of universal Christmas, in a spiritual sense...the entire process in spiritual science is actually a kind of Christmas festival, wherein the Christ becomes born in human wisdom.[335]

Rudolf Steiner elaborates further on this,

The anthroposophical spiritual science intends to contribute {to the Christmas festival}, so that this festival shall again be thusly understood...That is, when our thinking and feeling is so purified {from egotism} that what one person feels resounds in harmony with what others feel....When Buddhi, the Chrestos, is embodied in the human race, then the ideal of the sages of olden times, of Christianity, of anthroposophy will be fulfilled.

The animal can find gratification in the pleasure of the senses. But not so the human being; for the Life-spirit demands more {of us}. Buddhi is the sum total {that is, the quintessence} of the feeling aspect of the world...Why was the sixth degree initiate called a sun hero? Whoever had risen so high upon the ladder of spiritual knowledge must have developed, at least inwardly, such a life quality that this inner life proceeded according to the pattern of the divine rhythm {which is} in the entire cosmos.[336]

So, the sixth degree initiate is, in effect, a Christmas initiate !

What did one think occurred, in the soul of such a hero, who had found such a harmony? One viewed the matter like this: that now no longer did only an individual, separate soul live in the person; rather, in such a person something had arisen from the 'universal soul' {or Soul of the World}, which flows through the entire universe. This universal soul which flows through the entire universe was called in Greece, Chrestos.[337]

---

[335] GA 165 lect. Mar. 28th 1916.

[336] GA 54 lect. 14th Dec. 1905.
[337] ditto.

270

So the words Chrestos and Buddhi are the referring to the same thing, and since Rudolf Steiner is speaking of the "Christmas" – that is, the Holy-Nights festival – then these two terms from India and Greece are referring to Christ; meaning here the sun god or cosmic Christ. So the Holy Nights time is about what we know from anthroposophy as the Life-spirit; meaning especially the Life-spirit forces of the cosmic Christ.

We need not find it confusing that in the ancient Grecian culture the Life-Spirit which we have understood to be a part of the Sun, is viewed as also energies which stream across the cosmos, (possibly proceeding from the sun). For in the great Foundation Stone Meditation, the influence of the divine Life-spirit forces of the Christ are described as "grace-bestowing" (literally, 'en-gracing') and also going from horizon unto horizon (see the Appendix for more about this).

So in this verse we encounter the two views of the Chrestos or Buddhi or Life-spirit, namely as a core aspect of the sun, but also as energies streaming across our world and further out into the cosmos.[338] It is useful to note here that Rudolf Steiner once spoke of how this festival of the winter solstice time, revering the Life-spirit forces of the sun god, was widely celebrated in previous millennia,

> When we understand the ceremonies which were played out at the Christmas-Holy Nights festival in Asia, India and even in China, then we understand what actually resounds to us in the Christmas church bells.[339]

Now, if we recall the words quoted earlier, that the Holy Nights are about "a vivifying of inner etheric forces", then we can see more clearly that, as the above words are indicating, the Holy Nights or Yuletide, is a time when the Life-spirit of Christ, interwoven with that of the sun, are strongly present in the "world around one"; that is, in one's local wintry environs wherever one is in that hemisphere.

Now we can go further in understanding this description of the Christmas-Holy Nights festival, and imbue a well-

---

[338] To learn more about this meditation, see the author's T*he Foundation Stone Meditation - a new Commentary*
[339] Lecture, 21st Dec. 1903.

known religious expression, "Grace", with initiatory wisdom. For Rudolf Steiner also described the Holy Nights or Yuletide time as,

> "a festival of feeling in harmony with the entire cosmos {that is, the solar system}; a festival of feeling {the presence of} Grace".[340]

But of course "Grace" has now be revealed in a meaning far beyond ecclesiastical definitions. These words from Rudolf Steiner about Buddhi are very interesting for those seeking to understand the deeper meaning of the Gospels,

> Christ had meant, with the expression, 'Grace' nothing other than Buddhi (which descends down and draws our self towards it)".[341]

On another occasion he told an audience,

> Grace, in its original sense, is exactly the same as what one calls in theosophical {anthroposophical} language, 'Buddhi'.[342]

See the Appendix for more about the term Grace and the Foundation Stone Meditation.

No global 'world-Christmas-Yuletide'

One indicator of the difficulty for those encountering this subject is a term Rudolf Steiner uses, although only rarely: "world-Christmas" (meaning the Yuletide-Holy Nights). It appears that he used it only four times. None of these usages in his Complete Works refer to a **global** Holy-Nights-Christmas festival. Instead these all refer to people needing to recognize how this festival has a larger significance than is traditionally understood. The most commonly quoted of these four instances, is from a lecture given on 23rd Dec. 1923, in a lecture cycle called *Man and the World of Stars*.

This reference is used by those opposed to the new festival concept, to suggest there should be a global Christmas Day (which indeed there should be). But the people who suggest this, and thus don't want a seasonal

---

[340] Lect. 21st Dec. 1911.
[341] GA 266a, p.46.
[342] Archive document, lect. August 1905.

"Christmas", are actually merging in their minds, the 12-day Yuletide festival with this one-day church festival; and it is this error which creates their confusion.

For the German word for Christmas ('Weihnacht') actually has two meanings; usually it means the one-day Christmas Day, but since this occurs in the winter-time in Germany, where long ago the 12-day Yuletide festival was celebrated, it also can refer to this old Yuletide festival; and it often does with Rudolf Steiner.

The two types of festivals should not be merged; this helps us to understand what Rudolf Steiner means by a "world Christmas-Yuletide". The context tells us what is meant; for he explains in this lecture that the Yuletide-Christmas festival is actually something that **involves the natural world around your community** (your local environs (as part of the hemisphere), in its winter condition.

The term, 'world', in lectures by Rudolf Steiner about the seasons, can often mean the natural world around oneself, the nature environment in which one is living; as we don't really experience the entire hemisphere as we live and work in our daily lives. Thus in the reference from *Man and the World of Stars*, Rudolf Steiner, before using this expression, a 'world Christmas-Holy Nights', comments that,

> we can only become truly human beings through finding the spiritual part of us **in the world**.
> (emphasis mine A.A.)

By this term here he means the natural environment around about one. In this context, 'world' here means the local environs (as part of the hemisphere); exactly as it does throughout the Soul Calendar. So Rudolf Steiner does not mean a global Holy Nights festival, despite this being suggested at times by those opposed to the contrary view. The Holy-Nights (or Yuletide) festival can only be hemispherical, never global. So this lecture reinforces the message that the inner deeper meaning of the new festivals is found when we discover that the seasonal processes activate spiritual influences which are directly important to us.

But unfortunately, the last part of this sentence was defective, when the lecture was published in an English translation, and has caused confusion for decades. In the above sentence, "we can only become truly humans beings through finding the spiritual part of us, **in 'the world'"**, these last three words were deleted in the translation. The sentence lost the phrase, "in the world", so it read,

> we can only become truly humans beings through finding the spiritual part of us.

This error effectively prevented the actual message of Rudolf Steiner, about the winter-time condition of the hemisphere, from being communicated. But in addition, another error was made to the final sentence of his lecture. It is given incorrectly in English as,

> Then in the Holy Night, Christ will be born in the heart of each one of you, and you will again experience **together with all Mankind a World Christmas.** (emphasis mine A.A.)

However, the correct translation is,

> Then in the Christmas-Holy Night, Christ will be born in the heart of each one of you, and you will again experience in yourselves, **with the other people, a world Christmas-Holy Nights** {that is, a "local environs Yuletide").[343]

So, Steiner did not say, "together with all Mankind", which would mean a global Christmas-Holy Night or Yuletide event; but he said, "with the other people", meaning your friends and other people; and this occurring in your community, in your local environs, (and thus throughout your hemisphere).

With students of anthroposophy being falsely informed for decades, through erroneous translations, it is not surprising that the concept of the new cycle of festivals has proven to be very confusing. We need to mention here too, that Rudolf Steiner spoke of a "World Pentecost" festival. This term is quite correctly understood to mean a global festival, for that is what all the church festivals should be; they are global festivals. A church activity has no implications for the creating of the new hemispherical festivals.

---

[343] In German, „mit den andern Menschen" not: „mit die ganze Menschheit der Welt".

Leitmotifs of Epiphany.

With regard to the ecclesiastical festival cycle, Epiphany is an historical festival, its theme being the descent of the Christ being into the soul and spirit of Jesus of Nazareth. Through this immense event, the "light divine" (Spirit-self) and the spiritual sun (Life-spirit) forces of the Christ have now united to the Earth. And through the union of these forces to Jesus, the archetype of a Christmas initiate has been created, thus enabling all humankind to achieve this stage, in the far future.

Through the new festivals, born of anthroposophical wisdom, these two historical aspects of the traditional festival are metamorphosed into their contemporary present-day living reality. We note that January 6th is the date chosen for the traditional festival, and we realize that there is a deeply esoteric reason for this, as with the springtime dating of the Easter festival. In the new, esoteric Epiphany, we realize and celebrate the fact that on January 6th, the Holy Nights process reached its culmination, with the 'birth' of the Life-spirit forces in the womb of the Earth's soul, and also the culmination of the wondrous blessing or grace-bestowing interweaving that occurs between humankind and Christ Jesus.

Both these processes occur in deep, hidden depths of the physical body of the Earth, and also in our own ether body, during the isolated, withdrawn phase of the hemisphere's cycle. Thus, the new, esoteric Epiphany festival, as the culmination of the Holy Nights festival, or winter Christmas festival, occurs on the 7th of July in the southern hemisphere. Again Steiner's words provide confirmation for our elucidation of the Epiphany mystery:

> Thus {in the winter season} we live, together with the power of the plant seed, as it were, quite literally inside the earth, we penetrate the Earth. And if the winter has reached its midpoint, when the deepest darkness rules, then we feel precisely thereby that the external world does not restrain us from feeling ourselves united with the spirit, from feeling how, in the depths {of the earth}, into which we have withdrawn, spiritual light springs forth; that spiritual

light, for which mankind has received from Christ Jesus the mightiest impulse.[344]

In a private conversation with a clairvoyant student, Rudolf Steiner confirmed that deep in the Earth, amongst the evil substance of an ahrimanic nature, there is the germinal radiance of the spiritual sun.[345]

In pre-Christian times, initiates perceived the presence during winter, deep in the Earth, of Life-spirit forces. These had been absorbed from the sun during the summer. After the Epiphany and Easter events in old Palestine, the leader of the sun spirits, the Christ, united his Life-spirit radiance to the Earth,

> That which in earlier times could only be perceived through {awareness of} the 'dialogue' of the earth {hemisphere} with the cosmos {during winter}, that has descended and has appeared in a human being, the man Jesus of Nazareth.[346]

The following words present the essence of this Epiphany mystery, wherein the Christ forces came to the Earth. Through the nature of Christ Jesus, these forces can now be absorbed by humanity,

> Through the deed of Christ on Earth, the capacity was created in the human being to assimilate that which we call Buddhi {that is, the Life-spirit}.... That which has drawn into the physical, ethereal, and astral organism of Jesus of Nazareth is the common source of all of these 'spiritual sparks' {that is, Life-spirit} for humanity. This drew into Jesus of Nazareth, so that those who felt themselves united to Christ Jesus could assimilate the Buddhi element.[347]

Through the conscious experience of the Holy Nights, via the new Christian winter festival, the inexhaustible forces of life and love which the primal "soul of mankind" brought to the earth will arise ever more in each individual. True spiritual

---

[344] Lect. 21st Dec. 1909.
[345] From a conversation he had with Countess Keyseringk, at Koberwitz, in 1924.
[346] Lect. 13th Mar. 1917.
[347] Lect. 2nd. Dec. 1909.

love will arise in human hearts. It is, as I have mentioned, a special characteristic of the person who has achieved the inner birth of the Christ force, of the sixth degree initiate, to manifest, to ray forth, love into the world. Rudolf Steiner indicated that through the new Christmas festival this quality shall 'grace' humanity. That joyous mood of the historical Christmas which arises, at least in part, from what we feel about the nature of the Jesus child, namely, that it emanates to a sublime degree that beautiful love and purity which every infant has, is also especially relevant to the seasonal Holy Nights festival of each hemisphere.

On the basis of the spiritual realities which together create the reality of the winter in-breath, as I have presented the process, we may evaluate these words from a Steiner lecture on The Calendar of the Soul, given in May 1912:

> The festival of the divine being, that is, the Earth spirit, could never be placed in summer by a clairvoyantly knowing humanity; rather, it must be celebrated in the wintertime. In the 'hallowed time' {of the year} the soul feels itself united with the divine spiritual powers which then permeate the earth. The Christmas-Holy Nights festival **belongs in the winter,** just as St. John's festival belongs in the summer.[348]

These words establish the necessity that the Holy Nights of winter, that is, the seasonal Christmas festival, be celebrated in the winter of each hemisphere.

The above conclusions are fully affirmed as accurate by Steiner's key statements in the special core lecture on the seasonal cycle for both hemispheres, given in Oslo, in 1923.

The background to the lecture of 21st May, 1923 in Oslo.
There is a special background to this key lecture, which, as we shall soon see, tells us directly that the Holy Nights-Christmas (or Yuletide) takes place in the southern hemisphere, in June-July To fully grasp what he was teaching in this lecture, we need to know that Steiner's lecturing output is carefully chronicled, and his talks were

---

[348] Lect. 7th May 1912.

officially announced as either, 'Members', 'Semi-public', or 'Public', lectures. Lectures to Members were open only to members of the Anthroposophical Society; Rudolf Steiner could then speak on the reasonable assumption that the audience had some knowledge of anthroposophical ideas and were supportive of his intentions.

With 'semi-public' lectures, Members could invite friends along, who were positive towards the general direction of anthroposophical ideas. Lectures for the Public were held for people with no background knowledge; although these were often attended by Members. In public lectures, he would carefully introduce the spiritual-esoteric content, as many anthroposophical ideas, when first heard, were indeed startling.

In this 1923 trip to Oslo, which coincided with the time of Pentecost, Rudolf Steiner gave 12 lectures. The only Public talk was about education, given on the 15th October; there were 3 semi-public ones, and the rest, (7, including a festive Pentecost address) were all Members-only talks.

In the lecture on 21st May, his words are so definite about the Holy Nights being caused by the winter in-breath, and thus occurring in the southern hemisphere in June-July, that it is these words in particular which those who are opposed to the new festival concept would like to dismiss. One technique is to suggest that the words used by Steiner have another, unheard of, meaning (we shall examine this later) and another technique is to imply that this lecture is a 'public lecture', and therefore, by inference, is not so worthy, not so significant. Another approach is to suggest that there are no other lectures from Steiner in which he suggests that the Holy Nights belong in the winter in the south; we have already seen how inaccurate that conclusion is.

The second approach has been used recent recently by a Christian Community official, M. Samson, who refers to a preceding lecture, about Pentecost, given on 17th May, as a 'public lecture', and then goes on to write the following confusing words, "*it is the public lecture given during the lecture cycle {in Oslo} that is used to prove that the antipodeans have their Christmas in the winter*". [349]

---

[349] M.Samson, *"Festivals in the southern..."* p. 36.

Firstly, **neither** of the two lectures (on 17th & 21st May) were public ones.[350] Secondly, it is only the unique lecture of 21st which refers to the Antipodeans. And so indeed, it is this unique lecture which is especially used to prove the new festival cycle. Hence, when reading the sentence quoted above, which mixes up the two lectures in a confusing way, one comes to the impression that this key lecture of 21st May, is ('only') a public lecture. Then within the reader the conclusion forms that it can be ignored, or treated as less significant.[351]

But in fact, this especial lecture of the 21st May was very much a Members-only talk. It was given on the important occasion of the founding of the Norwegian Anthroposophical Society, and thus its esoteric content would be especially selected. So spiritually inspired was the occasion, and the nature of this lecture, that some of Rudolf Steiner's concluding remarks (which were not about the festivals) were omitted from the first publication of this lecture, in 1925.

Presumably this was done to safeguard against the public and opponents accessing the text. By 1923 various groups were strongly opposing Rudolf Steiner. However eventually, in 1934, Marie Steiner published the omitted text, and informed the Members about this earlier omission, in the Dornach *Anthroposophical News* of 7th Oct. 1934.

In such a special lecture Rudolf Steiner could state openly what he otherwise had only indicated in earlier years about the Holy Nights. This was a remarkable event, considering that the new festivals is a topic which, as he told an Australian enquirer, was not going to be comprehensible for some decades (see ps. 60-61).

During his time in Oslo, Rudolf Steiner built up a basis for the great statements to be made on the 21st. One of these Members' lectures was about the festival of Pentecost; this was a Members' lecture not a public one, as stated by Samson.[352] It was given on 17th May, some five days before the crucial lecture with its specific statements about the southern hemisphere. This lecture is described by Samson

---

[350] The status of these, and all of Steiner's lectures, are given in the Register published by the Anthroposophical Soc., "*Das Vortragswerk Rudolf Steiner*" Hans Schmidt, 2nd. edition, Dornach, 1978.

[351] Ibid. p. 36.

[352] Ibid. p. 41.

as primarily telling the audience that festivals can be global, thus celebrated in both hemispheres at the same time (as church festivals always are).[353]

But in fact, after speaking extensively about the original Pentecost event, Rudolf Steiner, towards the end of his talk, begins to prepare his audience for a radically new and inspiring definition of the 'Pentecostal' activity of the (Holy) Spirit, in our times, a definition that has nothing to do the churches. For he gently refers to the new festival cycle. In this Pentecost lecture, he creates a basis for his listeners to understand the powerful message about the two hemispheres that will be given to them in the climactic lecture on 21st May.

He points to the new festival concept, to the spiritual influences behind nature, and therefore to the seasonal cycle. In summary one sees that these remarks presented the moods and cycles of nature as a blessed gift to those people seeking to experience Christ, as the spirit of our Earth. This is just what he had said to Rev. Rittelmeyer, if we share Emil Bock's interpretation, (as we discussed on p.58). For at the end of his Pentecost talk, Steiner says this,

> Through spiritual science we must again learn to see the Spiritual behind all material things; the spiritual behind the stones, the spiritual behind the plant, the spiritual behind the clouds, the spiritual behind the stars, the spiritual behind the sun. When we again find the Spirit behind matter (as earlier humanity did) in its reality, **then we open our human soul also to the voice of Christ**, who wishes to speak to us, if we only wish to hear him.

This is not about a (global) church festival, but something else entirely; it is about the seasonal festivals as a way to the spirit and to Christ.

Then, three days later in this cycle of lectures, the day before the crucial talk, as he finishes his evening lecture, he tells his audience that in the morning, he wishes to discuss the **contemporary implications** of the Mystery of Golgotha for us today. In his own words,

---

[353] Ibid, p.36.

Then (tomorrow morning) we will want to place before our souls the actual Pentecost mystery, but in its significance for our actual contemporary times, and thereby bring our lecture cycle to an end.

The next day, May 21st, the key lecture is given with a focus on the spiritual significance of the seasonal cycle, and also how education and health are linked to a spiritual renewal. Here, Rudolf Steiner sums up, and also presents in essence, what he had taught over decades about the spiritual influences in the seasonal cycle by which we can be nurtured. He refers to the need that humanity has, to feel the spiritual reality of the seasons and then states,

> after the Resurrection, Christ Jesus has brought it about that the Pentecost-secret followed… Christ has sent the Spirit, the healing Spirit, thereby he has indicated that the human being is to have, from out of himself or herself, the Christ-experience.

Then Rudolf Steiner, who in this lecture has already spoken about the Holy Nights in the two hemispheres, and spring and autumn, speaks again of the seasonal cycle, especially spring and autumn, in relation to death and resurrection, saying,

> when people have gained the ability to create these {new} seasonal festivals, the human being will have attained, **from out of the present-day {holy} Spirit**, the power to give to themselves a festival (of the new seasonal kind).   (emphasis mine, AA)

In doing this, he was carrying out what he had announced the night before, namely; *"bringing before our souls the actual Pentecost mystery, but in its significance for our actual contemporary times"*.

In other words, the Christ-inspired Pentecost reality, in its contemporary way of manifesting, brings about that influence which enables us to create the new seasonal festivals ! Whereas lacking this Pentecostal inspiration, we would not be able to grasp or support the new festival concept. In the process of doing all this, he makes it clear that the Holy Nights-Yuletide time is **caused by the winter in-breath in each hemisphere,** in their respective winter-time. Let's now consider what he said.

The clear statement from Oslo, 21st May 1923, about the Holy Nights occurring in June in the Southern hemisphere.

> ....just consider, though, that when we here {in Europe} have St. John's festival, that is, when it is the case that our souls can follow the Earth-soul which {now} arises and 'unites' itself with the stars, ***then the Antipodes, the Antipodeans, have their Christmas-Holy Nights.***[354]

Steiner repeats this theme a few minutes later in the same lecture,

> Whilst {during summer} in the north{ern hemisphere} the Earth-soul goes forth, appearing to spiritual vision like a comet's tail which is drawing itself out toward heaven, **on the other side** {of the Earth} the Earth-soul withdraws back into the earth ***and it is Christmas-Holy Nights*** {*in June-July*}.[355]
>
> (*emphasis mine AA*)

Here we have, so clearly stated, from Rudolf Steiner, that the Christmas-Holy Nights **begin in late June in the southern hemisphere**. These teachings arose from his extensive spiritual research into the seasonal cycle of the year, in both the southern and northern hemispheres. Our careful, fully contextualized study in this book of his teachings on the phenomenon of the wintertime and that of the so-called Holy Nights, has already established this to be the case.

I have assessed the above quotation in the context of every statement in the 354 volumes about this festival and the wintertime. It becomes clear that the initiate discovered as he carried out his research, that the nights of both hemispheres around their winter solstice are hallowed.

But undeniably, the above statements also declare that the Holy Nights are **caused by the winter in-breath**. For it would have been probably quite incorrect to state, in 1923, that in the southern hemisphere the Holy-Nights Christmas festival

---

[354] When he says 'unites itself with the stars, he is being poetic, re-phrasing what he said a few minutes earlier, that "the earth-soul {in that hemisphere} "strives upwards, towards the stars".

[355] Lect. 21st May 1923 in *Man's Being, his Destiny and World-evolution.*

occurred in late June – **if** Steiner were referring to the human beings living there ! Today the statement would have been true for a number of the more insightful people in the southern hemisphere who are aware of this anthroposophical truth, **but this was probably not the case in 1923**.

However, the winter in-breath itself causes a sacred hallowed presence to permeate the hemisphere around the time of the winter solstice, whether people there participate consciously or not ! This is what Rudolf Steiner revealed when he said this, **for the Holy Nights, as part of the Christ-sustained seasonal festivals, is a festival celebrated by spiritual beings, not only people**. Hence Steiner states that **both** the southern hemisphere as a part of the globe, (he calls this, 'the Antipodes') **and also the people living there** (he calls them, 'the Antipodeans') undergo the Holy Nights or Yuletide, in late June-early July.

But, the people living there then would have included either none, or a very tiny number, of anthroposophists who were aware that the Holy Nights occur in late June ! Yet even so, they and all the other people in the southern hemisphere, **did undergo the Holy Nights festival then** – even though they did not consciously observe this as a festival. For the process happened back then, in 1923, and has happened long before and ever since, **because the winter in-breath brings it about** !

And this reveals what a truly esoteric (not ecclesiastical) festival is: the elemental beings, and the many nature sprites, and their rulers, the Spirits of the Elements, and the archangel Gabriel, as well as various higher divine beings, are all involved in experiencing and celebrating the particular sacred forces which are then so powerfully present. These spiritual beings are celebrating the presence of the cosmic Life-Spirit from Christ which is being interwoven into the hemisphere's own etheric body; and also bestowed, so far as possible, upon the etheric and astral bodies of the sleeping people.

The Holy Nights do occur in the southern hemisphere in late June – in and through the etheric and astral aura of the hemisphere, and this involves all the beings active therein.

Here we see how the 'conditions' of the wintertime hemisphere create, and are identical with, the festival.

At this point we need to note the second technique used by Christian Community clergy to obscure these words. Namely, that Rudolf Steiner, when using the words here, **"and it is Christmas-Yuletide {in June}"**, is somehow only saying that the wintry *conditions* of the southern hemisphere are the opposite to those of the northern hemisphere in its summer, so, he is not referring to the **festival** of Yuletide-Holy Nights as occurring then.[356] Such suggestions are a semantic exercise without any foundation. But to further weaken the power of these statements by Steiner, a third approach is used, "*Nowhere does Steiner explicitly state, as a result of his spiritual insights, that we need to celebrate Christmas in winter, in the southern hemisphere*".[357]

This is a puzzling declaration, since quite a number of such statements from Rudolf Steiner were already well known from the first edition of this book. These are copied in the Appendix at the end of the book; but here are a few of these statements, all of which necessarily explicitly point out, (which is the same as 'stating'), that once people sense the seasonal reality, and want to create festival, then that Christmas-Holy Nights festival, in the southern hemisphere, belongs in its winter,

> The Christmas-Holy Nights mystery, when it is understood as a mystery, belongs paramountly to winter.

> In the 'hallowed time' {of the year} the soul feels itself united with the divine spiritual powers which then permeate the earth. The Christmas-Holy Nights festival **belongs in the winter,** just as St. John's festival belongs in the summer.

> With the Holy Nights-Christmas time, we have to do with an earth {hemisphere} which is forsaken by the

---

[356] M. Debus, following Benesch, Community View, 2007, Christmas in Summer? "*..it can be that Steiner only meant 'winter' when he said Christmas*", & M. Samson, "*...Steiner is talking about the 'conditions*' not *...the festival*"...*Festivals in the south*....p.41. These two suggestions are achieved by formulating two conflicting meanings to impose on the unified, inseparable meaning of Steiner's words.

[357] Samson, M. *...Festivals in the south...* p. 41

heavens...so we have the Holy Nights-Christmas festival firmly placed in the calendar entirely according to earthly circumstances.

The Christmas-Holy Nights festival has not merely symbolical meaning, it also has natural significance... at this time {of the yearly cycle}, a force recedes from humankind which otherwise comes to it.

These extracts from his lectures show that opposition to the new seasonal festival idea indicates that a core anthroposophical-Pentecostal truth, namely that sacredness, of a Christ-allied kind, can be due to, or caused by, the natural yearly cycle, is being rejected. For the ecclesiastical point of view, such an attitude is entirely normal, and to be expected.

Fortunately, this error that the Holy Nights are a global calendar event, and not connected to the winter-time, was pre-empted by Rudolf Steiner on many occasions, for on a number of times he spoke of the Christmas-Holy Nights as being caused by the winter. A very clear example occurred especially in that lecture which we discussed earlier, given in 1917, where he revealed to his audience the annual meeting with Christ-Jesus, whilst we are asleep in the hemisphere's wintertime.

At that time, he specifically emphasised that it is the dynamics of the winter-time which actually creates the Holy Nights. In explaining this, Steiner was also teaching that we human beings still have a meaningful link to the spiritual influences active in the seasonal cycle of both hemispheres.

As we noted above, this does not contradict his other statements about our inner separation from the natural cycle. This is because the divine energies from the spiritual-sun active during the Holy Nights are so powerful,

> ...in regard to the meeting with Christ Jesus {in winter}, this occurrence **is an integral aspect of the *seasonal cycle* of the year**. If it were not united to the seasonal cycle of the year, then the {impossible} result would be, that one person could celebrate a Christmas-Holy Nights in December, another person in March, and so on... in regard to this Meeting, which is placed in the cycle of the natural year, and there the human being is also placed....in direct

connection with the natural cycle of the year. **In this matter the human being is placed within the *natural cycle* of the year**, whilst in regard to the past and the future, he has stepped out of the natural cycle of the year....[358] (emphasis mine AA)

As we have noted before, Rudolf Steiner teaches that in general we modern human beings are outside the seasonal cycle; but he also emphasizes how important it is that we re-connect to the seasonal cycle, so as to able directly to draw sacred spiritual influences from the seasons.

Now, in the 1917 lecture, and also in the above quote from the Oslo lecture of 1923, we learn how in fact human beings are not fully outside the seasonal cycle – when it comes to the **especially powerful influences** which make possible, the sacred time of the meeting with the Saviour, amidst the golden radiance of the Life-Spirit. Hence the Holy Nights occur in both hemispheres in their respective winter-time.

It is this same point which, as we noted earlier, occurs in the play *Hamlet*, and where we can detect surely the inspiring influence of the great Rosicrucian initiate, "*Some say 'gainst that season wherein the Saviour's birth is celebrated, no witch does take....so hallow'd and so gracious is the time*". Note that '*gracious*' here hints to us that Life-Spirit energies are present in the wintertime, for as we saw earlier, the term 'Grace' esoterically means the Life-Spirit.

Now we have noted the lecture extract about the meeting we have at night, once a year, wherein Christ offers that which builds up the Life-Spirit in the human being. At the end of that extract, Rudolf Steiner made this comment,

> The Christmas-Holy Nights time is bound to processes in the earth. For the human being, together with the earth {that is, the hemisphere} undergoes the 'Christmas-Holy Nights alteration' of the hemisphere.

His words, "the human being, together with the earth undergoes the 'Christmas-Holy Nights alteration' of the hemisphere" is really saying the same thing as he explained

---

[358] GA 175, lect. 27th Feb. 1917, p. 79, "..es ist ...gebunden an die Naturordnung..in unmittelbar Zusammenhang mit dem Naturlaufe.."

in the lecture in Oslo. Namely, that it is not only the human beings who undergo the Holy-Nights process in the wintertime, it is also the hemisphere itself (its etheric and astral and devachanic beings and energies) which is involved in this process. The **nature condition** of the hemisphere is that which in effect is the festival. That is, the new kind of festival is created from this basis. It is these words which so well summarize all that we have so far explored in this book, and shall be further exploring.

We need to know that on the 21st May, after revealing the winter in-breath as the basis of the Holy Nights-Yuletide, Rudolf Steiner comments to his audience that we are unable, as modern people, to effectively go along with, or draw spiritual nurture from, the seasonal cycle. But a very false impression is given here to readers by Samson, as he makes them aware of only the small section of this lecture where this is incapacity is noted, and then omits the key message, presented in large sections of the lecture, where Rudolf Steiner, as he did hundreds of times in his life's work, proceeds to explain to his audience, that it is essential for humanity to strive towards **re-awakening precisely this ability**,

> we **must not** keep on trying to ever more and more lose the awareness of the content of the festivals {in terms of the seasons} so that we no longer at all know why {for example} Easter is to be placed at the first Sunday after the first full moon of the springtime. [359]

You can sense here almost an urgent tone, as the initiate urges his audience to heal their modern, arid soul state. As we have already noted in this book, this dating formula actually makes Easter into a seasonal festival, occurring twice each year, once for each hemisphere. A little later Rudolf Steiner again emphasizes the deep spiritual importance of, and hence the latent ability to, re-create the capacity to be aligned to the natural seasonal cycle, as we noted in the beginning of our study (p.59),

> After the mystery of Golgotha, humanity must strive to make this experience of an en-souled, spiritualized

---

[359] This lecture is in GA 226, "*Man's Being, Destiny and World evolution.*

nature (thus the seasonal cycle with its various nature spirits) constitute the following of Christ...for the nature spirits can all be seen in the following of Christ, but without Him they cannot be seen.

As we have seen, it is through the new festivals that a much more conscious, living relationship between humanity and the Christ being, in his contemporary influence and activity in the spiritual life processes of the earth and humankind, will be established; this is another aspect to the 'reappearance' of Christ; and to the Pentecost outpouring of the spirit.

This sublime being reappears to our consciousness as the central, guiding being of the ethereal, astral (soul), and spiritual being of the Earth. Thus, humankind can be involved in the gradual development of the New Jerusalem, the future, nonmaterial Earth. Without humankind's active participation, the new Earth, the future spiritual development of the Earth, cannot develop. We are not only responsible for the future ecological health of the earth, but also its spiritual integrity !

Spiritual Ecology

At this point, we need to note that in this book, we are learning to understand Rudolf Steiner's **spiritual ecology**. This is a view which has an esoteric Christian-Rosicrucian wisdom underlying it. If awareness of the spiritual influences operative in the seasons, and how these form the basis of the new festivals is hindered, then a true spiritual ecology will be prevented; such attempts are not an expression of a 'spiritual ecology', but an imposition of religious attitudes and concerns onto the seasonal cycle.[360] The essential spiritual basis for a renewal of our link to nature, and care of our planet, will be undermined.

The new consciously esoteric seasonal festivals are not appropriate socially, where the mediating role of the priesthood is required for the spiritual nourishment of people with religious faith, who are not interested in the initiatory wisdom of Rudolf Steiner. The new festivals can only be established where those people are active who are

---

[360] F. Benesch & M. Samson's writings are not based in a 'spiritual ecology'.

288

undergoing an esoteric development process; or respectful of the wisdom that this offers.

The importance of the Christmas-Holy Nights festival cannot be over-emphasized; it is the holiest time of the year. It was the intention of Rudolf Steiner to assist humanity to develop a perception of the spiritual reality behind the seasonal cycle, a perception that would enable us to consciously participate in the seasonal processes, to assist in the spiritualization of the Earth. Steiner's early death prevented his carrying out this intention through deeply esoteric meditative sessions.

Concerning the significance of this new esoteric Christmas festival, Steiner taught that we need the experience of this festival in order to be able in the future to develop the new clairvoyance, or higher consciousness, that will be possible for humanity in the next cultural epoch.

In this next epoch, or zodiac age (of Aquarius in the north and Leo in the south),[361] Rudolf Steiner taught that the faculty of recalling, or knowing, one's past life will be possessed by some sectors of humanity. This faculty will be an expression of the dawning Christéd ego-hood of humankind; the birth of the higher ego in the personality will then (that is, from the thirty-sixth century onward) be possible.

If, however, the incarnations in this present age do not lay a foundation for this future higher consciousness, through striving to attain the Christmas initiation, then this future capacity will be imperfectly born in us,

> Those people alone will in the future age {be able to} remember correctly their present existence who have absorbed the Christ impulse, the fountain of true ego-hood.[362]

It was at this point that Steiner stressed that the purpose of the anthroposophical Christmas or Holy Nights festival is to enable humanity to absorb the Christ impulse, especially the Life-spirit, to bring about,

> ...the anthroposophical Christmas festival in our own soul, the birth of the Christ in us.[363]

---

[361] See the Appendix for more about the two future zodiac Ages.
[362] Lect. 26th Dec. 1909.
[363] Ibid.

Just as the conscious participation in the sacred processes occurring during each hemisphere's winter will bring about the "birth of the Christ" within the soul, so too, the Holy Nights will gradually bring about the transformation of the Earth itself. This shall occur to the extent that humanity achieves the Christmas-Holy Nights initiation stage. For every wintertime there occurs, as elucidated earlier in this chapter, the assimilation by the hemisphere's aura of devachanic ether forces, deep in the Earth, and these also permeate the human soul,

> The forces, which as divine-spiritual light forces from the sun, pass into the earth's aura in the time when the outer sun strength is weakest, entered the soul {of Olaf Åsteson...because} he had attuned his inner nature to this end.[364]

And so too, modern humanity can achieve this experience, by striving toward the goal of the sun initiation. Such a process, enabling the 'divinizing' of our ether body, invokes the blessing of the archangels, just as the transformation of the soul occurs with the help of the angels. The metamorphosis of our ether forces into Life-spirit is assisted by efforts made toward spiritual consciousness, spiritual thoughts; for our thoughts are carried to our brain by the ether body. Then there is continually a tendency toward the development of such higher thoughts of inspirational consciousness in our soul, even if this tendency remains subconscious.

Every night when we enter the spiritual world, this tendency becomes a helpful influence for the archangels, in their striving to accomplish the divinizing of the ether forces of humankind and the Earth.[365] From their activity shall arise the Life-spirit forces that the Earth will have in the New Jerusalem state and the 'Inspirational' consciousness that humankind will then attain.[366]

Such activity is possible for the archangels, for they have the same relationship to the Life-spirit stage as the angels have to the Spirit-self. That is, their consciousness functions on that sublime level continually, just we as human beings

---

[364] Lect. 31st Jan. 1915.
[365] Lect. 3rd June 1915.
[366] Ibid.

function as ego-ic beings. When materialism is very strongly present in humanity's thinking, then this process is hindered; if materialism were to totally triumph on the earth, then the future Earth would be a more dense, mineral organism, rather than a fine, ethereal planet, quickened by a radiant Life-spirit power.[367]

During the winter, when the focus of the activity is on the ether body of the hemisphere, and the possibility of attaining Inspirational consciousness is greater, the interaction between the archangels and humanity intensifies. Therefore, during the winter, effort toward spiritual consciousness, toward transcendental, inspirational thinking, is especially appropriate and valuable. Since such activity will give a direction to the enhanced thought life of winter,

> ....it is a beautiful thought to connect the Christmas festival with the time when the Earth {hemisphere} is closed off from the cosmos, when the human being, in earthly isolation, seeks to establish communion for {self-produced} thoughts with the divine-spiritual realm. And in that we understand what is here meant, we seek to protect ourselves from the ahrimanic powers.[368]

A little later in the same lecture, Rudolf Steiner presents this aspect of the winter Holy Nights-Christmas festival from the aspect of the thinking capacity,

> The Christmas festival is that {festival} wherein the person seeks to deepen inwardly, to spiritualize whatever knowledge he {or she} acquires about the world.

Such an activity counteracts the influence of the ahrimanic gnomes and also assists the tendency toward the Life-spirit stage of existence. It is through such activity as this that Inspiration is able to develop. In winter, any effort toward this development will be 'naturally' strengthened by the dynamic in the Earth-soul at that time, because the Earth-soul has its most intense 'awake' state then, so Inspirational consciousness permeates its being. This activity by

---

[367] Ibid.
[368] Lect. 23rd Dec. 1922.

291

humanity in turn assists the archangels in their work with the ether body of the earth, which activity comes to a peak in winter. For then, deep in the earth,

> ...forces are present, which so vivify the minerals, that they can {that is, shall} develop to the future Jupiter age {of the Earth, that is, the New Jerusalem}... a kind of viscous substance is created.[369]

These sparse words from a Steiner notebook reveal the consequence of the accumulation of Life-spirit forces in the Earth's interior; a less dense, more alive quality develops down there in the winter.

It becomes clear now that the sublime Holy Nights event of the meeting with Christ Jesus is not an event occurring across the globe in the manner of traditional Christian church festivals. Instead, the Holy Nights or Yuletide occurs for each hemisphere due to the way that cosmic spiritual forces are activated in each hemisphere in its winter time; forces which are integrated into the life processes of the Earth.

The Holy Nights around the winter solstice in June-July and in December-January are the wonderful expression of the guiding, nurturing activity of the indwelling Christ being, as the Spirit of the Earth. Through this specific intervention in the wintertime process, the meeting, the spiritual interweaving, between humankind and the archangelic hierarchy is brought into a relationship with the cosmic Christ.

In this way the development of the Life-spirit in the human being, from the cosmic life spirit forces of the Christ, may be achieved. This development is made possible through the divine forces present in Christ Jesus that derive from a great archangel. Jesus of Nazareth had achieved on Earth the Life-spirit stage already, as we have noted earlier in this chapter, "He manifests himself {now} through a being of the rank of the archangels".

Now we can appreciate the full significance of Steiner's words about the wintertime in-breath and its Holy Nights-Christmas process;

---

[369] In supplementary vol. to the Complete Works, No. 19. p.3.

So one can say {that} at Holy Nights-Christmastime {winter-time} the earth {hemisphere} has absorbed its soul forces into itself. It has, in the great annual breathing process, absorbed its soul organism into itself. The Christ impulse is then born in the earth's {hemisphere} inbreathed soul forces, in the interior of the Earth. He flows out into the cosmos, with the out-breathing in spring {in September and in March}.[370]

These words also reveal the importance of the Michael festival for the Holy Nights festival. Without the cleansing of the earth's astral forces by archangel Michael, in autumn, the Holy Nights mysteries cannot be fully accomplished,

Before the yearly cycle is once again ended with the approach of December {June in the south} which enables the Christ impulse to be born in the earth, the earth must be cleansed from the dragon. It must be cleansed from ahrimanic forces, by spiritual forces. The Michael power must unite with all that flows into the earth, as it inhales, between September and December {March and June in the south}. The purifying powers of Michael, conquering evil ahrimanic forces, must unite with this in-streaming breath in preparation for the Christmas festival... so that the birth of the Christ impulse can be accomplished....Michael battles for the purity of the earthly world.[371]

Thus the meditation for wintertime given to initiates, "Guard thyself from evil". Still it would be wrong for the Advent time, and the wintertime in general, to be centred on the theme of evil; the primary process during this time is the development in the earth soul of the spiritual light, which each winter may now enter humanity, as a result of the original Epiphany event,

But if the earth lives in this deepest outer darkness, we know that the Earth-soul experiences her light; she begins to awaken to the highest degree. The spiritual waking time is connected to the

[370] Lect. 31st Mar. 1923.
[371] Ibid.

Christmastime, and with this spiritual waking phase there should be united the commemoration of the spiritual awakening for earth's evolution, by Christ Jesus. From this derives the placing of the Christmas {that is, the Hallowed Nights} sanctification festival precisely at this time.[372]

The New Year's resolution.

After St. Sylvester's Eve, December 31st, the beginning of the New Year is celebrated by a variety of traditions, including the setting off of fireworks and the making of resolves. It is interesting to ask why this is, for as we have noted earlier, historically as well as in terms of the cycle of the seasons, the New Year really begins on the spring equinox, not in the middle of winter. In Europe, March 25th was New Year's day, for most nations, because that is when the renewal of the life forces of the hemisphere occur. January 1st has been New Year's Day for only about 250 years in central Europe, Russia, and England.

The change from the spring New Year to January 1st was first made in France, in 1564, by a mentally weak monarch, Charles the 9th; this decision was without any deep motivation, and was ignored by other countries for about 150 years. The Easter day of both hemispheres is the true New Year's day.

Nevertheless a significant phenomenon occurring on (or about) December 31st has been subconsciously perceived by humanity and expressed in the New Year's resolution tradition. This deep phenomenon was revealed, without commentary, by Rudolf Steiner, in a private conversation; he is reported to have said,

> On New Year's Eve, our folk-soul briefly releases us, as it were, and {consequently} what we then think, is perceived by the highest hierarchies, and has the power in it to be brought into reality.[373]

We may understand this mystery through a consideration of the Christmas winter process. A folk soul is a very real being, it is an archangel; the different, distinctive national

---

[372] Lect. 19th Dec. 1915.
[373] Conversation with H. Hahn, reported in *Das Goetheanum*, No.3, 4th January, 1990.

qualities of each nation derive from the influence of its guiding being, which is an archangel.

This being establishes its connection to us, via our ether body.[374] When the Spirit-self stage is attained, as in the fifth degree of initiation, the person is able to consciously experience and assist the folk soul. When the Life-spirit stage is achieved, then the capacity develops to experience and commune with the Earth-spirit; hence this stage was brought to its completion by an initiation in the midwinter time, when the Earth-spirit is closest to us.

During this time, the Chrestos process occurs, wherein Life-spirit radiance from the Christ being and from the sun, permeate the sleeping human soul. In other words, we are permeated by the spiritual essence of the ether forces from which the human ether body itself was formed. This process, in turn, would alter our relationship to that archangel which is our own folk soul. The 'release' from the folk soul brings us, however, into the sphere of influence of the cosmic Christ, who is the indwelling earth spirit.

So the folklore tradition of the New Year's resolution may be regarded as a pale reflection of what the soul naturally feels impelled to do during the holy nights of winter, that is, to find a goal in life which transcends the ideals and aspirations that we have as members of the various (and, at times, antagonistic) nations. It follows from what Rudolf Steiner told Hahn, that this New Year's Eve phenomenon occurs in the southern hemisphere on or about June 30th.

Understanding this mystery, we could direct the New Year's resolve toward assisting the intentions the Christ-being has for all humanity or toward achieving insight into how we may progress toward the realization of the higher self. This new year mystery is, then, a process deriving from the influence on us of the Life-spirit   forces of the Christ, and the process has the potential in the future to lead humanity back to a unified brotherhood and sisterhood, wherein divisive national and racial qualities are overcome,

> That which drew into the physical, ethereal, and soul organisms of Jesus of Nazareth, that...is the common fountain for the 'sparks of spirit' of humanity. Though the {lesser} gods could, through their influence, bring about the {existence of} communal

---

[374] See the lecture cycle, *The Mission of Individual Folk-souls.*

ethnic groups, the Christ is, for the entire world, a common indivisible spiritual being, so that thereby humanity could be united into a 'family' which encompasses the entire Earth.[375]

The number of different nations on Earth is defined, in esoteric tradition, as being 72. There is an ancient esoteric Christian text which appears to me to refer to the sublime mystery of the development of the Life-spirit in humanity. This is a process which as we have seen in this chapter, is strongly enhanced by a conscious involvement with the hemisphere's Christmas winter process. The ancient text is from the Gospel of Thomas,

> The Lord went into the dye-works of Levi. He took 72 different colours and threw them into a vat. Then he took them out, all neutral cloth colour, and he said: 'Even so has the Son of Man come as a dyer'.

The Three Kings festival.
Before summarizing the themes of the new winter Holy Nights festival, we need to consider the Three Kings festival. As the man Jesus became the central being of Christianity, the cosmic Epiphany festival was gradually replaced with the Three Kings day. By the third century AD, the Roman Empire had made inroads into the forests of east and central Europe, and Christianity spread with it. One convert amongst the Goths, Wulfilas, was exceptionally successful in converting his own people; eventually, many families of such Christian Germanic peoples had to be brought into areas within the borders of the Roman Empire, during the fourth century, for their protection.

Such events increased the need for a Christian midwinter festival, as the Germanic-Gothic people not only had their merry winter solstice festival, but also an awareness of the Holy Nights process in the earth. Further, as mentioned earlier, the Mithraic and other religions of southern Europe had midwinter festivals. Thus the Church decided to create a midwinter 'birth' festival of its own. A high church dignitary, Julius, was given the task of researching this in approximately A.D. 330; in A. D. 337 he became the Pope,

---

[375] Lect. 2nd Dec. 1906.

296

and decided that on December 25th the birth of 'Jesus Christ' should be celebrated. There was no universal, official, Christmas festival in Christianity before then. That is, one which celebrated the birth of Jesus. Such a festival came into existence in Rome, for the first time, in A.D. 354.

In the western or Roman church, which was now the official religion of the Roman Empire, the festivals were being formulated in a uniform manner, in which the real, cosmic Christ reality had no place. In letters, still extant, written to bishops in southern Europe, St. Augustine commanded them to cease celebrating Epiphany as the event in which the Christ descended upon Jesus. The Epiphany festival had to change from a commemoration of the descent of the cosmic Christ to something else; it became the festival of the 'manifestation' (epiphanoia) of the Jesus child (called the 'Christ child') to the Magi.

The basis for the Three King's day was created early in the fourth century, when Helena, mother of Emperor Constantine, journeyed to Palestine in search of sacred relics. Amongst such things as the claws of a pet crab of St. Peter, she also 'found' the bodies of the three Magi. These bones were taken to Constantinople. By the early fifth century, the western church fathers were presenting Epiphany as the visit of the three Magi to the child. By A.D. 600 the Eastern churches had accepted this definition of Epiphany, or at most, considered it as a commemoration of the 'blessing' of 'Christ' by God, during the baptism.

In the twelfth century, the cult of the three Magi intensified, the relics having been sent to Milan in A.D. 1158. In 1164, Kaiser Frederick conquered Milan, and sent the relics to Cologne. The Magi then acquired names and special features, and the bones, placed in an exquisite reliquary, became the object of veneration for large crowds of pilgrims. The Zarathustrian initiate priests, who were also potentates, became simply, 'kings'.

In the first centuries after Christ, the simple Gospel accounts were augmented with elaborate details, deeply esoteric, meant to assist people in celebrating certain aspects of the historical-ecclesiastical Christmas festival. Appearing in old apocryphal Gospels, such details were no doubt given to humanity by esoteric Christian sources. For example, neither the number 3 nor the specific gifts which the Magi brought are mentioned in the New Testament. Nor is the kings' racial origin not mentioned there.

But the apocryphal details indicate that the kings are to be considered representatives of the Lemurian, Atlantean, and Post-Atlantean 'epochs', of the different kinds of spiritual development that humanity achieved in those Ages. The three Magi, as Rudolf Steiner stated, represent the initiates of those civilizations: Caspar; the African, in whom live remnants of the Lemurian people. Balthasar; Indian, that is, Asiatic, expressing a similarity with Atlantean humanity. Melchior; Caucasian, representing the post-Atlantean times.

The gifts represent the spiritualization of the soul; gold for wisdom or the Spirit-self; myrrh, the triumph of life (of the Life-spirit stage) over death; frankincense, the (final) destruction of the lower self and the resurrection of the higher self, thus a self-sacrificing capacity, an aspect of the Spirit-human. Rudolf Steiner created the term 'Spirit-human' for the spiritual force that arises in us when the physical body is spiritualized.

A new look at Advent.
Little was said by Rudolf Steiner concerning Advent. As a traditional church festival, it is self-explanatory; it builds up a mood of receptivity to the Christmas festival. However, since the contemporary Christmas festival is a mixture of various aspects of the Holy Nights and Jesus-birth mysteries, we do need to reassess Advent. It could be used to prepare for the historical Christmas festival; for example, for celebration of the birth of the two Jesus children mentioned in the Gospels. In this sense, Advent topics could include the preparation that was undertaken for the births of the Jesus children down through the centuries in the Old Testament Judaic culture. Celebration of the historical Christmas could include, as a further aspect, observation of the 'preaching in the temple' in 12 AD, at which time the spiritual union of the two children occurred, only then the basis being created for a vessel for the sun god.

The only reference to Advent in a lecture by Rudolf Steiner is from the seasonal perspective. He referred to a historical development in the way that humanity would experience the time leading up to the Holy Nights. He indicated that the seasonal Holy Nights process was experienced in different ways, over the millennia, in the different cultural epochs. In this lecture, Steiner described the three-week Advent as an image of the main spiritual development process of the three cultural epochs that preceded the Graeco-Latin age wherein the Christ event occurred.

In particular he described the experience of the inner winter dynamic during those epochs. He concluded that the current three-week advent occurs so that,

> human beings {can} briefly once again recapitulate the way in which, in earlier times, the lights waxed after the Christmas time, and also the consequent 'living' in the light which followed on this.[376]

So, it derives from the knowledge of earlier initiates regarding the historical development of humanity's experience of the Holy Night's process. But since humanity now has no knowledge of these ancient experiences, it is perhaps right to form Advent, as regards the seasonal Holy Nights festival, into a preparation process for those deep and wondrous events which occur during the Holy Nights. This approach is preferable to the present practice with its unclear, abstract 'Christ child' theme.

Again it should be stressed that when those of us who live in the northern hemisphere become aware that the Christmas festival has been celebrated without conscious understanding, we have taken a very important step toward renewal of the festivals. But this awareness usually arises only when we journey to the southern hemisphere and find that, actually, we are not sure when to celebrate what ! To help minimize confusion or misunderstanding in the wider community regarding these new festivals, we need to clarify the terminology.

Thus 'Christmas Day' refers to the historical festival of the birth of Jesus; the 'Christmas winter' festival of twelve days is the Holy Nights festival, which occurs in the winter of each hemisphere. And 'Advent' can refer to the preparation for the historical Christmas festival, while another term can be chosen for the winter preparation time for the Holy Nights.

Nothing has does more to hinder the development of the contemporary Christian seasonal festivals than the

---

[376] Lect. 19th Dec. 1904. There is no evidence at all from Rudolf Steiner, to support a theory from S. Prokofieff, about Advent being linked to activity of evil spiritual beings during the wintertime.

persistence of the view that humanity is now freed from the spiritual forces behind nature and therefore no longer needs to bother with the spiritual processes that the inhabitants of the "middle kingdom", guided by the hierarchies, carry out during the seasons. This concept has been shown in these pages to be fundamentally incompatible with the teachings of Rudolf Steiner. For it is in re-establishing our relationship to the cycle of the year that we will be able to develop our own higher spiritual potential.

And, further, it is in this way that humanity may become conscious of, and a servant of, the intentions of the cosmic Christ. For the activity of the elementals and the archangels during the seasons is in the fullest sense of the term a Christ-permeated activity. The inspiration of a guiding archangel of the anthroposophical esoteric wisdom, Vidar, urges modern seekers of the spirit to consider the seasonal cycle of the year as a way to the risen Christ. It is this being Vidar, through whom the Christ reappears to humanity, and through whom also the new seasonal Christian festival impulse will be nurtured.[377]

Although the higher nature of the human being may be developed independently of the cycle of the year, it is surely the hope of the spiritual world that humanity will not spurn the opportunities offered during the yearly cycle to absorb and experience the high spiritual forces present in a particular season. Again, Rudolf Steiner,

> The spiritual state of the sun is at its most intensive in the wintertime, and therefore the conditions are then at the most favourable for those individuals who will to approach a deepening of the soul, which is connected with the spirit of the earth, and with the spirit in general. Therefore, those who are seeking a deepening of the soul can confirm for themselves that they will have the best experience in the thirteen days around the Christmas-Holy Nights time. Although modern people are already so placed that they are emancipated from the outer processes, so that the occult experiences can come at any time. But insofar as the outer world can nevertheless have an

---

[377] See my the *Rudolf Steiner Handbook* for more this archangel

influence, the time between Christmas and New Year is the most important of all.[378]

We should pause over these words, *"But insofar as the outer world can nevertheless have an influence, the time between Christmas and New Year is the most important of all"*. Here we learn yet again that although we are separated from nature inwardly, yet it is so important to seek alignment to the influences which are activated at the wintertime. Our modern arid soul-state does not prevent this, indeed it makes this effort all the more important.

The presence of the 'Christ sun' in the winter, that is, the Life-spirit forces which can metamorphose compassion into healing, creative love, is a sacred reality. And Rudolf Steiner indicated in private that the great individualities which guide human evolution as initiates have tasks with these divine Life-spirit forces during the Holy Nights. That the Holy Nights festival, through which we are permeated by the cosmic Christ with the creative power of love, actually occurs in winter is powerfully emphasized by Steiner in these words:

> It has arisen from a profound intuition that, that time when the human being should unite with that which Earth evolution should call into fullest consciousness, that is, the Christ-impulse, has been placed in the midwinter, and not in the summer, as the Christmas-Holy Nights festival.[379]

Christmas dates and themes of the historical festival cycle

Christmas Eve: December 24th, the day of Adam and Eve; the role of Maria and the Jesus Child of St. Luke in reversing the fall of humanity.

Christmas Day:
December 25th, the birth of the two Jesus children; the significance of the 'primal child of man'. This theme could be preceded by a preparatory Advent, especially in the southern hemisphere; but in the north the same days also

---

[378] GA 158, lect. 7th Jan. 1913.
[379] GA 162, lect. 23rd May 1915.

need to be available for the seasonal Holy Nights Advent (I have suggested that this latter Advent might be given another name), which is of greater importance.

Three Kings Day:
January 6th, further contemplation of the preparation for the birth of Jesus, especially as in St. Matthew's gospel; the events of the preaching in the temple.

Midwinter dates and themes of the new seasonal Christian festival cycle:

The Holy Nights Festival:
December 25th to January 6th in the northern hemisphere, June 25th to July 7th in the southern hemisphere.

We remember: on the third day after the winter solstice, the primal Jesus soul was born, and the Chrestos ritual was celebrated, for at this time the nights are hallowed.

We surmise: "Will not a truly devout hallowed nights mood once again permeate the earth's atmosphere when humanity...glimpses the great Hallowed Nights festival of the earth, through the birth of the Jesus child proclaimed in St. Luke?"[380] That is, when humanity realizes that this Jesus soul was born in winter because then the Life-spirit forces are strongest.

We contemplate and seek to experience: the Holy Nights of winter.
In the winter in-breath, the earth soul is intensely awake and is permeated by the divine, inner sun forces, the Christ sun.
Radiant life spirit solar forces are descending deep into the earth's interior.
Our ether body, like the plant roots, is permeated by these high ether forces; if our soul is prepared we may absorb these, thus regenerating it.
Our consciousness (thought life) is exposed to both an intensified egotism, and to illumined, inspirational thinking; clairvoyance reaches now to Spirit-land experiences.
The beings of the Earth-soul now become strongly aware of the stars and the forces which stream in from the cosmos to

---

[380] GA 150, Lect. 21st Dec. 1913.

the hemisphere; the zodiac Word resounds to the earth, bringing perception, too, of the archetypal force behind the mineral kingdom.

The light divine, the Life-spirit radiance of the Christ being, who is the spirit of the Earth, also permeates the earth now, and descends deep into it.

The sun may be seen at midnight; that is, a radiant star arises in the centre of the earth, from which a new Earth will be formed; the texture of the earth's interior softens.

We seek to experience: the birth of the Christ child, the Life-spirit in the hallowed forces of our soul.

Now at night we descend deep into the earth, where Christ Jesus, amidst the golden radiance of the Christ sun, graces us with Life- spirit powers.

Freed for a while from our folk soul, we may contemplate and resolve upon a spiritual goal; our resolve will be heard on high.

The Earth-soul is now deep in communion with the spiritual reality behind the zodiacal forces; we may participate in this by contemplation of the twelve-fold zodiac Word, the zodiac influences on all its levels.

The Epiphany Festival: January 6th in the northern hemisphere, July 7th in the southern hemisphere.

We remember: the cosmic Christ descended to the earth at the baptism, bringing to the Earth's firmament the Life-spirit.

We contemplate: during the Holy Nights, and culminating on the 12 day (13th night), the Christ sun may be assimilated into the Earth's core, and into our inner being.

CHAPTER NINE

THE FOUR ARCHANGELS AND THE NEW HEMISPHERIC FESTIVAL CYCLES

Of the many archangels, there are four, Michael, Raphael, Gabriel, and Uriel, who have especially significant tasks in the evolution of humanity. These four archangels are often mentioned in ancient esoteric texts. According to the Sibylline Oracles, "then shall come the servants of eternal god: Michael, Gabriel, Raphael, and Uriel. They shall lead all souls out of the misty darkness to... the throne of the immortal great god". (2:214) In another early Christian esoteric text, the risen Christ declares, "Now, the regent of the angels are Michael and Gabriel, Uriel, and Raphael; these archangels accompanied me {during my descent to the physical plane} unto the fifth heaven".[381]

In the springtime, the cosmic Christ mediates the solar life-ether into the earth and sacrifices his own light and life that humankind may have a measure of protection from luciferic and ahrimanic entities. Through this deed of Christ, the elemental forces in the Earth's aura during each hemisphere's springtime are enabled to remain in a wholesome balance, and we are free from either of the two extremes. In Steiner's words, humanity "enters the sphere of the balance in spring".[382]

Given the presence of this healing, equilibrating force from the Christ, it is the task of Raphael, the archangelic regent of spring, to guide the healing powers that humanity has needed ever since the fall brought imbalance and disorder into human nature. Through the 'Fall of Man', the illness-bringing influences of luciferic and ahrimanic beings gained access to humanity. A Hebraic esoteric text refers to the healing capacity of Raphael: "Raphael is one of the four 'presences' {before the throne of God}, and is set over all the diseases and wounds of man."[383]

---

[381] In the Epistula Epostolorum, C. Scmidt, trans. (Leipzig, J.C. Hin'rische Vlg, 1919.)
[382] In Supplementary vol. to the GA, no.19.
[383] The Book of Enoch 1:40.

304

When we can perceive the tendencies in the soul that take us away from a balanced, moderate way of being, then we can begin to understand the origin of our illness, and we can understand why the meditative expression for the springtime, in the ancient mysteries, was "know thyself". The activity of the archangel Raphael, through whom the cosmic, that is, atmospheric processes are guided, for the healing of humanity, only unfolds in the springtime season. Similarly, the sacrifice of the Christ being, which is undertaken to ensure the rejuvenation of the life-ether, a deed through which the crucifixion of Golgotha virtually reoccurs, only occurs in spring.

In summer, as we noted in Chapter Five, it is the archangel Uriel who becomes regent of the cosmic processes. The activity of Uriel with the inner sun forces and the will forces from the Earth's interior occurs only in summer, and only in that season has Uriel an effect on the forces of nature, on the cosmic environment and thereby on humanity.

Likewise, it is in the autumn that the archangel Michael becomes the regent of the cosmic processes, the processes that occur above the atmosphere, where cosmic influences are active. Then it is that Michael uses the meteoric iron to combat the ahrimanic influences manifesting in the sulphurous presence developed in the summer atmosphere. Hence, in Steiner's words, Michael is the cosmic spirit of the autumn. That the Michael festival must be placed in the autumn (see Chapter Six) is due to this fact, namely that the appropriate time to strive to have a festival through which the community may draw near to, and even experience, the activity of Michael in the spiritual life processes of the earth is when that archangel is active in the elemental and spiritual processes of the Earth's aura, that is, when the archangel is the cosmic spirit of the season.

This is true for all four guiding archangels. It is precisely at the season when the archangel is striving to guide the processes occurring in the Earth-soul, so as to enable the Christ intention to triumph, that our assistance is needed. And it is precisely then that we will have the possibility, despite the lack of clairvoyant consciousness, to sense the presence and nature of the archangel, thereby gradually forming a bridge to each of these sublime servants of the cosmic Christ.

During the winter of both hemispheres, the solar ether forces cease to permeate the Earth's ether body, and the lunar ether rays predominate in their influence on the life processes of the Earth. This influence varies according to the phases and motion of the moon around our planet, against the background of the zodiac stars. Hence in winter the hemisphere's ether body is intensely active, although not in the same way as in the springtime. And this activity is governed by the moon, which, like the Earth, is en-souled (hierarchical beings constitute part of its aura or soul-aspect).

According to ancient esoteric lore, which Rudolf Steiner confirmed as accurate, the archangelic regent of the moon is Gabriel. Hence this archangel is described as governing "the forces {life forces} of the Earth" in esoteric texts.[384] This activity of Gabriel in the earth's ether body was known to esoteric groups, as can be seen in early Christian iconography. From the sixth century onward, a staff became the symbol of an archangel.

But the staff of Gabriel was exceptional, being in effect 'the rod of life'; it had a flower and three leaves at the top. The flower represented the ether forces, since it is the presence of these subtle energies which differentiate rocks from living plants. And the choice of three leaves indicated that Gabriel is not just an aspect of the moon's soul (that is, astral forces), but is connected with the central spiritual powers of creation, the Trinity and their foremost sphere of manifestation, the sun. Eventually this wonderful symbolic staff became a bundle of lilies; these flowers are associated with the moon in esoteric tradition.

It should not be surprising, then, that Steiner named Gabriel as the archangel of winter, the cosmic spirit of the wintertime. All that which occurs in the ethers in winter is guided by this archangel. But in winter there are two processes. One involves the normal ether forces animated then, so that the springtime renewal can occur. This process, guided by the archangel Gabriel, includes the descent of all those souls who are going to be born during the coming twelve months, in that hemisphere.

It is during the months from the winter solstice to the spring equinox (late December to late March in the northern hemisphere, late June to late September in the southern

---

[384] The Book of Enoch, 40:90.

306

hemisphere) that the unborn are able to enter the Earth's aura, there to wait for the time of their conception. Steiner described this wondrous event as the yearly fertilization of the Earth.[385]

In the second wintertime process, the inner spiritual essence of the ethers, which have permeated the hemisphere during the summer, is now present deep in the earth. This Life-spirit radiance is united to the Life-spirit forces of the cosmic Christ, and through the activity of Christ Jesus we may receive this into our own being, transforming our ether body. We may assume that Gabriel is also active in this second process, depending on the extent to which the individual enables this to occur.

For as we know from the Gospel of St. Luke, when the child Jesus prepared to incarnate, he in whom the Life-spirit forces were 'naturally' present, it was through the specific intervention of archangel Gabriel that the conception took place. Hence all that we have considered concerning the Chrestos forces of the Holy Nights is intimately connected with archangel Gabriel.

The working together of the two archangels

It is important that we note a further aspect of the activity of these four archangels. We have so far considered their cosmic (or macrocosmic) activity, that is, their role in guiding various processes occurring in the Earth's soul. This is a cosmic role, for the archangel is then involved in activity arising through the interaction of the earth soul with the cosmos. It is this role that is a factor in the new festivals. However, each of the four archangels is also able to nurture life processes occurring in the human body.

These are **microcosmic** activities, and as with the cosmic activity, this microcosmic activity of the archangel only takes place when it is the guiding cosmic regent of the season; but in the case of the microcosmic activity, the archangel's effect is on the people living in the other hemisphere. It is as if forces from the archangel permeate the Earth, while it is active as seasonal regent, and work into the human beings living on the other side of the planet.

For example, in the springtime, Raphael is the cosmic spirit who is able to make healing forces available to humanity, because of the sacrificial deed of the Christ in

---

[385] Lect. 13th Oct. 1923.

springtime. At the same time, in the other hemisphere, it is autumn and Michael is the cosmic spirit or regent. But in this autumn hemisphere, we also find Raphael is exerting an influence. The difference is that in the autumn hemisphere he is active subtly **within human beings**, not out in the macrocosm, in the Earth-soul. In the autumn hemisphere his activity helps the human beings maintain the health of their breathing processes.

Likewise, at the time when Gabriel is the guiding regent for the winter hemisphere and Uriel is above the southern hemisphere during its St. John's Tide, then forces from Uriel are also active in the winter hemisphere, but within humanity, not in the Earth's soul and ether forces. And in that summer hemisphere, where Uriel is regent, forces from Gabriel – coming from the other side of the globe – exert a subtle influence on humankind's bodily organism.

The microcosmic influence from Gabriel is quite different from his wintertime activity with the ethers; it has to do with nutrition, that is, with the forming and nourishing of the body. In winter the microcosmic activity of Uriel, within humankind, influences the thinking powers in a subtle manner, it does not pervade the winter hemisphere generally.

Forces from the archangel Michael are also subtly active within humanity on the opposite side of the Earth, where it is springtime. When Michael is the regent of the autumn in the one hemisphere, then his forces, working within humanity in the springtime hemisphere, vivify the power of movement, that is, the capacity to use the limbs.

These four 'internal' influences of the archangels, which reach from the other side of the globe to be active inside us, will need to be included when we consider the themes of the new festivals, but they constitute only a secondary aspect of the seasonal dynamics. In the lecture in which he discusses this secondary process of the archangels, Rudolf Steiner elaborated by considering the microcosmic influence of Uriel in the winter (Holy Nights) time, wherein Gabriel is active as regent. Uriel's influence at that time, he said, is rightly thought of "when we say: from the force of Uriel we {now} have...the inner forces of our human head".

In Chapter Seven, one of the phenomena we considered, because it develops in the wintertime, is the enhanced state of our thinking life. That is, in the winter our capacity for inspirational thinking develops; it is this process which the microcosmic influences of Uriel may be able to enhance.

A further element comes with the realization that the degree of microcosmic influence an archangel is able to develop during a season is dependent upon the activity of the archangel which was active within the human organism during the preceding season. Thus, for example, the effect of Uriel in the thinking process of humanity in winter is 'passed on', so to speak, to Michael in the spring. Michael then metamorphoses these forces into the capacity to quicken our powers of movement.

It is important to realize that these subtle microcosmic influences are **not a major, but only a minor factor**, when creating the new festivals. It is already difficult for modern humanity to sense even the powerful macrocosmic influences of the archangel who is the powerful Regent of a given season. The purpose of the festival is help people sense the various spiritual forces active in that season. There is no other archangel out there during that season, powerfully determining the life-processes of the hemisphere. And it is these macrocosmic influences, in the etheric, astral and divine (devachanic) forces of the hemisphere, that are the focus of the festival.

The subtle influence of a second archangel, in the internal life-processes of people, cannot be a focus of the festival; we need the much more tangible macrocosmic role of the archangel, to have any chance to sense a resonance with what is happening in etheric and astral environs around us. It is precisely this that the Soul Calendar was written to make tangible to us. The internal or microcosmic influences are far too tenuous and subtle for a community to really experience, and then integrate into a festival as a major theme.

It is important here to note that when the concept of the new festival cycle is not understood, this theme, of two archangels being active in any one season, can lead to the erroneous conclusion that both hemispheres can celebrate a festival, such as Michaelmas, at the same time. This attitude arises from confusing the external, powerful, central dynamic of the archangel who is the Regent of a season, with the very much less perceptible, microcosmic influence of the archangel on the other hemisphere, inside a human being.

This confusion is carried along by a yearning, to support a uniform, global festival; this yearning is strengthened by the cultural-religious heritage of Christendom. One example of bringing about this confusion, from the Christian Community clergy, is when the activity of the archangel is presented as 'carrying along' the spiritual essence of Christmas, or Michael-mas, in the hemisphere's season, as if it were somehow **part of the Archangel's own being.** This core element is presented as an "Imagination", meaning an astral thought-form, "*the cosmic imagination would then be linked to the archangel, and not to the cosmic forces of the hemisphere.*"[386] And then, since the archangel is also active in the other hemisphere, microcosmically, the suggestion is made (M. Samson), that this mystical-religious 'imagination' (astral thought) of Christmas-Yuletide works through the Earth and nourishes the human digestive system.[387]

To see through the confusion which this idea spreads, one needs to realize that in reality, the archangel does not, **and cannot**, carry along in itself, the essence, the spiritual 'being-ness', of the festival (say Yuletide). This is because, as we have already seen in detail, **the festival is brought about by a condition of a hemisphere**, brought about by the seasonal cycle, and **involving many spirit beings**, including beings **far beyond the archangels**, and in the case of the Yuletide, the cosmic Christ himself.

Consequently there is no mystical Imagination or 'astral thought' which, on the other side of the planet, can transform itself into a microcosmic activity occurring inside the human being's body. In essence, by suggesting this erroneous idea, the actual difference between the microcosmic and the macrocosmic activity is obscured.

Another source of confusion here is to not only regard both archangelic influences as equal (the macrocosmic and the microcosmic), and to melt them together, but also to relate this unequal mixture to a very different view about the Earth, given by Rudolf Steiner.

This view presents the globe as a vast human being; having its northern third (the cool temperate zones) correlated to our head (or thinking), the middle third (with the equatorial regions) correlating to our emotions, and the lower or southern third to our will (the legs and feet of a vast human

---

[386] M. Samson, Festivals in the southern... p.107.
[387] Ibid.

being). This valid three-fold view is not compatible with, and not relevant to, the task of determining the theme of a seasonal festival.

Additional festival themes

In winter, archangel Gabriel is active, guiding the gnomes in their work with the life-ether, from which the material substances for the new plant and animal life will develop. For this process to develop fully, the moisture-forming chemical-ether is needed. This is possible through the increased activity of the moon's ether rays during the winter, in the hemisphere's ether aura. Active within this process also are solar ether forces, absorbed during the summer, and now drawn down below the ground.

Such elemental processes as these, which influence especially the root systems of the plants, also exert an influence on the brain functions of humanity (see Chapter Two). It is into this dynamic that Uriel's microcosmic influence would have some discreet resonance, assisting our thoughts to draw nearer to the state of inspiration. Further, the archangel Gabriel, as the archangel of the Annunciation, can be thought of as the guide of the person who seeks to consummate the Holy Nights process of assimilating the Life-spirit radiance from Christ Jesus.

This is the higher, esoteric activity during the winter nights of this archangel who two thousand years ago was active in preparing the divine ether body of the pristine 'child of mankind'. Surely one may conclude that Gabriel yearns to assist the rest of humanity to achieve this union with the inner sun Chrestos radiance.

Also, during this winter-time, that is, in each hemisphere, the yearly fertilization occurs, whereby all those souls who are to be born in the next twelve months descend into the moon sphere. That is, they draw near to the periphery of the hemisphere's ether layers; in effect, this means the life-ether layer, as that is the outermost layer, as we established in Chapter One. Rudolf Steiner's research confirmed that a soul preparing for the conception of its body, does indeed first enter the life-ether when forming its new ether body.[388]

The activity of Uriel in winter in the processes underlying brain activity is relevant to the Holy Nights festival in only a minor way; it forms a minor theme for the festival. Likewise

---

[388] GA 93a, lect. 18th Oct. 1905.

the influence of Gabriel in the summer, in the digestive processes of humanity, forms only a minor aspect to the new St. John's Tide festival.

The spiritual sunlight that in summer Uriel unites to the earth's out-breathed aura becomes the inner sun forces with which, six months later, Gabriel and Christ Jesus are active during the Holy Nights. This inner sun force is the esoteric basis for that initiation text (quoted in Chapter Five), which I quote again: "Then Gabriel and Uriel form a column of light, and go before the elect, into the sacred realm, and bid them to eat of the tree of life, and to put on white raiment".[389]

We discussed the themes of the new spring festival in Chapter Four, but we omitted at that point, the activity of the archangel Raphael. It is important to note that Raphael was revered for millennia as the archangel empowered with a healing ministry for humanity. Raphael, also called Mercury, was invoked by the initiated priests involved in healing work, in various ancient civilizations.

Through the presence in springtime of the cosmic Christ, who directs the solar life-ether into the earth and repels the forces emanating from fallen elemental beings, Raphael may unfold his healing powers. It is in the springtime that the life-ether or prana in the earth's atmosphere is most 'alive', most quickened, through the influence of the inflowing solar ether. This process has been guided by the Christ being over the ages, not just since the time of his union to the earth soul.

I have already considered in detail the activity of archangel Michael in autumn.

The new seasonal festivals

The Christ-attuned Spring festival. The physical body, as the vessel of human consciousness, is the focus of this festival; hence the sacrifice of the Christ to enable the solar life-ether to permeate the earth, repelling the influences of ahrimanic and luciferic beings. Archangel Raphael is the guiding regent of the elemental forces, and strengthens his healing powers.

---

[389] The Apocalypse of Elias:40.

St. John's Tide. The ego, especially the still unconscious will forces, is the focus; the sun gods draw near; the warmth and light-ethers predominate. Archangel Uriel draws elemental forces from the earth's interior up into the heights; human will is sifted.

Michaelmas. The astral body is now the concern of a festival; in it are the ahrimanic sulphurous presence and the cosmic iron, in which Michael sends his power. Preparation for the Holy Nights begins now.

The Holy Nights-Yuletide. The ether body's capacity to transform into Life- spirit is the theme of this festival; how with the help of Christ Jesus this radiance is brought near to us, as we descend with the winter in-breath into the earth. Under Gabriel's guidance the winter fertilization of the earth, and the meeting with the Chrestos radiance occurs.

Illustration 10 shows the cycle of new Christian seasonal festivals for both hemispheres. For the sake of economy, this diagram does not include the presence within humanity of the microcosmic influence of the archangels. Neither does Illustration 10 accurately represent the inherent difference between the northern and southern hemispheres. This difference does not affect the fundamental aspects of the new festival cycle; it is a difference more in quantity than in quality.

As Rudolf Steiner commented, the southern hemisphere having less land than the northern, the result is that one hemisphere is more awake in its winter phase than the other.[390] Presumably it is the northern hemisphere that is more awake, because there are many more beings, human, elemental, and divine, in the Earth's physical body in winter on that half of the globe.

Thus the comment that the one hemisphere is more asleep in its sleep phase than the other refers to the southern hemisphere. For in the summertime when the out-breath carries the ether and astral forces and beings into the heights, the sleep phase there would become especially marked, because in the time of the Earth's out-breath or sleep phase there is still some activity going on behind the nature maturation processes, and in the south there is less of this activity because there is less land. And with much of the southern hemisphere being ocean, which would have

---

[390] GA 150, lect. 8th June, 1913.

little involvement with the in- and out-breathing dynamic, the residual activity in the southern hemisphere, during summer, would indeed be minor.

New festivals and traditional festivals

Illustration 12 presents a revised calendar for the traditional Christian festivals. We begin with Easter, with its variable dating (as I have noted, Easter is today celebrated as a historical festival with a hidden springtime relevance), and connected with Easter are Ascension and Pentecost. These two festivals are likewise today historical festivals which, unknown to the exoteric cultural life, also have a certain seasonal relevance, which we will considered shortly.

In addition, we can add to a calendar of historical Christian festivals the dates of the historical Easter event, that is, the mystery of Golgotha, which occurred in A.D. 33 between the 3rd and 5th of April. Then forty days later, on May 15th, occurred the Ascension event, and 10 days later, on May 25th, the Pentecost event. The addition of these days may appear to be unnecessary, since the traditional, varying Easter festival does include them. However, there is a validity to remembering an event on the day that the event actually occurred. We will also examine this matter.

Next in the calendar is the commemoration of John the Baptist on June 24th; we have established that this date is in essence seasonal, although it is historically valid. Then on August 6th is the Transfiguration of Christ; the basis of this day's dating is probably historical. This festival commemorates a major event in the interaction between Jesus Christ and the three foremost disciples. Briefly (since the esoteric significance of the historical festivals is not the subject of this book), the event involved the raising of the disciples' consciousness to the spiritual world and hence to the actual nature of the sun god, Christ, in Jesus.

Then for August 15th on the calendar we could enter a festival to honour the achievements of Mary and to acknowledge her ongoing significance for humankind, having to do with her selfless, consciously spiritual approach to conception. As Rudolf Steiner pointed out, much depends on such an achievement. In September we enter on the calendar the festival of "Michael and All Angels". As we have established, there is profound validity in placing a festival of the archangel Michael in the autumn. It is not an historical festival, but to omit it from the calendar of today's ecclesiastical or cultural life would weaken the chance for future generations to consider the nature of this archangel and the autumn.

It is already a serious sign that the festival was changed in recent times to "Michael and All Angels". In December the situation is more complex. Since the twelve days of Christmas, the Holy Nights, are not really an accepted part of the normal traditional festival calendar, and are not historical, but seasonal, we just note that these nights may be regarded as beginning on December 24th and ending on January 6th. Thus in December, historically, there is on the 24th, the Day of Adam and Eve, wherein the 'Fall of Man' is contemplated, together with the fact that the 'child of mankind' did not fall; this day prepares one for the 25th, the commemoration of the birth of the child Jesus, as given in both Gospels. Other aspects of the childhood of Jesus are valid for the historical "Christmas," which is the birthday of Jesus. The finding of the child in the temple is a good example.

On the 6th of January this theme of the birthday of Jesus can be continued in connection with the visit of the Magi. I have explained why the designation 'Epiphany' is incorrect for commemoration of this event. The true Epiphany festival, historically has, as its theme the descent of the dove, the cosmic Christ. We have placed the true Epiphany festival in the new Christian seasonal cycle, wherein it is also metamorphosed to show that a seasonal Epiphany event occurs each winter toward the end of the Holy Nights.

However, if we wish to define a historical festival cycle for our own clarity, as well as to help others, then the historical Epiphany event does belong to the historical cycle. Thus there are two themes for the 6th of January – the three Magi (including their historic-symbolic significance) and the baptism in the Jordan.

The entries on the traditional festival calendar are for commemorative days; in some cases, the days do have a seasonal relevance, which, however, is understood to be of secondary importance. The seasonal relevance is to enable humanity in the future, when the time is right, to form a Michael or Easter or St. John festival as an esoteric Christian

Michaelmas
Cosmic Iron

Regent :
Archangel Michael

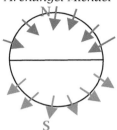

Esoteric Easter
Sun-god sacrifice

Regent:
Archangel Raphael

St. John's Tide
Sun forces & our will

Regent :
Archangel Uriel

Holy Nights
Chrestos

Regent :
Archangel Gabriel

Holy Nights
Chrestos

Regent :
Archangel Gabriel

Esoteric Easter
Sun-god sacrifice

Regent :
Archangel Raphael

St. John's Tide
Sun forces & our will

Regent :
Archangel Uriel

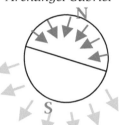

Michaelmas
Cosmic Iron

Regent :
Archangel Michael

10 The new esoterically 'Christian' seasonal festivals in both hemispheres

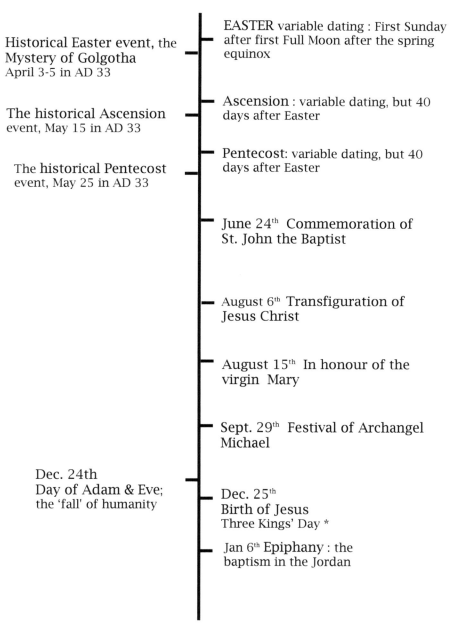

Historical Easter event, the
Mystery of Golgotha
April 3-5 in AD 33

EASTER variable dating : First Sunday
after first Full Moon after the spring
equinox

The historical Ascension
event, May 15 in AD 33

Ascension : variable dating, but 40
days after Easter

The historical Pentecost
event, May 25 in AD 33

Pentecost: variable dating, but 40
days after Easter

June 24th Commemoration of
St. John the Baptist

August 6th Transfiguration of
Jesus Christ

August 15th In honour of the
virgin Mary

Sept. 29th Festival of Archangel
Michael

Dec. 24th
Day of Adam & Eve;
the 'fall' of humanity

Dec. 25th
Birth of Jesus
Three Kings' Day *

Jan 6th Epiphany : the
baptism in the Jordan

* To transfer the Three Magi theme back to Dec. 25th, where it belongs,
i.e., an event to do the birth of Jesus, would enable the historical
festival cycle to have an unburdened day to contemplate the descent of
the cosmic Christ to the Earth: this is the true Epiphany event.

11 The traditional church calendar, revised

seasonal festival in the right season for each hemisphere. This situation is quite clear as regards the Easter festival. It is not so clear with the Ascension festival. I have noted that there was a definite day or days when the original Easter events took place, yet the Easter festival dating formula ignores this historical element; this is surely done to assist humanity, from the twentieth century onward, to realize that here is a contemporary interaction between the Christ being and the renewal of life in the spring.

So it is also with the Ascension festival; it could have been celebrated on the actual day of its occurrence, May 15th (AD 33), but instead it is connected to the springtime. To understand the deeper reason for this dating, we must briefly consider the meaning of the Ascension of Christ. Although the Christ being united his spiritual forces to the earth at the Mystery of Golgotha, it was not until forty days had passed that this event was completed, so to speak. The overcoming of the influences from luciferic beings took place at the resurrection; through this deed the future of the earth, of the physical-ethereal planet, was assured for humankind.

The luciferic beings seek to influence the human ether body; they tend to draw humanity up out of the earthly reality; both psychologically and even, in a subtle sense, physically, through the "levity" tendency which is in our ether body. They seek to prematurely spiritualize humanity. But important life processes on the Earth generally have a rhythm of forty. With the rhythm of forty, a cycle is completed.

As Steiner is reported to have pointed out, with all the processes in the Bible where the number 4 occurs, there is something wherein 'maya' is overcome.[391] The original ascension event, forty days after the resurrection, signified that the Christ forces had permeated the Earth's ether body, thus protecting humankind from the influences of Lucifer.[392] It has been shown (see Chapter Four) that every springtime, the original Easter event re-occurs, in a certain sense, for each hemisphere.

Verse 7 of the Soul Calendar indicates that the ascension process also needs to be reaffirmed about forty days after

[391] In the memoirs of Ludwig Kleeberg.
[392] In his lectures on Ascension and Pentecost, in *Festivals and their Meaning*.

the hemisphere's Easter festival. Now, however, the responsibility falls to the individual to summon up intuitive faculties, as the thinking life becomes less reliable:

> My self is threatening to flee,
> Attracted powerfully by cosmic light;
> Now enter, my divining,
> With strength into your rightful realm.
> Replace for me my thinking's power
> Which in the senses' shine
> Thus wills to lose itself.

Therefore, the Ascension can be commemorated as a historical event in a global festival, but also as a recurring seasonal event, the result of the same processes which underlie the esoteric Easter festival.

The Pentecost festival can also be part of a historical festival cycle, for it commemorates a most significant event in Christianity, namely that time when the conscious striving by the disciples to achieve the Spirit-self, through the inner nourishing which the Christ gave them, was blessed with a response from the spiritual worlds, from the holy spirit.

The placing of Pentecost ten days after the Ascension corresponds to the historical events; but with the variable timing of the Easter and Ascension festivals, Pentecost also is removed from its original historical date. As Rudolf Steiner pointed out, this is quite appropriate from the viewpoint of the symbolism involved. For Pentecost can then be considered to be a festival of flowers.

And just as flowers are the result of the plant's striving up to the light, as well as the descent of the rays of warm sunlight to the plant, so too the 'fiery flames' of the spirit which descended onto the disciples may be thought of as the response of the spiritual sun to the striving toward spirituality by the disciples. Hence, this varied timing of Pentecost, whereby it occurs in the spring, after the Ascension, has a deeply valid symbolic significance, namely, that of the plant which flowers in response to the rays of the sun. Further, the tandem timing of these three days represents the sequence of spiritual events whereby the Christ being brought healing and renewal to the earth.

First, through the Mystery of Golgotha, the continued healthy existence of the (physical) earth itself was assured. Likewise, through the springtime Easter sacrifice the physical body of humankind is imbued with the solar life-ether, protecting humankind from the 'Prince of this world'. Then in the Ascension event historically, and seasonally (each year), the ethereal forces of the earth and humanity are protected from luciferic influences. Finally, in the Pentecost event the soul (that is, astral forces) of the individual who seeks consciously to attain the Spirit-self can be permeated by the holy spirit. Hence in the historical, commemorative festival calendar Pentecost has a place, as do the mysteries of Golgotha and Ascension.

And Pentecost also has a place in the new seasonal Christian festival cycle, following the seasonal Christian spring festival. For these three festivals together also form, when understood esoterically, an important seasonal festival sequence in the spring. This we have seen as regards Easter, and we have now noted that the Ascension event has a seasonal reoccurrence. Thus, in the southern hemisphere, both these festivals occur in the spring. Concerning the Pentecost event, although as with the two proceeding festivals, its historical date should be noted, its springtime connection is also important.

Hence in the south it may be celebrated fifty days after the esoteric Easter spring festival. However, should a global Pentecost festival project be envisaged, in any one year (or years), then the southern hemisphere participants could coordinate with the northern hemisphere's springtime dating, since Pentecost is not the expression of an activity of the Christ reality in the actual hemispherical life processes of springtime.

Integrating the cycle of the traditional festivals and the new cycle

Illustration 12 displays the relationship of the two festival cycles. Across the centre is the historical-traditional sequence, across the top the seasonal cycle of the northern hemisphere, across the bottom the seasonal cycle of the southern hemisphere. In March or April, the esoteric Easter festival will be celebrated in the north, as the springtime out-breath develops. And following will come celebration of the seasonal Ascension (which coincides with the traditionally observed Ascension). Then will come Pentecost, appropriately placed in the springtime.

During these weeks the actual historical dates of the original Easter, Ascension, and Pentecost will have passed.

320

People in both hemispheres may wish to recall these momentous events on those dates, perhaps more as a private festival. The Michael festival will have been celebrated in the southern hemisphere by this time, not necessarily on the 29th of March, but at a time perhaps shortly after the autumn equinox. The holidays made available for the traditional Easter festival offer an opportunity for the Michael festival there in the south.

In June the north will have the St. John's Tide festival, while the south will enter the time of the Holy Nights-Yuletide of winter and the seasonal Epiphany. Then, the need will arise for people in the south to find the right themes or symbols for this festival, as distinct from those for the historical Christmas, that is, the birth of Jesus festival of December 25th (see later in this chapter).

In August the Transfiguration of Christ will be commemorated, and a festival to honour the Madonna could perhaps be observed; by this I do not mean any activity derived from the worship of Mary as in the Roman Catholic church. Both hemispheres will celebrate these festivals at the same time, for they are part of the historical cycle. In the church calendar (Catholic), the 15th of August is the day of the Assumption of the Virgin Mary.

What I suggest is perhaps a festival to contemplate the spiritual significance of events in the life of Mary that represent important spiritual processes. For example, behind the exoteric doctrine of the "bodily" presence of Mary in heaven, after her death, is a deep mystery connected with the spiritualization of the physical body. Likewise, the concept of an immaculate conception has profound significance. Such a festival may also indicate the contribution to humanity's spiritual development which womankind can bring.

In September, the north will celebrate the Michael festival, while the south will keep the esoteric Easter festival and then the seasonal Ascension and Pentecost. Then in December, the south will observe its St. John's festival as part of the esoteric seasonal festival cycle. A complex situation will develop at this time as the north enters into its seasonal Holy Nights and the globally acknowledged Christmas-Day event comes around. So amidst the summer and the observance of the St. John's festival, the historical

MARCH   APRIL   MAY   JUNE   JULY   AUGUST

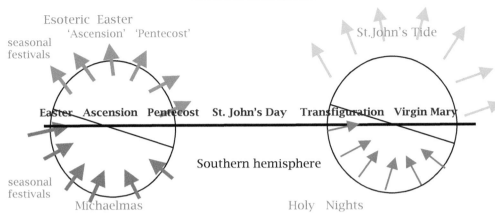

This diagram depicts how the global and the hemispherical-seasonal festival cycles can be integrated. Across the centre of the globes in brown are the historical church festivals; these are global, celebrated on the same day world-wide. (Adam & Eve day could be combined with the Jesus Birth day (Christmas Day) for practical reasons.
In magenta are the seasonal festivals for each hemisphere; these are 6 months apart from each other. About the 3 Kings' Day on 25th Dec; see illustration 11.

September   October   November   December   January   February

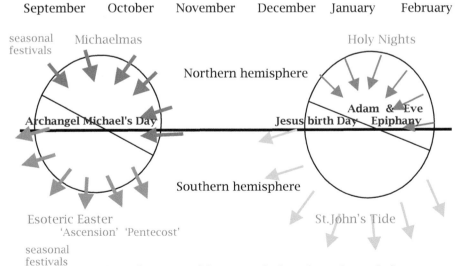

12   The revised historical-church cycle and the development from it of the new festivals.

Christmas-Day festival will be celebrated in the south as well as in the north.

On Christmas Day, and also on the evening before the 25th, a global commemoration of the birth of Jesus and the legend of Adam and Eve (that is, the fall and the need for the child of humankind to descend to earth) will occur. At the same time, again, the north will commence the Holy Nights, which will end on January 6th with an esoteric Epiphany contemplation.

In the south, much of what constitutes the festival of the Holy Nights (in the north) will naturally be absent during this time; but this seasonal festival in its fullness will be celebrated later there, in the southern winter (late June). In this way, with the two 'Christmas' days (24th & 25th Dec.) still celebrated globally, the family gatherings and outdoors enjoyments and gift giving (which are socially necessary), can all continue in the south in late December. And people from the southern hemisphere may actually exchange gifts, for example, with people from the north.

So will it be also with a Three Kings festivity on January 6th. But I do feel that where possible, the Three Kings motif could be worked in on or near to December 25th, so as to enable the historical Epiphany festival day to arise, unencumbered, on January 6th. As I mentioned earlier, Epiphany will also occur in the seasonal cycle at the end of the winter Holy Nights period for each hemisphere.

For those interested in the new festivals, an event in the historical cycle develops its full significance when its hidden seasonal relevance is discovered, enabling a new esoteric seasonal festival to arise. If this development is to take place in the future with Epiphany, then it must first be restored to the historical calendar. So on January 6th, the global historical Epiphany festival has its place, although for those who will be experiencing the southern Holy Nights festival which culminates in an Epiphany festival (in an esoteric seasonal sense), the historical Epiphany may be only briefly observed.

In the north, the Holy Nights will have their culminating Epiphany day. Illustration 14 portrays this situation that develops in December. In the north, the 24th will be the Day of Adam and Eve, a preparatory day for the 25th, when the historical fact of the need for the birth of the unfallen Jesus soul is contemplated. This observance will also occur for the south, but there the two days, the two themes, could be combined in one day, so that more time is available for the St. John's Tide festival. For example, the 24th (of December) and morning of the 25th could be for the historical Christmas day; then on the evening of the 25th or on the 26th of December, St. John's Tide could be celebrated.

In the north, Advent (or a seasonal equivalent under a new designation, so as not to confuse it with the historical preparation) will have already anticipated the Holy Nights. On January 6th, the Three Kings Day will occur; however, again, it could be nearer to the 25th in both hemispheres. Also on the 6th January, the Epiphany festival will culminate the Holy Nights in the north. For those who are not involved in the new festivals, it will retain its traditional, historical sense, in the south and the north.

The Three King's Day need not be observed by performing the Oberuferer Three King's Play; this play, derived from the normal medieval (Catholic) Christianity, is not as important as the other Oberuferer play, which has its origin in a somewhat esoteric Moravian/Bohemian Christianity.[393] The historical preparation for Christianity, and the inner preparation necessary to become a sun hero, are also valid themes for such a festival; and both are symbolized by the legendary traditions regarding the three Magi-their races, their gifts (see Chapter Eight).

There is the challenge in the north of consciously forming the themes for the historical birth of Jesus festival and the Holy Nights. Whereas in the south the challenge is to develop the festive activity appropriate to the Holy Nights without the convenience of the present-day Christmas customs. This is quite a challenge, but there is the advantage that in the south the Holy Nights occur at a time of little social or work stress, even if there are no official holidays allowed.

Also, the commercialism which has damaged the global Christmas festivities can be kept out of the southern Holy Nights. For example, the children could receive gifts which have a purely symbolic meaning and value.

Children's festivals and the new Holy Nights
The question of how to bring these new festivals to expression for children is better dealt with in an additional

---

[393] In GA 274, Rudolf Steiner's addresses for the Oberuferer Plays.

volume. For it is necessary in the first instance that adults experience and contemplate the new festivals. Then the right form for children's festivals can be found. A consideration of the matter of gift giving will provide some indications about children's festivals, that is, not the giving of presents between people, but the spiritual reality which is expressed in the mysterious figure of Father Christmas or the Christmas Man or Santa Claus.

This theme of Father Christmas leads to important considerations concerning the new Holy Nights festival; by examining this fascinating figure of Santa Claus, we can gain a clearer understanding of the major leitmotifs of the festival. Until the nineteenth century the Christmas Elf Man was just that – he was a wonderful, elfin-like youth (or adult entity) who brought presents to children on the night that Christmas began. In this figure was expressed the profound truth that it is through the cycle of the year, through the hallowed nature of the winter nights, that a gift, which has some connection with 'a child' and with the Christ reality, is given to humanity. This is a beautiful image of the gift to humanity of the divine power of active love which Christ Jesus mediates to the soul at night during the Holy Nights, that is, what is called here the Life-spirit.

However, the present-day Father Christmas or Santa Claus has lost much of this quality. This loss took place during the last century in North America, where the Dutch figure of Saint Nicholas, which is another version of the Christmas Elf Man, but much more down to earth, was merged with the Christmas Elf Man or elflike Christ Child (called in Germany Kris Kringle). All these versions of the Hallowed Nights gift to humanity were present in the United States, through its many emigrants.

But Saint Nicholas was an actual historical person, a saint of the fourth century, whose generosity, whose compassion eventually was used as a vehicle to express the Hallowed Nights mystery. Thus when the St. Nicholas cult figure was merged with other figures introduced by other non-Dutch immigrants, the result was the present-day, too human, rotund, ruddy-cheeked Dutch uncle figure.

The original Christmas gift giver, which I have called the Christmas Elf Man, was then an expression of the inner reality of the Holy Nights. As such, this part of the children's festival belongs to the winter; but this inclusion creates social problems in the south, if some children receive nothing while the others do have presents. One solution to this problem would be for the south (and the north, where the commercialized Christmas presents have little spiritual significance) to observe an additional seasonal present-giving ritual involving things with symbolic value.

The following story could serve as a basis for a simple ritual, wherein a golden star disc is given. And part of the Holy Nights decorations could include a figurine of the Black Madonna, a Madonna with an alert, majestic child, holding a star disc.

The legend of the Christ child and the cave with the golden star

Every winter, when the nights are longest and darkest, and the days are so cold, it seems as if the sun itself has gone far away from us. Then it is that the Christ child and the archangel Gabriel descend from heaven and hover above the snow-clad hills. For twelve days and thirteen nights they stay; thus begins the festival of the Holy Nights of winter.

On every night during this festival, the Christ child sends the Archangel Gabriel to meet every child on its journey to Dreamland, and to give each child a wonderful present; a golden star disc. It is made from the beams of the summer sun, like a golden dewdrop. But it glows with a wonderful golden radiance, it shines like a little star. This is the gift from the Christ child. When all the children have received their shining star discs, the archangel Gabriel guides them down to a secret cave, to a beautiful cave deep beneath a mountain.

There in this secret cave, made of glistening crystals, the Christ child waits, to greet each child, with its shining star disc. What a beautiful, mysterious cave it is !

It has twelve sides, of rainbow coloured crystals, and in the middle of each side stands a great column. Each column is covered with countless silvery stars. And in the centre of the cave a wonderful golden light is shining. It comes from a great star disc, which lies in the middle of the cave, just beneath the surface of its rocky floor.

"Dear children", says the Christ child, "would you like to help me make this golden star in the heart of the earth much brighter?" Then, the archangel Gabriel beckons to all the children and they go with him toward the centre of the cave. There each child places its star disc on the floor of the cave, around the great golden star disc. As they do this, the light of all their little star discs joins with that of the great star disc, and the cave becomes brighter. And then one of the star-covered columns begins to shine and sparkle with a silvery light. Then the Christ child smiles happily at the children, and archangel Gabriel leads them swiftly back up to the starry heavens, where their guiding angel is waiting to take them up to heaven.

As they rise high up in the night sky, they look down toward the earth and can see deep within it the soft gentle glow of the great star sun in the Christ child's cave. Also the column which has begun to glow and sparkle can be seen, too. Each night during the Holy Nights of winter, the archangel Gabriel gives to each child a star disc, and they journey down to the cave of the Christ child. By the twelfth day, all twelve columns are gleaming brightly, for the great star sun in the centre of the cave is aglow with a golden radiance.

CHAPTER TEN

THE SOUL CALENDAR AND THE TWO HEMISPHERES

The Soul Calendar verses are meditative and hence not so easy to grasp. But above all, unawareness in some official anthroposophical circles, that it is a guide to the seasonal cycle, starting in the springtime, in either hemisphere, may explain why its potential has not been realized in festival activity and in the renewal of festivals. A simple prose format would make for easier understanding but would be of limited value. For the Soul Calendar verses are designed to be meditated upon; through a meditative text many more esoteric truths can be made accessible to the users than through a straightforward logical treatise. Errors deriving from misunderstanding of the grammatical structure of the original German occur in some translations, and this of course adds to the difficulties.

Also, until there is knowledge as I have presented here of the fundamental concept behind the Soul Calendar, its verses will remain liable to mistranslation and misinterpretation. Without such insight into the spiritual reality of the seasonal cycle, it is difficult to know, for example, just when to start with verse 1 (the 'Easter' verse) in the southern hemisphere. Understanding Steiner's use of the term 'Easter' will aid us in resolving the problem of knowing when to start.

English and German-speaking people are often unaware that the term 'Easter' is peculiar to their cultures; elsewhere in the world, this term is seldom used. In other parts of the Christian world, 'Paschal' is the name of the festival commemorating the events of Golgotha. The word Paschal derives from the Aramaic term for the Old Testament lamb-sacrifice festival, which is the prophetic forerunner of the events on Golgotha hill.

Because of this derivation, Paschal is a better term than 'Easter' for the traditional Christian festival. The word Easter, intimately connected to the springtime, to the vivifying effect of the sun at (or after) the spring equinox, derives from the old Anglo-Saxon-Germanic peoples, has two meanings. It means, in the first place, "in the direction of the rising sun", that is, it referred to a direction, namely that point of the horizon where the sun is seen to rise. In this sense, 'Easter' is an extension of the word 'east'.

In the second place, amongst the Anglo-Saxons (and, presumably, the Celtic-Germanic tribes) this primal word became the name of a goddess. It is assumed that the Christian missionaries applied this term to the Paschal festival when they instituted it amongst these peoples, in accordance with church policy of adopting the names of popular festivals of pagan peoples. The festival of Eostre took place at about the time of the spring equinox.

Thus in the earliest Old High German texts, Ostara occurs as the name of the Paschal festival. And thus the term Easter is in fact quite naturally usable for the new Christian seasonal spring festival, since it directs our (European) attention to the life-renewing influences emanating from the re-born sun at the spring equinox. Rudolf Steiner often used the phrase 'the Mystery of Golgotha' instead of 'Easter' when speaking of the crucifixion and resurrection of Christ. But when speaking specifically of the springtime activity of the cosmic sun god in either hemisphere, he used the term Easter. This tendency is especially noticeable in the Soul Calendar, where the first verse has the title 'Easter mood', and yet refers to processes which are not connected at all to the historical events in Palestine, two thousand years ago.

The Soul Calendar in the southern hemisphere
It becomes clear, from this perspective, that the Soul Calendar is a contemplation guide to the new Christ-centred seasonal festivals. That the Soul Calendar is a hemispherical guide to the seasonal processes is obvious to those who use it in this way; but in addition, we actually have the words of Rudolf Steiner himself regarding the use of it in the southern hemisphere. This is reported by one of this students Fred Poeppig,[394] who specifically asked Rudolf Steiner how to use this Calendar in the south. Rudolf Steiner replied that it should be used according to the seasonal cycle of the southern hemisphere.[395]

---

[394] Fred R.E.A. Poeppig, 1900 -1974; lived in southern hemisphere at times; and served as a watchman over the ruins of the first Goetheanum.
[395] In *Abenteuer meines Lebens*, F. Poeppig, Novalis Verlag.

Tragically, the publishing of a version of the Soul Calendar was arranged in recent years, caused by the attitude that the purpose of the Soul Calendar can never be a seasonal guide for the separate cycle of the seasons of the hemispheres. In this version, Rudolf Steiner's specific phrases, which tell the reader the season to which season the verses apply, **have actually been removed,** (in effect, censored.) This is the version by William and Liselotte Mann.[396] When these words placed there by Rudolf Steiner himself, and integral to his book, were removed, the intention of the Soul Calendar was effectively thwarted.

The Soul Calendar is to start (with verse 1) in either hemisphere on the first Sunday after the first full moon after **that hemisphere's spring equinox day.** That is, verse One in the north will start in late March to late April, while in the south it will start in late September to late October. It is at that time when verse One is appropriate that the cosmic Christ ensures, through a sacrifice similar to that which this being underwent on Golgotha hill, two thousand years ago, that the solar life-ether forces do actually stream into the hemisphere's aura. As verse One indicates, it is through this activity that the consciousness (thought life) of humanity can rise above abstract, materialistic attitudes.

These processes, which result in the rejuvenation of the body as well as the freeing of our thinking (or consciousness) from ahrimanic influences are subconscious. But they are just as real – in some ways more real – than processes which are accessible to our normal consciousness. The joy the soul can experience in the springtime derives from its perception of these life-renewing activities.

Another problem with the Soul Calendar has been related to the special Easter dating formula. What do we do if the Easter verse is to commence unusually early or unusually late? Rudolf Steiner indicated that there is a transition from one dynamic to another which always involves three verses; one does not need to always have a precise definition regarding the day on which a verse is to be commenced and finished.

One can glance back at the preceding verse, and on into the following verse, in any one week, so to speak. But this is not a sufficiently clear guideline for the process of determining how to harmonize the Soul Calendar with the

---

[396] Published by Hawthorn Press, Stroud, UK, 1990.

very changeable 'Easter' date, since the Easter day of either hemisphere does not occur at the same time, but, depending on the moon's rhythms, occurs any time within a four-and-a-half-week period. That is, verse 1 could be due to start as much as four-and-a-half weeks later in one year than another. Only when verse One commences at about April 6th (in the north) or October 6th (in the south) can one use the 52 verses of the Soul Calendar without running out of weeks, or out of verses, before the Midsummer (St. John's Tide) verse, number 12.

That is, if verse One starts late, there are not enough weeks for the other ten verses that occur between Easter and St. John's Tide. Conversely, if verse One commences early, then there are too many weeks for the (ten) verses which exist after verse One to the midsummer verse. Since verse 12 must occur just after the summer solstice, and likewise the verses for the Holy Nights and the autumn equinox are to occur at these times, these non-mobile times provide the limits within which the varying date for verse One are to be arranged, see the following diagrams.

Likewise, the verses just prior to the Easter verse, those which relate to the spring equinox of the old year, those which lead up to the Easter verse, namely numbers 51 and 52, will be insufficient for all the weeks that occur; if the Easter day comes late. On the other hand, if this day comes early, then verses 51 and 52 will have no weeks allotted to them.

Summing up, if there are eleven weeks for verse 1 through to verse 11, then the use of the Soul Calendar is straightforward. But should verse One occur earlier than in the year when Rudolf Steiner gave it to the world (earlier than the 6th of April or October) then some kind of adjustment must be made.

If the 'Easter' day is late (perhaps not until late April or October) then there will still be the ten verses left but only about seven weeks to allot to these. This discrepancy can be dealt with by simply allotting less than seven days to each of these eleven verses. That is, one contemplates these ten verses during the seven-week period available.

Since the verses describe processes occurring between equinox and solstice, these processes still occur, but in a faster, more condensed manner in such years. Conversely, should verse 1 occur early, perhaps just a day or so after the spring equinox, then there will be about twelve weeks before the midsummer week, and only ten verses to experience over this time. This discrepancy can be dealt with by allotting more than seven days to each verse.

As we have noted, the moving date of the Easter day also affects the verses prior to verse One, the last verses of the Calendar, from the spring equinox through to verse One, in other words, verses 51 and 52. If verse One commences very early, that is, a day or two after the spring equinox, then verses 51, 52, and One will all apply in the one week ! That is, the processes which these verses express, the ingress of inner sunlight, the bringing in of solar life-ether through the Christ power, and the rejuvenation of physical-material substance, will occur very rapidly.

And then, as we have just noted, there will be twelve weeks for the ten verses that lead up to midsummer. This is the living reality of the earth, when lunar rhythms change the time periods, the middle kingdom undergoes a corresponding intensification (or slowing down) in its elemental processes. Thus, also, when verse One starts very late, then verses 51 and 52 will apply to the whole period of some four-and-a-half weeks between the spring equinox and the first Sunday after the first full moon.

The reader may ask, is such a procedure really a correct way to deal with this problem? The answer is openly given, but veiled, in Rudolf Steiner's own dating procedure in the three editions of the Soul Calendar that he caused to be published in his lifetime. For example, in the 1918 edition, verse 1 commenced earlier than in 1912, when the Soul Calendar was first issued. Steiner therefore suspended the 'rule' of always starting on a Sunday, and in order to fit the ten following verses (up to midsummer) into the approximately twelve weeks of time, he set out periods for verses occupying 8, 10, and 11 days.

In other words, he used the same system that I am proposing here, wherein the midsummer St. John's Tide timing and verse, like the Holy Nights verses and timing, are fixed points in the yearly cycle, and the movable Easter dating creates the need to condense or expand the verses into the time available. The rest of the year is in harmony with the time scale of the 1912 Soul Calendar, there are eleven verses and eleven weeks from solstice to equinox.

Such a process demands simply that the user of the Soul Calendar become conscious of the yearly cycle, in particular the flow of the moon's rhythms in relation to the sun.

Steiner placed this necessity before the first generation of the Soul Calendar's users in a veiled yet powerful way. His first edition, which starts on Easter Sunday, 1912, simply runs through for 52 weeks, ending on the day before Easter Sunday of 1913.

This is, in fact, absurd, since Easter Sunday in 1913 occurred some two weeks earlier than in 1912, that is, directly after the spring equinox. So verses 51 and 52 and verse One all had to be read in the one week. Not to do that would have meant finishing verse 52 some two weeks after Easter Sunday in 1913 !

Likewise, the 1918 edition runs through exactly 52 weeks, finishing in 1919 some 365 days after Easter Sunday of 1918; but since Easter in 1919 occurred late, an inattentive reader would have had a two-week gap between verse 52 and Easter Sunday of 1919. In other words, the year from one "Easter day" to the next is never 365 days in length, but rather ranges from about 335 days to 400 days.

The Soul Calendar is one of Rudolf Steiner's greatest achievements; it is a manual for developing communion with the divine beings who maintain the life and the spiritual dynamics of our planet. After some years of working with the Soul Calendar, one can experience, at first in retrospect, then in the present moment, increasingly tangible impressions of the 'Middle Kingdom". Such experiences grant a wondrous, enchanted mood to the daily routine, and result in, not only an enhanced attunement to the spiritual world, but also pragmatic commitment to environmental questions, in the fullest sense.

We will now look at three diagrams, designed to help you work out how to understand the distribution of the verses between verse One, the esoteric Easter verse and verse 12, for the summer solstice, varies.

There are three options:
Firstly: if the year is the same as when the Soul Calendar was printed.
 Secondly: when the time of Easter occurs very late, and some verses have to be shortened.
Thirdly: when Easter comes very early, and some verses have to be stretched.

1 : Easter occurs as in 1912

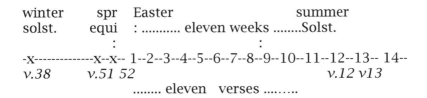

```
winter      spr   Easter                    summer
solst.      equi   : .......... eleven weeks ........Solst.
             :                     :
-x--------------x--x-- 1--2--3--4--5--6--7--8--9--10--11--12--13-- 14--
v.38        v.51 52                               v.12 v13
                   ........ eleven  verses ..........
```

2 : When Easter occurs very late

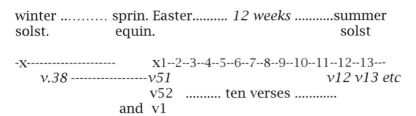

```
winter      spring      Easter              summer
solst.      equi         : ...... 8 1/2 weeks ......  solst

-x------------x--x-- 1--2---3-X-4--5--6--7--8--9--10--11--12--13--

v.38 ..  .v.51-52      v.1                       v12 v13
                   ...... eleven verses ...........
```

(So here verses 51 and 52 have several weeks to occupy, but verses 2 - 12 have only about 9 weeks to go into)

3 : When Easter occurs very early, 2 days after equinox

```
winter .......... sprin. Easter.......... 12 weeks ...........summer
solst.         equin.                              solst

-x--------------------        x1--2--3--4--5--6--7--8--9--10--11--12--13---
   v.38 ------------------v51                       v12 v13 etc
                          v52  .......... ten verses ............
                      and  v1
```

(So here, 3 verses occur in 1 week; and there are 10 verses for 12 weeks)

Other Questions

With the new seasonal festivals, the question arises regarding the situation of people living on the equator and in the polar regions. These questions are of little use to the quest to understand the living Earth. No specific statements are available from Rudolf Steiner on these questions. But it is important to note first that very few people live in the polar regions; any unusual conditions there do not affect many people. And the width of the equator, that is, the imagined point of meeting of the two hemispheres, hence a region which is neutral, which does not belong to either the southern or northern hemisphere aura, is very, very narrow.

Physical evidence from simple experiments on the ground, determining when water follows clock-wise or anti-clockwise down a drain, indicative of the etheric forces of the Earth, reveals that the equator is only about two yards wide. The astral equator may be even less broad, it is not possible to say.

Then we can remind ourselves that there are two causes for the seasonal phenomena. The extreme weather conditions of the equator and the polar regions are due primarily to one of these causes – the spatial, astronomical relationship of the earth to the sun. The equatorial regions have maximal exposure, the polar regions' minimal exposure.

But the full reality of a season is the result of the ascending and descending elemental (and spiritual) substance of the Earth's being, and the extent to which this process proceeds in the region of the poles and the equator will determine the inner seasonal reality in those areas. This inner elemental breathing is of course harmonized with the spatial movement of the Earth – it is hemispherical. Normally one would assume that the entire hemisphere is involved in the process. However, it is likely that the poles and the equatorial regions are not fully integrated into the yearly breathing, that they are regions with imbalanced rhythms on the **ethereal level**.

That is, the warmth and light-ethers in polar regions would have little influence during the long polar winters. But on the astral (soul) level, it appears from Steiner's comments, that these areas are predominantly involved in the yearly cycle. Hence the archangel Uriel is not constantly active over the equator, even though summer-like conditions exist there during most of the year. When the summer out-breath ends, then Uriel is no longer active over the hemisphere, even though the ether processes of the summer will continue, to some extent, in the warm conditions of the tropics.

And neither would Gabriel remain constantly active over the cold polar regions, for the actual in-breath process, on the astral level, in which Gabriel is active, only lasts for three months, across the hemisphere. It does appear that the breathing process encompasses the whole hemisphere, including the polar region as well as the equator, even if in an unbalanced rhythm. The yearly breathing can proceed and be difficult to physically perceive in areas where temperatures and so forth are constant.

The seasonal cycle and the cosmic Christ

It is difficult for us today to grasp the sheer fact of the spiritual reality underlying the seasonal cycle of the year. The contemporary Christian worldview derives from medieval times in Europe, when enormous effort was expended to develop a uniform, all-encompassing theological/philosophical definition of the Christ reality. Any viewpoints that could lead to differences in the practice of the Christian religion were deeply disliked and distrusted. For example, if the early British churches celebrated Easter at a different time of the spring, or Sicilian and Syrian churches celebrated Epiphany as the descent of the power of God upon Jesus, that is virtually acknowledging that Jesus became the Messiah only at the Baptism, then such divergences were intensely opposed.

There was at times much justification for the effort to achieve a uniform Christian worldview, for the cohesive integrated nature of Christianity depended upon the effort made to develop an accurate and universally respected view of basic dogmas. In this centuries-long struggle, both the deeper, more accurate, and the fallacious, dubious viewpoints that were not part of the mainstream of Christianity were rejected. In expanding to encompass the early Europeans, Christianity also had to battle against the nature worship of the Celts, the Germanic-Nordic peoples, and others.

The new hemispherical festivals could be viewed with suspicion because they may appear to threaten the globally celebrated traditional festivals. This anxiety is groundless, because the new festivals are intended not as replacements but as additions to the present global festivals. These, as we have seen, are not related to the life processes of the earth, to the spiritual reality that weaves through the seasonal cycle, hemispherically.

When we do grasp the spiritual reality behind the seasons, that the life process of each hemisphere has its own rhythmical cycle, we can develop a festival concept that may lead us to an experience of the Christ being. This festival activity is being nurtured, as are so many spiritual processes in humanity, by higher beings who serve the will of the world creator; in Christian terminology, they are called 'the hierarchies'. In particular, an archangel referred to in old Icelandic texts, Vidar, is given the task of inspiring the development of the new festivals. This same archangel is intimately involved in making possible the experience of the reappearance of Christ.

If we do not accept the spiritual reality behind the seasonal cycle, if we are not aware of the activity of the hierarchies and the cosmic Christ, through which the spiritual development of humanity and the earth is attained, then we will be unable to take full nourishment from Steiner's Soul Calendar.

The intent of the Soul Calendar's organization is that verse 51 be contemplated at the spring equinox, verse 38 at midwinter, and so forth. The verses are more than simply poetic meditations on spiritual realities remote from the daily reality of the changing seasons of the physical earth. Rudolf Steiner's Soul Calendar is a meditation manual for those who seek the contemporary reality of the Christ being, as the spirit of the Earth.

Until we develop awareness of this Christ-permeated spiritual alchemy, we may regard the seasonal nature processes as quite divorced from the Christ-being. We will regard the Soul Calendar verses for Easter, Christmas (that is, the Holy Nights), Michaelmas, and St. John's Tide as referring to festivals that are 'simply Christian', that is, quite separate from the seasons of either hemisphere. A major misunderstanding about the Soul Calendar is shown in the attitude that, "because the nature rhythm in the south does not coincide with the festivals", it is necessary to, in effect overlay a seasonal reading with a calendar reading. This statement has no actual meaning, as the seasonal; cycle is the cause of the processes which are the focus of new festivals.

But this confusion can lead people to include in addition to the seasonally appropriate verse, a verse from six months later. Thus verse 12, which is for the St. John's Tide festival (June 24th in the north) would need to be read in late June in the south, not just verses 37/38, which are the appropriate verses for the winter solstice. For only in this way could one ensure that the St. John's Tide verse, number 12, would be read at the right time, this is an attitude which presupposed, that the Christ reality is not aligned with the seasonal processes. This is a pointless exercise, unless one is striving to reflect back on the contrasting dynamics of the earlier season, as a kind of secondary focus.

What Rudolf Steiner meant when he stated that the Soul Calendar needs to be correlated to the southern hemisphere seasons is exactly the opposite. His emphasis was on ensuring that the verses coincide with the seasonal esoteric Christian festivals. The festival cycle which the Soul Calendar proclaims is hemispherical. Thus verses 37/38 need to be read in late June in the south, so that the winter Christmas or Holy Nights festival and the meeting with Christ Jesus amidst the Chrestos radiance can fully occur. The St. John's Tide verse (12) can safely wait until late December in the south, at which time the sun gods will, through Uriel, work further miracles of transformation with the elemental forces generated by human willing.

However, to accompany the present verse, seasonally speaking, with the verse of six months ago will assist the seeker in the task of more clearly sensing the inner reality of the present week, by throwing it into stark relief against its opposite. That the Soul Calendar verses refer to seasonal festivals is also established by the fact that when in the south it is read in 'reversed order', with the summer verses at summer solstice time, and likewise with the verses for the autumn equinox and winter solstice, then in springtime the cycle begins again with verse One, which is also designated the **"Easter" verse**.

But, significantly, this Easter verse in the Soul Calendar begins with the title **'Spring'**. About a century ago, Steiner thus proclaimed in the Soul Calendar, as well as various lectures, as we saw earlier, this inherent connection of the esoteric Easter with the springtime of both hemispheres.

338

Rather than disregarding the nature of the dynamics arising in each season, Steiner urged people to consciously seek to experience how archetypal these forces are with respect to the human soul. For we are sons and daughters of Mother-earth, and what develops in the Earth-soul during the year must also develop in us. Self-knowledge may be achieved through the new seasonal festivals, once the abstract attitude to the yearly cycle is overcome. Again, according to Steiner,

> Humankind was once connected to the processes of the macrocosm, but in order to gain consciousness of ourselves, we had to lose our connection to the spirit; so that in a future time {which has now dawned} our inner being could become strong enough to find again, as ego-ic beings, the spirit.[397]

Steiner elaborates this thought in his introduction to the Soul Calendar; he writes,

> Our inner {soul} processes, are now less connected to time, to the cycle of the year, but if we bring our own 'timeless' soul activity into correspondence with the temporal rhythms of the year, then great secrets of existence will unfold for us. The year becomes the great archetype of humankind's own soul processes, and thereby a fruitful source of self-knowledge.

The seasonal cycle is best experienced in the cool temperate climate zones; but from the research of Rudolf Steiner, one can conclude that the astral changes occur regardless of which climate zone one is in. But I remember well, from my childhood, the power of the seasonal cycle of the year in southern Australia, how the fiery-golden autumn colours gave way to the cold bare days. Soon the towering cumulo-nimbus snow clouds filled the grey skies, then, in June, and the landscape was clad with snow. Sometimes, driving blizzards came, which buried the sheep deep in a blanket of snow.

At times the snow fell gently, inviting a child to put on the balaclava and gloves, and to wander, enchanted, through its faery landscapes. Springtime brought floods, as melting

---

[397] GA 175, lect. 27th Feb. 1917.

snow and rain combined to create large lakes of water. Then the spring blossoms appeared, bringing radiant shades of green to the pastures, which gradually turned yellow, then brown, as the burning heat of summertime made the air shimmer and a drowsiness overcame both man and beast.

It is simply the case, that such physical manifestations of the elemental processes occurring during the year are most perceptible in the temperate climate zones. Since there is more land in the north, there will be larger areas where the climate is moderate, is cool enough to manifest the seasonal changes physically. But in the south, wherever the climate zone is appropriate, the seasons are very real. So the process of developing new seasonal festivals is, for both hemisphere important.

For only after lifetimes of endeavouring to work with the ether-astral reality of the seasonal cycle, will we be in a position to become co-creators with these beings, manifesting the will of the cosmic Christ on Earth. Further, there are, according to Rudolf Steiner, new elementals now coming into being to serve the Christ, beings with whom humanity may cooperatively work in the future. The way to deal with the changed conditions of the Earth in the future is to be found by working to develop an awareness of these beings and their guiding archangels; not by ignoring them.

For humanity to achieve this important capacity of cooperation, a new conscious, ego-controlled clairvoyance is needed. Rudolf Steiner pointed out that not only will we, in the future, need the help of these beings; now, in fact, they need our help. It is especially in autumn and spring that a conscious effort is called for, to help these beings avoid the influence of Ahriman and Lucifer.

In the far future, the Earth will be developing its ethereal counterpart, and most of humanity will be developing the capacity to live in ethereal bodies, quite consciously, while the material earth becomes harder and less alive. As the Earth begins to develop its new ether form, humanity will be called upon to become conscious co-creators with the gods, through cooperation with the inhabitants of the middle kingdom. For example, the motion of the Earth through space will be sensed by humanity at that future time precisely through their empathy with a certain kind of elemental being.

And further, another kind of elemental being will enable humanity to sense what kind of experiences the earth soul is undergoing as the Earth journeys through space. That is, the energies to which it is exposed, and the rhythm with which this occurs, will become part of humanity's life experience. People will achieve this perception and become involved in this process through developing the capacity to sense what the elemental beings are experiencing.[398]

The alternative future is the one that Ahriman is incubating, wherein people living in an artificial plastic-electronic environment focus their attention on physical galactic space. The new festivals can assist humanity to live into the realm of the ethers, the realm wherein we may being to glimpse the earth spirit.

There is no doubt that Rudolf Steiner came to the conclusion, on the basis of his extensive research, that the same rhythmical life process, the same breathing process, transpires in the south as in the north. The quotations I have presented in Chapters One and Nine reveal this conclusion. Again, Steiner said, for example, that "when on the one side {hemisphere} of the Earth there is the waking state {in winter}, then on the other side {in summer} there is the sleeping state, and vice versa".[399]

As I have noted, Rudolf Steiner was aware that the southern hemisphere's larger water mass produces a different dynamic. He found that although the yearly pulsation of life forces in the hemisphere's aura is not hindered, a greater 'sleep' state does prevail in the south while a more 'awake' state prevails in the north. But to some extent, the same nature beings are active in the breathing processes of both hemispheres. Rudolf Steiner told two audiences of how some nature spirits continuously encircle the Earth. These beings migrate between the hemispheres; moving from the northern hemisphere to the southern hemisphere and back again,

> The rhythmical dynamic is such that the earth spirits, when they depart from the northern hemisphere in summer, they draw toward the southern hemisphere... ascend in spring and summer into the heights, and {descend down} on to the other hemisphere.[400]

---

[398] GA 272, lect. 30th May, 1915.
[399] GA 143, lect. 16th May 1912.
[400] Ibid..

These are beings who have to remain in the autumn and winter in-breath phases, predominantly; see Illustration 13. As the winter season passes over into spring and then summer, these nature beings migrate as it were around to the other hemisphere, thus having a short exposure to the spring and summer out-breathing phases. Most of their year is spent in between the two hemisphere's in-breathing time of autumn and winter. Their activity forms a kind of bond in the seasonal processes of the two halves of the Earth.

Such considerations as these also highlight the subjective nature of the attitude expressed by certain groups in the southern hemisphere, that having been able to directly experience the seasonal cycle in the south, they have a better grasp of this theme than Rudolf Steiner, who was 'not able to experience the southern cycle'.

As we have seen throughout this book, the etheric energies of the two hemispheres are an integral part of the seasonal processes, and intimately interwoven with the astral aura of the planet. Although Steiner did not visit the southern hemisphere, the quotations I have presented, indicate that his spiritual research faculties were fully capable of examining the inner reality of the southern hemisphere's life cycle and other features.[401]

So it is that developing the new seasonal festival cycle is a task for people in both hemispheres. It is a Christian experience, in an esoteric sense. We need to do this work so that humankind can develop the capacity to deal with the challenges of the future. For example, learning to work with the life processes of the Earth so as to be capable of existing on an increasingly etherealized planet.

Through the development of the new festivals, we will enable ourselves to become ever more attuned to the reality and intentions of the cosmic Christ. Were the classical ecclesiastical observances to remain as the only kind of festivals, for both hemispheres, then this positive process could not take place. The classical festivals had to be placed abstractly in the living Earth's yearly cycle, because humanity was then in its 'hermits in the cosmos' stage, living on a flat Earth.

---

[401] He stated to G. Wachsmuth, that the great rock outcrop, Uluru, in central Australia was the place of the highest spiritual forces, in ancient Lemurian times.

But now, through the seasonal process of attunement, the cosmic Christ may gain ever greater capacity to guide humanity on into the golden future, the future that he wills to grant us. For it will be through the ever greater sensitivity in humanity to the ether-astral reality of the Earth, that we may participate with the cosmic Christ in the process of guiding the Earth as well as ourselves into the future. Here is the reappearance of the cosmic Christ in human consciousness.

May the new seasonal Christian festivals arise, as a true deeper Pentecost inspiration, so that humanity in both hemispheres may be united in participating consciously in the life drama of the Earth, which through the original Epiphany events is destined to become a star.

10 For their work in the Earth's ethers, some nature spirits are required to constantly avoid the spring & summer. As the spring approaches where they currently are, they migrate around to the other hemisphere's autumn & winter.

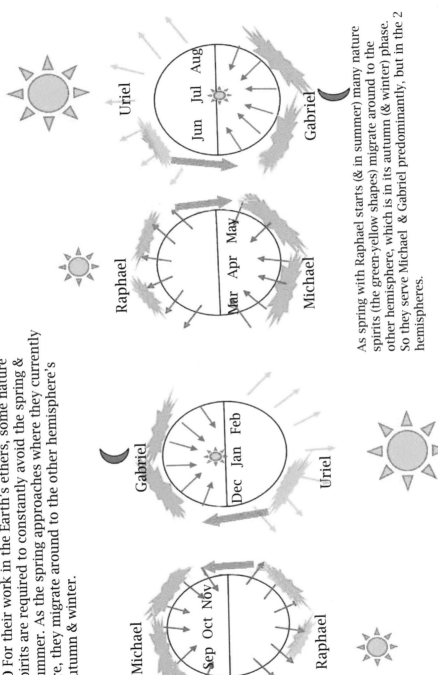

As spring with Raphael starts (& in summer) many nature spirits (the green-yellow shapes) migrate around to the other hemisphere, which is in its autumn (& winter) phase. So they serve Michael & Gabriel predominantly, but in the 2 hemispheres.

APPENDIX 1

A list of quotes showing that the Holy Nights-Yuletide festival belongs in the winter of either hemisphere

1 The external power of the sun is fully outpoured in the spring and summer sun. In that the physical power of the sun ever more declines, its spiritual power intensifies and becomes stronger and stronger toward Christmas-Holy Nights. (p.212)

2 The Holy Nights-Christmas (Yuletide) festival is placed from an old consciousness, in that time in which the sun draws its forces away most strongly from the earth {hemisphere}; in that time (season) when the earth, with all of its capacity, including what all this can signify for human beings; and is most especially in charge of itself. With the Holy Nights-Christmas time, we have to do with an earth {hemisphere} which is forsaken by the heavens...so we have the Holy Nights-Christmas festival firmly placed in the calendar entirely according to earthly circumstances. (P. 219)

3 The Christmas-Holy Nights mystery, when it is understood as a mystery, belongs paramountly to winter (p.230)

4 So we see that one can say: at Christmas time {that is, in the winter hemisphere}, the earth {hemisphere} has absorbed its soul forces into itself; it has in the great annual breathing process absorbed its soul organism into itself. The Christ impulse is born in the earth's (hemisphere's) inbreathed soul forces, in the interior of the Earth. Deep in the earth's core, each winter, the Life-spirit forces of the Christ being increase (p. 234)

5 In the key revelations about the meeting with Christ in the Holy Nights, such words as these are spoken:

Therefore, the special feeling which we connect with the Christmas mystery and its festival is in no way something arbitrary; rather, it is connected with the time of the year in which Christmas is placed. In those winter days, appointed to this festival, the human being is then, as is indeed the entire world around us {that is, the hemisphere} given over to the spirit............. In a profound sense, and this should not be blotted out by the materialistic abstract culture of today, Christmastime is bound to processes in the earth. For the human being, together with the earth {that is, their hemisphere} undergoes the 'Christmas-Holy Nights alteration' of the hemisphere.....

This meeting the human being has with the spiritual world, in the cycle of the year, on any point of the earth, in that time in which it is, for that point of the earth {i.e., hemisphere}, in fact, the Christmas wintertime.

6 The Christmas-Holy Nights festival has not merely symbolical meaning, it also has natural significance... at this time {of the yearly cycle}, a force recedes from humankind which otherwise comes to it. When the disciple is so far, he must heed this. The human being must develop the forces from within, which otherwise come from without. The source of this must be cultivated in wintertime... this is indicated in the placing of the festivals {in the yearly cycle}. (p. 263)

7 The festival of the divine being, that is, the Earth spirit, could never be placed in summer by a clairvoyantly knowing humanity; rather, it must be celebrated in the wintertime. In the 'hallowed time' {of the year} the soul feels itself united with the divine spiritual powers which then permeate the earth. The Christmas-Holy Nights festival **belongs in the winter,** just as St. John's festival belongs in the summer. (p. 271)

8 ....it is a beautiful thought to connect the Christmas festival with the time when the Earth {hemisphere} is closed off from the cosmos, when the human being, in earthly isolation, seeks to establish communion for {self-produced} thoughts with the divine-spiritual realm. And in that we understand what is here meant, we seek to protect ourselves from the ahrimanic powers. (p.284)

9 But if the earth lives in this deepest outer darkness, we know that the Earth-soul experiences her light; she begins to awaken to the highest degree. The spiritual waking time is connected to the Christmastime, and with this spiritual waking phase there should be united the commemoration of the spiritual awakening for earth's evolution, by Christ

346

Jesus. From this derives the placing of the Christmas {that is, the Hallowed Nights) sanctification festival precisely at this time. (p. 287)

10 It has arisen from a profound intuition that, that time when the human being should unite with that which Earth evolution should call into fullest consciousness, that is, the Christ-impulse, has been placed in the midwinter, and not in the summer, as the Christmas-Holy Nights festival. (p. 294)

APPENDIX 2

The zodiac age and the two hemispheres.

It is commonly accepted that the present zodiac age is that of Pisces and that later 'we' will be in the zodiac age of Aquarius. Human civilization is now subtly influenced by Piscean forces; this is a global dynamic. Rudolf Steiner confirmed this zodiac clock as a basis for the different epochs of civilization. Thus in the old Egyptian and Babylonian cultures the bull was a sacred religious symbol. For in that remote time, the sun had entered the sign of Taurus. After some two thousand years the sun entered the next sign, Aries, and the age of the ram began, the search for the Golden Fleece becoming the task for the initiates. Then, some centuries ago the sun entered the sign of Pisces, our present age.

But what does it mean, "the sun enters a sign"? Briefly, leaving aside astronomical considerations, it means that if in a particular year the sun is in front of, say, Gemini, on the morning of March 21, then because the sun changes its position slowly as regards the background of stars, after some years, when its position is again observed, on the morning of March 21, it will now be in the sign of Taurus.

But why was the sun's zodiac position on the 21st of March taken as the determining position? If another day of the year had been chosen for these yearly observations, say the 22nd of June, then the zodiac sign would have been quite different, it would have been the midsummer time and thus a different zodiac sign would have been behind the sun.

The 21st of March is, in the northern hemisphere, the spring equinox day, that time in the spring out-breathing when the hemisphere is especially receptive to the solar forces, which then bring the renewal of the life processes. In earlier times, humanity was aware that this situation has a significance regarding the influence of the zodiac forces. When the hemisphere is so receptive to the cosmos, then the zodiac influences 'behind' the sun also stream into the hemisphere, and become part of the creative forces renewing life on Earth.

It is therefore not surprising that Rudolf Steiner found that in earlier times people felt that the fresh young power

348

of the springtime united with the zodiac force 'behind' the sun.[402] They said to themselves that the zodiac force "is the bestower of the sun with its new vigour, it is the bestower of the new creative divine power".[403] In effect, the zodiac force behind the sun at the time when the hemisphere has its spring equinox is uniquely powerful, and it influences civilization in that hemisphere for as long as the sun, at the equinox, is in front of it.

This process has a cycle of 2,160 years, the length of time that the sun takes to move from one part of the zodiac to another. Although the northern hemisphere has moved from the Aries age into the Piscean age, and will next move into the age of Aquarius, in the southern hemisphere we are in the age of Virgo and will next move into the age of Leo. The qualities of the Piscean and Virgoan ages are not our present theme, but I have mentioned this subject as an example of how the reality of the cycle of the year will elude us so long as we think in an abstract way about the spiritual reality of the cosmos.

---

[402] In Theosophy of the Rosicrucians, lect. 3. (GA 99).
[403] Ibid.

APPENDIX 3

The Chrestos force and Foundation Stone.

One of the deepest, most inspired meditations from Rudolf Steiner on the Christ reality is an Epiphany Christmas verse, spoken during the northern hemisphere Holy Nights, called The Foundation Stone meditation. It includes these words:

> At the turning point of time the light of the Cosmos-spirit entered the stream of earthly being; darkness of night had run its course, day-radiant light streamed into human souls, light that en-warms simple shepherds' hearts, light that enlightens the wise heads of kings. Light divine, Christ sun, en-warm for us our hearts; enlighten for us our heads.

The light of the 'cosmos-spirit' is the supernal radiance of the devachanic or spiritual being of the cosmic Christ, who is then more precisely described as the 'light divine' and 'Christ sun', that is, the Spirit-self radiance and the Life-spirit or 'inner sun' forces of the cosmic Christ. In these words there is an indication of the role of the primal soul of humankind, now Christ Jesus, in the offering to humankind of the "light divine" to human hearts. The seasonal Christmas festival is and will be, therefore, a focus point for a central aspect of the Christ mystery, the assimilation and manifestation of the power of love in humanity, from the inexhaustible fountain of the Christ sun.

And this process, from which in the future a culture of sun initiates will arise, is that same process which anthroposophy offers to humankind, as we saw earlier.

The great spiritual event wherein the Foundation Stone meditation was given took place, as I have mentioned, during the Holy Nights of the northern hemisphere. The purpose of this gathering was to re-found the Anthroposophical Society, giving it a deeper, clearer understanding of its tasks for our times.

Hence, the meeting was held during that time of the year when the light of the cosmic Christ most strongly permeated the Earth's aura; if this gathering had been held in the southern hemisphere, then it would have taken place from 25th June to early July. In the light of the spiritual processes referred in these pages, from which the relationship of the

350

Christ impulse to the cycle of the year becomes evident, it is also possible to approach a profound truth of the Christian initiation wisdom presented in the Foundation Stone meditation.

This meditation consists of three main sections. The middle one concerns the 'middle sphere' of our nature, the feeling life, which is between thinking and willing, as it were. This section speaks of the possibility for the human being, when the feeling life is transformed and achieves an inner equilibrium, to unite with the "world ego." Such a transformation of the feeling life or soul mood is invoked by striving toward being attuned to the spiritual reality in which we are continually immersed, although we do not sense it.

The meditation urges us to practice 'contemplating' the spiritual realities behind the world by using our heart, the feeling life which manifests in us via the rhythmical system, our heartbeat and breathing. This activity, similar to the 'practice of the presence' of the mystics is, in effect, a striving to sensitize our feelings and therefore the ether body, by overcoming the self-centred emotions. When the imbalance or storms in the soul body are subdued, then this fine, subtle 'sensing-feeling' can arise.

Our normal sense perception and predisposition depend upon the ether body. When the soul attains a higher sensitivity, the ether body is then regenerated and serves as mediator of spiritual perceptions. Thus through the Christmas Foundation Stone meditation, another aspect of the inner sun initiation or Holy Nights can be understood, namely that in a person whose ether body has been "reborn" from the purified soul forces, the divine creative ether powers become accessible. And this development in turn creates a resonance or a merging with the inner heartbeat of the world, with the divine creative forces which have formed and maintain the life processes of the world.

These divine devachanic ether powers have a rhythmical quality, they manifest through rhythm; hence the presence of a rhythm in the life processes of creation, from the movements of the planets to the breeding habits of insects. The meditation expresses this aspect of the Christmas winter mystery in these words:

O Human Soul ! You live in the pulse of heart and lung, which leads you through the rhythms of time into the feeling of your own soul's being; practice spirit contemplation in inner equilibrium, where the on-surging world-evolving deeds unite your own ego to the ego of the world; then you shall truly feel within the dynamics of the human soul.

That is, the feeling life will be able to manifest the real, spiritual potential of the human soul and also to merge with the world soul. This section of the meditation refers, then, to a process which will eventually lead to the development of the Life-spirit or Buddhi.

That the attainment of the Life-spirit or Chrestos is now possible for all humankind, since the union of the cosmic Life-spirit forces of the Christ with the Earth, is expressed in the two lines of the meditation immediately following the extract I have just quoted: "For in the Earth's circumference, the Christ will reigns bestowing grace on souls, in the rhythms of the world."

That is, above the planet, spanning its horizons, the divine ether force or Life-spirit of the cosmic Christ is now present. Although some of this divine ether force draws down into the earth at winter, it is generally present behind the atmospheric ether layers. It manifests through, and maintains, the rhythmical life processes of the planet. This influence assists the development of the 'christed' humanity, those in whom the Life-spirit can manifest. Although the relevance of these two lines to the development of the Christmas initiation, to the achievement of Life-spirit, is not at first evident, when one knows that the term 'grace' refers to the Chrestos or Life-spirit forces, then the connection becomes clear.

Hence, the influence of the divine life-forces of the Christ are described as 'grace-bestowing' (literally, 'en-gracing'). We can remind ourselves here of Rudolf Steiner describing the Christmas-Holy Nights festival as,

> A festival of feeling in harmony with the entire cosmos {that is, the solar system}, a festival of feeling {the presence of} Grace.[404]

This revelation from Steiner concerning the word grace is itself of great importance for a deepened understanding of

---

[404] Lect. 21st Dec. 1911.

352

Christianity. He explained that through the law of karma, people achieve, after many lives, the spirit self. Beyond the spirit self, the Life-spirit is granted to humankind, as something new, something that flows into the soul from above. But, and this is one of the deepest secrets of the Christ reality, through the Christ impulse, a stream of Life-spirit may descend upon humanity before the working of karma has fully achieved its goal of the Spirit-self. It was possible for St. Paul to say, "From his fullness, we have received grace upon grace", because he himself had received this to such a degree.

Steiner indicated, further, that the power of the Christ permeating the earth gives to humankind the capacity to 'absorb' the Christ substance, so that the ether body becomes gradually a Life-spirit organism.

The next lines of the meditation refer to a sublime reality, the interaction between humankind and the hierarchies – in particular, the second hierarchy, the second grouping of hierarchical beings, which are also known as "the spirits of light". It is the work of these beings to mediate the Life-spirit forces of the Christ being to humanity. "You spirits of light, let from the East be enkindled what through the West is formed."

The west, which is the direction in which the sun is at its weakest, may be considered as a symbol of the moon forces, through which we enter in to earth existence, through which the physical body is formed. The east, being the direction from which the sun rises, is often used to represent the sun and its life-bestowing powers. Steiner revealed how, as we arise during sleep up into the spiritual realms, beyond the earth, we are permeated by forces from the second hierarchy.

These forces, which obviously derive from the light divine of the Christ being, course around the earth, going from east to west: "From the second hierarchy, as if going with the sun, there is actually this stream of forces; and this continually permeates, grace en-filled, the soul life of humanity".

Steiner referred to the presence of this divine Life-spirit radiance in "the circumference of the Earth" in another lecture in these words: "With Christ, a power has appeared, which will work into the farthest future, and this will weave that true, spiritual love as a force around the earth, which will actively live in all that lives on into the future".

Understanding the meditation in this way enables a central truth of the spiritual evolution of humanity to be contemplated. The Foundation Stone meditation extract is, in full, as follows:

> O human soul ! You live in the pulse of heart and lung, which leads you through the rhythms of time into the feeling of your own soul's being; practise Spirit Contemplation in inner equilibrium, where the on-surging world-evolving deeds do unite your own I to the cosmic I. Then you shall truly feel within the dynamics of the human soul. For in the Earth's circumference, the Christ-will reigns bestowing grace on souls, in the rhythms of the world. You spirits of light, let from the East be enkindled what through the West is formed

The Life-spirit forces permeate the soul during the nights, in the course of the twenty-four-hour rhythm of day and night, as we arise through the Earth's firmament. And in addition, during the rhythm of the year, that is, in the wintertime, some of these forces permeate us, when we are drawn down into the earth, where they too have descended.

Steiner quotes about: 2 hemispheres or the Holy Nights as a winter phenomenon for either hemisphere: 53,184,188, 201-2, 218, 225, 234, **247,** 248-49,259, 263-4, 285, 291 and 282-87 (the Oslo lecture)

Opposing statements:
Human beings are no longer nature-connected,   99
The two hemispheres don't really exist: Benesch,   55
The Earth's etheric body has no involvement in the
seasonal cycle: Benesch,   55
The term 'Christmas-Holy Nights', if applied by Steiner
to the south hemisphere in June, only means wintry
'conditions' occur then: Debus, Samson,   284
The German word for 'opposite' (*entgegengesetzt*), as in
"*opposite hemispheres*", doesn't mean they are opposite;
they are only 'inclining towards' each other: Samson, 84
Rudolf Steiner errs in defining the meteor showers as
the basis of autumn's Michael-ic reality: Samson,   173

Picture credits

1,2 3,10-13 : the author
4 Rudolf Steiner Verlag, Switzerland
5 Rudolf Steiner Verlag, Switzerland
6 Anthrowiki.at/Kabiren, via Creative Commons License
7 Wikipedia; courtesy of the British Museum
8 Courtesy of the Deutsches Brotmuseum, Ulm, Germany
9 From the author's private collection

Also by this author:

The Way to the Sacred   (2003)
The Foundation Stone Meditation: a new commentary (2005)
Dramatic Anthroposophy: Identification and contextualization
   of primary features of Rudolf Steiner's anthroposophy. (Ph.D.
   thesis, 2005)
Two Gems from Rudolf Steiner   (2014)
The Hellenistic Mysteries & Christianity   (2014)
Rudolf Steiner Handbook   (2014)
Horoscope Handbook - a Rudolf Steiner Approach   (2015)

See also Damien Pryor:

The nature & origin of the Tropical Zodiac
Stonehenge
The Externsteine
Lalibela
The Great Pyramid & the Sphinx

website: www.rudolfsteinerstudies.com

CPSIA information can be obtained
at www.ICGtesting.com
Printed in the USA
BVHW05s1659221018
530872BV00008B/208/P